MARKET POWER AND MARKET MANIPULATION IN ENERGY MARKETS

FROM THE CALIFORNIA CRISIS TO THE PRESENT

Gary Taylor, M.S., J.D.
Shaun Ledgerwood, Ph.D., J.D.
Romkaew Broehm, Ph.D.
Peter Fox-Penner, Ph.D.

Taylor, Gary (Consultant), author.

Market power and market manipulation in energy markets from the California crisis to the present / Gary Taylor, J.D.; Shaun Ledgerwood, Ph.D., J.D.; Romkaew Broehm, Ph.D.; Peter Fox-Penner, Ph.D.

pages cm

ISBN 978-0-910325-34-9

1. Electric utilities--Law and legislation--United States. 2. Electric utilities--Law and legislation--California. I. Ledgerwood, Shaun D., author. II. Broehm, Romkaew, author. III. Fox-Penner, Peter S., 1955- author. IV. Title.

KF2125.T39 2015

333.793'209794--dc23

2015003529

First Printing, March 2015

Printed in the United States of America

MARKET POWER
AND
MARKET MANIPULATION
IN
ENERGY MARKETS

FROM THE CALIFORNIA CRISIS TO THE PRESENT

Gary Taylor, M.S., J.D.
Shaun Ledgerwood, Ph.D., J.D.
Romkaew Broehm, Ph.D.
Peter Fox-Penner, Ph.D.

FOREWORD

This book explores the causes and subsequent failures of the California efforts at restructuring or deregulation of its electric power system in 2000-2001 and subsequent electric market manipulation cases to the present. One aspect of this exploration was to distinguish between market power and market manipulation. This distinction takes us through a number of revealing analyses, presumably because manipulation has tortious, or even criminal consequences, while market power is merely the undesirable vulnerability of an electric market to be administered in certain negative ways. The book mentions various techniques for detecting market power or manipulation as analogous to the medical state of "infection," which must be diagnosed and treated indirectly.

The greatest virtue of the book is the accuracy and depth of its analysis explained in ways understandable, for example, by authorities struggling in the field of electricity regulation. Another clarification of the nature of manipulation comes in the discussion of "intent"–always an element of manipulation and, in some cases, a derivative of Section 10-5 of the Securities and Exchange Act, which imports fraud into the analysis. Another central distinction between market power and manipulation is that manipulation involves improper actions in one market that affect profits in another (linked) market. On the other hand, market power as studied in traditional antitrust analyses is a phenomenon that occurs only in one, well-defined market. The book explains that manipulation usually requires fraud, while the exercise of market power requires only the withholding of supply to inflate price.

It is certainly not my purpose to attempt to summarize the contents of this extremely searching analysis but to give the reader a taste of its analytical depth explored in comprehensible prose. If the purpose of the book is to make the complex and multifarious elements of the California crash and the FERC's efforts to build an anti-manipulation enforcement program understandable to reasonably well-informed observers, it has succeeded.

One part of the book explores various aspects of market power and its causes. This focuses on how electric systems may be designed to suppress supply and increase price. This was certainly an element in the California crisis, although perhaps not a dominant one. The book also explores demand factors in market power. All of these tend to interfere with competitive prices, which are the touchstone of successful design.

This brings me to a fundamental and possibly most controversial comment on deregulation or restructuring generally. In my view, an important driving force in these efforts, though perhaps not the dominant element, has been ideology–the effort to conform control of electricity systems to the general scheme of capitalist economics. These market-centered ideas of general application in our society were developed originally with physical commodities rather than with electricity in mind. And, electricity can be conformed to the normal pattern only with some effort. This is reflected in the movement to competition as the sole (or dominant) regulator of electric power and the exclusion of extrinsic government authority. The whole thrust of deregulation was from fiat to competition–the essential basis of capitalism. The book may be interpreted to hint at this approach, although, not surprisingly, this is not explicit. Of course, the California restructuring was described (and referred to in this book) as deregulation, a word which properly characterizes the process.

My comments, of course, raise the question why deregulation should follow an ideological path and be pursued for ideological reasons. The answer is not hard to divine. The purpose of deregulation, as the word suggests, is to remove government from direct control of electric system prices and entry. Capitalism with its reliance on markets tends to dispense with direct government regulation of price/entry and to substitute the influence of the owners of capital. Specifically, competition among market participants substitutes for government regulation.

Capitalism has now emerged as almost the only viable economic system remaining after the collapse of the Soviet Union and its satellites. The only important exception to this conclusion is the vast but ambiguous economy of China, which is still nominally socialist, but more recent Chinese economic achievements have been accomplished mainly with profit incentives (although political interventions are still obviously present). Profit incentives and the absence or limitation of public control over private economic power are the essence of unfettered capitalism and pervade the story of the California crisis.

Deregulation the California way has thus created hazards that this book explores brilliantly.

Hon. Richard D. Cudahy

TABLE OF CONTENTS

Part II: Market Power and Manipulation in the Western Crisis

Chapter 4

Chapter 5

Chapter 7

Chapter 8

Part III

New Developments in Market Manipulation

Chapter 9

Market Power and Market Manipulation in Energy Markets: From the California Crisis to Present

Preface

More than a decade after the crisis in California and other western energy markets,[1] the Federal Energy Regulatory Commission (FERC), Commodity Futures Trading Commission (CFTC), and other agencies are opening large numbers of market manipulation cases pursuant to recently expanded regulatory authority. These investigations involve both physical and financial commodities and extend beyond electric power into natural gas, electricity, and gas derivatives, and many financial products unrelated to electric power. Our experience in analyzing and assessing trader behavior in regulatory proceedings arising from the Crisis, as well as many of the more recent enforcement actions, has provided insights that we hope can further the dialog regarding what constitutes manipulation and clarify the types of behavior that should or should not be targeted in enforcement actions.

We recognize that market analysis and the enforcement process are continuously evolving, and that our contributions are only one step along the path toward better power, commodity and financial market oversight and performance.

CA Book Acknowledgement

As this book will recount, our understanding of the elements and nuances of market power and manipulation has been informed to a substantial degree by our work over the last decade in litigation relating to the collapse of electricity markets in California in 2000-2001 and more recently through enforcement actions involving electricity and natural gas market manipulation. We are deeply indebted to many organizations and individuals that involved us as consultants and expert witnesses in those efforts.

1. The crisis started in California and spread throughout electric power markets in the West. Thus, various names have been applied to this series of events such as "California Energy Crisis," "Western Energy Market Crisis," "Western Crisis," and often just "Crisis." These will be used interchangeably throughout the book.

With regard to the proceedings related to the California Crisis these included the California Attorney General,[2] the California Public Utility Commission,[3] Pacific Gas & Electric, Southern California Edison, and the California Electricity Oversight Board. Therein we have been privileged to collaborate with an outstanding legal team led by David Gustafson of the California Attorney General's Office, Kevin McKeon of Hawke, McKeon and Sniscak, outside counsel for the Attorney General; Richard Roberts of Steptoe & Johnson, for SCE; and Stan Berman of Sidley & Austin for PG&E. We also received superb support from Joe Fagan of Day Pitney and from Paul Mohler. There were many other able attorneys involved, and we are indebted to them all.

We also would like to acknowledge the contributions of Dr. Carolyn Berry and our colleagues at The Brattle Group, Dr. Robert J. Reynolds, Jamie Read and Phil Hanser, fellow expert witnesses in the Crisis-related proceedings, and Frank Graves, head of Brattle's Utility Practice, who encouraged us to write the book. Special thanks also go to Paul Carpenter and Matt O'Loughlin, who started the project, and Johannes (Hannes) Pfeifenberger, the original project manager. Beyond these, an incredibly talented and dedicated array of Brattle employees has supported our work over a period of nearly thirteen years. Below we name many of them with our thanks.[4] Their number and the countless hours they worked bespeak the magnitude of the effort required.

We would also like to acknowledge the work of the many experts for the Parties and the FERC staff who were our opponents throughout these proceedings. While we frequently did not agree with their conclusions, over many long years they kept us on our toes.

In addition, we have had the pleasure to work both for and against many law firms and attorneys who strive to keep their clients compliant with the market manipulation rules and to vigorously represent those clients against allegations of manipulation. Specifically, we would like to thank Ken Irvin, Greg Lawrence and Paul Pantano of Cadwalader, Wickersham and Taft; Dan Mullen of Fried, Frank, Harris, Shriver & Jacobson; Charles Mills and Will Keyser of K&L Gates; Todd Mullins of McGuire Woods; Bob Fleishman of Morrison Foerster; Joseph Williams of Norton Rose Fulbright; Michael Spafford of Paul Hastings; John Estes of Skadden, Arps, Slate, Meagher & Flom; and John Ratliff and Roberto Grasso of Wilmer Cutler Pickering Hale and Dorr LLP.

Our experience would also not be complete but for our work with current and former regulators, as colleagues, clients, and occasionally as adversaries. At the CFTC, we would like to thank Matthew L. Hunter for his substantial thought leadership and contributions to this field,

2. Disputes over the "California Crisis" have spanned the tenures of three Attorneys General: Bill Lockyer, Jerry Brown and Kamala Harris.

3. The General Counsels for the CPUC since the commencement of the litigation have been Gary Cohen, Randall Wu and Frank Lindh.

4. This list includes only those that put in major time into our effort. There were over a hundred others involved as well.

as well as Mark Higgins (now at Barclays), Patrick Marquart, and Kate Sandstrom. At the FERC, we wish to thank David Applebaum, Keith Collins (now with the CAISO), Sean Collins, Larry Gasteiger, Wesley Heath, Jeffrey "Zeke" Honneycut, John Kroeger, Kathryn Kuhlen, Kelli Merwald, Bob Pease (now with Bracewell & Giuliani), Chris Peterson (now with EIA), Thomas Pinkston, Arnie Quinn, Lauren Rosenblatt (now with NV Energy), Justin Shellaway, and Lee Ann Watson. We would also like to thank Lucia Passamonti and Biagio De Filpo of the Italian Regulatory Authority for Electricity and Gas, as well as Devon Huber and Jonathan Scratch of the Market Assessment and Compliance Division of the IESO.

We thank Public Utilities Reports for agreeing to publish this work and for their cooperation throughout the project. Finally, we express our deep appreciation for the talented and dedicated core group that helped produce this book: Richard Sweet, Heidi Bishop, Marianne Gray, Marjorie Fischer, Debra Paolo, and our wonderful, intrepid book intern Karen Dildei.

We dedicate this book to our colleague, Adam Schumacher, who lasted through all-nighters with us from 2003 on, eventually becoming the coordinating hub of our endeavors in seeking relief for California ratepayers burdened with the costs of the Crisis. He remains part of our team in spirit from his current perch in North Dakota.

California Proceedings – The Brattle Group Colleagues

David Adler, Luke D. Archer, David Azari , Jenn Baka, Greg Basheda, Gunjan Bathla, Amrita Bhattacharyya, Justin Bledin, Adam Block, James Bohn, Ha Cao, Chris Castle, Martha Caulkins, Metin Celebi, Anne Chaisiriwatanasai, Chuck Chakraborty, Steven Chambers, Judy Chang, Darrell Chodorow, Melissa Chow, Marc Chupka, Michael DeLucia, Emily Devlin, Kent Diep, Rachel Eisenberg, Jose Antonio Garcia, Beth Gavin, Mariko Geronimo, Susan Guthrie, Jamie Hagerbaumer, Attila Hajos, Kevin C. Hearle, Emily Hertzer, Yonca Heyse, Caroline Hopkins, Nauman Ilias, Kevin J. Immonje, G. David Jackola, Tumer Kapan, Rachel Kilmer, Aaron Kuebler, Jennifer Lake, Quincy Liao, Sin Han Lo, Alexander Luttmann, Kamen Madjarov, Petya Madzharova, Brendan McVeigh, Yuan Mei, Elizabeth Miller, William Moss, Nancy Pine, Evan Pittman, Nicholas Powers, Benjamin Reddy, Conor Reidy, James D. Reitzes, Blake Reynolds, Grete Roed, Guillermo Sabbioni, Sanem Sergici, Monisha Shah, Jeffrey Shen, Holger Siebrecht, John Simpson, Stella Stergiopoulos, Shruti Talwar, Alexander Tenenbaum, Sharon Ulery, Sandeep Vaheesan, Shannon Wentworth, Joseph B. Wharton, Sarah Whitley, Robert W. Wilson, and Lisa Wood.

Part I

The Concepts of Market Power and Market Manipulation

CHAPTER 1

INTRODUCTION

The California Crisis – A Market Experiment in Shambles

On January 17, 2001, approximately one month after the Federal Energy Regulatory Commission (FERC or Commission) had made its initial attempt to defuse a looming crisis in the California power markets, the lights literally went out in one of the wealthiest and most technologically advanced regions on earth, and the earliest effort in the United States to restructure electric power markets along competitive lines was in shambles. The California Power Exchange (PX) and the California Independent System Operator (CAISO), institutions set up to administer markets in California, were reeling and soon ceased to function effectively.[1] Two of the world's largest investor-owned utilities (IOUs), Pacific Gas and Electric (PG&E) and Southern California Edison (SCE), faced financial ruin and lacked the trade credit to make daily energy purchases needed to meet customer loads. Reliability was compromised, and the power grid teetered on the verge of collapse for thirty days.

To avert disaster, the State of California stepped in to buy the energy supplies necessary to serve electricity customers and avoid crippling the state's economy. Through the California Department of Water Resources (CDWR), it purchased electricity in the wholesale power markets and supplied it to the IOUs or to the CAISO for operating its transmission network. Although later actions by the FERC and improving market conditions returned normalcy to electricity markets by the end of June 2001, CDWR incurred nearly $9 billion in energy purchase costs

1. The PX declared bankruptcy in March 2001, and the CAISO defaulted on its financial obligations in February 2001.

that were covered through long-term bonding that continues to burden California electricity users. Litigation over the "California Energy Crisis" continues as this book is written.

Much of the Commission's initial focus and that of the lion's share of the subsequent academic and practitioner debate was upon the issue of supplier market power (or the lack thereof) and flaws in the design of the PX and CAISO markets.[2] However, years of litigation have made clear that while market power and market design issues were factors at play during the Crisis, an important contributing cause was market manipulation using fraud-based schemes. Even after discovery of Enron memos describing its deceptive practices that were rapidly copied and modified by other suppliers, the FERC did not develop or adopt a clear framework for evaluating this sort of manipulative behavior. The Commission's traditional market power approach proved to be of limited use, and the FERC-approved tariffs failed even to mention market manipulation.

The meltdown of the California markets was one of the early collisions between the worlds of tariff or rule-based regulation designed to prevent or mitigate market power on the one hand and principle-based prohibitions against fraudulent behavior on the other. These two contrasting regimes differ in terms of legal authority, underlying market theory, implementation, and, indeed, even in terms of the culture of those operating within each of their traditional domains. Some of the difficulties in reconciling approaches for constraining the exercise of market power and fraudulent behavior became apparent in the Commission's efforts to contain the California Crisis, and we see the lessons learned from this experience as useful in establishing and maintaining effective oversight not only of today's electric power markets, but of natural gas and other markets as well.[3]

A New Era of Market Manipulation

After a decade, the California Crisis might seem old news, but manipulation in energy markets is certainly not. The Crisis and subsequent litigation completely reshaped the FERC's market oversight policies and helped to inform the Congressional authors of the Energy Policy Act of 2005 (EPAct), the Energy Independence and Security Act of 2007 (EISA), and the Dodd-Frank

2. We do not seek here to reopen this debate. We have long acknowledged that many factors contributed to the Crisis including tight supply and demand conditions and features of the PX and CAISO market design.

3. Some of the features that make power markets vulnerable to manipulation are also found in natural gas and other commodity markets and even certain financial markets as discussed in later chapters.

Wall Street Reform and Consumer Protection Act (Dodd-Frank).[4] In the aftermath of the Crisis, these bills granted the FERC and other federal agencies unprecedented authority to rectify manipulation in the electricity and natural gas markets.

While EPAct gave the FERC much larger enforcement powers than it had in 2001, it faces a new wave of regulatory challenges in an expanding and changing market that continues to be vulnerable to manipulation. The FERC's oversight is no longer limited to monitoring the buying and selling of physical gas and bulk power; it is increasingly looking at financial markets that now dwarf traditional physical energy exchanges. In both sets of markets, new instruments, trading hubs, and interconnections create more opportunities to improve profits through small manipulations of prices. Consequently, it is more difficult than ever before to separate manipulative behavior from legitimate trading in the market.

Current concern over manipulation is reflected in the substantial rise in the number of cases before the FERC and other regulators. Between 2010 and 2014, the Commission opened 35 investigations into market manipulation.[5] On July 30, 2013, the FERC reached its largest settlement to date when J.P. Morgan agreed to pay $410 million in penalties and disgorgement to ratepayers relating to allegations of manipulative behavior in several regional power markets.[6] The FERC Staff concluded that the firm's energy-trading unit engaged in 12 manipulative bidding strategies from 2010 to 2012 designed to enrich itself at the expense of consumers.[7]

The Commodity Futures Trading Commission (CFTC) has similarly stepped up enforcement actions as a result of the Dodd-Frank legislation. In 2012, for example, it obtained $14 million in penalties and disgorgement from Optiver and others for manipulation of New York Mercantile Exchange (NYMEX) oil and gas futures contracts and concealing the manipulation by making false statements in response to an inquiry from NYMEX.[8] At that point, CFTC leadership stressed that it has zero tolerance for "traders who try to gain an unlawful advantage by

4. Multiple members of Congress referenced the Crisis in the debates over the Energy Policy Act to advocate for stronger protections against manipulative behavior. Amendments to the Natural Gas Act and the Federal Power Act prohibiting market manipulation reflected these efforts (*see Energy Policy Act of 2005*, Sections 315 and 1283). For example, Sen. Cantwell remarked that the Crisis "has been devastating to California's economy" and that "this kind of market manipulation ought to be outlawed specifically in the Power Act today so this does not happen again" (Senator Cantwell (WA) (2003)). She made similar comments in 2007 regarding the EISA (*see* Senator Cantwell (WA) (2007)). The Dodd-Frank Wall Street Reform and Consumer Protection Act reinforced the authority of the FERC to prevent fraud and market manipulation. Sen. Bingaman reminded his colleagues that Congress specifically granted these powers in the aftermath of the California energy crisis (*see* Senator Bingaman (NM) (2010)).

5. FERC, Report on Enforcement, (2013), (2012), (2011), (2010).

6. FERC, 2013 Report on Enforcement, p. 5. This case is discussed in detail in Chapter 11.

7. *Id.*

8. Commodity Futures Trading Commission (CFTC) press release, April 19, 2012.

using sophisticated means to drive oil and gas futures prices in their favor,"[9] setting the tone for the new wave of manipulation investigations and enforcement actions to come.[10]

Although the recent wave of manipulation investigations involved behavior in disparate parts of the United States and separated from the California Crisis by more than a decade, in both old and new cases wholesale electric markets were suspected of failing to deliver effective competition and fair prices. In both old and new cases, regulators were required to analyze massive quantities of market data so as to distinguish between appropriate competitive outcomes and actions that improperly hurt competition or manipulated prices. In both old and new cases, regulators confronted market participants who argued that market manipulation was too subjective to be prohibited; that the sellers' actions were normal and pro-competitive; and that undoing observed price outcomes would harm rather than help economic efficiency. In every case, regulators were forced to evaluate these and other arguments and to strike an appropriate balance between overregulation and the prevention of inefficient and unfair trading.

The Purpose and Plan of this Book

In this book we draw on a decade of experience analyzing and debating the California Crisis before the FERC and similar work in the recent wave of power market manipulation proceedings. Our goal is to discuss the development and evolution of methods to determine whether and why electric markets are not working properly and how to distinguish between acceptable and unacceptable market behaviors be they the exercise of market power or fraud-based manipulation. We illustrate the roles played by market forces and "the fundamentals," market design (good and bad), information asymmetries, and data limitations, all of which may contribute substantially to market malfunction and complicate diagnosis of its causes.

In the course of this discussion, we shall address in some detail the similarities and differences between market power and fraud-based market manipulation in energy markets and how each of these phenomena may properly be diagnosed. To do this, we build on the seminal work of one of us (Ledgerwood), creating a framework that helps categorize different types of market manipulation and also helps with diagnostic and enforcement efforts. With a decade of decisions and rules regarding proper and improper market behavior, we focus the lens

9. *Id.*

10. In FY13 the CFTC obtained a record $1.7 billion in monetary sanctions and filed 82 actions, bringing the total number of actions between FY11 and FY13 to nearly double the number of actions brought during the prior three fiscal years. The FY2013 civil penalties include $700 million in *In re UBS AG et al.*, $325 million in *In re The Royal Bank of Scotland plc*, and $65 million in *In re ICAP Europe Ltd*, which all involved manipulation and false reporting related to LIBOR. Taking these FY13 cases together with the action against Barclays Bank in FY12, the CFTC's benchmark-related cases have yielded total penalties of just under $1.3 billion. (CFTC 2013).

provided by the framework upon the actions and strategies the FERC and other agencies have determined to reflect impermissible market manipulation.

Our objective in this book is not to re-enter the grand debate over what caused the California Crisis or whether regulation and government actions were the source, victim, or amplifier of this tragic set of events. Thousands of pages have been written attempting to divide the causes of high prices between poor design, genuine supply shortages, unhelpful government responses, and other factors. Scholarly publications include Will McNamara's analysis of the facts surrounding California's deregulation and lessons learned from California's model;[11] Professor James Sweeney's comprehensive review of the series of policy choices that were made prior to and during the Crisis;[12] Charles Cicchetti's (*et al.*) attempt to explain what went wrong in California's restructured energy markets and what must be done to restore the state's system;[13] and Jeremiah D. Lambert's discussion of corporate involvement in the Crisis.[14] Professors Severin Borenstein, Frank Wolak, and James Bushnell in multiple articles offer extensive debate of the market inefficiencies related to the Crisis;[15] Doctor Scott Harvey and Professors William Hogan provide analysis of the exercise of market power in the California markets;[16] Professor Paul Joskow's contributions focus on the quantitative analysis of the pricing behavior in the California electricity markets;[17] and Christopher Weare's report addresses the policy changes that can rebuild the state's energy market after the Crisis.[18] We have long acknowledged that the Crisis arose from multiple sources, only some of which involved market power or fraud-based market manipulation.

This book is organized into three parts. In Part I, consisting of Chapters 1-3, we provide necessary background knowledge about the concepts of and issues related to market power and market manipulation to inform the remainder of the book. In Part II, we treat the Crisis in California—or, more properly, the entire Western United States—at some length.[19] Chapter 4 offers a description of the state's market design following the restructuring efforts in the mid-1990s as well as an overview of market performance during the Crisis (May 2000–June 20, 2001). The Crisis remains by far the longest, most costly, and most extensively litigated meltdown in the annals of electric competition. Chapter 5 discusses this lengthy litigation process in depth. During the Crisis, sellers employed a wide variety of market manipulation strate-

11. *See* McNamara (2002).

12. *See* Sweeney (2002).

13. *See* Cicchetti, *et al.* (2004).

14. *See* Lambert (2006).

15. *See* Borenstein, *et al.* (2008); Borenstein (2002); Borenstein, Bushnell, and Wolak (2002); Borenstein, and Bushnell (2000); Bushnell (2003); Bushnell (2000); Wolak (2003a); and Wolak (2003b).

16. *See* Harvey, S.M. and W.W. Hogan (2001a) (hereinafter "H&H"); and H&H (2001b).

17. *See* Joskow and Kahn (2002a); Joskow (2001); and Joskow and Kahn (2002b).

18. *See* Weare (2003).

19. The electric power system in the western U.S. is highly integrated, so the problems in California affected adjacent regions, particularly the Pacific Northwest (PNW). Crisis-related litigation ultimately involved transactions throughout the West.

gies amidst a constantly changing set of market rules and fundamentals. The analyses of this behavior in Chapters 6 and 7 illustrate a wide variety of challenges in detecting and mitigating market power and market manipulation. Concluding Part II, Chapter 8 looks at the challenges regulators faced in responding to the Crisis and its aftermath.

As a result of the Crisis and other experience, the FERC, antitrust agencies, other market regulators, and market monitors have a better understanding of how power markets work and what is needed to ensure they remain relatively free of manipulation. Still, power market products and structures have evolved to become increasingly complex, and new trading strategies and enforcement challenges continue to present themselves. In Part III we examine some of these new challenges and introduce a framework for analyzing manipulation that we have found helpful for distinguishing between fraudulent and legitimate market behavior, and for understanding the difference between the traditional antitrust treatment of market power and enforcement actions against manipulative trading strategies in commodities and financial markets. Chapter 9 introduces this conceptual framework and Chapter 10 suggests processes for implementing it as an enforcement and compliance tool. Chapter 11 applies the framework to recent enforcement actions, illustrating its usefulness across agencies and cases.

Whether the strategies we see today are echoes of the trading first seen in the Crisis or tread unfamiliar ground, proper power market oversight remains an essential feature of the modern regulatory landscape. With too much enforcement, the markets themselves may be in jeopardy, rendered illiquid and ineffective by overcautious sellers and insufficient buyer interest. Conversely, as the Crisis amply illustrated, markets that cease to function well can cause massive economic dislocation, wealth transfers, and hardship. We conclude the book by elaborating on these lessons and our concerns going forward.

CHAPTER 2

MARKET POWER AND MARKET MANIPULATION: DEFINITIONS AND COMPARISON

Definitions of Market Power and Market Manipulation

This is a book about detecting and assessing the extent of market power and market manipulation, so it seems appropriate that we provide a brief overview of the definitions of market power and market manipulation to inform the remaining discussion.

Definitions of market power and market manipulation are statements about what they are, not necessarily what we observe to prove they exist. By analogy, there is a distinction between a disease—for example, the presence of a virus in one's bloodstream—and the symptoms of the disease. We cannot always observe the disease directly—we must infer its existence from tests and observation of the symptoms. Moreover, if we want to prevent the disease in the first place, we often need a different approach that applies preventive measures before the fact.

The same applies to market power and market manipulation. We cannot, for example, readily observe a firm's ability to raise prices within a single market.[1] We certainly cannot know in advance, with complete certainty, how much more ability the firm would have if it merged with a rival. Instead, we develop diagnostic tools much like the medical profession that can distinguish between markets "infected" by market power or manipulation and those that are not. This book is devoted to examining the tools and techniques we used to test for market power and manipulation in the California power crisis and in more recent cases.

1. We can often observe price increases, but we cannot usually know immediately whether they reflect changes in costs or other causal factors.

Market Power

Though the precise definitions of the term "market power" vary somewhat among economists, agencies, and courts, the economic concept of market power is well-established: it is the unilateral ability to raise prices without losing profits. The U.S. antitrust agencies (the Federal Trade Commission and the U.S. Department of Justice's Antitrust Division, 1997) consider market power the ability of a firm to profitably raise prices by a small but significant amount above competitive levels for a significant period of time.[2] Landes and Posner (1981) define market power as "the ability of a firm (or a group of firms, acting jointly) to raise price above the competitive level without losing so many sales so rapidly that the price increase is unprofitable and must be rescinded."[3] Areeda (1995) states market power in terms of "the ability to raise price by restricting output."[4] Kaplow (2011) considers the most workable definition to be "the ability to profitably elevate price (P) above the competitive level, which in the case of perfect competition would be a price equal to firms' marginal costs (MC), which would be equated through the competitive process. The extent of market power is accordingly the degree to which the profit-maximizing price exceeds the competitive level."[5]

These definitions—all quite similar—are echoed by the FERC. In *Citizen Power & Light Corp.*, the FERC defined a seller with market power "...when the seller can significantly influence price in the market by withholding service and excluding competitors for a significant period of time."[6] We explore these definitions, and how the FERC has implemented them, throughout the remainder of this volume.

The Supreme Court has adopted an economic definition of market power and it is widely used in appellate courts today.[7] In *National Collegiate Athletic Association v. Board of Regents of University of Oklahoma* (NCAA) the Court defined market power as "the ability to raise prices above those that would be charged in a competitive market."[8] This definition is distinct from the definition of monopoly power, which is "the power to control prices or exclude

2. *See* U.S. Department of Justice and Federal Trade Commission, 1997 Section 0.1.

3. Landes and Posner (1981).

4. Areeda *et al.* (1995), p. 86. The American Bar Association Section of Antitrust Law (2005), p. 1, n. 3 notes though that while "generally, a monopolist will reduce sales to increase price ... it is not always the case. For example, a monopolist need not restrict output to raise prices if it can employ perfect price discrimination."

5. Kaplow (2011), p. 245. Kaplow cites Areeda, P.E. *et al.* (2007), 109 (3rd ed.) ("Market power is the ability to raise price profitably by restricting output."); and Carlton (2007), 3: 3–27 ("One standard definition of market power is the ability to set price profitably above the competitive level, which is usually taken to mean marginal cost.").

6. Citizen Power & Light Corporation, *Order Noting Intervention, Accepting in Part and Denying in Part Request for Waivers, and Conditionally Accepting Rate Schedule,* Docket No. ER 89-401, August, 1989.

7. Werden (1998).

8. *Nat'l Collegiate Athletic Ass'n v. Bd. of Regents of Univ. of Oklahoma*, 468 U.S. 85, 1984; *see also Jefferson Parish Hosp. Dist. No. 2 v. Hyde*, 466 U.S. 2, 1984 ("As an economic matter, market power exists whenever prices can be raised above levels that would be charged in a competitive market."); *United States Steel Corp. v. Fortner Enterprises*, 429 U.S. 610, 1977 ("Market power is usually stated to be the ability of a single seller to raise price and restrict output.").

competition."[9] It is important to keep in mind that monopoly power and market power are related concepts but not the same. Monopoly power, at a minimum, requires a substantial degree of market power. However, even market power less than what is required for a monopoly can lead to violations of antitrust law,[10] and, as we will see later on, it can trigger market manipulation. Moreover, the exercise of market power is not limited to sellers; buy-side market power, or "monopsony power," can also exist and lead to reduced output and low prices relative to competitive levels.

Consistent with these various definitions, we define sell-side market power as *the ability of an individual supplier or group of suppliers to profitably[11] maintain[12] prices[13] above competitive levels for a significant[14] period of time.*[15] Thus, an exercise of market power occurs when a seller is able to increase and sustain its prices above competitive levels without experiencing such a large decrease in its sales volume that its overall profit falls.

Because a wide range of economists and jurists largely agree on the definition of market power, most recent discussions of the topic in energy markets concern the methods of diagnosing rather than defining it. By extension, this includes the metrics that are used to measure market power and standards for determining whether a particular market power metric (for example, the price-cost margin) exceeds permissible levels. As we will see, these questions were integral to our market power work on the Crisis and they remain integral to energy market power investigations today. These questions involve *how* we measure the amount of market power present, not what market power *is*, and they are the primary focus of our discussion in the following chapters.

9. *United States v. E.I. du Pont de Nemours & Co.*, 351 U.S. 377, 1956 (*Cellophane*); *see also Aspen Skiing Co. v. Aspen Highlands Skiing Corp.*, 472 U.S. 585, 1985. For qualifications of this definition, *see* Kaplow (2010) n. 13.

10. For example, while Section 2 of the Sherman Act requires monopoly power, Section 1 and attempted monopolization under Section 2 require less. *See* Fortner, 394 U.S., at 502, 1969.

11. Thus, our definition recognizes that both the ability and the incentive to raise prices are needed to trigger market power concerns.

12. Focusing only upon price increases could lead to the false impression that the firm does not have market power, because the current price level already reflects the exercise thereof. *See* American Bar Association (ABA) Section of Antitrust Law (2005) p. xii.

13. Economists would typically expand the meaning of "price" to include, for example, a reduction in quality. *See* Hay (1992).

14. "Given the unique nature of power markets, we note that a "significant period of time" might be as short as several dispatch periods during adverse market conditions." The Brattle Group (2007). As we discuss later, this is reflected in the Commission's use of pivotality as an indicator of market power.

15. *Id.*, p. 2.

Market Manipulation[16]

In contrast to market power, attempts to define market manipulation by jurists and economists have proven to be much more challenging and inconsistent. The FERC, CFTC, and Federal Trade Commission (FTC) have rules with anti-manipulation language based upon the U.S. Securities and Exchange Commission's (SEC) fraud-based Rule 10b-5 (17 C.F.R. § 240.10-5),[17] but they lack a clear definition of the term and there is little harmonization across the agencies about what types of behavior are covered.[18]

To complicate matters further, the CFTC has retained an "artificial price" standard based on the (pre-Dodd-Frank) Commodities Exchange Act (CEA), which also fails to provide guidance as to the definition of what constitutes manipulation.[19] The artificial price rule has proven extremely difficult to prosecute. In fact, only one successful case was brought during the 35 years following its passage, coincidentally against an electricity trader for using physical trades to manipulate the value of CFTC-jurisdictional contracts. *See DiPlacido v. CFTC*, 364 F. App'x 657, 657 (2d Cir. 2009). Nevertheless, the CFTC settled many cases for attempted manipulation under its then-existing authority. Dodd-Frank did not repeal the CFTC's artificial price rule, but rather added a fraud-based provision to bolster its powers. The CFTC is using its expanded authority to investigate a broad range of behavior, including an alleged physical power market manipulation in ERCOT that may have affected the value of CFTC-regulated derivatives.[20]

On its website, the SEC describes manipulation as "intentional conduct designed to deceive investors by controlling or artificially affecting the market for a security."[21] However, even this rather vague description is neither a legal interpretation nor a statement of SEC policy.

16. Portions of the following discussion are taken with permission from Ledgerwood and Carpenter (2012).

17. §240.10b-5 Employment of manipulative and deceptive devices.
It shall be unlawful for any person, directly or indirectly, by the use of any means or instrumentality of interstate commerce, or of the mails or of any facility of any national securities exchange,
(a) To employ any device, scheme, or artifice to defraud,
(b) To make any untrue statement of a material fact or to omit to state a material fact necessary in order to make the statements made, in the light of the circumstances under which they were made, not misleading, or
(c) To engage in any act, practice, or course of business which [*sic*] operates or would operate as a fraud or deceit upon any person, in connection with the purchase or sale of any security.

18. *See* e.g., *Commodity Exchange Act* (CEA) 2009; *Securities Exchange Act of 1934*, 2012; *Energy Policy Act of 2005*. A good summary of these definitions can be found in Pirrong (2010) and *infra*.

19. The artificial price refers to a price that was affected by factors other than supply and demand. Manipulation was undefined in the statute but has been defined by the federal courts. In *Frey v. CFTC*, 931 F.2d 1171, 1175 (7th Cir. 1991), manipulation is "an intentional exaction of a price determined by forces other than supply and demand." In *Volkart Brothers, Inc. v. Freeman*, 311 F.2d 52 (5th Cir. 1962), "manipulation has been construed as 'any and every operation or transaction or practice...calculated to produce a price distortion of any kind in any market either in itself or in relation to other markets.'" *CFTC v. Enron Corp., and Hunter Shively*, U.S. District Court for the Southern District of Texas Houston Division, Civil Action No. H-03-909.

20. *See* Alexander Osipovich, "GDF Suez faces CFTC market manipulation probe," available at *http://www.risk.net/energy-risk/news/2350187/ gdf-suez-faces-cftc-market-manipulation-probe* (June 24, 2014).

21. *See http://www.sec.gov/answers/tmanipul.htm.*

It is merely offered as guidance to investors.[22] Courts have similarly failed to provide clear direction. In *Cargill v. Hardin*, the Eighth Circuit declared: "the methods and techniques of manipulation are limited only by the ingenuity of man."[23] Professor Craig Pirrong (2010) notes that "a good deal of the confusion arises from the fact that there are at least two, very distinct, types of manipulative acts [i.e., market power and fraud-based manipulation]."[24] Rather than developing a precise definition for market manipulation based upon clear principles, most economists, regulators, and courts have decided on a case-by-case basis whether a particular type of conduct is or is not manipulative.[25] Indeed, authors such as Fischel and Ross (1991) have asserted that the manipulation standard of the (pre-Dodd-Frank) CEA was so vague that it created inefficiency by over-deterring legitimate trading behavior to prevent what was viewed by many at the time as a victimless crime.[26]

In 1993, Pirrong broke with this "we know it when we see it" line of thinking, positing that manipulations such as market corners are enabled through the exercise of market power and revealed in patterns of behavior that are distinguishable from competitive benchmarks.[27] His later articles and testimony continued to advocate for the use of regression analyses and other statistical tests to confirm these patterns in order to prove or disprove intent and to measure the price effect of manipulative behavior.[28] However, these works continued to explain the ability to execute a manipulation solely as a function either outright fraud or the exercise of market power. This perception led to his ultimate conclusion that fraud-based manipulation statutes do not apply to market-power manipulations.[29]

Aside from the works of Pirrong, the analytic focus of much of the relevant literature centered upon relatively narrow and often dissimilar types of manipulative behavior prosecuted under the SEC's fraud-based 10b-5 rule. For example, Gerard and Nanda (1993) discussed the manipulation of seasoned equity offerings using secondary markets;[30] Jarrow (1994) studied the manipulation opportunities created by the emerging availability of financial derivatives;[31] Aggarwal and Wu (2003) empirically tested SEC data to discern qualitative elements of stock price manipulations;[32] Attari, Mello, and Ruckes (2005) observed that strategic trading can

22. Securities and Exchange Commission, 2014.

23. Pirrong (2010), p. 3, citing *Cargill, Incorporated, et al. v. Clifford M. Hardin*, 452 F.2d 1154 (8th Cir. 1971).

24. *Id.*, p. 3.

25. *See* e.g., Federal Energy Regulatory Commission (FERC) Docket IN 12-4-000 (Rather, as we have recognized, the elements of manipulation are "determined by all the circumstances of a case." 2013 (footnote omitted)).

26. *See* Fischel and Ross (1991).

27. *See* Pirrong (1993).

28. *See* Pirrong (2004).

29. *See* Pirrong (2010). The desire to distinguish "market-power" manipulation from "fraud-based" manipulation is understandable given differences in their statutory origins.

30. *See* Gerard and Nanda (1993).

31. *See* Jarrow (1994).

32. *See* Aggarwal and Wu (2003). (Presented at the 64th Annual Meeting of the American Finance Association, 2004).

profit from liquidations by large arbitrageurs to manipulate markets;[33] Goldstein and Guembel concluded that strategic trading causes financial market prices to misrepresent equity values, thereby creating incentives to sell and enabling manipulations;[34] and Massa and Rehman determined that mutual funds exploit inside information to affiliate a bank's pending loans to large customers to build portfolios of those customer's securities timed to the closing of those loans.[35]

These treatments reflect the lack of a systematic method for consistently evaluating different cases of potentially manipulative conduct under the same statute and across different statutes. Some authors have made progress in establishing foundational principles for assessing whether or not behavior is manipulative. For example, Kyle and Viswanathan build on the earlier works of Allen and Gale,[36] Kumar and Seppi,[37] and others to provide a reconciliation of certain SEC and CFTC manipulation cases, ultimately finding manipulation occurs only from distortions of "allocational efficiency that relates to market informativeness and transactional efficiency that relates to market liquidity." This finding supports, and is supported by, the model we present in Chapter 9. However, such works to date have accepted the premise that all manipulations are the product of either outright fraud or the exercise of market power, thus providing no consistent guidance to rely upon in evaluating manipulative behavior. The framework we propose in Chapter 9 provides a vehicle for reconciling these issues. It relies upon the concept of uneconomic behavior as the bridge between outright fraud and the exercise of market power.

We propose a practical and intuitive definition of uneconomic behavior designed to execute a manipulation: *intentionally losing money on transactions that set (or make) a price*[38] *to benefit the value of related positions that tie to (or take) that price.*[39] This definition recognizes that the exercise of market power, as defined above, can be one particular form of manipulation that lends itself to a self-contained diagnostic framework, but that can also fit within our broader definition of manipulation. We further discuss the various triggers of manipulation in Chapter 9 and provide a framework designed to allow for an accurate diagnosis of market manipulation in both energy and non-energy markets consistent across all products, statutes, and agencies relevant to the implementation and enforcement of market manipulation rules.

---

33. *See* Attari, Mello, and Ruckes (2005).

34. *See* Goldstein and Guembel (2008).

35. *See* Massa and Rehman (2008).

36. *See* Kyle and Viswanathan (2008).

37. *See* Kumar and Seppi (1992).

38. The link between the losing and profitable transaction does not necessarily need to be an index price, but could also be, e.g., cross-market payments tied to the quantity traded. *See* Chapter 9 for further discussion.

39. For further discussion, *see* e.g., Ledgerwood *et al.* (2011a); Ledgerwood *et al.* (2011b).

The Role of Intent

"Intent" is an integral requirement in several manipulation statutes and therefore must be a part of any complete diagnostic process.[40] Except in relatively rare circumstances, a person is not guilty of a criminal offense unless the government not only proves the unlawful act (*actus reus*) of the crime, but also the defendant's *mens rea*.[41] The same applies to many civil actions. In civil enforcement actions under anti-manipulation statutes the courts have imposed an intent requirement despite the lack of explicit language in the statutes.[42] In *Ernst & Ernst v. Hochfelder* the Court limited the application of the SEC's Rule 10(b) (15 U.S.C. § 78j(b)) and 10b-5 to cases where the defendant showed "scienter," that is "intent to deceive, manipulate, or defraud."[43] It concluded that "[t]he words 'manipulative or deceptive' used in conjunction with 'device or contrivance' strongly suggest that § 10(b) [of the Securities and Exchange Act] was intended to proscribe *knowing* or *intentional* misconduct.... [The term] connotes *intentional* or *willful* conduct designed to deceive or defraud investors by controlling or artificially affecting the price of securities."[44]

The importance of the scienter requirement under rule 10(b) extends well beyond SEC enforcement proceedings as other statutes are modeled after and interpreted in accordance with the rule and related precedent. Sections 315 and 1283 of EPAct—which amended Section 4A of the Natural Gas Act (NGA) and Section 222 of the Federal Power Act (FPA) respectively—instructed the FERC to pattern its anti-manipulation rule (18 C.F.R. § 1c) after the SEC precedent (it did so in Order 670).[45] Pursuant to Section 811 of the EISA, the FTC also modeled the language of its prohibitions on market manipulation (16 C.F.R. § 317) after the SEC rule.[46] Note, however, that with regards to CFTC anti-manipulation rules, Section 753 of the Dodd-Frank Act expanded the reach of the CEA (7 U.S.C. § 9) by reducing the scienter standard for fraud-based manipulation to intentionally *or recklessly*.[47]

As economists, we recognize that a necessary aspect of establishing that manipulation has occurred involves the use of objective evidence as proof of intent. In Chapter 10, we discuss

40. By comparison, as explained in Chapter 9, the pure exercise of market power within a single market traditionally does not require a showing of intent.

41. *Mens rea* is the mental state—usually involving intent, knowledge, recklessness, or sometimes negligence—required by the definition of a particular offense.

42. Note that agencies generally refer alleged criminal violations to the DOJ for prosecution.

43. *See Ernst & Ernst v. Hochfelder*, 425 U.S. 185, 1976. Note that *Ernst* was a proceeding concerning a private civil action, but *see* Marcoux (2009) (The Court later ruled that scienter also must be established as an element for SEC civil actions to enjoin violations of *Securities Exchange Act of 1934* (Exchange Act) § 10(b) (15 U.S.C. § 78j(b)) and SEC Rule 10b-5 (17 C.F.R. § 240.10b-5). *Aaron v. SEC,* 446 U.S. 8, 1980).

44. *Ernst & Ernst v. Hochfelder*, 425 U.S. at 197.

45. *See* FERC, Docket RM 06-3-000, 2006.

46. *See* Federal Trade Commission, "16 .FR Part 317 Prohibitions on Market Manipulation; Final Rule," 2009.

47. *See* CFTC (2011a).

specific ways in which the proof of intent by various methods can be integrated with our proposed framework for diagnosing manipulation.

Distinguishing Between Market Power and Market Manipulation

The Sherman and Clayton Acts refer quite specifically to the activities we generally describe as monopolization, market dominance, and market power.[48] Moreover, the definitions of market power at the beginning of this chapter often hinge on forms of prohibited behavior, not the amount by which prices are affected. The laws forbidding market manipulation are much more general, seemingly including market power as one (but certainly not the only) means of manipulating markets. From the standpoint of economic analysis, should we think of market power as a subset of market manipulation, something entirely different, or an overlapping concept?[49]

Most discussions of harmful economic behavior in markets are rooted in the conceptual framework of market monopolization or fraud. The now-universal analysis of the deadweight loss from a monopolist's withholding of output to raise price is taught in nearly every microeconomics course and law school curriculum in the world. Perhaps more importantly, it is used frequently enough to be remembered by most practicing economists, lawyers, and judges.

As one would imagine, the elementary theory of market power was developed for the industrial goods of the 1900s. In a world of physical goods made by physical factories, ownership or control of physical production or distribution was the main means of acquiring power over price. Industrial goods are almost always storable, so control over the factories making widgets does not immediately translate into pricing power if buyers were able to stockpile the product. However, if storage is costly, the inevitable depletion of stockpiles ultimately ensures that control over production becomes control over price.

Economic analysis of market power also came of age well before the advent of modern finance and deregulated electric and gas markets. Commodity futures have been around since the 19th century, but they were originally created for agricultural commodities—markets that were often thought to be highly competitive in the physical control sense because it is believed

48. Section one of the Sherman Act forbids "restraint of trade" (15 U.S.C. § 1) and section two makes it a felony to "monopolize" or "attempt to monopolize" (15 U.S.C. § 2). The Clayton Act condemns tying arrangements, exclusive dealing contracts, and mergers that may "substantially lessen competition or tend to create a monopoly" (15 U.S.C. § § 12-27).

49. A similar question—whether it is a subset or an overlapping concept—can be asked about fraud and market manipulation. Analogous to market power, we look at fraud as an overlapping concept (or circle in the diagram below), that is, while it can be used to increase profits within a single market, it falls within the concept of market manipulation when the actions in one (*primary*) market impermissibly increase the profits in another (*linked*) market.

difficult for any one entity to create or acquire a large market share in such instruments. By comparison, modern-day financial derivatives are a relatively recent invention.

All this has led to an analytic heritage centered on the analysis of structure, conduct, and outcomes within one product and geographic market. Time entered the analysis primarily as the entry period—the length of time it took a new entrant to build, repurpose, or divert productive capacity. Within this time period—typically a matter of months or years—market power metrics such as market share were a relatively stable concept determined by product and geographic market boundaries. If you owned all of the factories that could make tractors, and there were no good substitutes for them in a 500-mile radius, your market power was largely assured in this area, at least for a while. The time to enter would be unquestionably important for judging the severity of the problem and the propriety of potential remedies, but within this period the market for tractors had a relatively stable collection of buyers and sellers.

Another feature of markets for storable goods with long entry periods is that information plays a relatively minor role in market behavior in the short term (the period during which the capital stock is fixed). Then, supply options cannot change, so the main drivers that affect price are near-term, non-structural changes in supply or demand that affect price—most likely temporarily.

The core distinction we make between market manipulation and market power is that market manipulation involves impermissible actions in one market (as antitrust practitioners would define it) that affect profits in another market. In simple terms, manipulation is engaging in actions in what we call *the primary market* that impermissibly increase profits in what we refer to as *the linked market.* In Chapter 9, we introduce a framework that formally classifies the elements necessary to identify market manipulation, but these elements revolve around actions in the primary market affecting a linked market. For example, an agricultural company might intentionally issue a false report about current wheat production to benefit its holding of wheat futures contracts. Here the current market for wheat is the primary market and the linked markets trade wheat futures.

In the framework we introduce, the exercise of market power is one action sellers may take in a primary market to affect prices in a linked market (the other two, as we explain in Chapter 9, are uneconomic trading and fraud). While this might imply that market power is nested within the concept of market manipulation—i.e., one subset of the behaviors that trigger market manipulation—we view the concepts more as overlapping, as shown in Figure 2-1.

Figure 2-1

**Market Power versus Market Manipulation:
Our Conceptualization**

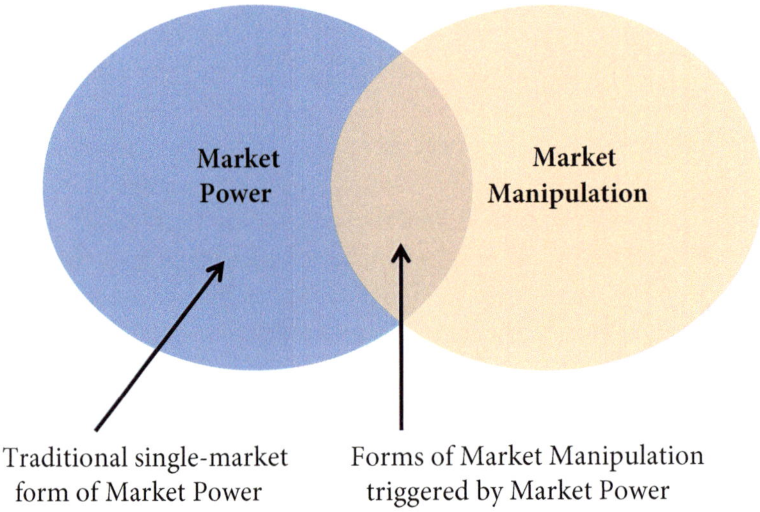

Market power is a phenomenon that occurs strictly within one well-defined market. The actions involve withholding the supply of the product, the price that increases is the price of the same product, and the buyers who are harmed are those who buy the product. If this is the only effect of the exercise of market power, we have the canonical, single-market form (left side of Figure 2-1). If the exercise of market power is intended to have impacts in markets beyond the primary market, it becomes part of a market manipulation.

We do not claim that ours is the only way economic analysts can integrate the twin concepts of market power and market manipulation, but we believe the conceptualization in Figure 2-1, combined with the framework formally introduced in Chapter 9, together constitute a view that is tractable and useful. For example, we do not wish to suggest that analyses in the market power tradition must limit themselves to products that have neither a time dimension nor time-based linkages to other antitrust markets. While we might prefer to analyze such situations with our later-described market manipulation framework, the same economic conclusion could be reached with a properly implemented antitrust analysis. The legal interpretation of the two analyses could differ, but the economic findings would be equivalent.[50]

In short, market manipulation is a broader concept than market power (or fraud), allowing for any sufficiently strong source of price linkage between two markets.[51] In modern-day econo-

50. Beyond the conceptual similarities, we note that many of the specific economic analytic techniques are used in traditional market power and market manipulation analyses. For example, in Chapter 9 we use the traditional tools of supply and demand analysis and the concept of deadweight losses to examine all forms of market manipulation.

51. Here we use the term "markets" loosely, for as shown in the later discussion of current manipulation cases, the linked, conditional outcome, such as a congestion or uplift payments by an RTO or CAISO, may not look much like a traditional market.

mies, a proliferation of financial and derivative contracts allows the price of nearly any visible commodity to be linked to the price of another. The tools of modern finance that enable these innovative risk-bearing instruments provide linkages that expand the ways in which buyers and sellers can profit in any number of markets from market distortions they themselves create in another market.

Noncompetitive Prices versus "Artificial" or Fraudulent Prices

In neoclassical microeconomics, the concept of market equilibrium and the ideal of (at least workably) competitive prices reign supreme. Economists look at market prices as the result of market structure and conduct—usually within a single, well-defined market—and ask whether the observed price is "competitive" or not. For markets without high levels of concentration, subadditive supplier costs, or some other inherent barrier to a competitive outcome, the prices are presumed to be "competitive" such that the efficiencies associated with perfect (or workable) competition attach. By comparison, where market power is present and exercised, the resulting price is "noncompetitive," such that some market efficiency is lost. However, both competitive and noncompetitive outcomes are the legitimate result of profit-maximizing behavior confined within a single market, though the latter may be subject to prohibitions under the antitrust laws or the FERC's regulatory regime.

By comparison, in market manipulation law and economics there are two relevant prohibitions, one against the creation of an "artificial price," the second against fraud.[52] While one might first think of an "artificial" price as the result of exercising market power so as to create a noncompetitive price, it is not. In the law of market manipulation, the true (non-artificial) price is the one that would occur if all sellers acted as profit maximizers within their own market. Acting strategically so as to distort information perceived by the market as to the true economic position of a trader—via quantities, prices, or any other information traders customarily rely on—leads to the creation of an artificial price. So, for example, a firm that has market power, but does not exercise it in order to act strategically, creates an artificial price even if it simultaneously refrains from an action that may be seen as prohibited or anticompetitive in an antitrust context.

Inherent in an act (or omission) used to distort market perceptions is the injection of false information into the marketplace, thus creating an artificial result that is inconsistent with a competitive outcome. Compare this with an exercise of market power by a seller, which

52. *See* CFTC (2011b). The CFTC retains both a fraud-based rule (Rule 180.1) and artificial price rule (Rule 180.2) in its anti-manipulation statute as amended by Dodd-Frank.

reduces output to generate a price increase. There is nothing fraudulent about this action, for the seller is simply setting its output at a level that maximizes its stand-alone profits within its product market. This distinction clarifies why different standards are ultimately needed to evaluate and deal with issues limited to the exercise of market power versus those associated with market manipulation.

While this can create a more complex enforcement picture, the difference between the two standards stems from an important difference in the purpose of rules that prevent market manipulation versus those that prevent market power exercised within one market. As explained above, the former is aimed solely at deadweight losses and wealth transfers in a single market setting, whereas the latter is intended to prevent economic harms created by distorting linkages between two different but ultimately related markets.

The reader should note that there are in fact different legal standards for proving a manipulation under artificial price and fraud-based rules. For example, the CFTC's artificial price rule requires proof (1) of the manipulator's ability, (2) intent to cause an artificial price, (3) that an artificial price was in fact created, and (4) that, in fact, the manipulator's actions caused the artificial price.[53] By comparison, fraud-based manipulation statutes require proof of (1) the use of a fraudulent device, scheme, or statement (2) in connection with a transaction jurisdictional to the regulator (3) used with the requisite scienter (intent).[54] As we will discuss in the chapters to come, the framework we propose provides an approach for assessing market manipulation that is equally useful in the detection, analysis, and proof (or disproof) of manipulation under either statutory standard, for it describes the cause and effect of the underlying behavior.

53. *Id.*, at 67660-67661.

54. The SEC's fraud-based Rule 10b-5 resides in 17 C.F.R. §240.10b-5. The FERC's anti-manipulation rule is codified in 18 C.F.R. §1c, 2010, as enabled by the Energy Policy Act of 2005, Pub. L. No. 109-58, 119 Stat. 594 *et seq.*, 2005, amending the Federal Power Act, 15 U.S.C. §717c-1 and the Natural Gas Act, 16 U.S.C. §824v(a). The FTC's anti-manipulation rule is codified in 16 C.F.R. Part 317, as enabled by Section 811 of Subtitle B of Title VIII of The Energy Independence and Security Act of 2007, 42 U.S.C. 17301-17305. All of these rules arise under the authority granted in 15 U.S.C. §78j(b), 2010.

CHAPTER 3

ISSUES IN IDENTIFYING AND DIAGNOSING MARKET POWER IN ELECTRIC POWER MARKETS

Special Features of Electricity Supply and Demand and Their Implications for Market Power and Manipulation

Unique Features of Electricity Supply

Several features of electric power production costs make electric power markets uniquely sensitive to small changes in supply. These features interact with peculiar demand characteristics to make electricity prices highly variable and electricity markets tempting targets for the exercise of market power and manipulation. They also complicate the diagnosis of the performance of power markets and the identification and measurement of market power.

At any one point in time, electric supply curves consist of the usable output from the set of power plants that can serve the geographic market of interest over the transmission system.[1] As with most production resources, power plants have a strict, finite usable output range. Over this range most plants have incremental costs[2] that are not difficult to calculate and, for non-renewable generators, are heavily dependent on the cost of fuel.

In most electric markets the market-clearing price is set by first stacking up the bids of power generators, which are equal to each plant's marginal cost under perfect competition, and then dispatching all plants from lowest to highest cost until the market's total demand for electric power in that time period is satisfied. Because each power plant has its own fuel contracts and its own technical and cost attributes, each one has relatively stable incremental costs over its

---

1. Defining the geographic market for electric power can be a tricky proposition, as discussed later in the chapter.
2. The term marginal or operating costs are also commonly used interchangeably with this term.

own output, but which differ quite significantly from other plants, especially plants of different types. Thus, the electric supply curve is not smooth—it is a series of stair-steps, some of which can be quite large, as shown in Figure 3-1.

Figure 3-1

An Illustrative Example of Supply Curves Reflecting Physical Withholding

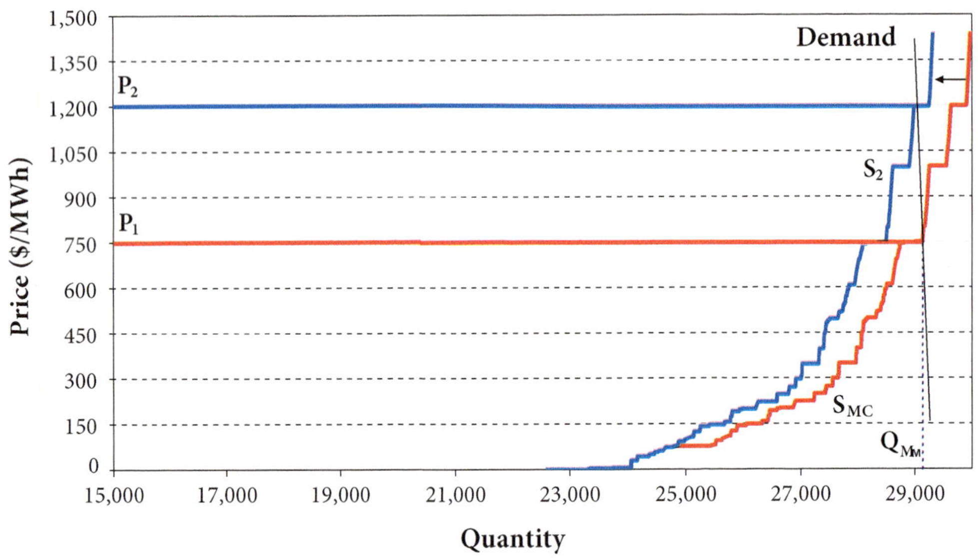

The unusually wide range of power production costs is due to the need to serve loads that vary substantially within a day without the benefit of stored supply.[3] So called "baseload" units have high capital costs, but low incremental costs. This sort of unit includes nuclear and run-of-the-river hydroelectric plants that run essentially all the time to supply the minimum power needs of a system. The highest levels of demand are met with "peaking" units, turbines or steam generators fired by natural gas that tend to have low capital costs, but high incremental operating costs.[4] In the West during the Crisis period, baseload incremental costs were almost always less than $30/MWh and often less than $20 per MWh, while old, inefficient gas-fired

3. The fact that electricity is generally non-storable is a major handicap in the operation of electric power systems. A prominent exception is hydroelectric systems with substantial reservoir capacity. Their ability to store electricity by impounding water makes them both extremely valuable and very influential in power markets.

4. Peaking units might operate very sporadically, some only in 5% of the hours in a year.

steam peakers running spot-price gas and requiring NO_x emission permits might cost well over $1,000 per MWh.[5]

As illustrated graphically in Figure 3-1, a supply curve with this shape can create strong incentives to physically withhold[6] supply under conditions when a small amount of withholding is sufficient to cause the market to rely upon a much higher-priced generator up one or more stair-steps from the marginal costs of the withholder.[7]

Suppliers can also profit from economic withholding, as depicted in Figure 3-2.[8] Suppose Supplier B offers to sell its output of 650 MW in the market at $300, instead of at its marginal cost of $150/MWh. Supplier B's bid, as shown in the red dashed line, becomes higher than that of Supplier C, who continues to bid into the market at its marginal cost of $200/MWh. Supplier B's elevated bid is still lower than Supplier D's bid of $350/MWh. This bidding behavior pushes the market price from $200/MWh to $300/MWh. Supplier B's bids only clear at 550 MW instead of the full 650 MW, leaving 100 MW idle. Its revenue, however, increases from $130,000 ($200 × 650) to $165,000 ($300 × 550). Such opportunities are a function of the unusual "chunkiness" of the power supply curve in most power markets.

5. At one point in December 2000, spot natural gas prices in Southern California hit $60 per MMBtu. These high prices were alleged to have been the result of market manipulation, but they were nonetheless the prices observed in spot gas transactions at the time. Fossil-fired units in Southern California had to purchase permits to cover their NO_x emissions.

6. Physical withholding occurs when a generator does not offer some portion of its generation when its output could have been sold economically at the market clearing price.

7. The payoff from physically withholding generation is obviously greater in the steeper, more price inelastic portions of the supply curve as the system approaches its capacity limits.

8. Economic withholding occurs when a generator's bid is too high to be dispatched even though its bid could have been dispatched if the generator had submitted its bid at its true marginal operating cost.

Figure 3-2

An Illustrative Example of Supplier's Economic Withholding

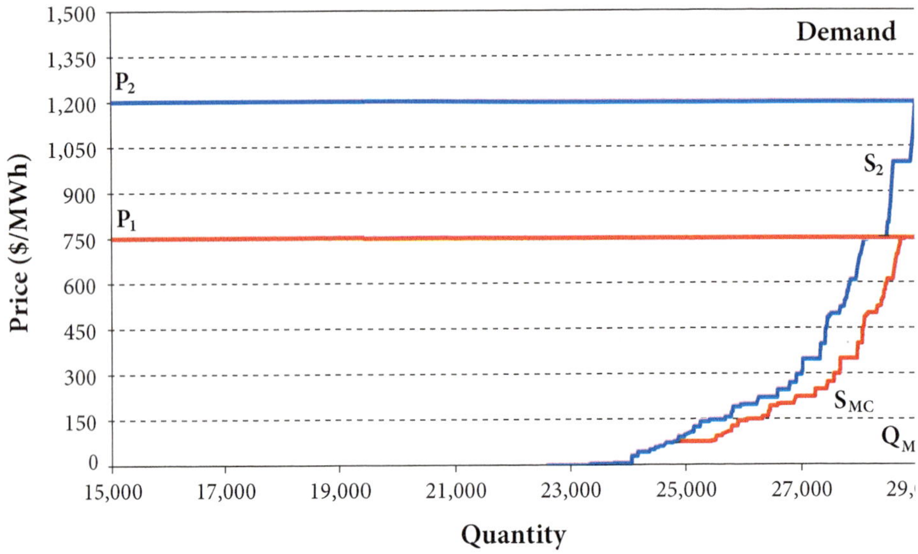

The sensitivity of wholesale power prices to the nature of the supply curve is exacerbated by physical constraints on the transmission needed to move energy from its sources to customer load. When one or more transmission links reach capacity, power flow over the link is constrained. This requires meeting load in a different, less optimal way (by adjusting generation or loads, or redispatch of the resources on the system) and may create submarkets in which there are few supply options. Thus prices in adjacent areas can differ substantially. Transmission constraints also give rise to "congestion" payments or revenues to holders of financial transmission rights (FTRs)[9] or to suppliers whose flows relieve congestion (counterflows). Redispatch of the power grid means that behavior affecting any particular transmission link or node on the system may also affect many other nodes in ways that may not be intuitive, but may nevertheless be appreciated by traders who watch the system in operation over time. These "network" characteristics of the system allow traders at times to transact at one node or location on the grid in order to influence outcomes affecting an existing position at another node or one based in differences in prices between nodes. This, as discussed in later chapters, is a feature of fraud-based manipulation.

From a market power perspective, however, the salient feature of transmission constraints is the reduction of the supply sources available to service the load in the region affected by the constraint. Such constraints, quite obviously, also complicate geographic market definition,

9. FTRs allow suppliers to hedge against fluctuations in congestion prices at the two points. They are thus essentially a form of fixed/variable swap.

particularly since they may be binding under system conditions that persist for only relatively brief periods of time. The ephemeral nature of transmission constraints, or system congestion, does not mean that they cannot be exploited, however, because the conditions in which they occur are foreseeable, and in some circumstances they may be created intentionally by the actions of market participants.

Unique Features of Electricity Demand

The traditional focus of market power discussions is on the supply side of the market, notably on the size and number of sellers (monopoly, duopoly, etc.). In electricity markets, the demand side of the market also plays a very important and unique role. Most importantly, customer demand is essentially fixed, as a practical matter over the time frames that are relevant in power markets. This has profound implications, as we shall see.

Most electric customers today—and all customers in California in 2000—did not actually see or pay the short-term wholesale price for power; they pay a retail price that is related to this immediate price, but typically in a highly-diluted and time-removed manner. At the time of the Crisis in California, the rates of the vast majority of the retail customers of the IOUs were totally insulated from wholesale price increases due to the rate freeze that was implemented as part of the California restructuring process.[10] Furthermore, to avoid blackouts consumers of electricity are generally regarded to have a very high short-run willingness to pay higher prices for electricity, also known as inelastic demand.[11] Anyone who has experienced a blackout or brownout, or has endured involuntary power conservation measures, knows the high cost of giving up electric power service, even for a few minutes.

Meanwhile, in all price-deregulated electric markets (including California's in 2000) a system operator immediately steps in to purchase (on behalf of all customers) any short-term deficit between the market's demand and the aggregate supply available in the market.[12] The system operator's charter typically instructs it to buy (or self-generate) sufficient power to meet any shortfall and prevent a blackout without regard to price. This was the case with the CAISO and later with California Energy Resources Scheduling (CERS).

The net effect of these demand-side features of electricity markets generally, and California markets during the Crisis in particular, is that individual customers are effectively insulated from most short-term wholesale electricity price changes and have no basis for adjusting their

10. The retail rates of SDG&E, as explained earlier, were briefly exposed to the run up in wholesale prices, resulting rapidly in the filing of a complaint with the FERC and the renewal of the rate freeze.

11. For a recent discussion of willingness to pay and elasticity estimates, *see* Fox-Penner and Zarakas, 2013.

12. The operation of this market in California is explained in more detail in Chapter 4.

short-term use of power based on such changes. In economic terms, there was (as of 2000–01) effectively little or no price elasticity of demand (also called price-responsiveness) in short-term *wholesale* prices.[13] In contrast to a typical demand curve for goods and services, which slopes downward somewhat gradually, electric demand is fixed and typically graphed (see Figure 3-1 and Figure 3-2) as an essentially vertical line at whatever quantity is required by the market during any given period (typically an hour, but sometimes less) in order to avoid a shortage-induced blackout. This is the amount of power (plus the required reserves) that the system operator had to assure regardless of the price sellers choose to charge.

This has rather profound consequences with regard to market power and understanding its role in the crisis. In the classical treatment of monopoly power, depicted in Figure 3-3, purchaser willingness to pay as reflected in the slope of the demand curve (demand elasticity) is a constraint upon the monopolist's incentive to raise prices. As the monopolist raises price, sales volume falls. Revenue gains from price increases are tempered by revenue losses from declining sales. As seen in Figure 3-3, this results in marginal revenues from additional sales that are well below the actual sales price. The more gently sloping the demand curve, the greater the volume loss from any attempted price increase, with a horizontal demand curve reflecting perfect competition where any attempt by an individual seller to increase price results in complete loss of sales volume.

13. From the very inception of electric deregulation it has been recognized that customers' inability to experience short-term prices would make them vulnerable to market power exercise and reduce the efficiency of markets. *See* Fox-Penner and Zarakas (2013). In the past several years electric markets have made great strides towards changing this, primarily by adopting pricing systems that allow retail prices to change rapidly (in a matter of hours) to reflect high wholesale prices. In addition, wholesale market operators have themselves become more sensitive to paying higher prices for power and usually attempt to reduce unusually high levels of aggregate demand through demand response programs before they generate or purchase shortfall supplies at very high prices. *See* the FERC Order No. 745 (134 FERC ¶ 61,187); FERC Staff, *2013 Assessment of Demand Response and Advance Metering*, Federal Energy Regulatory Commission, October 2013.

Figure 3-3

Demand and Supply Facing Seller in a Monopoly Market

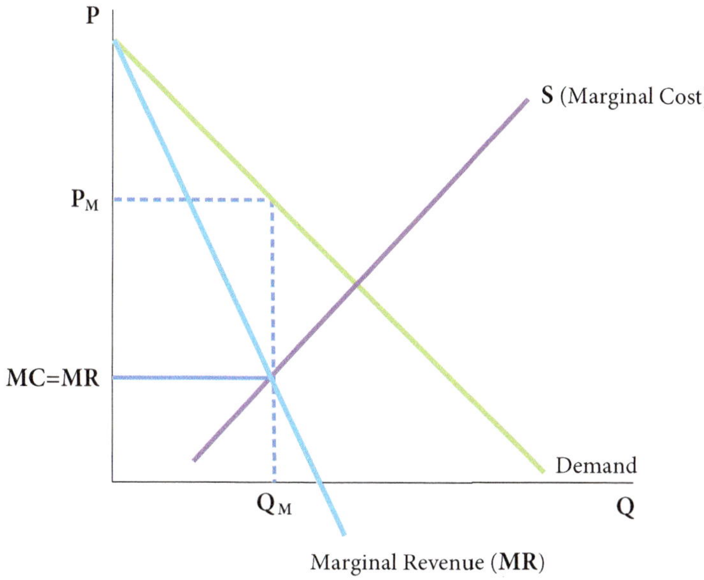

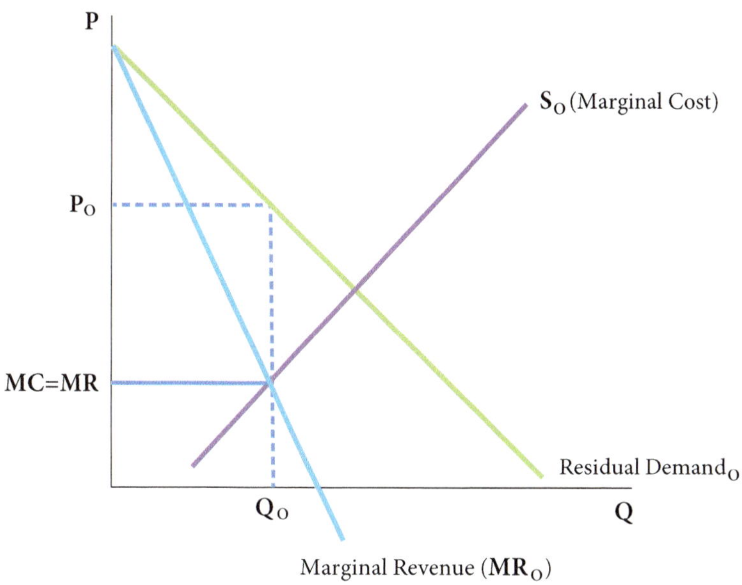

Because the demand curve is vertical in short-term electric power markets, the tempering influence of volume losses as a consequence of price increases is not present. The buyer must pay whatever it takes to serve load, that is, the aggregate demand at any given point in time. The power to raise price is essentially limitless. This can be seen through the Lerner Index (*L*), a well-known yardstick for measuring this market power. It is calculated as the percentage deviation of price from marginal cost, $\frac{P-MC}{P}$.

The index is zero when sellers possess no market power (P=MC), meaning the market is fully competitive. In contrast, a positive price-cost margin (P>MC) reflects some degree of sellers' market power.

The Lerner Index can also be expressed as the inverse of the price elasticity of demand facing the monopoly firm (ε_d).[14] Mathematically, it can be written as:

$$L = \frac{P-MC}{P} = \frac{-1}{\varepsilon_d} \qquad [1]$$

This equation implies that the lower the price elasticity of demand (in absolute value) facing the firm, the higher its price will be above the competitive price based upon marginal costs.[15] As the demand curve approaches vertical, elasticity approaches zero, suggesting the vastly increased pricing power of the monopolist.

In truth, neither pure competition nor pure monopoly is an accurate description of wholesale electricity markets after "deregulation." Although electricity is a commodity and sold by many sellers, power markets at times can still be dominated by a few sellers because of the features of electric power systems that effectively limit the number of suppliers.[16] For this reason many economists have thus used a "few supplier" or oligopoly model to analyze strategic behavior of sellers in electricity markets.[17] The key characteristic of an oligopoly is that each supplier recognizes that its profitability depends upon its rivals' actions in the market. Even though the suppliers do not formally coordinate their strategies, their unilateral profit-maximizing behavior becomes effectively coordinated. The oligopolistic firm recognizes that it cannot act entirely as a monopolist; its output decision depends on its rivals' output.

This interdependent behavior has been captured in many models, the most familiar of which is the Cournot model.[18] Given each firm's reaction to the rivals' output levels, the optimal output for a Cournot oligopoly depends on the number of sellers. As the number of firms increases, the Cournot optimal output approaches that of perfect competition, implying that the price

14. *See* Tirole (1988), p. 66.

15. Note that since demand curves are downward sloping (from left to right in graphic form), demand elasticity values are negative reflecting the fact that demand falls as price rises.

16. As discussed further below, temporal and geographic constraints in the scheduling and delivery of electricity can operate to severely reduce the number of suppliers who can deliver energy when and where it is needed on the system to serve customer demand.

17. *See* Schmalensee and Golub (1984); Green and Newbery (1992); Borenstein, Bushnell, and Stoft (2000); Oren (1997); Borenstein and Bushnell (1999); Wolfram (1998 and 1999); Wolak and Patrick (1996); Wolak (2000 and 2003b) utilized some form of the Cournot assumptions.

18. The Cournot model was developed and published by Antoine Augustin Cournot in 1838. *See* more discussion in Church and Ware (2000), Chapter 8 – Classical Models of Oligopoly.

declines towards marginal cost.[19] Thus in an oligopoly market the price would typically be greater than marginal cost but still lower than the monopoly price.

But here again, the vertical demand curve plays a key role. In an oligopoly market any individual seller's ability to raise price above marginal cost is limited by its market share. The Lerner Index in this case becomes:

$$L = \frac{P - MC_i}{P} = \frac{-S_i}{\varepsilon_d} \qquad [2]$$

where S_i is the market share of a firm i and MC_i is firm i's marginal cost. This equation indicates that despite the fact that any individual oligopolist's market share is less than one, its ability to elevate price over its marginal cost becomes unbounded as demand elasticity in the market approaches zero.[20]

Implications for Defining Electric Power Markets

Product Market Definition

Until now, we have referred to wholesale power as simply that—a product consisting of delivered electrical energy. Although this was not true in the Western power crisis, today's power markets often include markets for capacity as well as for ancillary services. Each of these products is tradable within complex market systems overseen by the FERC and other regulators, and the relationships between these different types of electrical products can be important in specific competitive analyses. However, the largest product type traded in power markets by far is electrical energy itself, so we generally limit our focus to this type of product.[21]

Physically speaking, electrical energy is a very homogenous product at any given point in time. Due to technical standards, all electricity placed onto the North American grid must meet very specific voltage and frequency standards. Thus, the only power one can sell or buy in North America is 60-hertz alternating current at a handful of voltages, mainly 120 and 240 volts.

While this might seem to create a simple task for defining products, the remaining dimensions of electric service as a product are what make the task complex. The essence of product market definition is the question of the degree to which a buyer can substitute different forms of power

19. *See* Cabral (2000), Chapter 9 – Market Structure and Market Power; Tirole (1988), pp. 218–221.

20. *Id.* For a more detailed treatment of the Lerner Index, *see* Landes and Posners (1981). Landes and Posner also pointed out the importance of defining relevant product and geographic markets, which we discuss later in this Chapter.

21. The relationship between products in the English markets is discussed by Newbery (1995).

for one another, in which case they are in the same product market. We therefore must inquire as to what dimensions differentiate power purchases from each other and the degree to which there is substitution between them.

First, from the perspective of electric consumers, supply that is available next week or next year is of absolutely no use to demand now. In other words, there is no substitutability of supply across time (which is simply another way of saying that neither sellers nor buyers can store power economically). Thus, as an initial matter, *markets for electricity must always be denominated by time*—more specifically, the time of power delivery.

In bulk power markets the primary energy product delineator is therefore the timing and duration of the delivery period.[22] Electricity can be purchased over any period ranging from one hour to twenty or more years. "Spot market" electric power trades occur over delivery periods of one hour to several days, while "long-term" trades are typically classified as one year or longer. In between these two clearly-defined product types are weekly, monthly, or part-of-month transactions. There are robust bilateral markets at recognized trading hubs such as the California-Oregon border (COB), Mid-Columbia (Mid-C), and Palo Verde (PV) where standardized contracts in which specified volumes[23] are purchased and sold at fixed prices[24] over various durations such as monthly, quarterly, or annually.[25] Whereas short-term arrangements tend to be standardized, there can be considerable flexibility in longer-term transactions. For example, for a one hour sale there is almost always a single (constant) level of power supplied at a single location on the power grid at a fixed price. In a twenty-year contract, the seller and buyer typically have complex provisions for selecting and adjusting the prices, amount of power supplied, the delivery location, the rights to resell unneeded power, and many other provisions.

The degree to which these products can substitute for each other in any particular market is a very complex question. First, the substitution can only occur in one direction. One can arrange for contracts that supply next year's power months in advance, but once a customer has a short-term need for power (say, 100 MW needed for delivery tomorrow) there is not enough time—nor a long enough established need—to negotiate a ten-year contract.

Less abstractly, there are always extremely important risk management and regulatory restrictions on the degree to which spot and long-term purchases can substitute for each other. Most electricity buyers do not or cannot rely too much on short-term or long-term purchases. This is especially important because (a) electric markets are always time-denominated, as noted

22. As noted above, there are also markets within the bulk power sector for capacity and ancillary services. These are also time-denominated and have their own distinct technical and economic features.

23. These are generally in multiples of 25 MW.

24. These products may specify delivery of energy during peak or off-peak periods or over all hours.

25. These standardized arrangements are typically deliverable at the transmission facilities in the vicinity of the relevant trading hub.

above, and (b) the amount of electricity demanded in total in any market, and demanded by nearly every individual customer, changes substantially hour to hour and across the seasons. Thus, no electric customer or system could rationally buy their highest level of use at a constant level for any period of time unless they were set up to resell instantly the surplus between their momentary demand and the higher constant amount they purchased long term.[26] As a practical matter, as the time for actual dispatch approaches, the energy transacted in longer-duration arrangements is already committed to load and thus is not a substitute for supply remaining uncommitted for the next hour or two. The electrons may be fungible, but the various commitments are not.

Geographic Market Definition

The geographic market for electricity for any buyer is determined by the set of generators that can compete to sell to that buyer. In the wholesale power market that set is determined by the capacity of the transmission system between that buyer and nearby power generators.[27]

The technical attributes of transmission grids dictate that power cannot be directed along specific transmission paths, instead flowing from generators to loads across the network paths of lowest impedance. These flows change on a minute-by-minute basis, which is only logical, because customer electrical demand may change minute-by-minute, and the grid operator must balance total supply with total demand. As power plants in a variety of locations are constantly dispatched up or down to meet changing demands in hundreds of locations on the transmission grid, it is easy to see why flows on each segment of the grid are also changing in magnitude and sometimes direction.

Since we know electric markets are always time-denominated, and further denominated by the duration of the product purchased, the more refined way to describe a geographic market for one buyer's bulk power is this: *At the particular time of delivery, and for the desired duration of the transaction, and for the specific location of the customer, which sellers with uncommitted supply can find sufficient transmission capacity on the system to be able to deliver power to that customer at roughly the same price?*

In physical-goods markets, the limits of the geographic market are set by the costs of shipping the product to the buyer. As sellers get farther and farther from the buyer, shipping becomes either prohibitively expensive or infeasible; such expensive or infeasible shippers are no longer part of the geographic market. On the transmission system the limits are analogous. "Shipping

26. *See* Fox-Penner *et al.* (2002), p. 308 for more discussion of this point. This is the corollary to needing different kinds of generation to follow varying load.

27. For additional discussion, *see* Moss and Fox-Penner (2005); Gilbert, Neuhoff, and Newbery (2004); Stoft (1999); Joskow and Tirole (2000); and many works by Professor William Hogan (available at *http://www.whogan.com/*).

costs" on the power grid are roughly set not by the geographic distance between generator and buyer, but rather by the electrical losses incurred between the two points, which are a function of many technical features in addition to distance. The feasibility of shipping is similarly a complex determination made with computer simulations that are constantly updated to reflect conditions over a wide portion of the nearby grid.

Fortunately, it is usually not necessary to do a separate analysis of all of these aspects of the electric geographic market on a customer-by-customer basis. Based on the results of transmission simulation models, it is usually possible to delineate some geographic areas in which, for many time and delivery periods, all customers have roughly the same access to the same set of generators. These areas are typically the boundaries of areas controlled by each of the grid operating authorities in North America, formally known as Control Areas or Balancing Authority Areas (BAAs). For example, the New York Independent System Operator (NYISO) controls the New York state as a single balancing area.

However, it is never sufficient simply to assert that a BAA is a proper geographic market without further analysis. Where there is ample transmission capacity from other BAAs, the geographic market may include generators in a number of these areas. Conversely, there are often time periods during which transmission limits within a BAA constrain the set of generators who can supply power to a customer to one "zone" within the area. In the case of the NYISO, the Long Island zone (Zone K), for example, is often congested and is thereby analyzed as a separate geographic market.

As Chapter 4 will explain, this problem was a significant factor during the California Crisis. The California Independent System Operator (CAISO) operated a BAA that roughly covered all parts of the state other than the cities of Sacramento and Los Angeles.[28] The CAISO BAA had transmission links to these two cities as well as Arizona, Nevada, and the PNW. During some hours of the Crisis these areas were part of the geographic market for spot power, but during others the transmission lines were full or out of service and the geographic market was effectively reduced to suppliers at a single delivery point. Just as importantly, within the California BAA there were three different zones that sometimes became separate geographic markets unto themselves. It therefore becomes impossible to specify the geographic market for bulk power during the California Crisis unless one further specifies the time period of interest and then takes a careful look at transmission availability into and within the CAISO BAA.

28. There were numerous other smaller municipal utility and agricultural districts that, although within the boundaries of the CAISO, were not part of the CAISO.

Other Market Power Related Issues

Supplier Entry

In every competitive analysis, the potential for entry of new suppliers serves as an essential potential check on the exercise of market power by existing sellers. This is true in electric power markets as well, but the entry period is unusually long—typically at least two years—relative to the trading period for spot power—typically today or tomorrow. In other words, if a power market becomes structurally non-competitive, it could take quite some time before entry was able to improve competition. The long time frame for plant development reflects not only the development and construction periods involved, but also lengthy environmental and siting approval processes required. The Western Power Crisis began in May 2000; the first new plants to be built following the crisis—built under the most urgent conditions—did not start operating until July 2001. Furthermore, these plants were already under development at the time and so were not really directly responsive to the Crisis.

Information Availability and Repeat Games

There are a finite number of power plants in any one area—and lots of public information on them. Information on generating unit types (even make and model numbers), operating characteristics and heat rates are available along with outage information so that every power generator in any area usually knows quite a lot about all of its competing generators. Fuel costs can easily be estimated. All this information comes from a variety of sources, including a wide variety of real-time data feeds.

Hour after hour with minor variations the same set of generators and transmission links are used to meet stationary loads that vary over time in a fairly predictable fashion. Generating capacities and costs, expected weather conditions and loads, and transmission links and looming constraints are internalized by every credible trading operation. Over time traders not only learn how the system operates under various conditions, but also how their competitors tend to behave under those conditions. In such circumstances it is generally less difficult for traders to experiment with and test new manipulation strategies or to pursue profits through coordinated behavior. Thus, electric markets are inherently well-suited to tacit collusion and other types of joint behavior that may impede strong competition.[29]

---

29. *See* Borenstein and Bushnell (1999) for a good early discussion of this aspect of power markets. The authors modeled the California markets prior to the crisis, correctly foretelling some of the problems that later occurred.

Identifying Market Power in Wholesale Electricity Markets

Market power is a matter of degree. Economists have developed various techniques to assess the degree of market power using information about ownership structure, pricing, and profitability. There is no single best metric to measure market power. Combinations of market power tests are often used in reaching a conclusion whether a seller has or exercises market power. The three types of market power diagnostic measures are structure, performance, and conduct-based tests. The first category is focused on dimensions of market structure, which is used to predict behavior of sellers and their performances. The second category, a performance-based measure, examines the degree in which a firm's price departs from its marginal cost. The third category analyzes behavior of sellers (or buyers) in a market and makes inferences about market power from such conduct. As the foregoing section suggests, the features of electric power markets require some recalibration of traditional approaches.

Structural Approaches

Structural tests are of particular significance in electric power markets because there is no presumption of competition. The FERC continues to regulate power markets to guard against undue market power and to assure just and reasonable rates, though not by fixing prices in advance. Under the scheme that the Commission has developed, a supplier must qualify to price at market-based rates (MBR) by demonstrating that it is not in a position to exercise market power. This requires *ex ante* assessment of whether or not a candidate supplier would have market power were it given the authority to negotiate and sell at a price on a market basis constrained only by competition. This predictive assessment precludes the use of approaches relying upon actual market performance or supplier conduct.

Structural analyses draw inferences regarding potential market outcomes from the number and size of all suppliers within defined product and geographic markets. Market power does not exist in a market with many small sellers and no barriers to entry. However, the number of firms cannot be a sole indicator of the market competitiveness since the distribution of firm size also matters. Early in its efforts to liberalize power markets and qualify sellers to price at market rates, the Commission relied upon a simple demonstration that the seller did not have a market share larger than 20% of the relevant market, defined according to FERC's rules that relied upon a very narrow and simplistic geographic market definition and did not recognize transmission constraints. While this approach constrained the market power of the incumbent utility systems in their former monopoly service territories, it did little else and was abandoned after the Crisis.[30]

The Herfindahl-Hirschman Index (HHI)

A more reliable index of market power can be obtained by measuring the degree to which the output in a relevant market is produced and sold by a few large firms. The Herfindahl-Hirschman Index is such a measure that is frequently relied upon by both the FERC and U.S. antitrust agencies in assessing potential mergers.[31] The HHI is the calculated sum of each seller's market share squared. The value of HHI varies from close to zero to 10,000. When a market is occupied by one firm, the HHI is 10,000 (100^2); but when a market has 100 small firms with one percent market share each, the HHI is 100 ($1^2+1^2+1^2+1^2+\ldots$..).

The HHI threshold used for the FERC's market-based rate approval is 2,500.[32] This is consistent with the DOJ's established HHI safe harbor threshold in *Oil Pipelines Deregulation Report of the U.S. Department of Justice* (1986)[33] and the 2010 DOJ/FTC Guidelines. The 2,500 HHI value is based on equal market shares of four firms in a relevant market ($25^2 + 25^2 + 25^2 + 25^2$). If the HHI value is greater than 2500, the market is considered to be at "high risk" for having market power.

As indicated above, the FERC also utilizes the HHI values before and after a merger and acquisition (M&A) transaction to gauge potential adverse competitive impacts in a relevant market. A large increase in the size of market concentration runs the risk of incurring social costs that exceed possible gains enjoyed by a larger firm. The FERC adopted the HHI thresholds from the 1992 U.S. Department of Justice and Federal Trade Commission (DOJ/FTC) Horizontal Merger Guideline, which based on HHI values divides markets into three types:[34]

- The market deems to be competitive or not concentrated if the HHI is below 1,000. Regardless of any changes in the HHI, the transaction is unlikely to have adverse impact.

---

30. Chapter 6 contains an expanded discussion of these topics.

31. Other than in considering applications for MBR authority, *ex ante* structural measures are commonly relied upon in considering the potential competitive impacts of proposed mergers.

32. In the final step of the FERC's current horizontal market power analysis for market-based rate applicants, the Commission examines together the HHI, market share, and pivotal supplier statistics if a seller failed the FERC's preliminary screens.

33. *Oil Pipelines Deregulation Report of the U.S. Department of Justice*, 1986, p. 30.

34. *Id.*; U.S. Department of Justice and Federal Trade Commission 1992. The DOJ/FTC reclassified the HHI types in the 2010 *Horizontal Merger Guidelines* (DOJ/FTC Guidelines). Under the 2010 DOJ/FTC Guidelines, a market with the HHI below 1,500 is considered to be an unconcentrated market. If the HHI is between 1,500 and 2,500, the market deems to be moderately concentrated. When the HHI is above 2,500, the market is highly concentrated. However, the FERC continues to use the 1992 thresholds. *http://www.ftc.gov/sites/defalut/files/attachments/merger-review/100819hmg.pdf*

- If the HHI is between 1,000 and 1,800, the market deems to be moderately concentrated. The M&A potentially raises significant competitive concerns if the change in HHI is greater than 100.

- When the HHI is above 1,800, the market is highly concentrated. In this case a proposed merger or acquisition raises potentially significant competitive concerns if the change in HHI is greater than 50.[35]

The index does have some predictive value in electric power markets. A very large number of firms with small market shares are more likely to compete aggressively. But as the number of firms decline, coordination of prices above competitive levels becomes easier. Thus, a highly concentrated market facilitates explicit or implicit collusion to restrict output and raise prices.

The Pivotal Supplier Index (PSI)

As discussed above, electric power markets are dynamic, varying substantially from hour to hour with conditions on the power grid. The relevant market definition and the number of competitors may also change substantially from hour to hour, particularly when the load on the system approaches capacity. For this reason a measure more suited to highly specific time-denominated markets called the Pivotal Supplier Index has been developed.

A potential seller is called pivotal when the total market demand for electric power cannot be met in a particular hour without some portion of the supply held by that seller. In other words, buyers of electricity in a given hour must buy at least some of their power from a pivotal supplier or they will have to take emergency measures to deal with a shortfall in electricity supply. Electric power economists have developed a simple quantitative index (the Pivotal Supplier Index or PSI) whose value establishes whether a supplier is or is not pivotal in a defined market—i.e., when the supply of the relevant product from every supplier and the level of demand ("Load") are known. As detailed in Chapter 6, the PSI formula for any particular supplier compares: (1) the amount of capacity held by that supplier to (2) the capacity net of load held by all suppliers in the market (the "supply margin"). If the supply margin is greater than the amount of capacity offered by the supplier being evaluated, PSI is less than one and buyers have supply alternatives. But if the PSI is greater than one, the supplier is pivotal, and its resources would be required in whole or in part to satisfy demand in the market.

In markets for goods that cannot be stored nor demand deferred, sellers who are pivotal have the ability to raise price. These conditions apply to electricity markets. In power markets, since buyers *must* purchase supplies equal to their load or they will experience blackouts, buyers will

35. *Order Reaffirming Commission Policy and Terminating Proceeding*, 138 ¶ 61,109, 2012, p. 34. FERC Merger Policy Statement; *see also FPA Section 203 Supplemental Policy Statement*, FERC Stats. & Regs. ¶ 31,253, 2007 (Supplemental Policy Statement).

have no choice but to accept the pivotal supplier's prices.[36] The higher the PSI, the greater is the ability of the supplier to influence market prices. When a generation supplier knows that it is pivotal, it acquires enormous bargaining power over buyers in the market.

Because the pivotal supplier test can reflect market conditions and dynamics at any particular point in time (in particular, times when the system is approaching its limits), and because empirical studies indicate that the pivotal supplier test is one of the more reliable indicators of electricity seller market power,[37] the FERC adopted this index as its most stringent test of whether sellers should be given MBR approval in the FERC Interim Generation Market Power Order issued on April 14, 2004, and later in its Order No. 697.[38] Obviously, this was too late for the western power crisis. Under the FERC rule, when the PSI is less than one, the seller passes the screen, and vice versa. The FERC also concluded that pivotal suppliers would be expected to exercise market power:

> Thus, the pivotal supplier screen measures market power at peak times, and particularly in spot markets. If demand cannot be met without some contribution of supply by the applicant, the applicant is pivotal. In markets with very little demand elasticity, a pivotal supplier could extract significant monopoly rents during peak periods because customers have few, if any, alternatives.[39]

In addition, a number of RTOs have also adopted the pivotal supplier test to identify conditions conducive to the exercise market power.[40] In all of these current test frameworks, when a supplier is found to be pivotal its power prices are controlled or reset; in other words, the FERC does not allow sellers who are pivotal to set prices because these prices reflect impermissible levels of market power.

To gauge the competitiveness of the CAISO market, the CAISO Market Surveillance Unit (MSU) used another form of pivotal supplier analysis known as the Residual Supplier Index

36. In modern electric markets, buyers can sometimes reduce their demand in response to higher prices without risking blackouts (Demand Response or DR).

37. *See Independent System Operator New England Inc.* Docket No. RT04-2-000 (2004). Federal Energy Regulatory Commission Electric Tariff No. 3. *Midwest Independent System Operator,* Business Practices Manual for Market Monitoring and Mitigation, 2005; *California ISO,* Conformed MRTU Tariff (2007b) available at *http://caiso.com/201c/201cc3142dab0.html. See also Prepared Direct Testimony of Casey, K.* Docket No. ER06-615-000, before the Federal Energy Regulatory Commission. *ERCOT Texas Nodal Protocols* Section 3 - Management Activities for the ERCOT System, 2007. *Analysis of the Three Pivotal Supplier Test: March 1st through December 31, 2006,* PJM Market Monitoring Unit, 2007. *See also* The Brattle Group (2007), p. 112.

38. The Commission initially adopted the PSI as an interim approach for analyzing generation market power in the 2004 MBR Order. The core element of the generation market power analysis adopted in Order No. 697 is the same as that in the 2004 MBR Order.

39. *See AEP Power Mkt'g, et al.,* 107 FERC ¶ 61,018, 2004, p. 72.

40. These RTOs, which have adopted and implemented the concept of the Pivotal Supplier Index (PSI) test in some form, include: PJM, Midwest-ISO, the ISO-New England, the CAISO and the Electric Reliability Council of Texas (ERCOT). All of these RTOs implement a single firm pivotal supplier test, with the exception of PJM and CAISO which implements a three firm pivotal supplier test.

(RSI).[41] The RSI is a measure of supply sufficiency in the market in relation to buyer's demand *excluding supply available from the seller being tested.* For example, if for one hour the amount of supply in a market is 110 megawatts without counting Seller A's capacity, and the total market demand is 100 megawatts, the RSI is 110/100 or 1.1. An RSI less than one indicates that all suppliers other than Seller A are unable to meet demand, and that Seller A is pivotal—i.e., necessary to meet demand. The use of PSI to measure seller market power in the California markets during the Western Crisis is presented in Chapter 6.

Performance-Based Measures

Performance-based tests examine the relationship between market prices and production costs under actual historical market conditions. The use of price-cost margins to infer market power measure is based on the Lerner Index concept discussed earlier in the chapter.

Many economists, including those looking at the California Crisis, have applied this approach to evaluate firm-specific conduct as well as a market-wide performance. Wolak (2003) applied a version of Equation [2] to measure firm-specific market power in the California power market from 1998 to 2000. Wolak calculated the price elasticity of residual demand faced by each of the five largest power suppliers in California (Big-5) and found that the average hourly markup (Lerner Index) of each firm during Summer 2000 was significantly higher than those of Summer 1998 and Summer 1999, suggesting that each of the Big-5 suppliers exercise market power in Summer 2000.[42]

Joskow and Kahn (2001 and 2002), Wolak, Nordhaus, and Shapiro (2000), and Hildebrandt (2000) identified market-level market power in California during 2000. They estimated competitive wholesale market benchmark prices and compared them to the actual market prices. They calculated the benchmark prices by simulating the California day-ahead market as if the market were to operate under perfect competition. In their analyses, suppliers submitted bids based on their marginal operating costs.[43] Both studies found that the California wholesale power market was not workably competitive. There was a significant gap between the competitive benchmark prices and actual market prices from June through September 2000. The gap could not fully be explained by market fundamentals since these factors were used in the calculation of each power plant's marginal cost.

41. *See* CAISO, Market Surveillance Unit, *Annual Report on Market Issues and Performance*, June 1999, pp. 7-4 – 7-5.

42. *Id.*, Table 1.

43. They constructed hourly supply curves using California power plants' operating characteristic data (such as capacity and heat rate) along with actual variable costs (such as fuel prices, variable operating and maintenance (VOM) and emission costs).

This use of competitive benchmark prices to identify market power by Joskow and Kahn sparked a debate over the use of simulations to model the competitive prices. Harvey and Hogan warned that simulation models were limited in their ability to isolate effects of market power from other factors such as higher costs, increased demand, or capacity constraints.[44] They emphasized that it was "equally important to identify the sensitivity of that estimate to changes in assumption that might reflect errors in the model" and concluded that the simulated prices included actual prices.[45] The differences that do exist could have resulted from competitive behavior or the exercise of market power, but the model was not able to make that determination.[46] In their earlier study, Harvey and Hogan claimed that price spikes in part were attributable to California's "unique" market design that predictably caused even a perfectly competitive firm to submit bids far above its marginal production costs.[47]

In assessing the competitiveness of the California power markets during the Western Crisis, the authors also studied the magnitude of the deviations between the actual power prices during the Crisis and what they would have been if the prices were derived from marginal costs of marginal units. Some part of our analysis is discussed in Appendix 6B in Chapter 6.

It is important to note the limitations of the Lerner Index and other price/cost analyses as measures of market power. This type of analysis does not recognize that some of the deviation of price from marginal cost can come from scarcity and the need to cover fixed costs.[48] As we shall see, this posed significant problems in assessing market performance during the Crisis and remains a challenge today.

Scarcity's Effect on Markets

Scarcity and market power are not mutually exclusive explanations of high prices. Scarcity conditions can set the stage for sellers to exercise market power by driving the electric power system toward its capacity limits and into the portion of the supply curve where, as outlined above, even small amounts of withholding may cause very large price increases. Scarcity conditions clearly do not preclude market power but they do complicate its measurement by raising questions about how much of any price-cost margin is attributable to market power and how much reflects true scarcity.

---

44. Harvey and Hogan (2002).

45. *Supra* n. 36 at 2.

46. *Supra* n. 36 at 3.

47. Harvey and Hogan (2000).

48. Because some types of generation such as peaking units have high production costs and are used relatively infrequently, fixed cost recovery can be challenging unless prices when they are running are well above marginal production costs.

Scarcity rents are reflected in the margins above sellers' costs that they receive as the market efficiently allocates supplies that are insufficient to meet demand at the marginal cost of production (that would otherwise determine the competitive price). From a regulator's perspective separating useful scarcity rents from "undue" market power is unusually important in electric markets. The foregoing discussion indicates that features of electric power markets, particularly those in California during the Crisis, make them quite susceptible to the exercise of market power by suppliers. On the other hand, legitimate scarcity rents were necessary in California's liberalized markets to elicit the investment needed to meet customer demands and assure reliable operation of the electric power system. But distinguishing between the two in practice is no easy task. To understand why, we return briefly to the basics.

In strongly competitive markets where the amount of supply is sufficient to meet demand, and each seller is so proportionately small, the market clearing price is equal to the marginal costs of the supplier whose offering clears the market. This is the traditional supply-demand picture, shown in Figure 3-4.

Figure 3-4

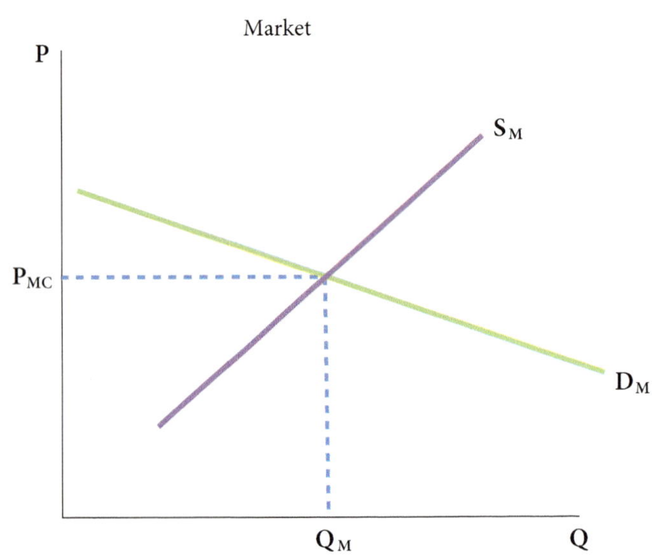

Physical scarcity occurs when the supply and demand curves do not intersect, as illustrated in Figure 3-5. Some consumers are willing to pay more than the price at which supply is offered at the limit of availability.

Figure 3-5

A Simple Market with a Shortage

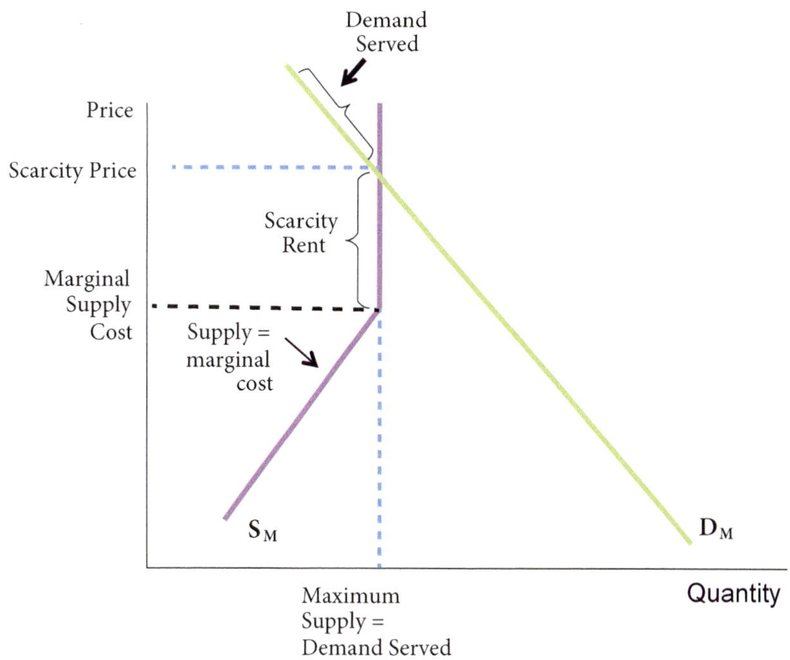

In this situation supply is allocated by the market to the customers who are willing to pay the highest price, those at the upper portions of the demand curve. This is efficient because supply goes to the customers who value the product most and are thus willing to pay the most for it. However, as Figure 3-5 illustrates, the price is set at the level of the willingness to pay of the last customer served.

This has three notable consequences reflected in this graphic representation of the market outcome. First, some customers willing to pay a price at or above the maximum supplier offer price (that is, the marginal cost of the least efficient/most expensive supplier) remain unserved. Second, all suppliers in the market get a "scarcity rent" equal to the difference between marginal cost of the least efficient supplier and the price set by the willingness to pay of the last customer served. These rents provide an attractive incentive for potential entrants to develop the new generation sources needed to relieve the shortage. Finally, the fact that the outcome shown in Figure 3-5 with price exceeding marginal cost looks just like that of the monopoly outcome in Figure 3-3 complicates the assessment of market performance.

It is worth pausing to ask why anything is wrong with this last outcome. A limited supply has been awarded solely to buyers who are most willing to pay for it. That would seem to satisfy the essential core of efficient market exchange. The general societal answer—and the reason electricity remains subject to price controls nearly everywhere in the world—is that it is not considered equitable or socially advantageous to award goods *regarded as necessities* only to the wealthiest buyers whenever shortages loom.[49]

There are many, many goods and services provided by processes that do not use scarcity rents to allocate demand under any conditions. Most public goods are available to all buyers at pre-controlled prices, and many private goods (for example, movie tickets) are allocated on a first-come, first-served basis rather than auctioned to the highest bidder. For the purpose of this discussion, however, what is of interest is that even in markets where price is allowed to allocate demand under ordinary conditions, governments typically put limits on market (i.e., scarcity-based) allocation under some circumstances, notably shortages. When there are shortages of essential commodities, such as water or medicine, governments often employ their emergency powers to ration these goods rather than allow them to be sold to the highest bidder. In fact, most states have price-gouging statutes that automatically limit market pricing when shortages occur.[50]

In electricity markets, there is another important reason not to rely upon prices to allocate scarce supplies. For technical reasons, during true shortages, power systems as currently developed do not have the ability to find the buyers willing to pay most and charge them the new price that aligns supply and demand. Yet operating the electric grid requires that supply and demand be balanced at all times. Since it is not yet administratively feasible to ration power only to the wealthiest buyers in a shortage, nor is it viewed as desirable, high prices are not the main tool used to allocate electricity when there are genuine physical shortages. At the time of the Crisis, the CAISO had a limited ability to divert supply away from a set of customers that had signed on for discounted interruptible service. Once these customers had been interrupted, however, the only remaining option was to reduce or curtail service (brownouts or blackouts) on a rolling, or eventually, a system-wide basis.[51] This only emphasizes the need to assure that scarcity rather than market power is driving margins over costs.

When the FERC made its first key decision to allow "market-based pricing," it made a momentous shift from an allocation scheme in which every buyer paid sellers the same regulated price to one in which prices and scarcity were allowed to allocate available supply to whomever would pay most for it when supplies got tight. However, the FERC also placed several controls on pricing in the California markets. Although these controls were quickly revealed to be deficient, a topic we return to at length in Chapter 7, at the conceptual level they illustrate that

49. Electricity is obviously among these. In fact, most utility distribution companies serving retail customers in the U.S. have subsidy programs to assure service to those customers least able to pay for it.

50. Thirty-four states have some type of prohibition on "price-gouging." The typical form of these laws is to prevent sellers from raising prices more than 10–20% during a shortage or emergency. In some cases, the statutes ban price increases that are simply judged "unjustified" or "excessive" in emergencies. *See List of State Anti-Price Gouging Laws*, Knowledge Problem, November 3, 2012 at *http://knowledgeproblem.com/2012/11/03/list-of-price-gouging-laws/*; and Price Gouging, October 8, 2014 at *http://www.ncsl.org/programs/energy/lawgouging.htm*.

51. Currently various approaches and technologies are being developed to facilitate demand response that would help respond to temporary shortfalls in supply. Even these, however, would not solve longer-term scarcity issues.

the FERC clearly followed widespread precedent and established boundaries at which scarcity-based pricing was to stop for public-interest reasons.

The first of these boundaries was price caps on both the PX and CAISO spot markets. We discuss the details of these shifting caps in Part II, and the point here is simply that these price cap levels were judged to be the point beyond which market-determined prices were no longer net beneficial. Similarly, the FERC required that each seller be tested in advance to see whether they had market power. These tests, which initially were extraordinarily ineffective in the context of the California markets, are discussed further in Chapter 6. Despite their ineffectiveness, these tests were nonetheless evidence of the Commission's appropriate goal of preventing sellers from taking advantage of scarcity to increase prices further through the exercise of market power.

Scarcity in California's Market Design

Scarcity pricing (i.e., prices that include scarcity rents) has become especially contentious in electric power markets due to the unique nature of the migration from regulated electric rates to market-determined ("deregulated") prices. Under FERC regulation, wholesale electricity supply has typically been divided into two distinct products, energy and capacity. Energy is the actual momentary power product, while capacity is the ability to provide that power when requested.

When the FERC set regulated prices for these two products, it priced energy as just the cost of making one incremental unit of power in an existing generator—mainly the cost of fuel, labor, and other supplies. Of course, this energy price could also be called the energy cost (since prices equaled costs under this form of regulation) and could also be seen as an approximate incremental or marginal cost. FERC then set the capacity price equal to the average per-unit cost of owning a generator, i.e., the average per-unit capital cost, including return on investment. These two charges together allowed generators to earn back both their capital and energy costs, including reasonable profits, but no more.

When the California markets were created early in the move toward deregulation, the design included only energy markets (hence the name "energy-only markets," a label still used today). By construction this meant that the only way for generators on the margin to recoup the value of their plant investment was to charge more than just the cost of making power, i.e., marginal cost or the traditional regulated energy price. Put differently, scarcity rents were an essential, if tacit, element in the California market design—it was the margin above energy costs that paid capacity costs and profit.

This posed a dilemma for the FERC in its response to the California Crisis. While the Commission's job was to prevent "unjust and unreasonable" prices, it had to allow some scarcity pricing. If it allowed too little, some generators might not continue to invest in supplying the market. But, as we have seen, scarcity sets the stage for the exercise of market power, leaving the FERC to determine when margins over costs went beyond the level necessary to ensure the investment required to serve customer demand in the long run. Much of the debate over whether prices were excessive during the Crisis centered on this question.

Conduct-Based Measures

A conduct test analyzes suppliers' specific behaviors. In a non-competitive market, a seller has the ability and incentive to restrain output to raise price. Under conduct-based measures, one directly assesses seller withholding acts including physical withholding and economic withholding. As noted earlier, physical withholding occurs when a generator fails to offer its supplies even when they could have economically been sold at the market price. Economic withholding, on the other hand, occurs when a generator's bid is too high to be dispatched even though its bid could have been dispatched had the generator submitted its bid at its true marginal operating cost.

With information available on generator capacities and operating costs, it is possible to observe directly when they do not produce all that they could when it was economic to do so. Where this is detected the investigation must focus on the reason for any apparent shortfall. Was it the result of a forced or planned outage or due to the lack of emission permits? If there were no physical or other reasons for shortfalls in economic production, were there patterns in such shortfalls consistent with withholding to raise prices?

Here again the analysis is complicated by the vertical demand curve in power markets and the fact that scarcity conditions contributed to the elevation in prices. The vertical demand curve meant that little withholding was required to alter prices, thus making detection difficult. Furthermore, scarcity confuses attribution of price increases to market power in statistical analyses.

With regard to economic withholding, because the PX and CAISO retained information on bids, it was possible to assess supplier bidding behavior. Supplier bids could be compared to generation costs and reviewed for patterns consistent with efforts to elevate prices. Two challenges arose in this type of analysis. One was the fact that many bidders were not generators, but rather marketers reselling power purchased from unspecified sources. Another was the issue of opportunity costs, raised primarily by hydroelectric producers able to displace energy from one period to another.[52]

In Chapter 6 we discuss the analyses undertaken to address these questions and challenges.

---

52. A hydro producer with reservoir capacity could hold water in its reservoir to run through its generator at the most opportune time to produce. Such a producer thus might bid a high price in January, for example, based upon expected prices or even quoted forward prices for June, July, and August, when prices are typically at their peak.

Part II: Market Power and Manipulation in the Western Crisis

CHAPTER 4

OVERVIEW OF THE CALIFORNIA MARKETS AND THE WESTERN POWER CRISIS

Establishment of the California Markets

Seeking to lower some of the highest electricity prices in the nation, the California Public Utilities Commission (CPUC) voted in December 1995 to deregulate California's electricity industry.[1]

> Our debates have revealed the broadest consensus that our rates are too high and must be brought into alignment with regional averages if California is to sustain a competitive posture as we enter the twenty-first century.[2]

The decision required the three California IOUs—PG&E, SCE, and San Diego Gas & Electric Company (SDG&E)—to break up their integrated monopoly retail sales franchises by divesting substantial portions of their fossil-fueled generation located within their service territories and by transferring control of their transmission assets to an independent system operator, the CAISO. The plan also required the creation of two entities that were to be the foundation of competitive electricity markets in California—PX and the CAISO. The CPUC

---

1. *Order Instituting Rulemaking on the Commission's Proposed Policies Governing Restructuring California's Electric Services Industry and Reforming Regulation,* The California Public Utility Commission Decision 95-12-063, December 20, 1995, p. 5. The order was modified in Decision 96-01-009, January 10, 1996.

2. *Id.*

scheme allowed the three IOUs to recover their stranded costs through a Competitive Transition Charge (CTC)[3] and capped their retail rates at 1996 levels.

In September 1996, the California legislature embraced the CPUC restructuring framework with some modifications in the Assembly Bill 1890 (AB 1890). The key modifications were rolling back electricity rates the IOUs were allowed to charge by 10 percent and freezing these rates until March 31, 2002. It was projected that even at the reduced rates, the IOUs would easily recover their stranded costs through the CTC before the 2002 deadline. The California Energy Commission (CEC) forecasted an average wholesale market-clearing price of $28.50/MWh in 2000 and $31/MWh in 2001 with a reserve margin of at least 12 percent.[4] They obviously did not anticipate the financial distress that would be encountered by the IOUs and their consumers due to high prices in the California wholesale power markets.

When the PX and CAISO markets commenced on March 31, 1998,[5] PG&E, SCE, and SDG&E divested their thermal generating capacity in California mostly to five companies—Allegheny Energy Supply (AES), Duke Energy Corporation (Duke), Dynegy Inc. (Dynegy), Reliant Energy Company (Reliant), and Southern Company Energy Marketing (later sold to Mirant). The divestitures aimed to mitigate potential market power of the incumbent IOUs in the deregulated markets.

These five companies purchased 17,700 MW of generation, approximately 31 percent of the total capacity (56,000 MW) in the California market. The IOUs retained their hydroelectric and nuclear generation, totaling approximately 12,400 MW.[6] Qualifying Facilities (QFs) owned about 9,500 MW, about 17 percent.[7] The remaining capacity was owned by relatively small companies.[8] The ownership breakdown of California generating capacity is shown in Figure 4-1. The output of the QFs was sold to the IOUs under long-term contracts. None of the divestitures included sales commitments back to the IOUs to cushion the transition to deregulated supply markets.

3. Stranded costs arose when the revenues realized in the forced sale of generation assets did not cover their depreciated values on the IOUs' books. The CTC was to be collected from the difference between the retail sales revenues and aggregate wholesale power costs, which included costs of energy, ancillary services, transmission, distribution, and regulatory services.

4. Electricity Analysis Office and Energy Information & Analysis Division, *Market Clearing Prices Under Alternative Resource Scenarios 2000-2010,* California Energy Commission, February 2000, pp. 8, 27.

5. The FERC approved the California's new wholesale market structure on March 30, 1998. *See* 82 FERC ¶61,327, 1998 and 82 FERC ¶61,328, 1998.

6. SCE retained a total of 2,800 MW (1,600 MW of nuclear and 1,200 MW of hydro generation) in California and 2,200 MW of capacity in Arizona and New Mexico. PG&E retained roughly 7,000 MW (2,300 MW of nuclear, 4,000 MW of hydro, and 600 MW of thermal generation). SDG&E kept 500 MW of its jointly owned nuclear power station.

7. The QFs were generally small, independent suppliers.

8. In 1999, PG&E divested an additional 14 geothermal power plants to Calpine.

Figure 4-1

Ownership Breakdown of California Generating Capacity by April 1, 1998

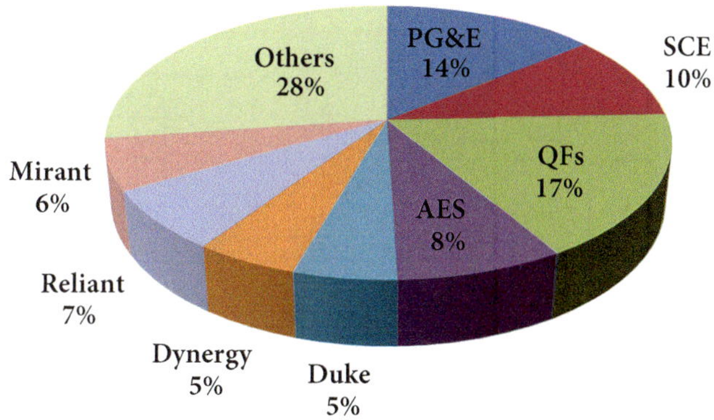

The structure of the California markets was unique both in its design and operation.[9] The PX was responsible for the wholesale power procurement while the CAISO managed the transmission system and ultimately balanced supply and demand fluctuations in its service area in real-time (RT) in order to maintain system reliability. The PX and CAISO were designed as sequential spot power markets. The IOUs would procure most of their power needs in the PX day-ahead market and rely on the CAISO Imbalance Energy (real-time) market only to address incremental fluctuations in supply or demand, as shown in Figure 4-2. Their operations, together, would ensure the reliable delivery of power to load in California. To obtain energy, ancillary services, and transmission, both relied on market-based pricing established via single market-clearing price auctions. However, when the CAISO found supply offers insufficient to cover its energy and reserve requirements, it was allowed to buy power "out-of-market" from neighboring utilities or power marketers via bilateral transactions outside its auction process.[10]

9. The California market design was the product of extended debate over various proposals. In April 1994 the CPUC announced in a Rulemaking Proceeding its intent to restructure the state's electricity market. The IOUs offered competing proposals during the proceedings. The "Direct Access Model" relied on bilateral contracts and the "PoolCo Model" used a centralized spot market to secure generation. In May 1995 the CPUC issued majority and minority policy preference statements, supporting the PoolCo Model and Direct Access Model respectively. In response to these proposals, major stakeholders (SCE, the California Manufacturers Association (CMA), the California Large Energy Consumers Association (CLECA), and the Independent Energy Producers (IEP)) issued a Memorandum of Understanding (MOU, available at *http://www.ucei.berkeley.edu/Restructuring%20 Archive/MOU.pdf*) in September 1995, suggesting functional separation of the proposed independent system operator (ISO) and a power exchange (PX). Consumer and environmental interest groups expressed concerns related to affordability and conservation, renewable energy, and energy efficiency programs. *See* Blumstein, Friedman, and Green, (August 2002). Professor Hogan laid out further arguments against the proposal in "A Wholesale Pool Spot Market Must be Administered by the Independent System Operator: Avoiding the Separation Fallacy" (October 1995). The CPUC ultimately decided to follow the September 1995 MOU and create two distinct entities to perform the spot market and transmission functions. See California Public Utilities Commission Decision 95-12-063, December 20, 1995, available at *http://www.cpuc.ca.gov/PUC/energy/Retail+Electric+Markets+and+Finance/Electric+ Markets/Historical+Information/D9512063/General.htm.*

10. Outside the PX and ISO power in the West was traded bilaterally at individually negotiated prices. These transactions typically were arranged directly with counterparties or through brokerage firms. The purchased energy was customarily delivered at one of five popular trading hubs on the WECC transmission grid: Mid-Columbia (Mid-C), the California-Oregon border (COB), Mead, Four Corners, and Palo Verde (PV).

Figure 4-2

PX and CAISO Market Structures

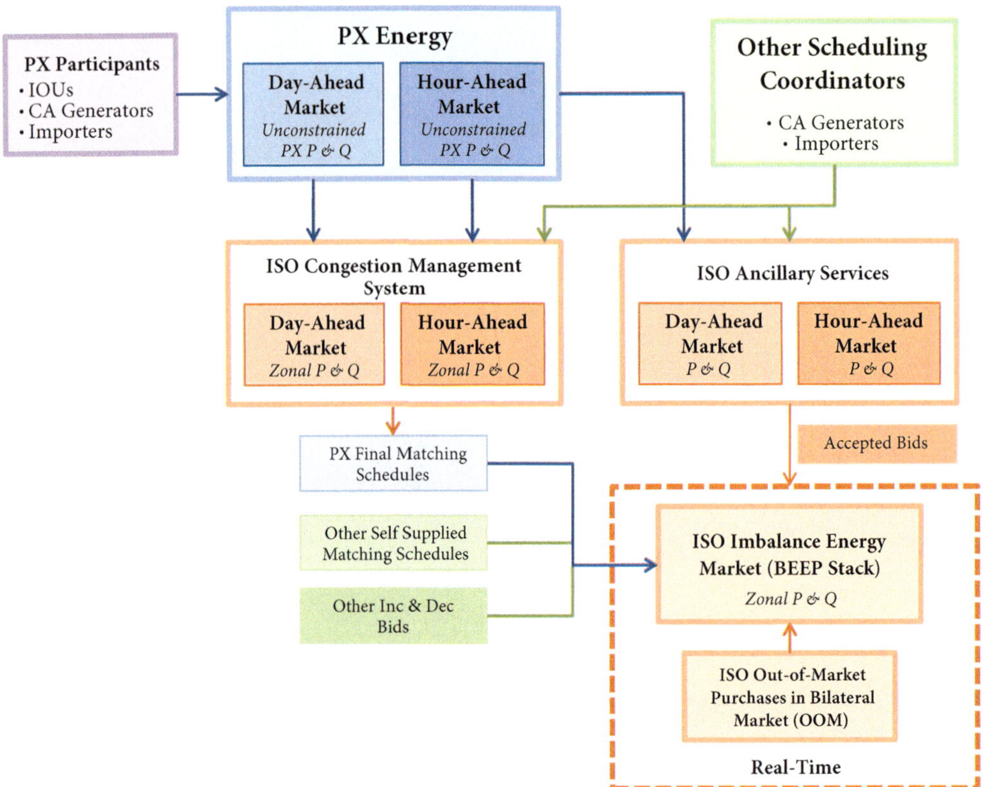

Basic Operations of PX and CAISO Markets

The Power Exchange (PX)

The PX operated a spot power pool that provided a centralized clearinghouse for buyers and sellers of electricity. It operated day-ahead hourly energy auctions for following-day power delivery as well as hour-ahead (HA) energy auctions for same-day power delivery. The PX day-ahead (DA) market opened at 6:00 a.m. and closed at 1:00 p.m. to set 24 hourly prices and quantities for the next day. The hour-ahead trading offered three auction periods. Following the close of the DA market, HA auctions started at 4:00 p.m. for power delivery in hours ending (HE) 1:00 a.m. through 10:00 a.m. on the following day, at 6:00 a.m. on the day-of (DO) market day of delivery for HE 11:00 a.m. through 4:00 p.m. delivery, and finally at noon on the day of delivery for HE 5:00 p.m. through mid-night of the same day. The HA market was designed specifically to allow the PX Scheduling Coordinators to alter their day-ahead demand and supply accepted schedules for changes in their forecasts, and thus minimize real-time imbalances.[11]

For each hourly auction, Scheduling Coordinators submitted their demand and/or supply schedules to the PX. The PX aggregated market participants' demand and supply schedules and determined a single uncongested market clearing price (UMCP) applicable to all purchases and "market-clearing" quantity (Q) as illustrated in Figure 4-3.

Figure 4-3

Illustrative Example of Hourly PX Aggregate Demand and Supply Curves

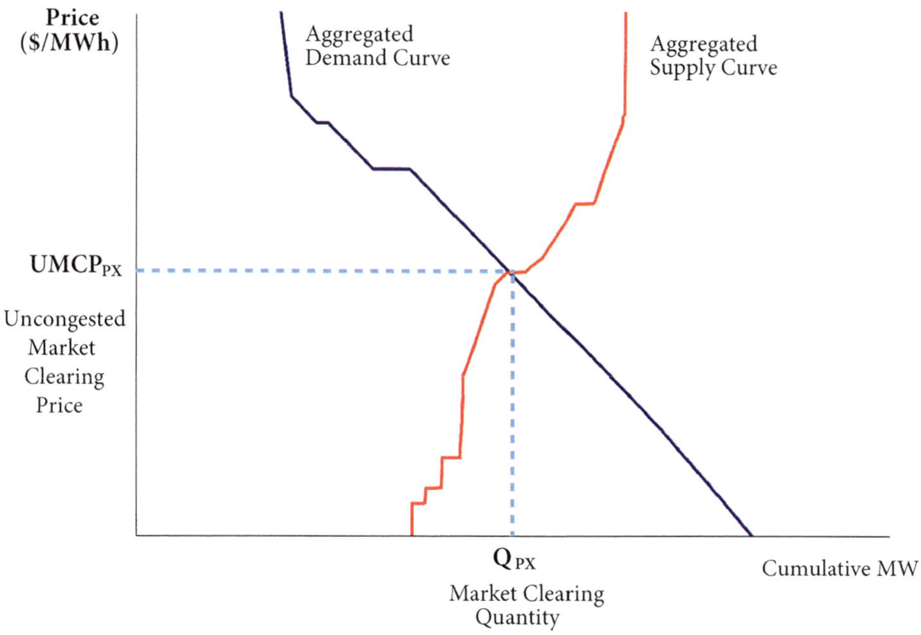

To procure transmission services for delivering the market clearing quantities (Q_{PX}) to load points, the PX first asked winning buyers and sellers to submit schedules for their accepted bids and offers.[12] The PX then submitted these schedules, known as Preferred Schedules, along with associated adjustment bids and offers to the CAISO's DA and HA congestion management markets. Adjustment bids were quantity and price pairs that reflected prices and volumes at and over which purchasers or sellers would be willing to increase or decrease from their

11. *Cal PX Primer, The Basics: How the California Power Exchange Works, California Power Exchange,* Version 6, December 1999.

12. Sellers scheduled from their chosen supply sources to PX delivery points and buyers scheduled from PX delivery points to their chosen loads. These schedules "balanced" in aggregate at the PX market-clearing quantity.

Preferred Schedules. The CAISO used these adjustment bids to alter receipts and deliveries to clear congestion on the system. The adjustments made by the CAISO to relieve congestion at various locations would determine the PX final prices of delivered energy in the CAISO system. If there was no congestion on the CAISO transmission system, the PX day-ahead price and cleared quantity would stay the same as the $UMCP_{PX}$ and Q_{PX}. But when the CAISO determined that congestion existed in a given hour, the PX final prices would deviate from the $UMCP_{PX}$. They could vary by the CAISO zones, which, at the time, were comprised of SP15 (South of Path 15), NP15 (North of Path 15), and ZP26 (area between SP15 and NP15), as shown in Figure 4-4.

Figure 4-4

CAISO Transmission System

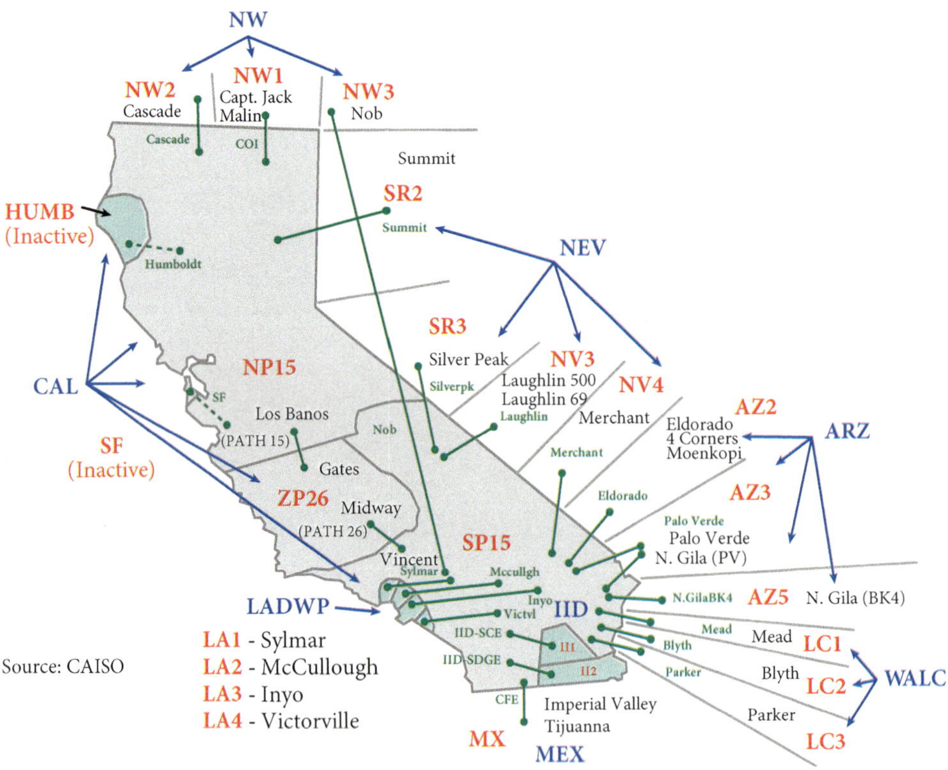

Source: CAISO

The California Independent System Operator (CAISO)

After the restructuring, the PG&E, SCE, and SDG&E balancing authority areas (BAAs) were combined to form the CAISO BAA. To ensure reliability of its system according to the Western Electricity Coordinating Council (WECC) reliability standards, the CAISO acted as a system operator that controlled and balanced the power flows in its transmission system on a continuous basis. Its main responsibilities involved (1) providing non-discriminatory transmission access, (2) having adequate ancillary services to satisfy the (WECC's) reliability requirements, and (3) adjusting generation to address energy imbalances in RT. The CAISO managed all of these reliability responsibilities through market mechanisms.

CAISO Transmission Markets

The CAISO provided DA and HA congestion management markets for the PX and other Scheduling Coordinators who wanted to utilize CAISO's transmission system to deliver power inside of or wheel power out of or through its BAA. In each congestion management market, the CAISO accepted hourly matching demand and supply schedules from its Scheduling Coordinators (or transmission customers). Each supply schedule included a Scheduling Coordinator's sources of generation, location of the resources, associated amounts, and its willingness to increase or decrease supply schedules expressed through adjustment bids. Each demand schedule indicated a Scheduling Coordinator's demand at each load point. The PX, on behalf of its winning buyers and suppliers, was among many Scheduling Coordinators that submitted schedules in the CAISO's congestion management markets.[13]

The CAISO determined, based on all unit-specific supply bids and location-specific demand bids submitted by its Scheduling Coordinators, where congestion would occur on its system. Congestion could occur on a transmission path when the Preferred Schedules submitted to the CAISO required power flows that exceeded a particular transmission path's available transfer capacity. In those cases, the CAISO charged all users of the congested path a transmission fee. This fee was determined based on a price differential of two scheduling points, a point of receipt and a point of delivery, such as Path 15 or NW1 shown on Figure 4-4. As discussed above, the CAISO determined a price at each scheduling point based on Scheduling Coordinators' adjustment bids, which reflected their willingness to charge/pay to increase or decrease their generation/load schedules. Its software, which modeled the electrical properties of the transmission system, would determine whether the DA (or HA) schedules were physically feasible. If they were not, the CAISO would reschedule the generation and/or loads, in accordance with the loads' and generators' adjustment bids, to avoid power flows in excess of the transmission capability. These adjusted schedules and CAISO-determined transmission fees modified zonal market clearing prices and the final schedules. The last (highest-priced) adjustment bid needed to relieve congestion in a zone generally set that zone's post-congestion zonal price. This forced the final day-ahead price to diverge from the PX's UMCP.

It is noteworthy that the CAISO's congestion management process did not address actual congestion, but rather congestion *expected* as a result of DA and HA schedules. Relieving

13. By Summer 2000, there were approximately 100 Scheduling Coordinators in the CAISO markets.

congestion was really about solving conflicts in the scheduled flows before they happened. Thus, being able to rely upon the accuracy and truthfulness of information submitted by Scheduling Coordinators was critical for reliable operation of the power grid. As we discuss in Chapter 7, Enron and other suppliers pursued strategies that intentionally misrepresented load and/or generation in schedules submitted to the CAISO during the Crisis.

CAISO Ancillary Services Markets

Ancillary services are those services necessary to support transmission of power from resources to loads while maintaining reliable operation of a transmission system within and among BAAs. The CAISO procured four types of ancillary services through DA and HA markets.[14] These included Regulation, Spinning Reserves, Non-Spinning Reserves, and Replacement Reserves. The demand for each type of reserve was determined by the CAISO based on its load forecasts. Supplier bids, which were submitted simultaneously for all of the various service types, had to contain a capacity and an energy component.

For each hour, the CAISO held auctions for each service and rewarded winning suppliers a market-clearing capacity price for making capacity available to the CAISO. Then if the supplier was called upon to deliver energy, they were also paid in addition the CAISO imbalance energy (real-time) market-clearing price. For instance, if a supplier's spinning reserve bids of 50 MW were accepted by the CAISO and the spinning reserve market-clearing price was $750/MWh, the supplier would be paid $750 per MW and the energy portion of the accepted spinning reserve bids would be entered into the BEEP stack for the Imbalance Energy market. If the energy bids were then taken in the Imbalance Energy market at the RT price of $750/MWh, the supplier would earn a total of $1,500/MWh.

The CAISO ancillary services markets were cleared sequentially, with the highest quality service, Regulation, first, followed by Spinning Reserves, Non-Spinning Reserves, and lastly the lowest quality reserve, Replacement Reserves. Bids to supply resources qualified to provide Regulation not accepted in the Regulation auction would be automatically included in a Spinning Reserve supply stack. If they continued to be unaccepted, their bids would be put in a Non-Spinning Reserve supply stack. If a unit is awarded capacity in one market, any bids from the unit to supply ancillary services in subsequent markets were adjusted to account for the capacity awarded to the unit in a previous market. Thus, participants did not need to decide in detail in which market they would like to bid, unless their units were physically constrained to one or another market.[15]

14. The CAISO also used Voltage Support/Reactive Power and Black Start but these products are inherently local and thereby procured by the CAISO through a long-term contract process with cost-based pricing.

15. Resources could only cascade downward to auctions with less stringent requirements. A resource that met only the requirements for Replacement Reserves, for example, could not be bid into the auctions for Non-Spinning Reserves.

CAISO Imbalance Energy Market

To balance fluctuations of load and generation in RT, the CAISO operated Imbalance Energy markets that were cleared at 10-minute intervals. Scheduling Coordinators submitted their matching demand and supply schedules that had already been adjusted for congestion, along with Supplemental Energy bids. These bids could be either in a form of "incremental" (inc) or "decremental" (dec) bids. An inc bid represented a price or prices at which a Scheduling Coordinator would be willing to increase its supply while a dec bid represented a Scheduling Coordinator's willingness to pay to reduce its supply or increase its demand.

The CAISO combined these Supplemental Energy bids and the energy bids associated with winning ancillary services offerings into a system-wide bid curve known as Balancing Energy Ex-Post Price (BEEP) Stack. In any 10-minute interval, if additional energy was needed in real time, the CAISO would dispatch the next lowest energy bid on the BEEP stack. But if there was an oversupply in the market, the CAISO would call upon the highest-priced dec bid to take supply from the CAISO imbalance energy market instead. The 10-minute imbalance energy price was set at the price of the last accepted inc or dec bid.

When the CAISO system was constrained due to transmission congestion, meaning that transmission was fully utilized and not available to deliver energy from point A to point B within the CAISO, the BEEP Stack would be separated by zones, i.e., SP15, NP15, and ZP26. Since the CAISO could not get lower cost energy from one zone to deliver into another zone, the CAISO would dispatch more expensive resources in the congested zone. In this circumstance the CAISO 10-minute imbalance energy prices would be split by zone and the imbalance energy price in the congested zone would be higher than that in the uncongested zones.[16]

A key feature of the real-time imbalance energy market was that it had to meet fluctuations in the CAISO's supply and demand instantaneously or its system would collapse. If the required quantity of electricity increased 100 MW, in order to avoid system collapse, the CAISO had to purchase another 100 MW, regardless of the price charged. Thus, unlike the PX demand curve shown in Figure 4-3 the CAISO's ultimate demand curve was essentially vertical ("Price Inelastic Demand Curve") rather than the traditional downward sloping demand curve, as shown in Figure 4-5.

16. Transmission constraints made the units located in the congested zone or imports at uncongested interfaces the only ones physically capable of meeting the energy need. Consequently, the bids from such resources had to be taken even if lower priced bids were available from other suppliers for resources foreclosed by the transmission constraint.

Figure 4-5

Illustrative Example of Hourly CAISO Demand and Supply Curves in Imbalance

Energy (Real-Time) Market

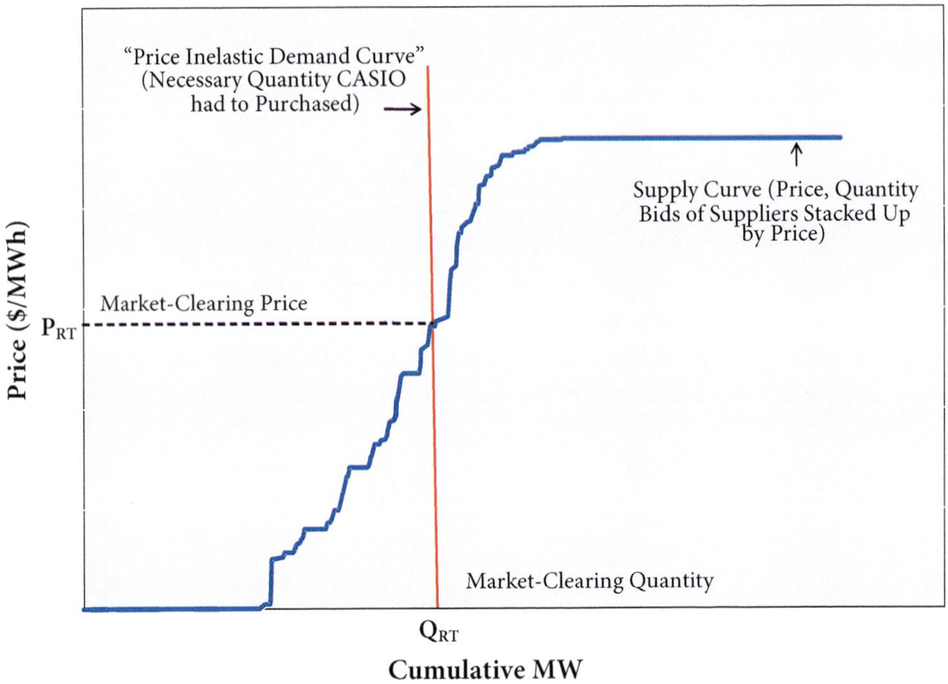

The implication of perfectly inelastic demand, as discussed in the previous chapter, is that prices are very sensitive to supplier withholding, either physical or economic. Furthermore, there is no loss of volume to constrain supplier-driven price increases. Without market power mitigation measures, purchasers' exposure to supplier market power in RT would be a significant threat.

Initially, the CAISO put two market power mitigation measures in place. First, it imposed cost-based rate contracts upon Reliability Must-Run (RMR) units. The CAISO determined which and when the RMR units needed to be on-line either to (1) satisfy the WECC's reliability criteria requirements, (2) meet local load, or (3) provide voltage support. These RMR units therefore were deemed to have local market power. Second, the CAISO imposed a bid cap of $125/MWh. This cap was raised to $250/MWh in May 1998 and continued to change over time. It was $750/MWh from September 30, 1999 to July 1, 2000, $500/MWh from July 1 to August 6, 2000, and $250/MWh from August 7 to December 8, 2000. After December 8, there were what have been called "soft caps" at $250/MWh and then $150/MWh. These caps or break points limited the market-clearing price but allowed suppliers to be paid on an "as bid" above the cap in order to acquire the energy needed to meet load. The soft cap approach did far more damage than good, and it is explained in Chapter 5.

To ensure the reliability of its system, the CAISO also had an emergency tool at its disposal. It could make out-of-market (OOM) purchases in the bilateral markets outside the CAISO to supply any expected real-time deficiencies in energy or reserves.[17] These OOM purchases were not subject to the CAISO price cap.[18]

Pursuant to AB 1890, the three California IOUs were restricted to buy and sell energy only through the PX and the CAISO auction spot markets. They could neither purchase nor sell their power in bilateral spot and forward markets inside or outside California. When they were authorized by the CPUC to use forward contracts in mid-1999, they could only procure them from the PX Block Forward Market (BFM). This limitation upon access to other active spot and futures power in the region deprived them of options that would have reduced their exposure to volatile spot prices in the PX and CAISO. The fact that essentially all California IOU's demand had to be supplied from the PX and CAISO markets left the IOUs exceptionally vulnerable to manipulation of these markets.

Issues in the First Two Years of Operation

In the first two years of operations (April 1998-December 1999), the PX and CAISO energy markets ran about as smoothly as one would expect from a workably competitive market. The PX monthly average prices ranged from $12.50/MWh to $49.01/MWh while the CAISO monthly average prices stayed between $10.94/MWh and $78.54/MWh, as shown in Figure 4-6. High prices only appeared sporadically in summer months. The hourly PX and CAISO prices rarely exceeded $100/MWh. Nevertheless, this does not imply that the CAISO did not face any challenges. The CAISO Market Surveillance Unit (MSU), the Market Surveillance Committee of the CAISO (MSC), and academic professors reported that significant market power was present during periods of peak demand in July to September of both 1998 and 1999.[19] Their analyses indicated that market prices were in excess of the marginal cost of the highest-cost unit operating (also known as "marginal unit"). They also noted market design flaws, software deficiencies, and regulatory barriers to price responsive retail customers

17. *See* ISO Tariff § 2.3.5.1.5 (2000).

18. Although the tariff authorized purchases above the price cap, the CAISO very rarely had to exceed the cap in OOM purchases.

19. Market Surveillance Unit, *Annual Report on Market Issues and Performance,* California ISO, June 1999. *See* Wolak, Nordhaus, and Shapiro (2000). Borenstein, Bushnell, and Wolak (1999).

caused by the CTC recovery mechanism (given retail rate freeze) and the limits on IOUs forward procurement.[20]

Figure 4-6

PX and CAISO Monthly Average Energy Prices April 1998-December 1999

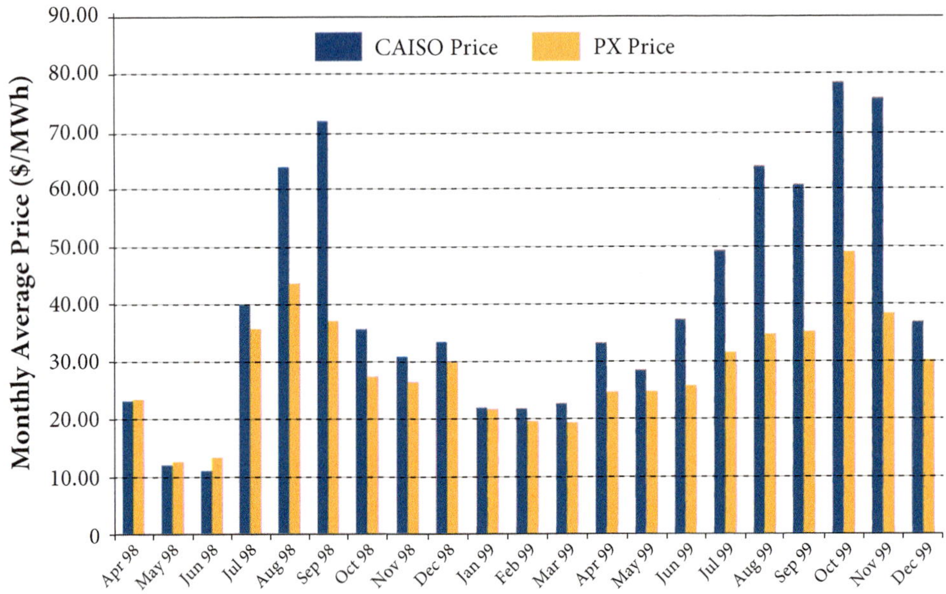

Initially there were also serious problems in the ancillary services markets. Many suppliers found the PX energy markets more attractive since they did not have authority to sell ancillary services at market-based rates, and their ancillary services bids were thus subject to cost-based rates in the range of $5/MWh to $12/MWh. In response to the resulting inadequate supply of ancillary services, particularly for Regulation, the CAISO had to call upon the costly RMR contracts due to their high reliability payment rates. In mid-May 1998, the CAISO adopted the Regulation Energy Payment Adjustment (REPA), a temporary emergency price adder paid to Regulation suppliers.[21] Under REPA, Regulation suppliers would receive an energy adder that was the higher of $20/MW or the CAISO hourly imbalance energy price. The introduction of REPA improved bid sufficiency levels significantly.[22]

20. *Id.*, pp. 4-7.

21. The REPA payment was stopped in November 1998 when the FERC granted market-based rate authority for all ancillary services sales.

22. *See* Wolak (1999), p. 49.

Figure 4-7

Hourly Average Zonal Prices of Regulation and Replacement Reserves

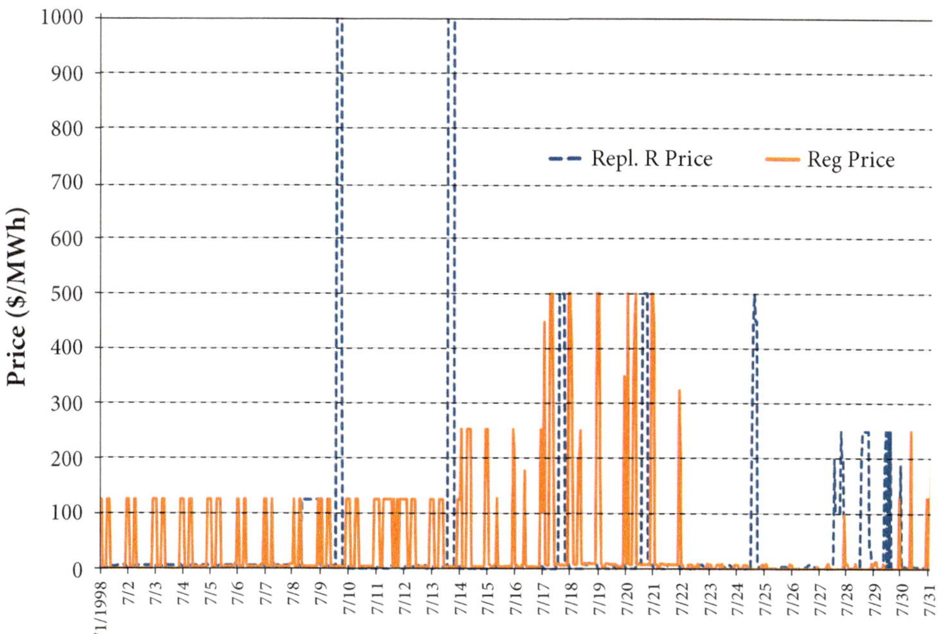

Prices are average zonal prices. On July 9, Replacement Reserve Prices HE 15-17 were $2,500/MWh and reached $5,000 from HE 14-18 on July 13.

Once the FERC granted market-based authority to ancillary services suppliers at the end of June 1998, the ancillary services prices became more volatile, as shown in Figure 4-7. The SP15 prices for Replacement Reserves spiked up to $5,000/MW on July 9 and reached $9,999/MW on July 13 while the prices in NP15 stayed below $2/MW.

The CAISO immediately submitted an emergency filing with the FERC to impose a damage control price cap of $500/MW on all ancillary services markets, starting on July 14. The cap was then lowered to $250/MW to be in line with the price cap in the Imbalance Energy market on July 25, 1998. In addition, the CAISO adopted a number of reforms to its ancillary services market rules. Changes relevant to the Crisis included:

- Adoption of "Rational Buyer" protocols that enabled the CAISO to purchase additional quantities of higher quality reserves for lower quality reserves if they were available at lower prices;[23]

23. The (MSC) of CAISO recommended this in its August 1998 Report, the CAISO filed the changes at the FERC on March 1, 1999 and implemented on August 17, 1999. Not all of the MSC recommendations were adopted by the CAISO.

- Accept ance of out-of-state bids into the CAISO ancillary services markets, beginning on August 6, 1998 with a limit of 25 percent of the CAISO's requirement. This limit was raised to 50 percent in June 1999.[24]

- Deferring up to 10 percent of its day-ahead ancillary services requirements to the HA market to promote more liquidity of the HA market and reduce ancillary services costs.

Following these changes, the ancillary services markets normalized.

The Crisis—Phase I (May 2000-December 2000)

Changes in market rules made in 1998 and 1999 did not prevent price spikes in 2000. The California energy markets showed the first signs of turmoil in late April and early May 2000. The price in SP15 first hit the $750 per MW cap in the CAISO RT market at 1:00 p.m. on April 26, 2000. SP15 prices also reached the cap several times during peak hours on May 1 and 3, 2000 as shown in Figure 4-8-Panel A. Pricing in the north, shown in Figure 4-8-Panel B, did not spike so strongly in early May, but shared the episodes at the cap in late May. Prices in both NP15 and SP15 jumped to the cap again on June 13, 2000 and did so repeatedly throughout the remainder of the month.[25] This was the initial wave of what would develop into the Crisis in California and western energy markets. The CAISO Department of Market Analysis noted in its June 9, 2000 memorandum on the then recent increase in energy prices that in May the prices in real-time and hour-ahead ancillary services markets hit the $750/MWh cap 23 times.[26] The monthly average PX and CAISO energy prices rose to $50.39/MWh and $76.87/MWh, respectively. They were more than 100 percent higher than those of a year before.

As price spikes became more frequent in June, the monthly average prices in the PX and CAISO rose to $132.35/MWh and $262.73/MWh, respectively. These monthly prices were more than 400 percent of June 1999 levels. The constrained PX day-ahead price rocketed to $1,099 per MWh during peak hours on June 28, 2000.

On July 1, 2000, the CAISO lowered the price caps from $750/MWh to $500/MWh. The price cap did not improve the market conditions as high power prices became more prevalent. Although the energy prices came down in the first half of July, they climbed back to the price

24. Market Surveillance Unit, Section 2.8.9 Market Design Modifications, *Annual Report on Market Issues and Performance,* California ISO, June 1999, pp. 2-15.

25. Prices hit the cap in both markets 34 times from June 13-29, 2000 and prices in many other hours were above $700 per MWh.

26. Anjali Sheffrin, Director of Market Analysis, *Market Analysis Report,* CAISO, dated June 9, 2000.

cap in late July. The CAISO, gravely concerned about runaway pricing, again lowered its cap to $250/MWh on August 8. But the energy prices in August stayed above $200/MWh for more than 40 percent of all hours. As shown in the figures, from this point through the beginning of October, prices regularly hit the cap in both regions, perhaps a bit more frequently in the north.

Figure 4-8-Panel A

SP15 PX and CAISO Hourly Energy Prices

May 2000-September 2000

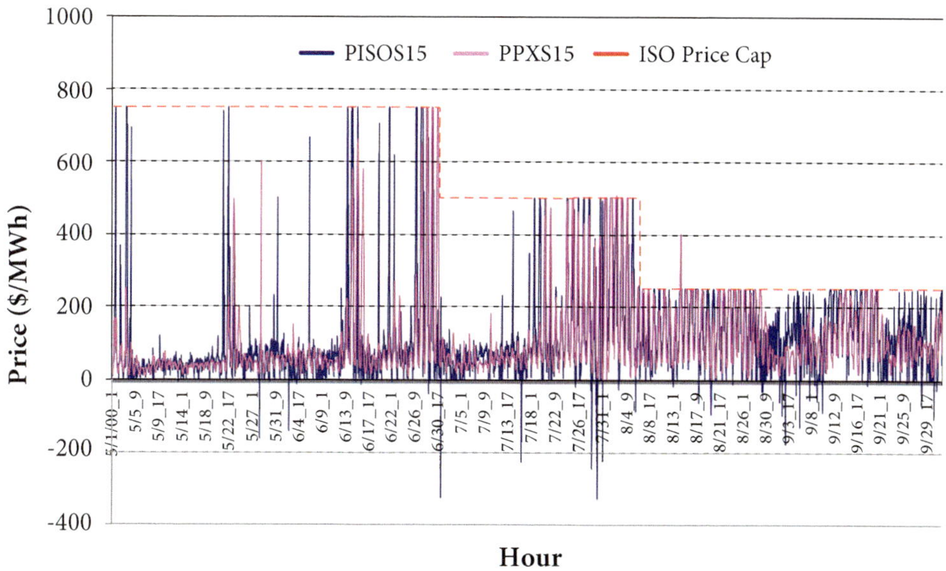

Figure 4-8 Panel B

NP15 PX and CAISO Hourly Energy Prices

May 2000-September 2000

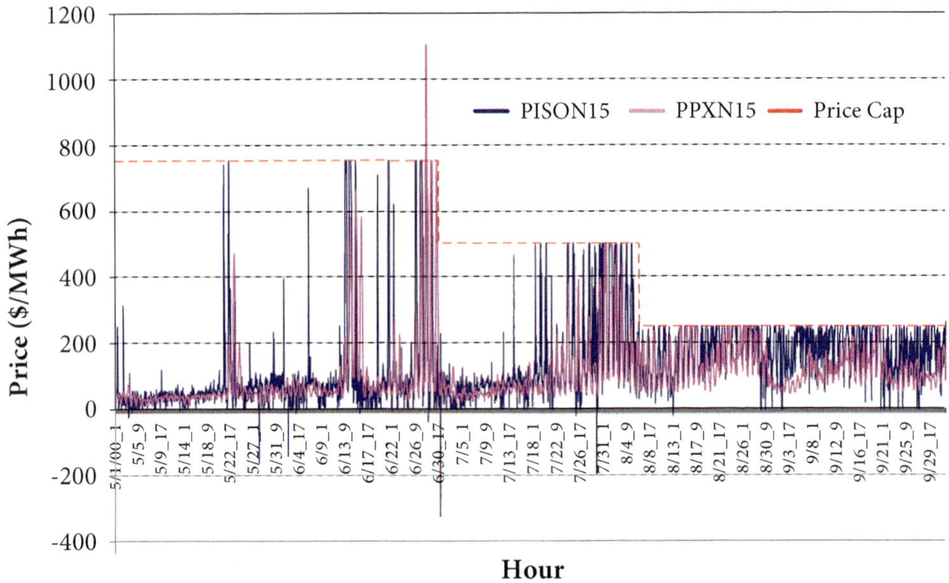

In November, average prices in the PX and CAISO markets rose sharply to $182/MWh and $173/MWh, respectively, after they had tapered off in October. The prices of ancillary services also jumped significantly, particularly for Replacement Reserves. The monthly average price of Replacement Reserves was $48.69/MWh, almost seven times higher than the October price and almost 40 times the average price of the same service in November of previous years. The CAISO faced a dearth of bids into its RT market forcing it to increase OOM purchases. On average, the CAISO purchased approximately 995 MW of OOM energy per on-peak hour at an average price of $245/MWh.[27]

27. Although OOM purchases were not subject to the price cap, through November the CAISO appears to have been able to purchase its needs at prices below the then prevailing $250 cap.

Figure 4-9

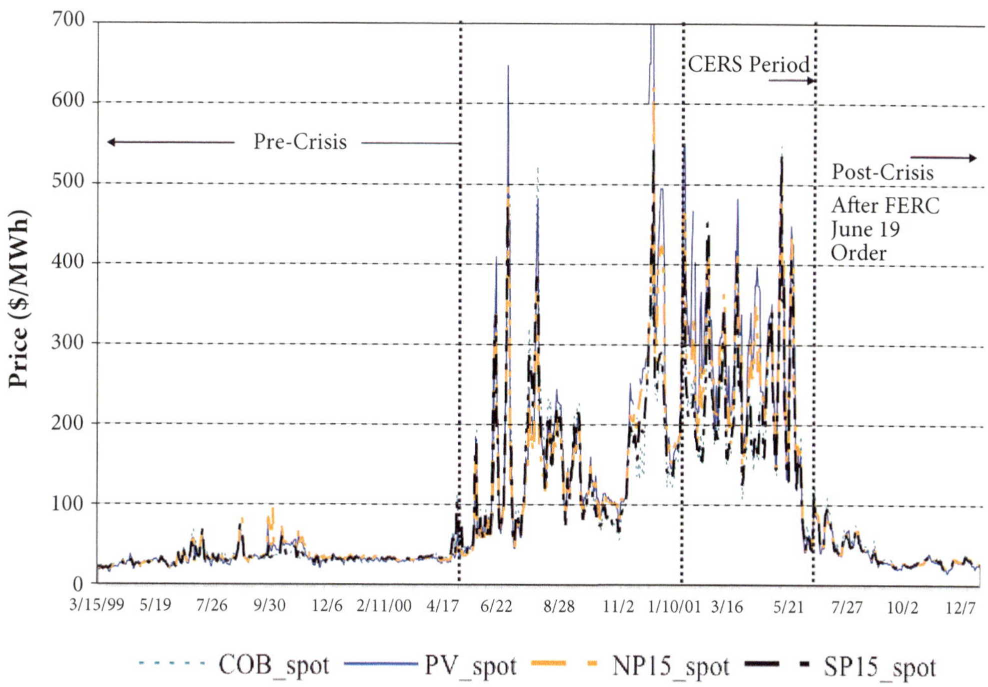

Data: PMW

The CAISO's situation worsened in December. On December 8, the Commission at the CAISO's request imposed a $250 "soft" price cap applicable to both the PX and the CAISO.[28] Traders responded by purchasing out of the PX at capped prices and selling the energy to the CAISO as OOM at prices that reached $1,000 or more per MWh.[29] The problem intensified when on December 15 the FERC ordered the CAISO to set the soft cap[30] at $150/MWh.[31] The bilateral power prices transacted outside the PX and CAISO markets fell briefly below $150 per MWh following the Order but quickly returned to excessive levels, as shown in Figure 4-9. The CAISO's OOM purchases rapidly rose to 2,246 MW per on-peak hour with an average OOM price of $382/MWh.

At this time the retail rates of PG&E and SCE were still frozen because they had not yet fully recovered their stranded costs. They thus had to absorb the huge run up in power prices, and their financial positions declined rapidly. PG&E, in fact, filed for bankruptcy while SCE had to sell its transmission assets to the State. Although the December 15, 2000 Order allowed the

28. *See Order Accepting Tariff Amendment on an Emergency Basis*, Docket No. ER01-607-000, 93 FERC ¶ 61,239, December 8, 2000. (*Direct Testimony of Gerald A. Taylor*, Docket No. EL01-10-085, Exh. No. CAT-41, September 21, 2012 (hereinafter Taylor Testimony 2012); Exh. No. CAT-048.)

29. As we discuss in Chapter 7, this required fraudulent misrepresentation of the source of the energy.

30. The difference between soft and hard price caps is that for a soft cap a supplier may bid higher than $150/MWh as long as the supplier could demonstrate that his/her variable operating cost was higher than a soft cap level.

31. *San Diego Gas & Elec. Co., et al.*, 93 FERC ¶ 61,294, December 15, 2000 (December 15, 2000 Order).

IOUs to hedge against high spot prices by buying forward outside the PX, their financial positions had deteriorated to the point that they lacked the credit necessary to buy power in the bilateral markets. Their inability to meet their obligations to suppliers including the PX and CAISO lead to the complete collapse of the California markets by the end of January 2001.

The Crisis—
Phase II (January 2001 through June 2001)

With the principal buyers, the IOUs, no longer creditworthy, the State of California acted to restore order to the markets and protect consumers. On January 17, 2000, in the midst of blackouts on the CAISO power grid, the California governor issued an emergency proclamation authorizing the California Department of Water Resources (CDWR), a state agency with experience in power procurement,[32] to begin purchasing the IOUs' "net short," the energy needed beyond what they could produce themselves in order to meet the demands of their consumers.[33] The authorization was affirmed by legislation on January 19 in Senate Bill 7X and later extended in Assembly Bill 1X on February 1.[34] To purchase this power, CDWR was appropriated $400 million under the authority granted in SB7X.[35]

Initially, there were no long-term supply arrangements, so the entire net short of the IOUs had to be procured on a short-term basis, largely in the bilateral spot markets. Table 4-1 shows that from January 17 through June 20 of 2001, approximately two thirds of CERS' total purchases were in the short-term DO, HA, DA, and Balance-of-Month (BOM) markets.

32. CDWR ran the California's extensive water system that both generated electricity (some of which was sold) and purchased energy to run its pumping operations.

33. Emergency Proclamation, Governor Gray Davis, January 17, 2001.

34. AB 1X extended the purchasing authority through December 31, 2002.

35. *See* Letter dated January 20, 2001 from Raymond D. Hart, Deputy Director of CDWR, and Terry M. Winter, President and Chief Executive Officer of the CAISO, to the California Generators. (Taylor Testimony 2012, Exh. No. CAT-41; Exh. No. CAT-58.) Later CDWR's funding was increased to cover its massive energy purchases.

Table 4-1

Summary of CERS Purchases by Provision (1/17/01 - 6/20/01)

Market Subtype	Quantity Level (MWh)	Quantity % of Total	Cost Level ($)	Cost % of Total	Average Price ($/MWh)
Spot Transactions					
RT	7,959,401.0	25.8%	$2,813,756,173.9	37.2%	$353 .5
DA	8,824,780.0	28.6%	$2,069,302,550.7	27.3%	$234.5
HA	989,051.0	3.2%	$215,959,803.1	2.9%	$218.4
BOM	2,647,787.0	8.6%	$651,984,518.6	8.6%	$246.2
Total Spot Transactions	20,421,019.0	66.2%	$5,751,003,046.3	76.0%	$281.6
Long-Term/ Medium-Term Contracts					
B1ockForwardContract	6,753,346.5	21.9%	$1,313,930,357.3	17.4%	$194.6
LTPurchase	3,694,844.0	12.0%	$502,992,435.0	6.6%	$ 136.1
Total Long-Term/ Medium-Term Contract	10,448,190.5	33 .8%	$1,816,922,792.3	24.0%	$ 173.9
Total Energy	30,869,209.5	100.0%	$7,567,925,838.6	1000%	$245.2
Exchange					
Exchange In	375,592.0				
Exchange Out	-447,512.0				
Nel Exchange	-71,920.0				

Notes and Sources: Workpaper CERS Transaction Data

Because nearly 40 percent of these short-term purchases were in RT, CERS was often racing the clock to procure the energy that was needed only an hour or two later. As shown in Table 4-2, the amount of power that CERS needed to procure in RT to satisfy the California IOUs load *averaged* over 3,300 MW during peak hours in February 2001, enough energy to serve more than 2.3 million homes. In several other months the shortfall in peak and off-peak periods often represented the consumption of one to two million residences. Any failure to acquire this electricity meant compromising the reliability of California's power grid, a fact amply demonstrated by the blackouts that occurred despite CERS' efforts.[36] Over time, CERS

36. In addition to January 17, and 18, Stage 3 emergencies and blackouts on the CAISO system were experienced on March 19 and 20 affecting over 1.5 million customers, and again on May 7 and 8. The CAISO had three stages of emergency alerts, of which Stage 3 was the highest, indicating that the system had insufficient reserves to handle a significant outage. Any loss or reduction in supply would require curtailment of firm customers, a blackout. In the first six months of 2001, Stage 3 emergencies were declared on 38 days. From its inception to the present, the CAISO declared a Stage 3 emergency on only one other day, December 7, 2000, as the California markets spiraled toward collapse.

negotiated various longer-term arrangements that reduced the amount of energy that had to be procured in this sort of last minute scramble.

Table 4-2

Average Forecast CERS Net Short (MW)

	NP15		SP15	
Month	**On-Peak**	**Off-Peak**	**On-Peak**	**Off-Peak**
February	2,014	1,569	1,310	1,166
March	1,035	1,270	1,058	834
April	932	986	931	1,135
May	1,418	1,380	1,069	478
June	403	558	142	435

The need for such large real-time purchases was in part due to the fact during the CERS Period (January 17, 2001 to June 20, 2001) suppliers outside California essentially ceased bidding into the CAISO Imbalance Energy market.[37] This was of considerable concern because California was heavily dependent upon imported energy to meet in-state demand.[38] Further exacerbating the situation, unmet demand in RT was typically in the northern zone, and south-to-north congestion on Paths 15 and 26 often limited transmission access to NP15 from the south. These factors left CERS in real-time seeking power in the Pacific Northwest where the few suppliers that would deal with CERS demanded very high prices. As shown in Table 4-3, spot power prices paid by CERS in the PNW, the vast majority of which were in RT, averaged $391 per MWh, nearly ten times the pre-Crisis price and over $160 above the average price of $227 CERS paid in its other short-term purchases.

37. This was in part due to the CAISO's lack of creditworthiness and the fact that imports to the BEEP had to be bid in on a price-taker basis and were thus constrained by the price cap.

38. California imported approximately 50 TWh each year between 1996 and 1999, or approximately 20 percent of the total consumption of 250 TWh.

Table 4-3

Summary of CERS Spot Purchases in the Pacific Northwest Markets During the CERS Period

Market Subtype	Quantity Level (MWh)	Quantity % of Total	Cost Level ($)	Cost % of Total	Average Price ($/MWh)
Spot Transactions					
RT	5,968,245	87.7%	$2,333,370,513	87.8%	$391
DA	702,436	10.3%	$265,133,609	10.0%	$377
HA	27,800	0.4%	$13,900,000	0.5%	$500
BOM	103,400	1.5%	43,970,280	1.7%	$425
Total Spot Transactions	6,801,881	100.0%	$2,656,374,402	100.0%	$391

Notes and Sources: Workpaper CERS Transaction Data

All in all CERS incurred staggering costs. In the course of 151 days it paid over $7.5 billion to acquire the energy needed to keep the CAISO system in operation, over $50 million each day to serve the IOUs' net short and keep the lights on in California.

To put the Western Crisis in perspective, it helps to compare western power prices with those in other areas of the country. Figure 4-10 presents a comparison of DA energy prices traded in the WECC, specifically at COB and Mid-C (hereafter "COB/Mid-C") with historical (DA) energy prices traded at the Into Cinergy hub in the Midwest of the U.S. The striking feature of this graph is that the extraordinarily high power prices at COB/Mid-C stretched out across 416 days while the episodes of extremely high prices at the Into Cinergy hub rarely lasted ten days.[39]

39. A similar conclusion can be reached when compared with power prices in PJM West, NYISO, and ISO-New England.

Figure 4-10

Day-Ahead Prices Cinergy vs. COB/Mid-C

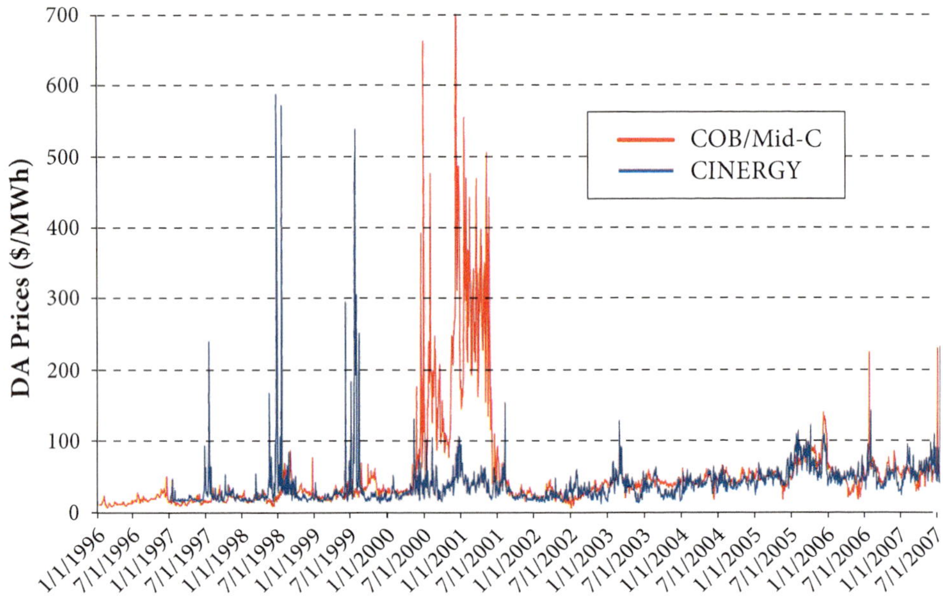

Sources: PMW and ICE

A price spike is generally caused by unexpected power plant outages and/or high demand driven by extreme temperatures. Once a power plant is back on line or a more normal temperature returns, prices typically fall back to ordinary levels. This is illustrated in the experience in the recent Polar Vertex event in January 2014. The power prices in many markets such as those shown for PJM in Figure 4-11 jumped to the price cap of $1,000/MWh for 4 hours on January 28, 2014 as the gas price spiked up to $81/mmBtu.[40] Given the unanticipated changes in supply and demand conditions that often occur, such short-lived price spikes are expected even in competitive power markets.

40. This was the gas price at Texas Eastern, M-3. Given this gas price, the implied heat rate (the heat rate inferred for the price setting unit determined by dividing the electricity price by the gas price) was approximately 12,500 Btu per kWh, which was very close to the heat rate of a gas peaking unit.

Figure 4-11

Day-Ahead LMPs in PJM East (January 1, 2014 – April 30, 2014)

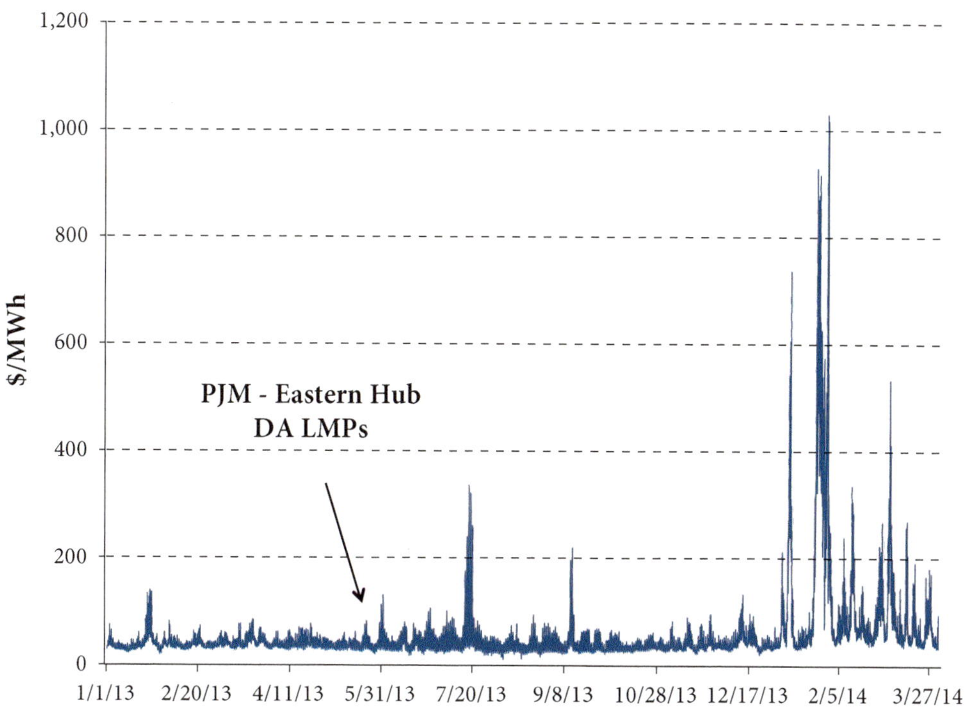

Source: Hourly electricity prices taken from Ventyx

The persistence of high power prices in California and the rest of the West during the Crisis have attracted enormous attention and concern and sparked a decade of litigation. The roots of the Crisis were complex. As implied by Figure 4-10, the sustained high prices were not simply the result of market fundamentals (such as hot weather, poor hydro conditions, high natural gas prices, high emission costs, plants' forced outages, and low net imports) that yielded scarcity conditions. Scarcity certainly contributed along with other factors we discuss, such as market design flaws and lack of demand response. Of particular importance, however, was supplier behavior that took advantage of these conditions. Numerous studies by the MSC, the CAISO Department of Market Analysis (DMA), the PX Market Monitoring Committee (MMC), academia, and the authors have concluded that prices were elevated by strategies devised by Enron and other suppliers to manipulate the markets that are treated in later chapters.

CHAPTER 5

LITIGATION HISTORY

The Commission's efforts to deal with the Crisis in western power markets can be divided into two phases. The first, which ran from August 2000 through December 2001, is virtually devoid of any discussion or treatment of supplier behavior. The second, beginning in February 2002 and continuing even now as this book is being written, was initiated in response to the then startling revelation of Enron's colorfully named manipulation schemes. We review these two phases not to provide a detailed account of the Commission's activities, which has been done elsewhere, but rather to highlight certain aspects that limited its effectiveness and are instructive with regard to its current attempts to address manipulative market behavior.

Phase I

The lengthy dispute over the Western Energy Crisis was initiated by SDG&E with a complaint filed with the FERC on August 2, 2000. Because SDG&E had recovered its stranded costs, its retail electricity rates, unlike those of SCE and PG&E, were no longer frozen.[1] As a result, SDG&E ratepayers were exposed directly to increases in the company's cost of acquiring electricity in the PX and CAISO wholesale markets. As chronicled in Chapter 4, in May of 2000 wholesale acquisition costs in the PX and CAISO suddenly doubled from those in May 1999. June wholesale prices in the PX and CAISO were on average four times their levels in 1999. The staggering impact of these increases on SDG&E customers led to their filing of the complaint and ultimately to the re-imposition of the retail rate freeze.[2]

The SDG&E complaint sought a $250 cap on bids into the energy and ancillary services markets in the PX and CAISO. This was to be imposed through a condition in the market-based-rate authority granted by the Commission to qualified electricity suppliers and was to last until

1. As discussed in the previous chapter, the IOUs were allowed to recover the "stranded" costs resulting from their sales of generation assets through the difference between their wholesale electricity purchase costs and their retail rates. The *quid pro quo* for stranded cost recovery was a retail rate freeze. Upon recovery of the stranded costs, the rate freeze was to end, thus allowing changes in wholesale purchase costs to be flowed through to retail customers. By the beginning of the Crisis in May 2000, SDG&E had recovered its stranded costs, while SCE and PG&E had not.

2. The outcry from SDG&E customers and officials in San Diego led to legislation that re-established the rate freeze. *See Direct Testimony of Michael Peter Florio, Docket No. EL01-10-085*, Exh. No. CAT-001, September 21, 2012.

the Commission could establish that the PX and CAISO markets were workably competitive.[3] In support of its complaint, SDG&E argued that the structure of the California markets was defective and that the PX and CAISO markets were not workably competitive, as demonstrated by prices far in excess of those in previous periods. The CPUC intervened along with SCE and PG&E in support of SDG&E's petition and suppliers intervened *en masse* in opposition.

August 23, 2000 Order

On August 23, 2000, the Commission responded to the complaint with an order that denied SDG&E's request for immediate bid caps in the PX and CAISO markets on the grounds that there was not sufficient evidence to support such an action.[4] However, the Commission did institute its own proceeding under §206 of the Federal Power Act (FPA) and consolidated it with the SDG&E docket. The Commission also instructed the FERC Staff to accelerate an ongoing informal review of electricity market performance throughout the U.S. and to conclude an assessment of California and other western power markets as soon as possible. The order indicated that the Commission intended to issue further orders should the Staff investigation find evidence to justify them and established a refund effective 60 days following the publication of the Order in the Federal Register.

The Commission's establishment of its own investigation had the effect of shunting SDG&E and other intervener/buyers to the sidelines. Although the Order noted that a purpose in opening its own §206 proceeding was to initiate "a formal evidentiary process where all interested parties are assured an opportunity to present evidence and arguments on the record before the Commission…,"[5] this never occurred in the original proceeding itself. The Order included a provision that a public hearing should be held in the consolidated dockets, but this provision was held in abeyance pending further orders.[6] Later orders, as discussed below, limited participation by aggrieved parties to commenting upon Commission remedial proposals. Thus, in its effort to "resolve as expeditiously as possible" performance issues in the PX and CAISO, the Commission relied almost exclusively upon analyses by the Commission Staff. Staff's investigation, which proceeded behind closed doors, culminated in a report dated

3. *See*, Order Initiating Hearing Proceedings to Investigate Justness and Reasonableness of Rates of Public Utility Sellers in California ISO and PX Markets, *San Diego Gas & Electric Company v. Sellers of Energy and Ancillary Services Into Markets Operated by the California Independent System Operator and the California Power Exchange*, Docket No. EL00-95-000, *Investigation of Practices of the California, Independent System Operator and the California Power Exchange*, Docket No. EL00-98-000, 92 FERC ¶61,172, August 23, 2000, at 61,604. (Order Initiating Hearing Proceedings 2000).

4. This denial was effectively moot because on August 7, shortly following the filing of the SDG&E complaint, the CAISO under its own authority reduced the price cap in the CAISO imbalance market to $250, which had the effect of also capping prices in the PX DA and HA markets.

5. Order Initiating Hearing Proceedings, *op. cit.*, at 61,605, n. 5.

6. *Id.* at 61,609-10.

November 1, 2000.[7] This was an unfortunate tack, since it deprived the Commission of evidence from market participants that might have yielded a deeper understanding of what was going on in the marketplace.

As the Staff Report makes clear, the Staff was quite handicapped in its efforts:

> This was an informal investigation. As such, staff did not depose market participants or others as it might as part of a formal investigation. Given the purpose, to find the general cause of the unusual prices and market activity, this was not necessary.
>
> * * *
>
> This investigation was conducted on an expedited basis so there was not enough time to address all issues in depth. This report is intended to provide the Commission with "the big picture."[8]

There was no attempt at formal discovery. Staff personnel conducted interviews with market participants, the CPUC, outside economists,[9] PX and CAISO personnel, and reviewed public data kept by the Commission[10] and other publicly available information. They also had available reports and analyses by PX and CAISO market monitors that evaluated price cost markups in their markets. As a practical matter, the Staff's work had to be completed in six to seven weeks.[11] In short, Staff had very little time and no reliable data that would allow assessment of individual supplier market behavior.

It is not surprising, then, that the Staff Report drew no conclusions about market power or manipulative behavior by suppliers. It identified as possible causes of high electricity prices in the PX and CAISO three factors: 1) tight supply and demand conditions; 2) problems with the design of PX and CAISO markets; and 3) market power. With regard to market power, the evidence was in the form of bids and prices above marginal costs, and the Staff cautioned that the impacts of market power and scarcity are difficult to separate and that market power may be exacerbated by magnified or flawed market rules.[12] On the available evidence, the Staff could not reach a conclusion with regard to the actual exercise of market power, but argued

7. *See Staff Report to the Federal Energy Regulatory Commission on Western Markets and the Causes of the Summer 2000 Price Abnormalities*, FERC Staff, November 1, 2000. (Staff Summer 2000 Report).

8. Staff Summer 2000 Report, pp. 1-1, 1-4.

9. Ironically, the only outside economists interviewed other than those serving as market monitors, were Dr. Richard Tabors and Professor William Hogan, who at the time respectively represented Enron and Mirant, major suppliers in the California markets.

10. Later in the proceedings related to the Crisis, it became clear that the data collected by the Commission in its oversight role was insufficient to support analyses of individual supplier behavior.

11. The Report had to be available (at least in draft form) for the Commission to use in developing its order of November 1, 2000.

12. Staff Summer 2000 Report, pp. 1-4, Section 6.

that mitigation might be appropriate nonetheless because of the ***potential*** for the exercise of market power:

> Mitigation…may be appropriate even in the absence of findings of market power exercise by specific sellers or buyers, if there are clear incentives for its exercise, and there are potentially large impacts that cannot be adequately separated from the effects of scarcity.[13]

The lack of a manipulation concept beyond market power also worked with the incomplete picture of market activities to blunt concerns that might have led the Commission to quickly uncover manipulative schemes that did not rely upon market power. The Staff was aware of allegations that generators in California were "gaming the system" by selling and exporting energy to entities outside California that also supplied replacement reserves to the CAISO through imports in real-time, sales that in high demand hours in June allowed the importer to collect $1,500/MWh, double the price cap in the CAISO.[14] The Staff interpreted this activity through the lens of market power:

> These exporting practices are permitted under the rules and are not necessarily a market power problem.
>
> * * *
>
> It becomes a problem if it is associated with a pattern of withholding resources from the market in order to drive up the prices.[15]

What the Staff might have found with a bit more digging was that in many cases the exporting and importing entities were the same, with an out-of-state entity acting merely as a middleman for scheduling purposes with the CAISO. This was the scheme that later became known by the Enron-inspired sobriquet "Ricochet." Its profitability derived not from an exercise of market power, but rather from the fraudulent misrepresentation of energy generated in California as an import so that it could qualify improperly for sale to the CAISO as Replacement Reserves or Supplemental Energy.[16] The Staff's concept of illicit behavior was simply too narrow. Anything other than market power was not considered a problem.

---

13. *Id.* p. 5-18.
14. *Id.* p. 5-17.
15. *Id.*
16. Ricochet and other manipulative schemes used during the Crisis are discussed in Chapter 7.

Commission's Initial Attempt to Quell the Crisis: The Orders in November and December, 2000

The Commission's initial stab at normalizing the PX and CAISO markets came in two orders in late 2000. The first, issued on November 1, proposed various remedial measures that were then implemented in slightly modified form in the second order dated December 15. The Commission's analysis of the causes of the poor performance of the California markets closely mirrored the Staff Report. It noted that supply and demand conditions were such that prices would be expected to rise. These conditions, in conjunction with dysfunctional market rules, made it possible for sellers to exercise market power to further elevate prices above just and reasonable levels. The Commission, as suggested by the Staff, found these circumstances sufficient for remedial action.[17]

In the Commission's view, market fundamentals and weaknesses in the design of the California markets were the core of the problem. The design defects had been hidden by favorable market conditions in the initial years of PX and CAISO operations and only became apparent as demand outstripped supply in 2000. Scarcity allowed even smaller suppliers to affect prices in the single price auction markets of the PX and CAISO,[18] where the major IOUs under the market rules were required to obtain their electricity.

Given this understanding of the nature of the impediments to well-functioning markets, the Commission saw little need to look further into supplier behavior. Removing these impediments would eliminate any threat of the exercise of market power. The Commission was confident that a full evidentiary hearing was not needed,[19] and it should proceed to propose measures to mitigate market dysfunction by reducing IOU exposure to the spot markets, particularly the volatile CAISO imbalance market, and to restrain potential market power.

There were three primary elements in the Commission's proposal directed at mitigating prices:[20]

- Removal of the requirement that the IOUs buy and sell exclusively through the PX;
- Imposition of a requirement to preschedule load and generation with the CAISO and an "underscheduling" penalty for relying too heavily on the CAISO Imbalance Energy Market; and

17. *Market Order Proposing Remedies for California Wholesale Electrics, Docket No. EL00-95-000*, 93 FERC ¶ 61,121, November 1, 2000 p. 19. (November 2000 Order).

18. *Id.* p. 50.

19. Noting the need for expeditious resolution of the Crisis, the Commission concluded that only a "paper" hearing was necessary in which participants were allowed three weeks to file comments on the proposed remedial measures along with supporting arguments and evidence. *Id.* p. 43.

20. The order also addressed a wide range of other measures including replacement of the PX and ISO stakeholder governing boards, redesign of the ISO's congestion management system, consideration of demand response programs, removal of disincentives to forward contracting, expedited siting of generation and transmission, eliminating double payment for reserves, etc.

- Implementation of a temporary soft cap of $150 on clearing prices in the PX and CAISO auction markets above which offers taken to meet load would be paid on an "as bid" basis, but would not affect the auction price.[21]

The Commission saw two advantages in relieving the IOUs of the obligation to buy and sell through the PX. First, freedom from the PX obligation would allow them to acquire the output of their own generation at cost and to further reduce their exposure to the spot markets through forward contracting. Second, forward contracts would limit the profits from elevating spot prices and thus erode potential supplier market power. The underscheduling penalty was intended to motivate load serving entities to avoid purchases in the highly volatile CAISO real-time Imbalance Energy market and reduce the volumes acquired from the CAISO to levels contemplated in the initial market design. The $150 "break point" would allow higher-priced bids to be taken for energy necessary to meet California load but would limit the impacts of such purchases upon the clearing prices in PX and CAISO single-price auction markets during the period it would take to implement the reforms proposed in the order.[22]

The November 2000 Order addressed refunds in a very measured fashion. While the Commission asserted its authority to impose refunds, it declined to propose them despite having found unjust and unreasonable rates, noting that refunds were discretionary and not a fundamental solution to the problems in California markets. It observed that any imposition of refunds would have to balance consumer and supplier interests and would have to recognize sellers' legitimate costs, including opportunity costs. Consistent with its view that scarcity was at the root of the problem and that additional supply was the ultimate solution, the Commission was reluctant to recommend measures that might undermine the financial stability of sellers and their participation in the California electricity markets.[23]

After reviewing comments from participants in the proceeding, the Commission implemented remedial measures on December 15, 2000. Despite serious concerns from all quarters, the Commission, with only slight modifications,[24] went forward with its November proposals. The Crisis posed an existential threat to the development of competitive power markets, and the Commission felt compelled to move expeditiously to preserve market credibility:

> Simply put, we must not only stop the current electric market hemorrhaging and restore credibility to the electric markets in the West, but we must ensure that this situation does not recur.

21. Bids were not limited by the cap, which only applied to market clearing prices. When bids above the cap were taken, the suppliers paid above the cap were required to file a report justifying the price.

22. Consistent with the breakpoint or "soft cap" approach, the Commission rejected requests by the PX and CAISO to implement or extend hard price caps in their markets. The $150 break point was to remain in effect for 24 months.

23. November 2000 Order, p. 38.

24. For example, the Commission provided protection for small generators regarding the underscheduling penalty and disallowed opportunity costs as a basis for marketers to justify bids in excess of the $150 breakpoint.

> Given the gravity of the situation and the need to expeditiously implement remedies that will avert recurrence of the problems in California last summer as well as the problems in the past few weeks, our order today is forward looking. ...Today we concentrate on the implementation of those market reforms that are needed immediately.[25]

Moving forward quickly with remedies meant rejecting a myriad of objections raised to the Commission's proposals.[26] Three of these are of particular relevance to an assessment of the Commission's effectiveness in overseeing the markets. The first such objection was that the Commission's $150 breakpoint would not be effective in dealing with the cited cause of the Crisis: market power.[27] The second was the concern that the Commission's promotion of forward contracting would prolong the impacts of the poorly performing spot markets.[28] The third major objection was to the Commission's rush to judgment, with opponents arguing that the Commission should temporarily stabilize the markets with price caps while it investigated supplier behavior more fully.[29]

The Commission's response to concerns regarding the breakpoint was that it is really the third line of defense in constraining prices. Correction of the structural problems through removing the PX restriction, thus allowing forward contracting, and reducing reliance upon the RT market by addressing the underscheduling problem would mitigate market power. The real purpose of the breakpoint was that the pay-as-bid prices above $150 would help by drawing in needed supply without impacting all of the purchases made by the CAISO.

Although the Commission recognized that spot prices could affect forward prices,[30] it nonetheless promoted forward contracting. In order to assure term contract prices were just and reasonable it established a $74 per MWh "benchmark" for five-year contracts against which contracts could be compared. This "benchmark" was not the re-imposition of fixed (regulated) wholesale rate, but rather something between a recommendation and warning from the Commission. In addition, FERC promised vigilant monitoring until effective remedial measures could be implemented.

In rejecting pleas for further discovery and thorough investigation of supplier behavior, the Commission conceded that the Staff investigation was at the "big picture" level, but considered

25. December 15, 2000 Order, p. 3.

26. In fact, the Commission noted vigorous objections from both buyers and sellers as an indication that it was striking the right balance in its approach.

27. This criticism came from among others, the ISO's Market Monitor. Their analysis detailed how traders would easily avoid the price cap and predicted that the Commission's proposals would both allow prices to skyrocket and lead to the demise of the PX and transparent prices. *See* Wolak, Nordhaus, and Shapiro (2000b).

28. Ironically one of the commentators raising this threat was Professor William Hogan, who represented suppliers. He correctly predicted that contracts signed during a period market dysfunction would wind up like the "stranded" natural gas contracts of the previous decade. *See* Chandley, Harvey, and Hogan (2000).

29. This was the position of the California Public Utilities Commission. *See* December 15, 2000 Order, p. 62.

30. November 2000 Order, p. 50.

this enough, as it established scarcity and poor market design as the clear culprits in market dysfunction and that addressing these issues would take care of potential market power.

Market Collapse

As predicted by the CAISO Market Monitors and detailed in Chapter 4, these initial measures failed utterly to return the markets to normalcy. Prices again skyrocketed. Volumes cleared in the PX plummeted, and it effectively ceased to function and soon declared bankruptcy. California's two largest utility companies, some of the largest in the world, became unable to pay their bills. Not only did they lack the credit to enter into the forward contracts the Commission had seen as their protection against spot market exposure, they could not pay for their spot market purchases. With the IOUs unable to cover their payables to the CAISO, it became financially nonviable. There were no remaining intermediaries with the trade credit required to purchase from electricity suppliers, and the entire electric power grid teetered on the brink of collapse from credit rather than physical shortages.

Facing a threat that could literally have brought its economy to a halt, the State of California stepped into the breach to keep electricity flowing. The agency charged with plugging the dike was the CDWR. While the Department had some experience in buying and selling electricity as an adjunct to operating the state's extensive water system,[31] it was ill-equipped suddenly to become one of the largest procurers of electricity in the world. To undertake this critical task CDWR established the California Energy Resources Division, CERS, which commenced operations with no office space, no equipment, no systems or policies and a few seconded personnel. On little but a shoestring, CERS was charged both with buying spot market supplies sufficient to meet the hourly net short of the IOUs and with securing longer-term electricity purchase contracts that would reduce reliance upon volatile spot markets as the Commission had promoted in its December 15, 2000 Order.

Undertaking these two tasks simultaneously was immensely challenging. When CERS stepped in late on January 17, 2001, the CAISO was in a Stage 3 emergency alert, and there were blackouts. Although blackouts ended on the 18th, Stage 3 emergency conditions persisted 24 hours a day for the next 30 days, requiring a mad daily scramble for energy by CERS just to keep the lights on.[32] While conditions eased somewhat after mid-February, the CAISO operated close to the edge, with Stage 3 emergencies and blackouts occurring on March 19-20 and May 7-8, 2001.[33] During the period from January 17 to June 20, 2001, CERS purchased 30.8 mil-

31. CDWR bought electricity to run its pumps, and sold surplus electricity produced by generators in some of the dams on the state's extensive water system. These transactions were typically not the sort of short-term "spot" transactions needed to meet the net short of the utility companies.

32. Realistically this challenge was hour-by-hour through the peak load periods of the day, as load varied from one hour to the next.

33. As noted earlier, virtually all of the Stage 3 emergencies ever declared by the CAISO occurred during the Crisis.

lion MWh[34] at an average price of $245/MWh, about five times the average price before and after the Crisis.

The Commission Restores Order to the Markets: The Orders of April and June 2001

With the system reeling, the Commission sought again to stabilize the markets in orders issued on April 26 and June 19, 2001. In contrast to the Commission's earlier orders, the April 26, 2001 Order proposed three measures that dealt directly with supplier market power.[35] The first was a price mitigation mechanism, which established a maximum market clearing price in the CAISO real-time market based upon marginal cost of the least efficient gas-fired generation dispatched[36] to constrain prices of all sellers within the CAISO[37] during periods of reserve deficiency.[38] The second was a requirement that all generators within the boundaries of the CAISO, including not only jurisdictional utilities with Participating Generator Agreements, but also governmental entities selling into the CAISO or using its transmission, bid any available generation into the CAISO's real-time market (a "must-offer requirement"). The third element was the modification of all participating suppliers' MBR authorizations to include refund liability for anticompetitive bidding in the CAISO real-time market.

The June 19 Order not only retained these key provisions, but it also extended them significantly in response to comments on the April 26 proposal. The price mitigation mechanism was increased in scope in two dimensions. It was expanded geographically to cover all transactions in the entire western power grid. Prices in bilateral transactions outside the CAISO[39] were required to be below the CAISO's mitigated price. The mitigation measure was also applied in modified form to cover all hours, not just those in which there were reserve deficiencies. In non-reserve deficiency hours prices were capped at 85% of the mitigated price in the last previous Stage 1 emergency in the CAISO. The reach of the "must offer" provision of the April 26

34. This is roughly 8,300 MW per hour around the clock, equivalent to the average load of a large utility system.

35. *Order Establishing Prospective Mitigation and Monitoring Plan for the California Wholesale Electric Markets and Establishing an Investigation of Public Utility Rates in Wholesale Western Energy Markets*, 95 FERC ¶61,115, April 26, 2001. The Order also proposed measures to enhance the CAISO's ability to manage generating unit planned outages.

36. The formula for the "Proxy Price" proposed in the April 26 Order reflected fuel costs (the product of an average natural gas cost in the relevant unit's heat rate) plus emissions permit costs and a $2 per MWh to cover O&M costs. The later order on June 19 changed the calculation by eliminating the emissions costs (which were to be billed as incurred to the ISO) and increasing the O&M adder to $6 per MWh. The CAISO was also ordered to collect and pay to suppliers a 10 percent mark-up on the market clearing price to reflect credit risk, but this charge was not included in prices outside the CAISO.

37. The mitigated price did not apply to suppliers from outside the CAISO. Generators, but not marketers, could place higher bids if they could be justified on the basis of costs.

38. Reserves were considered deficient when they fell below 7% of load.

39. Bilateral transactions within the CAISO, which had not been addressed in the April 26 proposal, were also covered.

order, which required that uncommitted generation capacity be bid into the CAISO or other local real-time market, was also expanded to the entire western grid.

These changes recognized the integrated nature of western power markets and, along with the other elements of the Order, cut off most of the avenues through which suppliers had sought to elevate prices. Price mitigation applied west-wide around the clock. The must offer requirement made withholding visible, and the anticompetitive bidding prohibition in seller MBRs made even economic withholding subject to remedial measures.

The writing was on the wall. As illustrated graphically in Figure 5-1, forward prices for the coming summer of 2001(Q3 2001) began a steady decline about the time of the April 26, 2001 Order and fell precipitously over the next two months. After the June 19, 2001 Order, spot prices, and price volatility quickly returned to pre-Crisis levels. The Crisis was for the most part over.[40]

40. The impacts of the Crisis, however, persisted for over a decade in the form of carrying costs of long-term bonds issued to finance CERS' electricity purchases on behalf of IOU customers and in reduced credit ratings and increased borrowing costs for the State of California more generally. The former were borne directly by electricity consumers in California, while the latter were suffered by all California taxpayers.

Figure 5-1

Commission Refund Methodology: The Orders July and December 2001

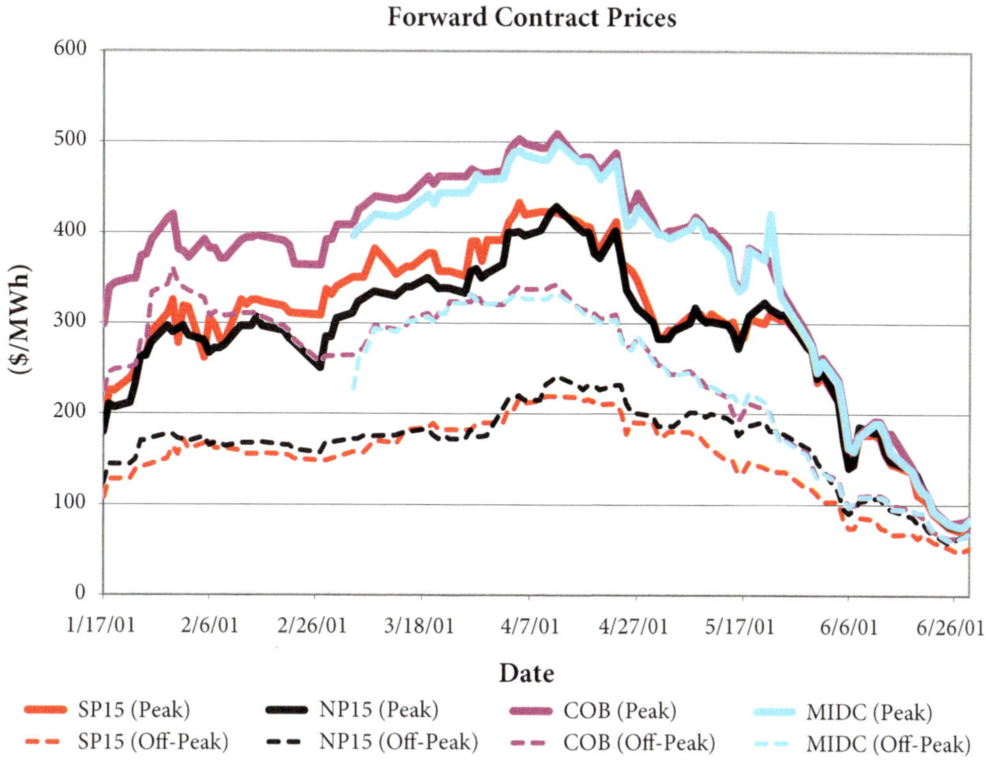

Source: NatSource

On July 25, 2001, the Commission issued an order establishing the approach for determining refunds. The scope of the refund remedy was quite limited in terms of both the time period covered and in the types of transactions for which refunds might be owed. Although the Crisis began in May 2000, the "Refund Period" ran only from October 2, 2000 through June 20, 2001. The Commission's reluctance to order refunds for the initial stages of the Crisis was based in its interpretation of the authority granted in the provisions of Section 206 of the FPA. The procedure in Section 206 established a "Refund Effective Date" 60 days after the filing of a complaint leading to a finding that the rates challenged were unjust and unreasonable. Following this procedure, the Commission settled upon October 2, 60 days after the filing of SDG&E's original complaint, as the earliest day upon which refunds could be required.[41]

41. The Commission had initially set the refund date of October 29, 2000, 60 days after the publication of its order of August 23, 2000 in the Federal Register, but altered this in its November 2000 Order.

In a manner curiously inconsistent with the prospective price mitigation it had just ordered on June 19,[42] the Commission also ruled with one rather peculiar exception, that only transactions in the PX and CAISO auction markets would be subject to refund liability. The exception was bilateral purchases made out-of-market by the CAISO. The rationale for limiting potential refunds to auction-based transactions in the PX and CAISO was the fact that it was only these transactions that were challenged in the SDG&E complaint that initiated the proceeding. These constraints upon potential refunds left many transactions during the Crisis, perhaps the majority, without a remedy. These included all transactions affected by the Crisis prior to October 2, 2000, and all bilateral transactions in the west other than the OOM purchases of the CAISO.[43]

The refund methodology followed closely the approach used in establishing prospective price mitigation in the June 19 Order. Refunds were to be determined by the difference between price charged and a competitive proxy price in each hour. Again, the proxy price calculation included fuel costs based upon natural gas costs[44] and the heat rate of the least efficient unit dispatched in any given hour plus $6 per MWh for O&M costs and a 10 percent adjustment for credit risk. Demonstrable emission costs were allowed as an offset to calculated refunds.

On December 19, 2001, the Commission issued an order that finalized the refund methodology along with other measures it had ordered in response to the Crisis.[45] The only substantive change in the refund calculation was the opportunity to show that calculated refunds would result in a total revenue shortfall for transactions in the California markets during the Refund Period. The Commission recognized the possibility that its refund procedure might rely upon proxy prices that were below the actual costs of some suppliers.

> ...we recognize that sellers have never had an opportunity to present evidence of their marginal costs, and also that the true impact of the refund formula on sellers' bottom lines will not be known until the conclusion of the refund hearing. Therefore, in order to assure adequate process, the Commission will provide an opportunity after the conclusion of the refund hearing for marketers and those reselling purchased power or selling hydroelectric power to submit evidence as to whether the refund methodology results in an overall revenue shortfall for their transactions in the CAISO and PX spot markets during the refund period.[46]

---

42. As discussed above, the Commission applied its price mitigation mechanism west-wide and included both auction-based and bilateral market spot transactions.

43. As discussed later, mandates from the Ninth Circuit Court of Appeals eventually forced the Commission to abandon this very restrictive approach.

44. In this case daily natural gas prices in the region relevant to the marginal generation were used.

45. Among the other adjustments made in this order were exclusion of governmental entities from the price mitigation and must offer requirements and elimination of the underscheduling penalty.

46. December 19, 2001 Order, pp. 168-169.

This late modification is a reflection of the problem presented by a remedy, resetting the price, designed to address overcharges by a vertically integrated monopoly seller in very different circumstances—that is, where there are many sellers and energy may have passed through many intermediaries upstream of its final sale to a consuming load.[47] In such a case, the final seller may have purchased energy at a price above the mitigated market price, and this may have been true of the upstream seller as well. This gives rise to the possibility of so-called "ripple" claims that could have led the Commission down the proverbial rabbit hole. While the "cost offset" approach cut off ripple claims and simplified the Commission's job,[48] it necessarily reduced refunds below the level that would make purchasers whole.[49]

Phase 2

Somewhat ironically, as the Commission was no doubt putting the finishing touches on its December 19, 2001 Order, Enron filed for bankruptcy.[50] Among the many sensational revelations flowing from Enron's collapse were memos reflecting discussions among Enron traders and the company's legal counsel describing manipulative strategies Enron employed to exploit the PX and CAISO markets during the Crisis. These memos explain the workings of schemes with colorful names like Death Star, Ricochet, Get Shorty, and Fat Boy used by Enron traders to move prices and to sell services and collect congestion payments under false pretenses.[51] According to the memos, Enron also plied their strategies for and with other suppliers.

With evidence mounting that manipulation had contributed to the Crisis, the Commission opened another investigation on February 13, 2002. In what must have been an awkward moment the Commission instructed its Staff to do the following:

> ...undertake a fact-finding investigation into whether any entity, including Enron Corporation ..., manipulated short-term prices in electric energy or natural gas markets in the West ... for the period January 1, 2000, forward.[52]

47. In the WECC at the time it was not uncommon for energy to change hands three or more times between source and sink.

48. Even so, there were numerous cost offset claims that consumed vast amounts of time and resources.

49. The authors discuss the difficulties in resetting price in Fox-Penner *et al.* (2002).

50. Enron filed for bankruptcy on December 2, 2001.

51. Evidence of Enron manipulation had been mounting even before Enron's lawyers released three memos discussing Enron trading practices and their potential ramifications in light of regulatory investigations and possible sanctions under the CAISO Tariff. We have relied for the purpose of references on the version written by Christian Yoder and Stephen Hall to Richard Sanders entitled *Traders Strategies in the California Wholesale Power Markets/ISO Sanctions*, and dated December 6, 2000.

52. *Order Directing Staff Investigation*, 98 FERC ¶ 61,165, February 13, 2002, p. 1.

The issue of supplier behavior, which the Commission had intentionally overlooked previously, was now the main attraction. Further embarrassment soon followed when the Commission had to admit that the transaction data it had collected quarterly from suppliers for years for the purpose of monitoring market activity was insufficient for assessing individual supplier behavior. In a letter dated March 5, 2002, after noting that in ordering the investigation it had empowered its General Counsel to gather information, the Commission explained:

> In the course of conducting the fact-finding investigation, Staff reviewed the wholesale sales information filed by jurisdictional sellers in their quarterly reports. Staff determined that the information contained in the reports is not useful for the fact-finding investigation.[53]

That the Commission had not previously been in a position to effectively oversee individual trader behavior was conceded in testimony before Congress by Patrick Woods, who became the Chairman of the Commission in the summer of 2001. In reviewing the status of FERC oversight of the electric power industry Chairman Wood stated:

> For restructuring of the power industry to be successful and yield benefits for customers, however, there must be some basic preconditions: Sufficient energy infrastructure, balanced market rules, and vigilant market oversight.
>
> Upon joining the Commission last summer, I concluded that none of these preconditions was firmly in place in the electric industry.[54]

He went on to outline the steps that had been taken since his arrival to bolster the Commission's monitoring and oversight starting with a "mindset change at the top," a commitment by the Commission itself to assure necessary supervision.

Having collected and reviewed the necessary transaction information sought in the March letter request, the Commission Staff released its Initial Report on potential manipulation in western power and natural gas markets. Importantly, this report concluded that certain supplier behavior violated the Market Monitoring and Information Protocol (MMIP) provisions of the PX and CAISO tariffs.[55] These tariff sections, commonly referred to as the "gaming provisions," are explained further in a moment. After further Staff investigation and analysis of trad-

53. Letter from: Donald J. Gelinas, Associate Director, FERC Office of Markets, Tariffs and Rates, to: All Jurisdictional Sellers and Non-Jurisdictional Sellers in the West, Docket No PA02-2-000, March 5, 2002 p. 1. The letter then went on to detail the information that would have to be provided in a specified electronic format by all sellers in the West by April 2, 2002.

54. *Asleep at the Switch: FERC'S Oversight of Enron Corporation*, Transcript of Hearings before the Committee on Governmental Affairs, U.S. Senate, Volume 1, November 12, 2002, U.S. Government Printing Office, Washington, D.C., 2003, Testimony of the Honorable Patrick H. Wood, III, p. 42.

55. *See Initial Report on Company-Specific Separate Proceeding and Generic Reevaluations; Published Natural Gas Price Data; and Enron Trading Strategies: Fact-Finding Investigation of Potential Manipulation of Electric and Natural Gas Prices*, Docket No. PA02-2-000, issued in August 2002.

ing activity by the CAISO using screens based upon the findings of the Initial Report, the Staff published its Final Report on March 26, 2003.[56] The Final Report reached several significant conclusions, among them that: 1) natural gas prices had been artificially elevated affecting electricity prices; 2) reported natural gas prices in California should not be used to establish just and reasonable electricity prices; 3) strategies undertaken by Enron and other companies were in violation of the anti-gaming provisions of the PX and CAISO Tariffs; 4) elevated spot electricity prices affected forward prices relied upon in establishing prices in long-term contracts; and 5) spot electricity prices were affected by economic withholding through inflated bidding. On the basis of analyses of Enron trading strategies done by the CAISO staff the Staff recommended further proceedings against Enron and other specified suppliers.

Between the Initial and Final Reports, the Commission issued an order in response to a remand from the Ninth Circuit Court of Appeals allowing parties in Crisis-related dockets 100 days to "...conduct additional discovery into market manipulation" by sellers during the Crisis and to undertake discovery, submit evidence, and propose findings of fact to the Commission by the end of February 2003.[57] The Commission also afforded the parties the opportunity to respond to submissions by adverse parties by March 17.[58] Finally, on April 2, 2003, the Commission allowed the parties to file briefs on Staff's position that the provisions of the California CAISO Tariff could provide the basis for remedial action concerning the manipulative activities alleged.[59]

The submissions by the ultimate buyers in the PX and CAISO markets were massive. They detailed allegations of manipulative behavior. They analyzed trading data to establish the widespread use of Enron-type manipulative schemes by many participants in the PX and CAISO markets. They provided evidentiary confirmation from supplier documents, e-mails, and phone conversations of the intentional pursuit of manipulative strategies and of cooperation in manipulative gaming strategies among suppliers. Finally, they pointed out the impacts of widespread manipulation upon the California energy markets and the reliability of the CAISO system. The breadth and depth of their showing far exceeded what the Commission Staff had been able to muster.[60]

---

56. *Final Report on Price Manipulation in Western Markets: Fact-Finding Investigation of Potential Manipulation of Electric and Natural Gas Prices*, Docket No. PA02-2-000, March 26, 2003.

57. *San Diego Gas & Elec. Co. v. Sellers of Energy and Ancillary Serv., et al.*, 101 FERC ¶ 61,186 (2002). The evidence became known as "The 100 Days Evidence."

58. The Commission later delayed the filing dates three days and issued ancillary notices and orders.

59. As discussed later, the MMIP was not part of the main body of the ISO Tariff, its provisions were fairly general in nature and it did not specifically mention manipulation.

60. *See*, for example, *Prepared Testimony of Dr. Peter Fox-Penner on behalf of the California Parties, Docket No. EL00-95-000*, Exh. No. CA-001, February 25, 2003.

The Enron Orders

On June 25, 2003 the Commission issued four orders based upon the Staff investigation and the 100 Days Evidence submitted by participants in the Crisis-related proceedings. The first, the so called Gaming Order, required various suppliers to show cause why they should not be found to have engaged in Enron-type manipulation strategies in violation of specified sections of the MMIP of the CAISO Tariff.[61] The second, referred to as the Partnership Order, demanded that named parties show cause why they should not be found to have been in league with Enron in executing its manipulative schemes.[62] The third order revoked Enron's authorization to sell electric power and natural gas at market-based rates (MBRs) because of its manipulative activities in electric power and natural gas markets.[63] A final order instituted an investigation of non-competitive bidding practices.[64]

These orders appeared to shake the very foundations of liberalized electric power markets all across the U.S. In the Gaming Order, twenty-two firms were alleged to have engaged in Enron's "Ricochet" strategy involving fraudulent exports; sixty-five sellers were alleged to have "gamed" the CAISO's congestion management system (using Enron strategies called Death Star and Load Shift); and twenty-six suppliers were alleged to have misrepresented their capabilities to sell ancillary services they could not provide (Enron's "Get Shorty"). The Partnership Order named ten entities, many of them non-jurisdictional municipal utilities, cooperatives or irrigation districts, which allegedly cooperated with Enron, wittingly or unwittingly, in executing Enron manipulation strategies. The Enron MBR Revocation Order concluded that the "gaming" activities of Enron affiliates involved fraud and misrepresentation and thus were inconsistent not only with the PX and CAISO Tariffs, but also with obligations implicit in their market-based rate authority for electricity sales and their blanket marketing certificates for sales of natural gas.

Virtually every seller named in the Commission's show cause orders disputed their guilt. In filings responding to the original 100 Days evidence as well as to the show cause orders, sellers generally disputed that the so-called Enron strategies were in fact tariff violations, instead arguing that these were legitimate profit-seeking trading acts allowed under the CAISO and PX tariffs. They also raised a host of other factual, technical, and economic objections.

---

61. *See Order to Show Cause Concerning Gaming and/or Anomalous Market Behavior* (hereinafter Gaming Order 2003), 103 FERC ¶61,345, June 25, 2003.

62. *See Order to Show Cause Concerning Gaming and/or Anomalous Market Behavior Through Use of Partnerships, Alliances or Other Arrangements and Directing Submissions* (Partnership Order), 103 FERC ¶61,346, June 25, 2003. Except for providing a very concrete demonstration of Enron's realization that manipulative activities are best implemented in physicals markets, thus requiring Enron's cooperation with many entities that controlled physical assets, the Partnership Order is of little interest and will be discussed further only in passing.

63. *See Order Revoking Market-Based Rate Authorities and Terminating Blanket Marketing Certificates* (Enron MBR Revocation Order), 103 FERC ¶61,343, June 25, 2003.

64. *See Order Requiring Demonstration that Certain Bids Did Not Constitute Anomalous Market Behavior*, 103 FERC ¶61,347, June 25, 2000. This investigation was conducted by the Staff and concluded without the participation of purchasers.

The Gaming Order

In the Gaming Order, the Commission took several steps forward. As a starting point, it established the "gaming" and "anomalous market behavior" provisions of the MMIPs in the PX and CAISO Tariffs as valid bases for direct remedial actions by the Commission. Suppliers quickly argued that these provisions were intended only to guide PX and CAISO market monitors and in any event were too vague to serve as a standard for judging supplier conduct.[65] While the anomalous market behavior provisions described certain specific conduct such as withholding generation capacity and bidding patterns inconsistent with prevailing market conditions, the gaming section left a lot of room for interpretation:

> …taking unfair advantage of the rules and procedures set forth in the PX or CAISO Tariffs, Protocols or Activity Rules, or of transmission constraints in periods in which exist substantial Congestion, to the detriment of the efficiency of, and of consumers in, the CAISO Markets.[66]

Nevertheless, the Commission held that the MMIP fairly established "rules of the road" sufficient to put suppliers on notice of proscribed activities.

The Commission then found that certain of the Enron trading strategies violated the provision of the PX and CAISO Tariffs and thus that remedial action would be appropriate for suppliers that engaged in them. These included a subset of the strategy Enron called Ricochet, which the Commission officially labeled False Import, congestion-related strategies such as Death Star and Load Shift and strategies involving improper sales of ancillary services like Get Shorty and Double Selling. Other Enron schemes like Fat Boy, relabeled False Load by the FERC, were held to involve tariff violations, but the Commission for equitable reasons chose not to require show cause filings. Finally, the Commission found that some of the Enron practices, such as Export of California Power and legitimate arbitrage of ancillary services markets, were not tariff violations.

The Commission also extended the period to be addressed in the show cause inquiry and for potential monetary remedies back to January 2000 so that it encompassed the entire Crisis. Profit disgorgement was seen as the applicable remedy for any tariff violations from January 2000 through June 20, 2001. This, as noted in the order, opened not only the possibility of refunds in the earlier period but also for additional refunds in excess of those previously implemented for the original Refund Period running from October 2, 2000 through June 20, 2001.

Although it moved in the right direction in the Gaming Order, the Commission missed an excellent opportunity to articulate a definition of gaming/manipulation and establish the legal

65. *See* Gaming Order 2003, ¶ 21.

66. California Independent System Operator Tariff, Market Monitoring and Information Protocol § 2.1.3, (Issued June 1, 1998).

authority for remedial action. Instead, it relied solely upon the strategies described in the Enron memos to define reprehensible behavior, and lacking a clear concept of manipulation, even interpreted these in far too narrow a fashion.[67]

Overly narrow definitions of gaming practices, however, was but a minor aspect of the handicap created by the Commission's exclusive reliance upon the Enron memos for definitions of manipulative schemes. This severely limited the scope of the investigation and initially foreclosed consideration of a wide range of other trading strategies that were just as fraudulent and damaging as those illuminated in the memos.[68]

The Enron MBR Revocation Order

The Commission's failure in the Gaming Order to articulate a definition of manipulative gaming was puzzling in light of the Enron MBR Revocation Order issued the same day. In this Order the Commission focused directly on the fraudulent nature of Enron's trading activities:

> 50. The Enron Entities contend that the Commission has not shown that their actions resulted in gaming or unjust and unreasonable rates. While the Show Cause Order properly made no findings of market manipulation and unjust and unreasonable rates, as the parties had not yet had an opportunity to respond, the Commission is now prepared to make such findings for the reasons discussed below.
>
> 51. The Enron Entities do not dispute the facts set forth in the Show Cause Order (and the Final Staff Report that was incorporated by reference) i.e., that they engaged in the conduct referenced and that they failed to report their influence/control over other entities' facilities. Rather, they argue that these "improper" actions did not constitute gaming or result in unjust and unreasonable rates. We disagree.
>
> 52. We have previously explained that companies failing to adhere to proper standards are subject to immediate revocation of their market-based rate authority. The Show Cause Order elaborated that "implicit in Commission orders granting market-based rates is a presumption that a company's behavior will not involve fraud, deception or misrepresentation."[69]

The Commission went on to find that Enron "...engaged in gaming in the form of inappropriate trading strategies" and the result was "...manipulated prices in the California market and

67. Descriptions of the Enron strategies are found in Chapter 7, where we also point out the shortcomings of the Commission's definitions.

68. Later a mandate from the Ninth Circuit Court of Appeals forced the Commission to allow participants in the Crisis-related proceedings to define and pursue other manipulative trading strategies.

69. Enron MBR Revocation Order.

congestion fees in excess of what Enron would have received with accurate schedules and bids." Here the Commission has clearly equated "gaming" as used in the MMIP of the PX and CAISO tariffs with manipulation based upon fraud.

In its discussion of Enron manipulation of natural gas markets, the Commission recognized a "fraud on the market" concept in which trades are intended to mislead other market participants. The Order describes ploys in which traders sought to move prices in the physical gas markets in order to benefit a derivative position. The specific mechanism underlying these ploys was the use of spurious trades on Enron's electronic trading platform known as the Enron Online (EOL):

> One of the most egregious examples of abuse through EOL resulted in the manipulation of natural gas prices at the Henry Hub located in Louisiana on at least one occasion to profit from positions taken in the over-the-counter (OTC) financial derivatives markets (OTC markets).[70] [Footnotes omitted.]

As explained by the Commission, Enron traders set the stage by taking large short OTC swap positions on EOL. Next Enron pushed physical gas prices, and, hence, the swap prices down.

> The EOL market maker then began to lower the prices and sold a very large amount of gas at rapidly falling prices. The falling of the physical price then further pushed down the OTC swap price, generating significant profits for the financial traders. These profits greatly exceeded the losses that were generated from the buying and selling of the physical gas.[71]

The Commission reasoned that such trading could "mislead the market in a number of ways, including by sending false price signals to other market participants and making the market at particular points appear more liquid than it really is."[72] Such "fraudulent trading" compromised Commission objectives:

> Clearly, the creation of false price signals ... is contrary to the goal of allowing gas purchasers to make purchasing decisions "in accord with market conditions."[73]

In later chapters we lay out a definition of manipulation and discuss a conceptual model for applying it. Here we merely observe that when the Commission issued the Gaming and Enron MBR Revocation Orders, it appeared to have all of the intellectual building blocks necessary

70. Enron MBR Revocation Order, ¶ 63.

71. *Id.* ¶ 65. The Commission observed although the price change in the physical markets was only about $.10/MMBtu, Enron traders made $3.2 million on the day due to the leverage from their large financial position.

72. *Id.* ¶ 68.

73. *Id.* ¶ 68.

to specify a framework for dealing more generally with the types of manipulative strategies employed by Enron and numerous other suppliers. It had equated the gaming prohibited under the PX and CAISO Tariffs with manipulation. Manipulation, in turn, involved transactions based upon fraud and misrepresentation. Finally, fraud could come in the form of filing false schedules or misrepresentation of the nature or source of the product or service sold or in the form of trades intended to mislead other market participants or the CAISO in order to influence a price or other outcome (such as a congestion payment, for example) in a way that would benefit the trader injecting the false information into the marketplace.

A fraud-based approach differs significantly from the Commission's traditional focus upon market power and would have provided both a broader set of tools to use in dealing with the Crisis as well as a much clearer picture of the types of trader behavior to target. Unfortunately, the Commission did not seize the moment to establish the boundaries of manipulation, but instead relied upon the Enron memos to define unacceptable behaviors.

The actual ordering provisions of the Gaming Order divided the investigation into seller-specific proceedings and directed the CAISO to provide transaction data regarding alleged gaming transactions to the relevant sellers (Identified Entities) within 21 days of the Order. The Identified Entities then had 45 days to respond to show cause allegations. A hearing was to take place within 15 days of the filing of the show cause responses.

In the period following the suppliers' responses to the show cause orders, most of the Identified Entities reached settlements with the FERC Trial Staff, which dismissed several of the key arguments made. These settlements were opposed by the purchasers as being too narrow in terms of the range of manipulative activity addressed and in terms of the small monetary penalties that the Staff required and the suppliers agreed to pay. Many of these dismissals seized upon the Commission's narrow definitions in the Gaming Order to conclude that there was no evidence of illicit activity. False Import allegations were dismissed, for example, because the imported energy was not sold to the CAISO at a price above the cap.[74] The hearing ordered by the Commission never took place.

Ninth Circuit Remands

For the next several years the parties were engaged in motions for rehearing, cost-recovery filings, and petitions to the Ninth Circuit Court of Appeals. Throughout these proceedings the Commission maintained a very circumscribed approach that relied upon specific, narrow definitions of illicit gaming practices, limited refund relief to the period beginning on

74. As discussed in Chapter 7, the CAISO rarely purchased at prices above the cap, even in its OOM purchases, leaving very few potential False Import violations under the Commission's definition.

October 2, 2000, and refused to consider manipulation of prices in bilateral purchases made by CERS on behalf of the CAISO between January 17 and June 20, 2001. The trajectory of the proceedings changed, however, in response to two decisions from the appeals court. The first allowed sellers to seek refunds for the summer of 2000 and opened the door to potential relief for manipulative strategies other than those that had been defined by the Commission.[75] The second put most of the CERS purchases back on the table by reviving claims by purchasers in the PNW where CERS had purchased much of the high-priced energy needed to meet the demands of California consumers during the Crisis.[76] These decisions led to evidentiary hearings that finally gave purchasers the opportunity to air their claims.

Proceedings under the CPUC Remand

In *CPUC* the Ninth Circuit made two game-changing rulings. First, it found that although the Commission had properly established the Refund Effective Date under §206 of the FPA as October 2, 2001, it had improperly failed to recognize that relief for the period prior to October 2, was available under §309 of the Act if suppliers had failed to comply with applicable tariffs. Second, the Court held that aggrieved parties were not bound by decisions made by FERC in its prosecutorial role as to what was or was not a tariff violation. Because the Commission had defined Gaming Practices in prosecuting its own action, the court held that these should not prevent purchasers from seeking to prove and secure relief from other potential tariff violations.

In response to the Ninth Circuit mandate, the Commission ordered an evidentiary hearing "... to develop a record on possible tariff violations during the period prior to October 2, 2000." The Commission also rebuffed claims from suppliers that the Commission had already adjudicated manipulation claims or that they had been conclusively resolved through settlements with FERC Staff, relying on the Ninth Circuit's ruling that:

> A party's valid request for relief cannot be denied purely on the basis that the agency is considering its own enforcement action that may impart a portion of the relief sought. If an aggrieved party tenders sufficient evidence that tariffs have been violated, then it is entitled to have FERC adjudicate whether the tariff has been violated and what relief is appropriate.[77]

---

75. *Pub. Util. Com'n of the State of Cal. v. FERC,* 462 F.3d 1027, 9th Cir. 2006, (CPUC Decision). On April 15, 2009, the Ninth Circuit issued its mandate for Commission action on this remand. *See Pub. Util. Com'n of the State of Cal. v. FERC,* slip op. No. 01-71051, Apr. 15, 2009.

76. See *City of Seattle v. FERC,* 499 F. 3rd (Ninth Circuit 2007). The second subsection following explains these proceedings in more detail.

77. *Order on Requests for Rehearing and Clarification, and Motions to Dismiss,* 135 FERC ¶ 61,183, ¶ 16, quoting *CPUC,* May 26, 2011, p. 1051.

The hearing commenced on April 11, 2012, more than a decade after the Crisis was over. There were nearly sixty days of testimony from 31 witnesses over a three month period. Purchasers' experts (including several of the authors) provided voluminous, detailed evidence of manipulative trading strategies based largely upon fraud and misrepresentation that violated the CAISO and other relevant tariffs but did not necessarily hue to the definitions recognized by the FERC in the Gaming Order. The evidence proffered included not only analyses of trading data to demonstrate manipulative trading patterns, but also documentary evidence of trader strategies and intent. Supplier fact witnesses testified that their trading was in pursuit of legitimate business interests and in many cases simply reflected trader efforts to arbitrage price differences among markets. Eminent academic economists opined that prices in the summer of 2000 could be explained by then prevailing scarcity conditions. Curiously the Staff took the position that several of Complainants' proofs should be discounted because they failed to show tariff violations that comported with the Commission's original definitions in the Gaming Order.

After considering 10,000 pages of hearing transcript and nearly 1,000 exhibits submitted in the hearings, the Administrative Law Judge (ALJ) concluded that the Complainants had made a *prima facie* showing on a transaction-by-transaction basis that Respondent suppliers had engaged in manipulative activities that violated applicable tariffs and that the majority of these transactions impacted prices in the California markets.[78] Conversely, the ALJ rejected Respondents' generalized arguments and found that sellers had failed to rebut Complainants' detailed showing on a similar basis and thus had not sustained their burden of persuasion.[79] Thus the proof of manipulative tariff violations and their impact upon prices stood against Respondent's challenge. On November 14, 2014 the Commission affirmed Judge Baten's initial findings on virtually every count and ordered a process for establishing refunds.[80] In Chapter 7, we examine the main manipulation strategies in detail.

Proceedings under the Puget Remand

In the wake of the SDG&E complaint and the Commission's order of August 23, 2000 instituting its own investigation, Puget Sound Energy, Inc. (Puget) filed a complaint on October 26, 2000, petitioning the Commission for a prospective price cap on sales of energy or capacity in the PNW wholesale power markets. The Commission initially dismissed Puget's complaint, but upon further consideration established a preliminary evidentiary hearing to develop a record on whether the rates for bilateral spot market sales in the PNW during the relevant

78. *See Initial Decision,* Docket No. EL00-95-248, 142 FERC ¶ 63,011, February 15, 2013, ¶¶ 1, 12-14.

79. *Id.*, ¶ 73.

80. San Diego Gas & Electric Company, *et al., Order Affirming Factual Findings, Directing Compliance Filing and Ordering Refunds* (Opinion No. 536), Docket No. EL00-95-248, 149 FERC ¶ 61,116 (November 10, 2014).

2period might have been unjust and unreasonable. A hearing was held in September 2001.[81] Shortly thereafter the ALJ recommended that the Commission not order refunds for transactions at issue in the PNW and further determined that sales to CERS were outside the scope of the proceeding.

On December 19, 2002, the Commission, consistent with its handling of the California proceedings, reopened the record to provide time for additional discovery, to allow participants in the proceeding to submit additional evidence of market misconduct and to propose new and/or modified findings of fact. The Commission later extended the deadline for submissions until March 20, 2003. Following a hearing, in an order issued June 25, 2003, the Commission determined that it had already provided the relief originally requested by Puget in its June 19, 2001 Order that imposed prospective price caps throughout the Western United States. In declining refunds, the Commission concluded that "even if prices were unjust and unreasonable, it is not possible to fashion a remedy that would be equitable to all the participants in the PNW market." In subsequent orders denying rehearing, the Commission affirmed the ALJ's finding that sales to CERS were outside the scope of the proceeding.[82]

On appeal, the Ninth Circuit held in a decision dated August 24, 2007, that the Commission had abused its discretion in denying relief for transactions involving energy purchased in the PNW that was ultimately consumed in California. The Court ordered the Commission on remand to consider those purchases, including the purchases of energy made by CERS, in its determination of whether refunds were warranted. The Ninth Circuit also directed the Commission to examine in detail the voluminous new evidence of market manipulation submitted in the 100 Days proceedings after the ALJ made the initial factual findings and to account for such evidence in any future orders regarding the award or denial of refunds.

The Commission responded to the decision in an Order on Remand on October 3, 2011. This Order established an evidentiary hearing and was noteworthy from a couple of perspectives. The Order, for example, noted that although the appeals court had directed the Commission "... to examine in detail the new evidence of market manipulation, submitted after the ALJ made factual findings and account for such evidence in any future orders regarding the award or denial of refunds...", it was nevertheless constrained in dealing with manipulative activity during the Crisis:

> Whether any sellers in this case engaged in unlawful market activity in the spot market must be determined based on the relevant laws, regulations, orders, and tariffs in effect at the time of the Western energy crisis. The Western energy crisis predated and, in fact, was one of the motivations for the anti-manipulation provisions of the Energy Policy Act of 2005. In addition, ***at the time of the crisis, neither the Commission's***

81. It must be kept in mind that at this time complaining parties had not had any Commission ordered discovery opportunities.

82. *See Puget Sound Energy, Inc.*, 103 FERC ¶ 61,348, June 25, 2003; *Order, reh'g denied*, 105 FERC ¶ 61,183, November 10, 2003.

> ***regulations nor its grants of market-based rate authority contained market behavior rules prohibiting market manipulation or defining prohibited market manipulation.***[83] [Emphasis added, footnotes omitted.]

This is odd, as discussed previously, in light of the Commission's Enron MBR Revocation Order in which a prohibition against fraud was deemed implicit in grants of MBR authority and manipulation was seen, at least in some cases, to be based upon either outright fraud or a fraud on the market concept. It is also inconsistent with the Commission's reliance upon vaguely specified gaming and anomalous market behavior provisions of the MMIPs of the PX and CAISO tariffs in its Gaming Order.

The treatment of CERS purchases in the Order on Remand was also significant. The Commission followed the dictates of the Ninth Circuit and allowed CERS to provide evidence and seek redress for purchases it made in the PNW. However, it determined that, unlike identical OOM bilateral purchases by the CAISO,[84] CERS purchases would be presumed just and reasonable under the *Mobile-Sierra (M-S)* Doctrine. As a practical matter, this significantly raised the bar in terms of the showing required of CERS to make a sufficient case for relief.

The *M-S* Doctrine is a judicial construct based upon a clause in § 206 of the FPA which recognizes that rates can be set by agreement between buyers and sellers in a contract. This clause has been interpreted as a restraint upon the ability of parties to a contract to challenge the prices established therein on the grounds that they are unjust and unreasonable. The public interest rationale for protection of contract rates is that long-term contracts allow buyers to hedge against spot price volatility, while they assure a reliable stream of revenue to sellers that can be used to support the financing required for investments in long-lived generation facilities. Undertaken fairly, such contracts reflect an arms-length allocation of price risk between buyers and sellers that should not be subject to regulatory revision during the term of the agreement merely because one of the parties becomes unhappy with the outcome.

Relying upon this rationale, the courts have implemented the *M-S* Doctrine as a rebuttable presumption that long-term contract rates are just and reasonable. The presumption can be overcome upon a showing that the contract rates are contrary to the public interest.[85] The governing case from the U.S. Supreme Court, *Morgan Stanley*, also reasoned that the *M-S* presumption would not apply if the formation of the contract were tainted by fraud, duress, or

83. *See Order on Remand, Puget Sound Energy, Inc.*, 137 FERC ¶ 61,001, Docket No. EL91-10-026, October 3, 2011.

84. The CAISO's OOM purchases were typically made at Palo Verde or COB at the interfaces with other control areas. Later, when poor credit prevented OOM purchases by the CAISO, CERS made such purchases at these locations and simultaneously transferred the energy to the CAISO under identical terms. Under the Commission's ruling, the CAISO purchases from CERS were judged under the just and reasonable standard, while the CERS purchases of the same energy under the same terms from third parties, were presumed *ab initio* just and reasonable under the *M-S* doctrine.

85. The courts have noted that rates are more likely to be contrary to the public interest where they place a substantial burden on electricity consumers who are not party to the contract.

bad faith by one of the parties or that the negotiations were impacted by market manipulation or other significant market disruption.[86]

In ruling that *M-S* should apply to the CERS purchase contracts in the PNW, the Commission made a significant leap in the application of the doctrine. No court has applied the doctrine to short-duration, spot price transactions of the sort through which CERS made purchases in the PNW. While spot price purchases were governed by a contract, the duration of CERS transactions was typically a day or less, often just an hour or two, and prices were negotiated orally based on brief trader conversations. Such contracts do not provide any of the benefits in terms of risk mitigation or price certainty relied upon by courts in considering the public's interest in preserving bilaterally negotiated long-term contract prices. The spot power prices paid under these rapid-fire oral agreements reflected, in fact, the very price volatility that the courts found it beneficial to *avoid* through traditional, price-hedging long-term contracting. Thus they did nothing to assure stable revenue streams that suppliers could rely upon in raising investment capital. Furthermore, unlike long-term agreements, there was no potential for the use of a regulatory process opportunistically to revise the terms of an ongoing arrangement.[87]

Regardless of whether or not applying the *M-S* Doctrine to spot price contracts is good policy, as discussed later, its impact on the *Puget* proceeding was considerable. It required that Complainants' proofs address each of over 900 contracts individually in terms of two issues: 1) whether the *M-S* presumption of just and reasonable rates should not apply because negotiations were tainted by fraud, duress, bad faith, or market manipulation; and 2) whether the *M-S* presumption, if applicable, was overcome by evidence that contract prices were not in the public interest due to the burden the contracts placed upon consumers.

The hearing ordered by the Commission commenced on August 27, 2013, and ended on October 24, 2013, with testimony by 33 witnesses during 24 hearing days over 7 weeks (excluding a two-week recess). The California Parties provided evidence on a contract-by-contract basis that each of the Respondent sellers had engaged in manipulative trading activities and price discrimination and that their negotiations with CERS reflected fraud, duress, and bad faith. As in the earlier hearing, the trading schemes shown by witnesses for the buyers sometimes differed from those defined by the Commission in the Gaming Order. Suppliers again claimed that scarcity of supply explained high prices and that their activities were in pursuit of legitimate business interests.

86. *Morgan Stanley Capital Group, Inc. v. Pub. Util. Dist. No. 1 of Snohomish County*, 554 U.S. 527, 2008.

87. In a long-term contract established during a period of high spot prices, for example, the contract price is typically below spot prices in the initial years of the agreement, but exceeds expected future spot prices in the later part of the contract term. The contract thus balances benefits to the buyer in the earlier part of the contract term against benefits to the seller in the latter part. The *M-S* Doctrine prevents a buyer in these circumstances from enjoying the benefits of the contract price in the early years of the term and then opportunistically obtaining regulatory relief in the later period because the price is too high to be considered just and reasonable. This would not only deprive the seller of the benefit of the negotiated bargain, but it might also leave it with a stranded generating unit developed to service the sale commitment.

Subsequent to the hearing, settlements with some of the suppliers companies left only Marketer B and Marketer C to be addressed by the ALJ, Ms. Bobbie McCartney. In her opinion, rendered on March 28, 2014, she found that Complaints had made their case that many of the Marketer B contracts were affected by manipulative False Exports[88] and that most of Marketer B's contracts reflected fraud, duress, or bad faith in dealing with CERS. As to these contracts the *M-S* Doctrine would not apply. She further held that evidence offered by Marketer B did not effectively rebut the showing by complaining buyers. In contrast, the ALJ concluded that Complainants had failed to prove their allegation that Marketer C's dealings with CERS had involved fraud, duress, or bad faith.[89]

The Initial Decision is of particular interest because of its treatment of whether the pricing in the Respondents' contracts with CERS was contrary to the public interest because of the burden such contracts placed upon consumers. The ALJ acknowledged that any particular spot price contract was of such short duration and transacted such a small volume in comparison to the overall market that it was extremely unlikely, if not virtually impossible, that it would place a measurable burden upon consumers.

She thus reasoned that the dictates of the FPA and *Morgan Stanley* required that in weighing public harm the contracts of each supplier should be considered not individually, but rather in aggregate. She refused to go further, however, and rejected the argument made by the Complainants that market prices elevated by manipulation and market dysfunction would make the prices in all contracts negotiated by Respondents during the Crisis inconsistent with the public interest.[90, 91]

The citations provided by the ALJ for the Commission's rejection of reliance upon the impact of others' sales, the Order on Rehearing, ¶¶ 26 and 30,[92] do not support this position. Neither addresses the issue of an excessive burden upon consumers.[93]

The Supreme Court in *Morgan Stanley* made very clear that exogenous circumstances including markets disrupted by misbehavior by others are relevant in assessing consumer burden:

88. False Export is the term experts for buyers applied to strategies that laundered energy generated in California through a putative export so that it could be misrepresented as coming from outside the CAISO for resale in the CAISO RT energy market or as OOM energy either to the CAISO or later to CERS.

89. Complainants had not alleged that Marketer C had engaged in any manipulative trading strategies.

90. Despite the holding that a supplier's contracts should be considered together in weighing their impact upon consumers, the ID found that neither the Marketer B nor the Marketer C contracts placed a sufficient burden on consumers to find them contrary to the public interest. *See* ID, ¶¶ 1,702, 1,710.

91. ID, ¶¶ 1694, 1696.

92. *Puget Sound Energy, Inc.*, 137 FERC ¶ 61,001, 2011, p.2 (Order on Remand), *order on reh'g*, 143 FERC ¶ 61,020, 2013, p. 2 (Order on Rehearing).

93. *Id.* ¶ 26 discusses avoiding the M-S presumptions, which according to *Morgan Stanley*, should focus in behavior of the parties, but does not address overcoming the presumption which turns instead upon the resulting burden borne by consumers.

> The dissent criticizes the Commission's decision because it took into account under the heading "totality of the circumstances" only the circumstances of the contract formation, not "circumstances exogenous to contract negotiations, including natural disasters and market manipulation by entities not parties to the challenged contract." Those considerations are relevant to whether the contracts impose an "excessive burden" on consumers relative to what they would have paid absent the contracts. It is precisely our uncertainty whether the Commission considered those "circumstances exogenous to contract negotiations," discussed in Part III of our opinion, that causes us to approve the remand to FERC.[94]

As discussed in Chapter 8, the Commission's interpretation of the *M-S Doctrine* could create serious limitations on its oversight of electricity markets.

94. *Morgan Stanley*, 554 U.S. 527, 2008, p. 549, fn. 4.

CHAPTER 6

MARKET POWER VS SCARCITY IN THE CALIFORNIA CRISIS

As noted in Chapters 3 and 4, sellers in the California power markets were given the authority to sell at prices established by the market, based on tests that they lacked undue market power. As we explain further below, these tests—conducted once every three years—were totally incapable of fulfilling their function.

When the Crisis occurred, the only other prohibition on market power was a loosely-worded tariff provision on seller bidding behavior in the PX and CAISO spot markets. The CAISO tariff had a section prohibiting what it called *anomalous bidding*; "bidding behavior that departs from normal competitive behavior."[1] The tariff noted that this included "pricing and bidding patterns that are inconsistent with prevailing supply and demand conditions, e.g., prices and bids that appear consistently excessive or otherwise inconsistent with such conditions."[2]

With these as our only formal guides, we analyzed market power during the crisis using a wide variety of tests and tools. All these methods were presented before the FERC in various proceedings related to the California Crisis of 2000–2001 investigation on behalf of the California buyers.[3]

---

1. CAISO Market Monitoring & Information Protocol, California Independent System Operator Corporation, FERC Electric Tariff, Original Volume No. III, August 16, 2000 (hereinafter CAISO MMIP) § 2.1.1.

2. *Id.* § 2.1.1.5.

3. The California buyers include Southern California Edison (SCE), Pacific Gas and Electric (PG&E), the People of the State of California *ex rel.* Bill Lockyer, Attorney General (California AG), the California Public Utilities Commission (CPUC), and the California Electricity Oversight Board (CEOB), (collectively the California Parties). Examples of the proceedings are FERC Docket Nos. EL00-95, *et al.*, EL03-180, *et al.*, EL03-137, *et al.*, Docket No. EL09-56, and Docket No. EL00-10.

Market Definition

As explained in Chapter 3, determining whether a seller is likely to have market power begins with defining the relevant product and geographic markets.

The Relevant Product Markets

In wholesale electricity markets, a variety of products are offered based on product durations. A buyer can buy a yearly product more than a year in advance for power delivery every hour and every day for a one year timeframe. Similarly, a buyer can buy quarterly, monthly, weekly, day-ahead, hour-ahead, and "real-time" energy products for power delivery, as illustrated in Figure 6-1. Day-ahead, hour-ahead, and real-time energy products are considered spot products while yearly, quarterly, and monthly products are forward products.

Forward products are often used in hedging, that is, as a means of ensuring that transactions for commodities, in this case electricity, delivered in the future occur at a known price so that both consumers and producers are protected against the risk of spot price volatility.[4] For most forward products the amount sold and delivered is fixed in advance for all hours as specified in the contract.

Figure 6-1

Illustrative Timeline of Product Markets

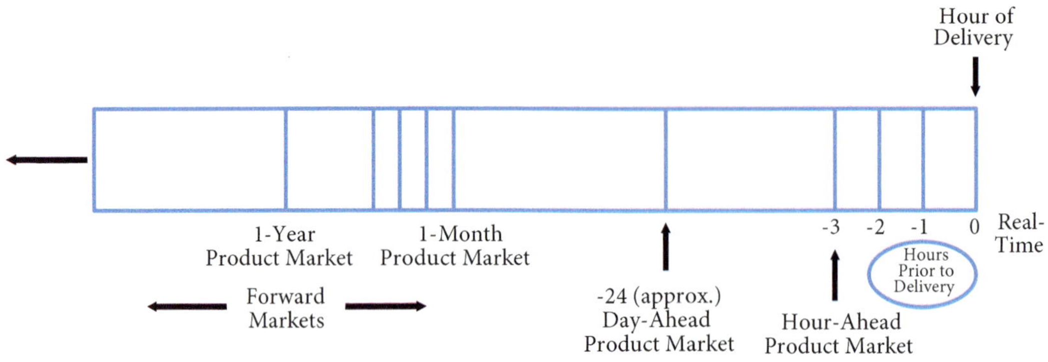

Without controversy, all forward power products with delivery duration of one month or longer are considered different than spot power products. As explained in Chapter 3, the degree of substitutability of the forward products for spot power is limited by the time sequence of each market, regulatory rules, and product specifications. For example, on January 28, 2014

4. Firms use forward markets to reduce the uncertainty of their costs (buyers) or revenues (sellers).

many parts of the U.S. experienced a cold snap caused by a polar vortex. Day-ahead electricity prices skyrocketed, reaching over $800 per MWh in several ISO/RTO markets. If a buyer had not already hedged spot power for delivery in January or for that week, the buyer would have no substitute for high-priced spot power purchases. None of the longer-term forward products would be available for fast enough delivery. Buyers or sellers therefore can rely on forward power products as close substitutes to spot power products only well in advance of the delivery hour. Due to this limit on substitutability, there is wide agreement that spot and longer-term power products belong in distinct markets.

Within the California spot markets—i.e., the combination of DA, HA, and RT markets—the product market boundaries were far less clear. Theoretically, in a workably competitive market these products are close enough substitutes that attempts to raise the price of one product are defeated by the availability of the other(s). Any price differentials across interchangeable products would be arbitraged away by buyers and sellers. However, this was not the case in the highly dysfunctional spot power markets in California and the Pacific Northwest. The price differentials between the different types of spot power during the crisis were extremely unusual.

We focused on price differentials between day-ahead and real-time products because they comprised the vast majority of spot purchases and sales during this period.[5] These are reflected in Figure 6-2 and Table 6-1. Figure 6-2 presents in graphic form the difference between that RT and DA prices for delivery in NP15 from January 1 to October 1, 2000. The figure shows that, prior to the beginning of the Crisis in May, RT and DA prices rarely diverged, but that this changed dramatically once the Crisis began. In many instances, crisis-period differentials exceeded $100 per MWh.

5. For example, during the CERS Period, CERS bought approximately 82 percent of its spot purchases in the day-ahead and real-time bilateral markets. Similarly, in Summer and Fall 2000 the HA market played a very small role.

Figure 6-2

NP15 RT-DA Price Differentials January 1 to October 1, 2000

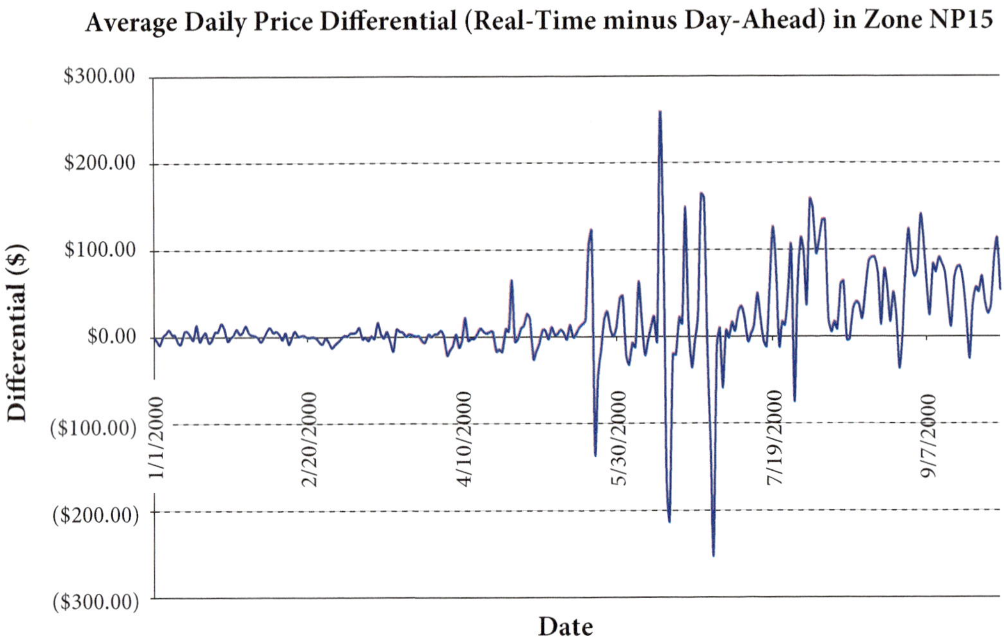

Table 6-1 compares day-ahead and real-time price differentials in NP15 and SP15 during the Pre-Crisis, Crisis-Pre-CERS, and CERS Periods. (The first two columns of the table identify the pricing periods.) The average price differentials between these two products in NP15 were $20.50 per MWh and $109.09 per MWh during the Crisis-Pre CERS and CERS Period, respectively. The magnitude of the price differentials in SP15 was smaller than that of NP15 in the same period but was clearly substantial in the CERS Period.[6]

6. We found that the degree of the product market separation in SP15 was quite strong for the May–October 2000 period. The average price differential between day-ahead and real-time products in SP15 was approximately $9.25 per MWh over the May–October period while that for NP-15 was approximately $33 per MWh.

Table 6-1

Day-Ahead and Real-Time Price Differentials California vs. Eastern ISO/RTO Markets

Region	Time Period	Price Metrics	Average RT - DA Differential ($/MWh)	Standard Deviation of Differential ($/MWh)
California Comparisons				
NP15, Pre-Crisis	4/1/98 - 4/30/00	NP15 CAISO BEEP Energy Price - NP15 PX DA Price	$0.77	$13.42
SP15, Pre-Crisis	4/1/98 - 4/30/00	SP15 CAISO BEEP Energy Price - SP15 PX DA Price	$0.10	$12.54
NP15, Crisis, Pre-CERS	5/1/00 - 12/31/00	NP15 CAISO BEEP Energy Price - NP15 PX DA Price	$20.50	$71.26
SP15, Crisis, Pre-CERS	5/1/00 - 12/31/00	SP15 CAISO BEEP Energy Price - SP15 PX DA Price	$3.33	$57.02
NP15, CERS Period	1/18/01 - 6/19/01	NP15 RT CERS Energy Price - NP15 CERS DA Price	$109.09	$112.88
SP15 CERS Perid	1/18/01 - 6/19/01	SP15 RT CERS Energy Price - SP15 CERS DA Price	$31.22	$78.66
Other Centralized U.S. Markets				
ISO-New England	3/1/2003 - 10/30/07	Internal Hub RT Price - Internal Hub DA Price	-$1.32	$10.74
New York ISO	1/1/2000 - 10/30/07	NYISO Reference RT Price - NYISO Reference DA Price	-$2.88	$13.99
PJM	6/1/2000 - 10/30/07	West Internal Hub RT Price - West Internal Hub DA Price	-$0.66	$9.42
Midwest ISO	4/1/2005 - 10/30/07	Cinergy Hub RT Price - Cinergy Hub DA Price	-$1.01	$9.59

Notes:
Daily prices calculated as average of 24 hourly prices.
Average and standard deviation of differential calculated across daily prices.
CAISO BEEP Energy Price is defined as RT prices in the CAISO imbalance energy market.

The Crisis-period differences are quite stark when compared with the similar price differentials in other ISOs/RTOs in the Eastern Interconnection, shown in the bottom section of Table 6-1. The day-ahead and real-time product markets of these Eastern ISOs/RTOs routinely converged; their average price differentials were relatively small, suggesting that each Eastern ISO/RTO's day-ahead and real-time products can be treated as the same relevant product market.

From the standpoint of product definition, the persistent California price differentials posed a conundrum. As in all other ISO/RTO spot markets, the California market's DA and RT products were *intended* to be very close substitutes. When the California markets were working well, as were all the other ISO/RTOs, this substitutability was evident. Yet during the Crisis something was *not* allowing the standard equilibration between California's two major spot energy markets.

In fact, during times of high market stress the differences between the DA and RT markets become more apparent and potentially more important from the product definition standpoint. For example, from May 2000 to January 2001 the DA energy market was a separate auction from the real-time energy market or the CAISO Imbalance Energy market. As explained in Chapter 4, the Power Exchange or PX had its own rules for bids and offers, its own FERC tariff, its own maximum price (which remained unchanged during the Crisis), and many buyers and sellers. Starting in January 2001, the DA energy market became purely bilateral, with the majority of California's buying done by CERS, a single public counterparty, on behalf of the

IOUs and the CAISO.[7] In both cases, the set of sellers included many power marketers (pure traders with no generation owned) as well as generator owners.

Meanwhile, the RT market operated according to the CAISO's lengthy tariff. Throughout the Crisis, the sole buyer was the CAISO, but the rules under which the CAISO purchased varied dramatically across various periods within the Crisis. The maximum allowed price was lowered twice during Summer 2000;[8] the algorithm for setting the clearing price was changed substantially in Fall, 2000; a "soft-cap" was adopted setting maximum prices starting in December 2000; and various other market rule changes were ordered by the FERC throughout the Crisis period. Moreover, this market allowed only sellers who physically controlled generators and importers to sell in its auction.

Finally, it was obvious that the time sequencing of the markets and differences in the demand characteristics suggested that the mechanics of market power exercise would have to be different in the two markets. If, for example, a seller sought to exercise market power in the DA market, that seller would face a buyer's downward sloping demand curve derived from the aggregate bids to purchase from all buyers.[9] The seller's calculus for whether to withhold and seek to raise prices profitability therefore follows the usual form, comparing the gains from higher prices (if any) to the losses from failing to sell the withheld power.[10]

In the RT market, the demand for electric power was dictated by the immediate needs of the CAISO to serve load and assure reliability. The quantity demanded was not price-sensitive; to the contrary, it was essentially a vertical demand curve. As explained in Chapter 3, price-inelastic (vertical) demand curves are highly vulnerable to the exercise of market power, and in some cases withholding is not necessary—only the threat of withholding is sufficient to raise price. Moreover, once the RT market has been reached it is too late to go back and buy DA power—it is no longer a usable substitute for power needed within the next forty-five minutes.

As a result of all of these factors, we sometimes chose to treat DA and RT spot power as separate products. While it is clear that there was an extremely high level of substitution and interdependence between these two products, the nature of the interaction was clearly something far less than unfettered arbitrage. Were we to have combined the two products into one market, we would have overlooked the reality that prices were not converging (for whatever combination of reasons) as well as many differences in detailed product attributes that may have been key to understanding what was happening. Indeed, our primary theory of market power (explained further below) was that it was exercised sequentially in the DA and RT markets;

7. The PX market ceased to function in mid-January 2001 and closed at the end of the month.

8. *See* Chapters 4 and 7 for more detail.

9. Buyer demand bids also reflected the fact that they could wait until RT and purchase from the BEEP at capped prices.

10. This calculation would cover its overall gain in both the day-ahead and real-time market. See a numerical example in the two-stage withholding example section of this chapter.

under this theory, combining the products obscures the mechanism we saw as the best explanation of seller behavior. However, it is also the case that some analyses, such as Borenstein, Bushnell, and Wolak (2000), Joskow and Kahn (2001), and Hildebrandt (2001) collapsed the DA and RT products into a single spot product.

When used as a distinct product, RT energy covered all energy offered into the CAISO BEEP Stack—formally, the Imbalance Energy market—including accepted and unaccepted bids of suppliers inside and outside California, as well as real-time out-of-market (OOM) energy that was purchased either by CAISO or CERS bilaterally at the last minute. Although imbalance and OOM energy were procured in two very different ways—the former in an hourly auction and the latter in a bilateral market—they both provided the resources required by the CAISO to keep the grid operating reliably. From the seller's perspective, these sales represented the last chance (in time) to sell power, for any given hour, and sellers that lacked hydro storage had to choose whether to bid into the BEEP Stack or sell bilaterally to CERS (during the CERS period) if they desired to place uncommitted generation.

Another consideration when defining a relevant product was whether the product market varied by season or time of day. For instance, during fall and spring, thermal and nuclear power plants may be taken off-line for maintenance or refueling. Pumped storage hydro power plants are usually available only during high load hours. Load also varies by hour and season. Therefore, defining the relevant product market too broadly, such as only capturing an average hour, may miss the critical periods during which pivotal firms can exercise market power. For our analyses presented in these case studies, we applied our market power tests on an hourly basis, although in some circumstances the available data only allowed us to perform the test on a daily basis. In other words, in our most refined tests we treated every hour of the Crisis as a separate product market.

The decision to separate the product markets into RT and DA energy was not without controversy. In at least one proceeding, FERC Staff disagreed with this definition as "too narrow."[11] However, specific disputes about product market definition were overshadowed by larger disagreements over the various types of analysis we used to diagnose market power. In some cases these analyses examined only the RT or DA market; in others the two were combined, but the disagreements over these analyses were seldom framed as merely a question of product market boundaries.

11. *Testimony of David Savitski, Docket No. EL01-10-085*, February 5, 2013. Dr. Savitski went beyond combining DA and RT energy to define the product market to include multi-day, balance-of-month, and longer forward products. (pp. 36-37).

Relevant Geographic Markets

As explained in Chapter 3, in the electric power industry a single BAA[12] or the footprint of an ISO/RTO is the logical starting point for a geographic market, but is not automatically correct. Within one BAA or RTO, constraints in the transmission system may limit power flow from one area to another within the BAA, making the geographic market smaller.

In fact, this was the case in the California market. In the CAISO, a major internal transmission link known as Path 15 connects the SP15 and NP15.[13] When congested, this path splits the two zones. Whenever Path 15 was limited, regardless of the direction of the constraint, the markets in the north and south separated—i.e., became distinct geographic markets—because suppliers in one of the two regions were prevented from selling to meet load in the other.

For the purpose of defining relevant geographic markets for our market power analyses, we examined the CAISO congestion patterns in Summer 2000[14] and the CERS Period by observing price differentials between NP15 and SP15. Figure 6-3, which shows Summer CAISO hourly real-time price differentials between NP15 and SP15 zones, suggests that Path 15 was sporadically congested from May through most of July and heavily congested in the south to north (S-N) direction starting at the end of July 2000. The price differential appears to be very persistent, particularly later in the period, with the price spread often approaching or exceeding $200 per MWh.

12. *See* Chapter 4 for definition.

13. Congestion on Path 26 also played a role, generally throwing the third zone, ZP26, in with one of the other zones, depending upon the circumstances.

14. For our purposes, Summer 2000 refers to the period between May 1, 2000 and October 2, 2000.

Figure 6- 3

CAISO RT Price Differentials between NP15 and SP15
May 1, 2000 to October 2, 2000

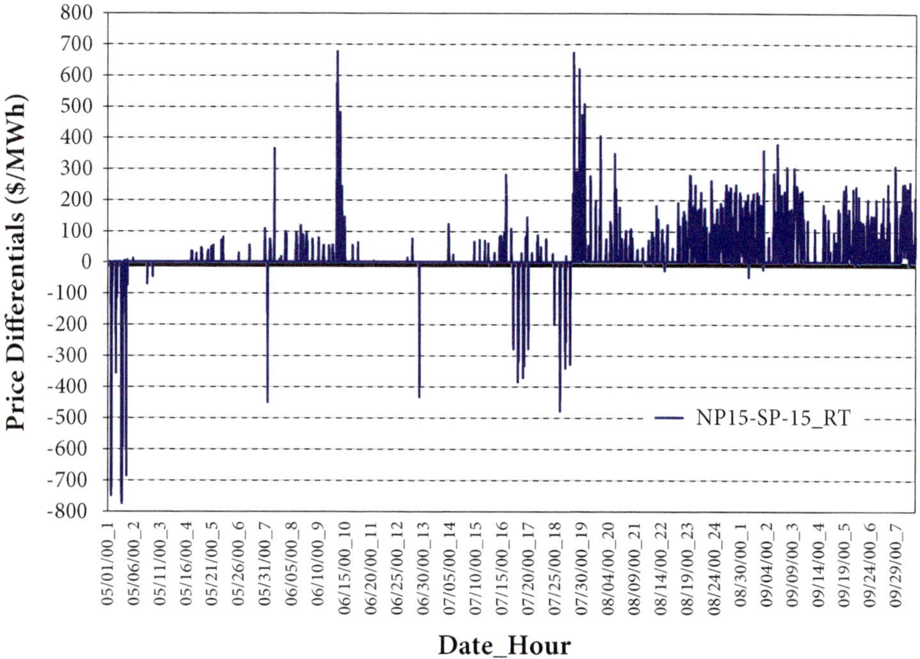

For the CERS Period, we found that Path 15 was congested 45 percent of the days during this period. As shown in Table 6-2, market separation occurred frequently in January and February when Path 15 was congested in the south-to-north direction for both day-ahead and real-time markets. Real-time congestion during this period was also extremely frequent, especially during peak hours.

Table 6-2

Frequency of Path 15 Congestion in DA Scheduling and RT Product Markets (CERS Period)

Month	Number of Hours	DA S-N Congestion on Path 15		RT Congestion	
		Hours	% of Total	Hours	% of Total
January	336	118	35%	308	92%
February	672	303	45%	447	67%
March	744	40	5%	123	17%
April	719	36	5%	284	39%
May	744	2	0%	78	10%
June	456	4	1%	33	7%
CERS Period	**3,671**	**503**	**14%**	**1,273**	**35%**

Our market power tests incorporated these geographic market dynamics. During uncongested periods, when the overall CAISO market area was intact, we applied market power tests to the CAISO as a single market. During periods when Path 15 congestion split the CAISO, we tested separately for the NP15 and SP15 zones.

Whether we divided the CAISO or did not, all our geographic markets included—on an hour-by-hour basis—transmission import capacity available to the spot market (i.e., that was not reserved for long-term transactions).[15] To distinguish the actual geographic markets we were defining from the names of the two ISO zones (NP15, SP15), we use the term Market Area to refer to the former. The NP15 ("Northern") Market Area included the CAISO north of Path 15 and the Pacific Northwest portion of the WECC, while the SP15 ("Southern") Market Area covered the CAISO south of Path 15 and the southwestern part of the WECC. Potential supply from WECC was always limited to the available transmission transfer capability into the relevant portion of the CAISO.

In summary, we defined hourly markets for power throughout the Crisis period. DA and RT products were treated separately, recognizing that they remained partial substitutes within a complex set of shifting regulatory rules and market conditions. Depending on congestion

15. The availability of transmission import capacity was another factor that prompted us to define RT and DA as different product markets. In the DA markets, individual sellers had to reserve and buy their own transmission capacity to deliver their power and were therefore limited to what was unreserved as of the day before delivery. In the RT market, the CAISO itself was the buyer and was able to use any transmission capacity it observed was not utilized, regardless of whether it had been previously reserved. Thus, RT transmission could be effectively larger than the capacity available to the DA market.

patterns and transmission availability, each product in each hour also had geographic markets that were either the entire CAISO or the Northern and Southern Market Areas. While our product market definitions provoked a little disagreement, our geographic definition was widely accepted. Most of all, this was only the start of the real debate.

Structural Test Case Studies

FERC's Hub-and-Spoke Test

The core of the market power test used by the FERC as of 2000 was a simple, mechanically prescribed calculation of annual peak hour market share, i.e., the percentage of all relevant product in the market owned or controlled by the seller seeking market-based authority. Although the FERC claimed that it did not use a "bright line" numerical threshold, sellers with a share below 20 percent were deemed to lack generation market power and allowed to negotiate prices freely under all market conditions.

Prior to 2000, the FERC had laid out an evolving set of detailed instructions in various Orders as to how to define product and geographic markets for use in hub-and-spoke tests. The two relevant products the FERC defined were *installed capacity* and *uncommitted capacity*. Installed capacity was simply the total rated number of megawatts of capacity owned or controlled by sellers, i.e., the rated capacity of their generators. Uncommitted capacity was defined as a seller's installed capacity less the amount of that capacity sold to others on a long-term basis or dedicated to native load service. For each of these defined products, the sellers' percentage share was calculated based on conditions during the single highest-demand hour of the prior calendar year (the peak hour).

For the purposes of this calculation, the FERC defined the relevant geographic markets as the BAA in which the seller's owned and controlled generation was located and all first-tier (immediately adjacent) BAAs that were directly interconnected to it. The total supply in each relevant market was then estimated by simply summing up all of the available capacity (for the uncommitted capacity measure defined in a manner we described above) of every generating plant owner.

The remarkable feature of these rules for computing hub-and-spoke market shares was that the total market included all of the capacity in adjacent electrically connected BAAs regardless of how much transmission capacity was available between the adjacent BAAs and the BAA in which the MBR applicant was located. Typically, the transmission capacity between BAAs is only five to ten percent of the total generation capacity within each BAA. Moreover, much of this capacity is typically reserved for long-term transactions and is therefore not available for spot market transactions, the product of interest. There was no consideration of transmission costs between the two BAAs. Thus, the FERC's rules for drawing geographic market boundaries included vastly more capacity than was realistically available to buyers. The FERC allowed anyone objecting to this approach to argue for a smaller geographic market, but in practice few, if any, opposed deregulated (market-based) rates when they were granted.[16]

While seriously over-inclusive, the Hub-and-Spoke (H&S) test was also under-inclusive, particularly as applied to power markets in the West. North/South transmission links among western BAAs were developed over time to take advantage of significant load diversity between northern and southern regions. Canadian generators could supply summer peaking utilities in Southern California or Arizona who, in turn, could help meet winter peaking needs in Washington State and British Columbia. Because the H&S test considered only generation in adjacent BAAs, it effectively ignored the fact that distant suppliers were significant players in the California markets during the Crisis, particularly in RT.

Beyond the fact that the test did not consider whether alternative suppliers could physically or economically reach a relevant market, it ignored the time dimensions of the electricity system. The test examined one snapshot of market share taken during the single hour of annual peak demand, rather than taking many readings performed during different spot market periods and conditions.

Spot market conditions can vary greatly during the day, month, and season due to fluctuations in the demand for, and available supply of, wholesale power. For this reason, any appropriate testing for market power should examine multiple snapshots covering a variety of system conditions. Yet at that time, the FERC tested for market power only for the single hour of peak demand in each year. Today, the FERC's tests examine peak hours in all four seasons, with an option to examine ten or more different system conditions using a more sophisticated market power model. Further, currently in all organized markets and at the FERC, much more market monitoring occurs, as summarized below. In some markets, market monitors now perform market power tests on every seller in *every hour*.[17]

Finally, the test entirely ignored the prices at which alternative suppliers could offer energy by calculating their market shares without considering their marginal costs. This is the opposite of the FERC's market power test for approving M&A transactions, known as the delivered

16. Once they were granted, the process of revoking the authority to sell at market-based rates was a full-blown administrative proceeding. In the wake of the California crisis, only one seller's market-based authority was revoked after a lengthy proceeding, that of Enron.

17. Both PJM and CAISO use a three-pivotal supplier test to assess the degree to which the supply from three suppliers is required to relieve a transmission constraint. The test is applied on an hourly or even five-minute basis in PJM while the CAISO utilizes the test on an annual or seasonal basis. If they fail this *ex-ante* test, their offers would be mitigated.

price test (DPT).[18] The DPT analysis, which has been used by the FERC since 1996, is careful to exclude potential competitors whose marginal costs plus transmission costs exceed the market prices in markets being examined by more than 5 percent. The FERC's failure in the Hub-and-Spoke test to properly exclude high-priced supplies from its market share calculation means that it systematically overstated the size of the overall market and thus often understated the market shares it used to measure the potential market power of MBR applicants.

The practical result of this test procedure was to render it nearly impossible for suppliers to fail, other than incumbent franchised utilities in their own service territories (and even most of these passed the test). Essentially every owner of generation in California and the rest of Western U.S. passed, and all were granted "market-based rate authority." This included the five generation companies who had purchased most of the generators formerly owned by PG&E and SCE.

Pivotal Supplier Tests

The deficiencies in the Hub and Spoke test made it wholly unusable to measure market power in the California markets in any meaningful way. As a vastly superior structural test, we turned to the pivotal supplier test, also referred to as the pivotal supplier index or PSI.

The unilateral pivotal supplier test compares the amount of capacity controlled by a particular supplier, Supplier *i*, to the difference between total supply (including imports and Supplier *i*) and hourly real-time demand in the market. The difference between total supply and hourly real-time demand is referred to as the "supply margin."

The construction of the PSI test as an indication of a single firm's potential gain from exercising market power can be written as:

$$PSI_{ih} = \frac{\sum\limits_{i \neq j} Supply_i}{\left(\sum\limits_{j=1}^{n} Supply_j - Load_h\right)}$$

If the PSI ratio is greater than 1, the supplier is pivotal. It is noteworthy that in electric markets a seller's incentive to exercise market power can occur prior to its becoming pivotal, that is, when the PSI is below 1. We explain this point further below.

If a supplier is unilaterally pivotal, the supplier is capable of "naming its price" because by definition, its supply is essential to meet market demand. Without it, electric system operators must "shed load"—stop serving some or all customers in their area via rotating or non-rotating

18. *See* Appendix A of *Merger Policy Statement* (Order 592).

blackouts. This is also true when two or more suppliers jointly became pivotal, that is, (a) when combined, their resources are required to meet load; and (b) the sellers act in awareness of this fact.[19]

The PSI calculation we presented in the California Crisis proceedings was a somewhat complex exercise. First, unlike the current FERC *ex-ante* market power test used in approving sellers' market-based rate authority, this PSI test was an *ex-post* analysis. The data were retrospective and based on actual sales and offer data such as suppliers' submitted and accepted bids in the CAISO RT market. Second, the "normal" supply sources, the RT market offers and the ISO's OOM purchases, did not reflect some supplies or loads that came from various market manipulation strategies in the PX and CAISO markets. To accurately capture each hour's market size and the offerings of the supplier(s) being examined, the real-time demand and the BEEP data needed to be adjusted, as explained further in Appendix 6A. These sources of RT energy were the relevant product.[20]

We found that during the Western Crisis period one or more sellers failed the unilateral PSI test during hours in 41 of the 154 days in the Summer period. We found both unilateral and jointly pivotal suppliers in the CAISO real-time market, as shown in Table 6-3.[21] This was the largest set of PSI test failures we had ever seen in any power market anywhere, and remains so to this day.

Table 6-3

Pivotal Supplier Results
Real-Time Market—May 1, 2000 to October 1, 2000

	Number of Pivotal Days		
	Days in Sample	Unilateral Failures	Joint Failures
	[1]	[2]	[3]
CAISO	153	23	46
NP15	122	22	52
SP15	122	5	13
Non-Overlapping Total	**154**	**41**	**76**

Sources and Notes: See Workpapers_Pivotality_Summer00_2010.xls

[3]: Note that sellers who offered only price-taker bids in any hour are conservatively not counted as jointly pivotal even when they and another seller jointly fail the joint pivotal supplier test.

19. As discussed in Chapter 3, the repeat nature of electric power markets allows suppliers to learn and become aware of the positions of other suppliers.

20. For the CERS Period, the scope of the real-time product extended to cover OOM purchases procured by CERS.

21. To avoid double counting, our results reported in Table 6-3 do *not* report jointly pivotal supplier-hours where one of the jointly pivotal suppliers is also unilaterally pivotal.

Figure 6-4

Plot of Unilateral PSI on RT OOM Weighted Average Prices over Peak Hours

CAISO CERS Period

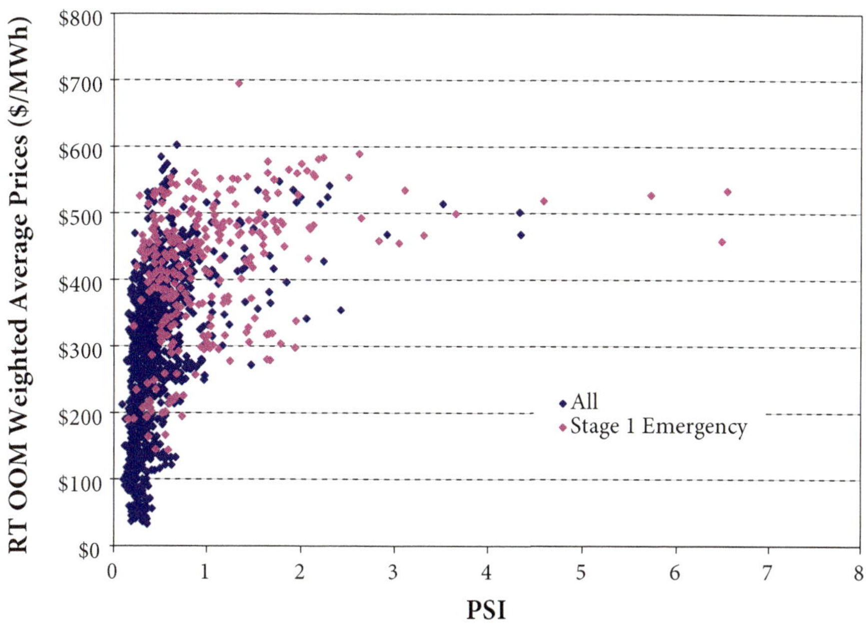

One additional finding was that the PSI is not a bright-line, one-zero test. Figure 6-4 shows that the relationship between test results and market prices is stronger and more visible when plotting PSI values on a continuous basis. Under emergency conditions, suppliers with PSI below but close to one may find that they have power to set prices even though their supply is technically not *required*. Dr. Robert J. Reynolds, a witness for the California Parties, demonstrated this same relationship econometrically during the CERS period.[22]

The CAISO Market Surveillance Unit (MSU) also did not use a binary PSI test to form its own non-binding opinion as to whether a supplier had market power or a market was non-competitive. Instead, the MSU converted the PSI test into a mirror-image index called the Residual Supplier Index (RSI). An RSI below one is arithmetically identical to a seller being pivotal, while the seller will be pivotal under the PSI if its PSI value is greater than one. Based on its experience, the MSU suggested different levels of RSI for different degrees of market

22. In performing his econometrics, Dr. Reynolds ran a regression of prices paid by CERS on the RSI values. *See Rebuttal Testimony of Robert Reynolds, Docket No. EL02-71*, Exhibit No. CLP-128, Appendix-C, December 2009.

power, as shown in Figure 6-5.[23] For instance, when the RSI falls below 110 percent or 1.1, they believed a firm attained "high" market power.

Figure 6-5

CAISO Residual Supply Index and Market Power

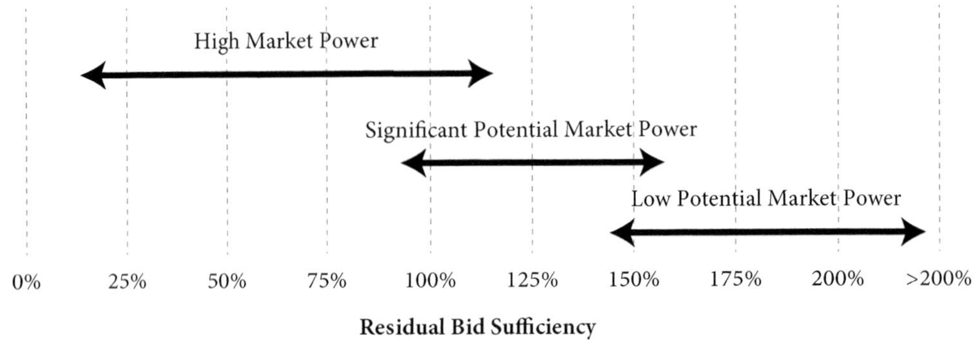

The MSU proposed to FERC a rule of thumb that designated markets as non-competitive in instances where the RSI was less than or equal to a level of 110 percent in more than five percent of the relevant hours in a given year.[24] When we applied this rule to our analysis by converting our PSI results into RSI values, we found that during the Summer 2000, RSI levels fell below 1.10 in close to seven percent of all hours, exceeding the MSU's threshold for failing to be workably competitive, as shown in the left panel of Figure 6-6. During the CERS period, RSI was below 1.10 in about 31 percent of period hours, indicating significant structural deficiencies, as shown in the right panel of Figure 6-6.

23. Annual Report on Market Issues and Performance, CAISO Market Surveillance Unit, Section 7.2 Pivotal Supplier Analysis, June 1999, p. 7-4.

24. *See http://www.caiso.com/docs/2002/12/05/2002120508555221628.pdf.*

Figure 6-6

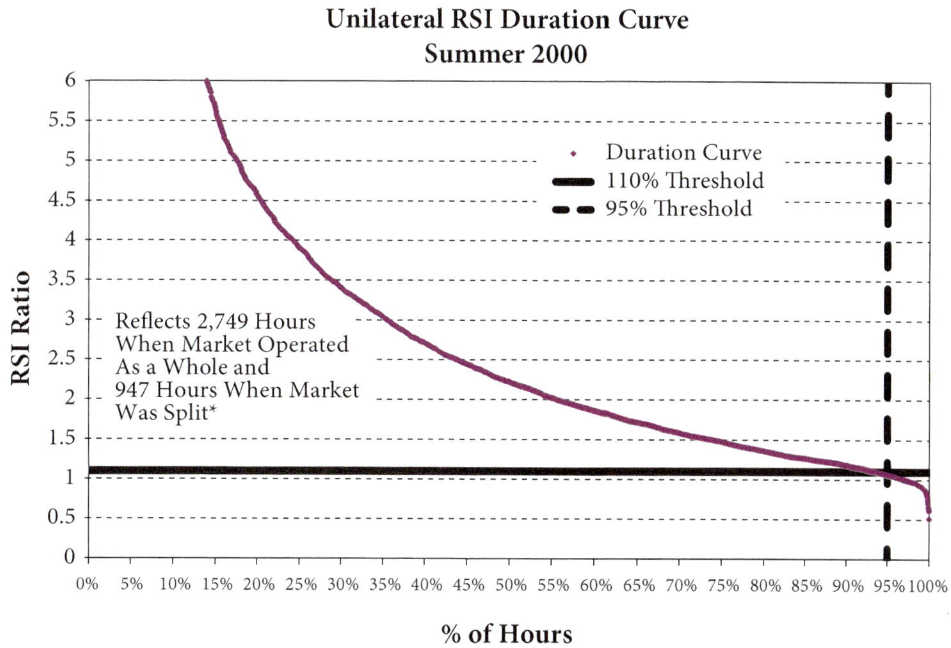

*When market was split, the minimum of the RSIs in the North and South was selected for inclusion in the duration curve.
Source: *Summer00_Pivotality_Details_2010.xls*

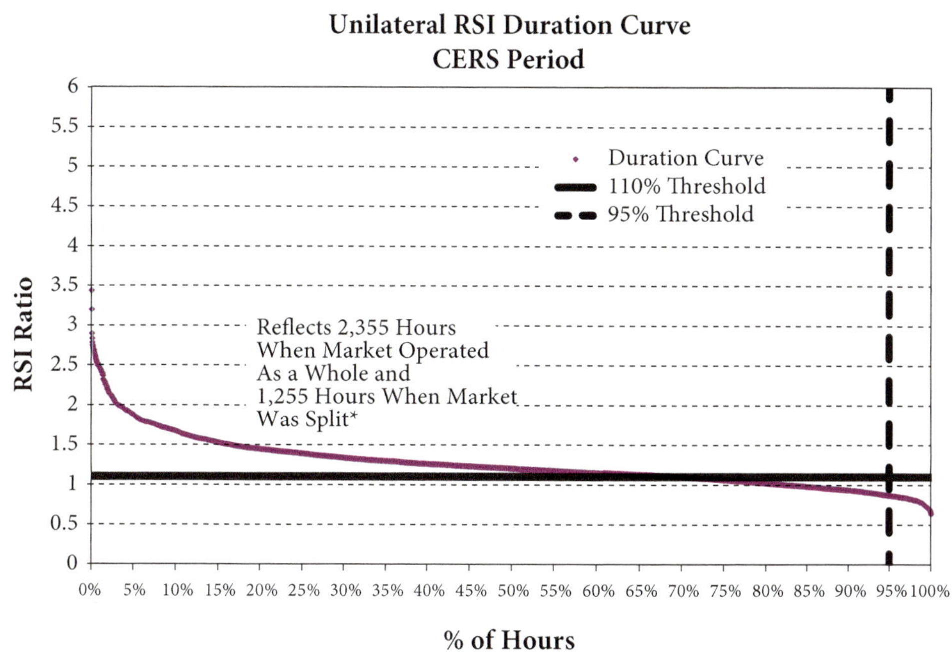

*When market was split, the minimum of the RSIs in the North and South was selected for inclusion in the duration curve.
Source: *CERS_Pivotality_Details_022010.xls*

Other Views of PSI Tests

Sellers' primary experts, Professor William Hogan and Dr. Scott Harvey (H&H), objected strongly to the validity of our PSI tests. Their most important objection was that these tests—even if correct—simply indicated that a seller's supply was necessary to supply the market. This fact alone, they argued, did not establish that any seller actually withheld supply or exercised market power—only that such a seller *could*, in theory, do so profitably. Thus, they argued that PSI tests alone proved nothing actionable, and that proof of actual withholding behavior was necessary. They further noted that power marketers merely bought and resold power every hour, and therefore had insufficient control over generation to effectuate withholding.[25]

Our reply to these criticisms had several dimensions. First, we agreed that proof of actual withholding was important, and we and our colleagues presented several major analyses of seller conduct during the Crisis described later in this chapter. However, we also noted that where the demand curve is vertical, the mechanism for exercising market power is not necessarily outright withholding. Instead, a pivotal seller simply "names its price" and the ISO must pay it. Indeed, this was precisely the reason we examined whether sellers were pivotal in the RT market; being pivotal would enable them either to raise bids in the BEEP that would have to be accepted or to bargain successfully for higher prices in OOM transactions with no other competition and no need to lose profit by withholding any otherwise-saleable units.

Beyond these conceptual replies, our motivation for presenting PSI results was to show the Commission that the potential or ability for sellers to exercise market power in the California markets exceeded the amount that the Commission allowed sellers to possess based on its own pre-approved tests. By November 2001, the Commission was using a form of the PSI test to pre-approve the ability of new generators to sell at market-based rates.[26] In one such test, the Commission found that an affiliate of American Electric Power failed what was essentially a pivotal supplier test for the single peak hour of the test year. The Commission concluded that this test failure alone warranted further analysis or mitigation of the AEP affiliate's potential market power.[27] We attempted to convince the Commission that its PSI test was not only useful as an *ex-ante* tool, but also as a de-facto measure that demonstrated that various sellers during the Crisis had market power sufficient to elevate prices.

---

25. They also raised questions regarding computational methods. These arguments were made in many filings; one good summary is the *Affidavit of Scott M. Harvey and William W. Hogan on Behalf of the Competitive Suppliers Group, Docket No. EL00-95-000*, August 4, 2009, p. 11. Also see H&H, (2005); H&H (2002); H&H (2001a); H&H, (2001b); H&H,(2000); *see also California Power Exchange Corporation Market Compliance Unit, Price Movements in California Electricity Markets: Analysis of Price Activity*: May–June 2000 (September 29, 2000).

26. The Commission applied a new screen called the Supply Margin Assessment (SMA) to market-based rate applications and triennial reviews on an interim basis. *See AEP Power Mkt'g, Inc., Docket No. ER96-2495-015 et al., Entergy Services, Inc., Docket No. ER91-569, and Southern Company Energy Marketing, L.P., Docket No. ER97-4166-008.*

27. *See AEP Power Mkt'g, Inc.*, 97 FERC ¶ 61,219, 2001. In this Order, the Commission imposed mitigation measures on AEP after it was found that the company failed the new Supply Margin Assessment tests during the single hour of peak demand.

Despite our compelling findings, our use of PSI tests proved to be entirely unsuccessful in persuading the Commission to act. Throughout the California proceedings, the Commission ruled that, "for reasons of fairness and notice," the only market power standard it could apply to sellers was the one that was used to approve sellers' market-based rate authority in the first place, i.e., the hub-and-spoke test.[28] While as economists we found these PSI tests useful and persuasive—and the Commission soon adopted them throughout the U.S. for precisely the purpose we used them for—the Commission never used them as a basis for assessing seller market power during the Crisis.

Conduct-Based Tests and "Two-Stage" Withholding

Two-Stage Withholding Mechanism

In a power market that clears sequentially, such as the California PX and ISO markets, how would one expect market power to be exercised? In this type of market structure, sellers who meet the necessary qualifications are free to choose where to offer their supply and face no obligation to sell in either of the two markets. They would be expected to choose the combination of markets that offers them the greatest profit. In a competitive market, this behavior merely reflects sellers pursuing arbitrage opportunities by favoring the higher priced market, creating efficiency from an economic perspective.

The mechanism that we expected a seller possessing undue market power to employ in this market structure was to withdraw or even buy energy out of the DA market, and then offer the withdrawals at high prices—with a bit of real or threatened withholding—in the real-time market.[29] This approach is illustrated graphically in Figure 6-7, which shows a simplified DA market in Panel A and a RT market in Panel B. The DA market has a downward sloping demand, as the PX buyers (IOUs) submitted sloping demand schedules to the PX, while the

28. *See* 125 FERC ¶61,016, ¶ 30, pp.15-16, October 6, 2010, later affirmed in *135* FERC ¶61,113, May 4, 2011. If the Commission had other disagreements with our use of these tests, as did Professor Hogan and Dr. Harvey, it did not speak to them.

29. In the California proceedings, we sometimes referred to sellers' decision to shift sales from the DA market to the RT market as "withholding" from the DA market. This elicited the strongest of objections from seller experts, who reminded the Commission that this was a completely nonstandard use of the term. These experts noted that the traditional use of the term refers to not selling a product at all, foregoing all profits on the sale of the withheld quantity. In contrast, this is an instance where (in a manner the sellers argued was procompetitive), sellers did not forego sales but merely sold them in the RT market rather than the DA market. They were not withheld, they were shifted. Our use of the term was meant to refer to the overall process, but for clarity here we use the terms *withdraw* and *shift* for sellers' actions in the DA market and reserve withholding for the traditionally-defined act of not selling at all.

RT market had a vertical demand because the CAISO had to purchase all imbalance power to meet its system needs in each hour regardless of price.

Figure 6-7

Withdrawing Power in DA Market and Exporting to RT Market

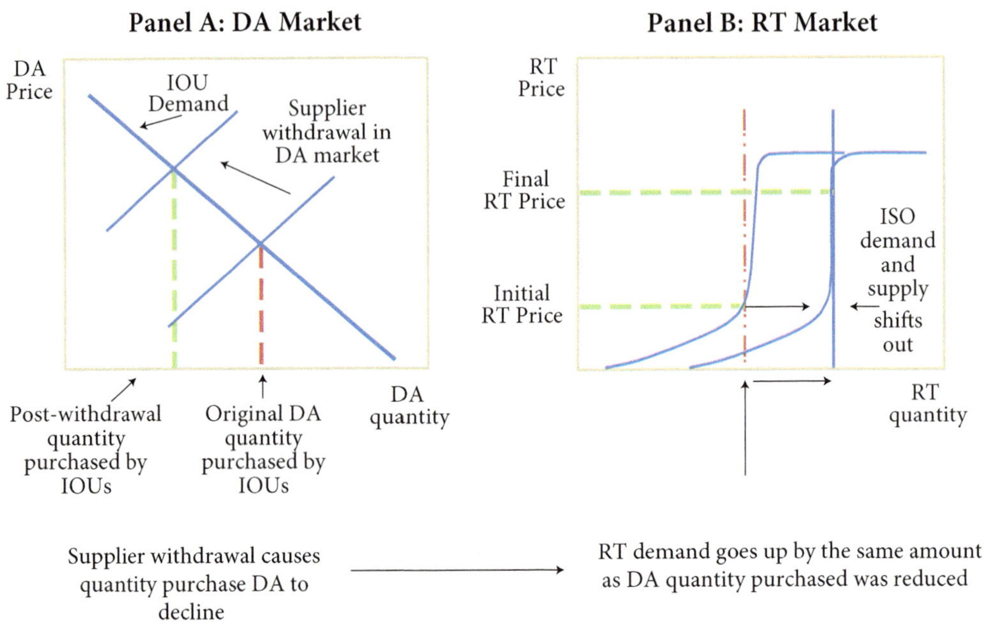

Note result: Both DA and RT prices were increased by DA withdrawal

Suppose for a moment that a seller suspects that it has a much better chance of exercising market power profitably in the RT market as RT demand increases. This is logical, because the larger the amount of RT demand, the higher the chance that any one seller's RT supply is essential. The seller decides to shift supplies that it could sell profitably in the DA market to offer more of its power in the RT market. The DA supply curve would shift to the left. As a result, the DA price would rise and the quantity cleared in the DA market would decrease from "Original DA Quantity purchased by IOUs" to "Post-Withdrawal Quantity purchased by IOUs."

This seller conduct has two implications for the RT market: 1) the demand for power would rise in the RT market; and 2) the seller would shift supply that it did not offer in the DA market to the RT market. The former would imply that the CAISO would need to procure more power in the RT market. The RT market price would also rise. As shown in Panel B, the price would increase from "Initial RT Price" to "Final RT Price." Note that the impact of this strategy, i.e., shifting supply from the DA market to the RT market, is to raise prices in both the DA and RT markets, although some of this RT price increase may be offset if the DA supply is bid into the RT market. However, if the RT market was structurally non-competitive, as our PSI tests indicated, once sellers shifted their supply into it they would now be selling a single-price market where any one seller's successful effort to raise the market-clearing price would benefit all sellers because the RT market was a single-price auction. We observed that as the market tightened, seller bids in RT were elevated, increasing the steepness of the supply curve. Thus, shifting supply into the RT market (normally a benign action) allowed sellers to "ride the coat tails" of *any sellers* in the RT market who had undue market power, as those sellers would set the market-clearing price paid to everyone.

If the DA energy market were workably competitive with additional supply available at or near market clearing prices, choosing not to sell in the DA energy market in order to wait for higher prices in the RT product market would not work because other suppliers would stand by ready to step in with little impact on the DA price. Buyers would have met most of their needs from other DA suppliers, and would consequently have sought little (only their balancing needs) in the RT market.[30] Thus a withdrawing seller would generally have gained little opportunity to profit in the RT market. However, if the RT market was ripe for market power exercise by *anyone,* it would remain higher-priced than the DA market over the long term, as in fact occurred.

This "two-stage" withholding mechanism is what theory predicts a seller with undue market power would do—either shift supplies out of the DA market and then seek to elevate prices in RT by withholding either physically or economically in the ISO RT market, or simply count on someone bigger and more pivotal to do it for you.[31] The majority of our market power tests centered on proving that this overall mechanism was in fact what occurred during the crisis. To do this, we proceeded in two major steps.

Dr. Gary Stern of Southern California Edison first analyzed the reduction of supply in the PX DA energy market during Summer 2000.[32] As noted above, the sole act of withdrawing power from the DA market in order to sell into the RT market, when the latter was persistently clearing at a higher price, is a normal act of arbitrage, not the exercise of market power. However, when the shifting of DA supply is so large as to help render the RT market structurally non-competitive, and in this expanded RT market withholding and threats to withhold occurred, the shifting of supply takes on a different character: it becomes part of an overall effort to create a RT market in which undue market power could be exercised.

This highlights the importance of the second step of our process, which was to show the prevalence of withholding by some sellers in the RT market. We did this via two types of withholding calculations, one examining the entire market, led by Dr. Robert J. Reynolds, and the

30. This, of course, is the way the DA and RT (balance) markets were intended to work.

31. In the CERS Period, pivotal sellers simply demanded higher prices from CERS in bilateral negotiations. CERS had no choice but to accept them.

32. *Prepared Direct Testimony of Dr. Gary Stern, Docket No. EL00-95 et al.,* Exh. Nos. CA-3 and CA-4, February 24, 2003. Also *see Prepared Rebuttal Testimony of Dr. Gary Stern, Docket No. EL00-95 et al.,* Exh. No. CAX-350, March 2012.

second examining specific sellers' economic withholding via the nature of their offers into the RT auction, led by Dr. Carolyn Berry.

Withdrawals from the Day-Ahead Market

There are several signs that sellers shifted their supplies out of the PX market during Summer 2000. The first sign is that the PX DA market faced increasingly tight supply conditions; there was insufficient supply offered in the market even though buyers offered higher prices. Dr. Stern compared the monthly PX DA aggregated supply curves between Summer 1999 and Summer 2000 and found that sellers offered substantially less power in 2000. The insufficient supply ranged from 2,000 MW to 8,000 MW, resulting in the IOUs' inability to procure sufficient power for their forecasted demand.[33]

To illustrate these insufficient supply conditions, Figure 6-8 compares the PX DA demand and supply curves in hour 17 on July 27, 2000 with that in the same hour on July 29, 1999. As seen in this figure, buyers were willing to buy more power at higher prices in this 2000 hour compared with that the same hour in 1999; the July 27, 2000 demand curve (solid blue line) lies above the July 29, 1999 demand curve (dashed blue line). At the same time, sellers were willing to sell less. The supply curve for the 2000 hour (solid red line) lies to the left of the July 29, 1999 (dashed red line). For instance, to procure 30,000 MW, the PX buyers had to pay approximately $425 per MWh in 2000 compared with $30 per MWh in 1999. To procure 34,000 MW of power in this 2000 hour, the buyers would have needed to pay $1,500 per MWh.

33. *Id.*

Figure 6-8

PX DA Aggregated Demand and Supply Curves

Hour 17 of July 27, 2000 and July 29, 2000

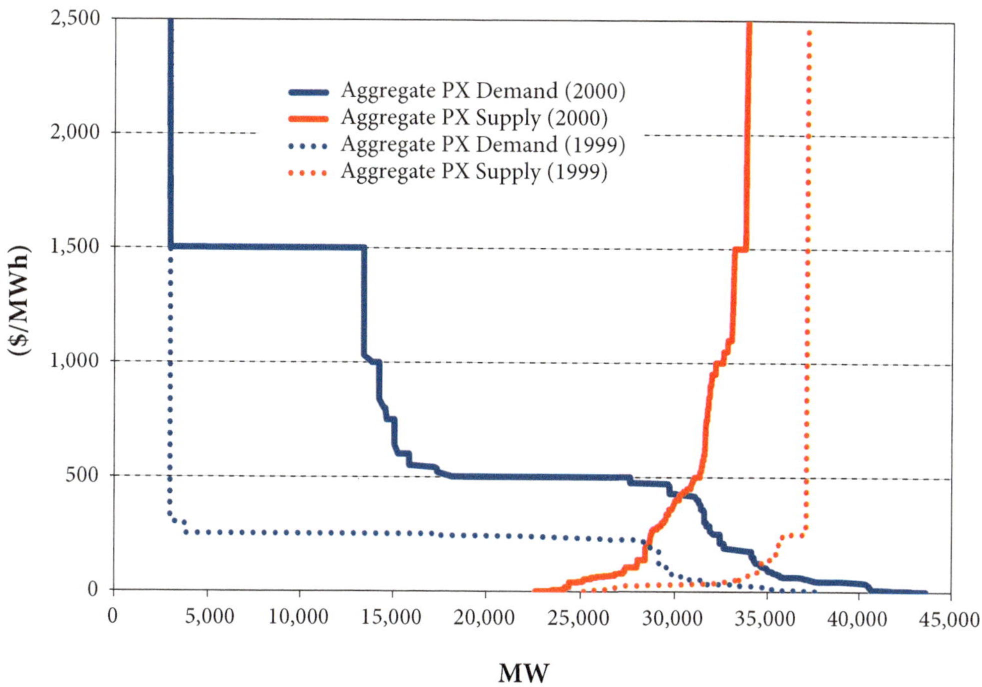

Supply insufficiency in the PX DA market during Summer 2000 was quite pervasive. In over 80 percent of on-peak hours during the period of May through October 2000, the total supply offered at any price was insufficient to cover the CAISO DA forecasted load. The average insufficient supply was approximately 4,116 MW per on-peak hour, quadruple the 1999 size. Dr. Stern performed an analysis showing that even if the IOUs had offered to pay $2,500 per MWh (the PX price cap) for all of their demand in the PX DA market, there would still have been insufficient supply in the DA PX market for a significant number of hours over the summer.[34] The bidding in this fashion would have raised the net buying cost of the IOUs by $6.7 billion for the period from May through September 2000.[35]

Another troubling sign of sellers shifting out of the DA market was an observed increase in the price elasticity of supply. The monthly averages of the price elasticity of supply in the PX

34. *See Prepared Rebuttal Testimony of Dr. Gary Stern*, Exh. No. CAX-350 at Section X.

35. *Id.*

DA market during Summer 2000 ranged from 0.06 to 0.15,[36] substantially lower than those of 1999 for the same period, which ranged from 0.15 to 0.23. This suggests the DA sellers demanded much higher prices to induce them to supply additional power in Summer 2000.

Sellers and the FERC Staff saw the situation differently. They accused the IOUs of engaging in "underscheduling" because the IOUs did not buy 100 percent of their forecasted demand in the PX day-ahead and hour-ahead market.[37] In fact, in the December 2000 Order, the FERC required market buyers to schedule 95 percent of their loads on a DA basis; otherwise they would pay penalties.[38] The California Parties refuted the allegation and pointed out that the amounts that the IOUs could buy out of the market were the outcomes of the PX auction process since the buyers demand in the PX market was a downward sloping demand curve.[39]

Real-Time Withholding

As noted above, proof of the two-stage exercise of market power in the California markets required that withholding, or the threat thereof, be demonstrated. The first such demonstration, led by Dr. Reynolds, was an examination of the behavior of the five largest in-state generation companies.[40] Together, these companies owned about 17,000 MW of thermal generating plants. Through discovery and public records, it was possible to construct an estimate of the marginal cost of each generating unit in each of the five sellers' portfolios on an hour-by-hour basis. It was then possible to compare the marginal cost of each unit to the hourly RT market-clearing price and also to determine the amount dispatched by the generating unit in that hour. If a generating unit sat idle during an hour in which its marginal cost was below the market-clearing price, Dr. Reynolds concluded that the seller was withholding in that hour.[41]

---

36. The price elasticity of supply was calculated as the percentage change in PX DA market prices around the market clearing price and quantity for each on-peak hour if the demand were to increase by 1,000 MW.

37. *See*, for example, *Prepared Testimony of Joseph P. Kalt* on Behalf of MPS Merchant Services, Inc. (f/k/a Aquila Power Corp.) and Illinova Energy Partners, Inc., Exh. No. MI-1 October 25, 2011, p. 26; *Testimony of Jeffrey Tranen on Behalf of Shell Energy North America* (U.S.) L.P., Exh. No. SNA-3, October 25, 2011 p. 21; *Prepared Direct and Answering Testimony of Commission Staff Witness James S. Ballard*, Exh. No. S-9, January 2012, pp. 15-16.

38. *Order Directing Remedies for Wholesale California Electric Markets*, 93 ¶ 61,294, December 2000, at p. 5 and pp. 42-45.

39. *Prepared Rebuttal Testimony of Dr. Gary A. Stern On behalf of the California Parties*, Exh. No. CAX-350, March 2012. The PX Tariff, in fact, required the IOUs to submit downward sloping demand bids. *See* PX FERC Electric Tariff No. 2 § 3.3, Third Revised Volume No. 1.

40. *Prepared Testimony of Robert J. Reynolds, Docket No. EL00-95-000*, Exh. No. CA-5, February 27, 2003. This analysis followed a series of earlier studies published by Professor Paul Joskow and Dr. Edward Kahn that estimated withholding by these generators (Joskow and Kahn, 2000, 2001, 2002, hereinafter "J&K"). J&K were not involved in the FERC proceedings on the Crisis and therefore were limited to using publicly-available data. Along with this limitation, J&K's original (2000) study was criticized strongly by H&H as having a variety of analytical shortcomings; J&K disagreed strongly in the subsequent (2001, 2002) papers. (For H&H's critique, *See Answering Testimony of William W. Hogan on behalf of the Competitive Supplier Group, Docket No. EL95-00-248*, October 2011, Exh. No. CSG-1 (hereinafter Hogan Testimony 2011).

41. In this context, note that undispatched generation following the close of the RT market indicates that the generator was not selling either into the DA or the RT market. In this sense, Dr. Reynolds amalgamated all forms of DA and RT energy into a single product market, nullifying criticisms that the product definition may have been too narrow.

More completely, Dr. Reynolds measured withholding (or "unbid producible capacity") as the hourly amount of each generating unit's capacity whose marginal cost was lower than the RT market price cap, less the maximum supply offered by that unit.[42] The maximum supply offered by the unit was the sum of its scheduled output (i.e., the amount it had contracted to sell to any buyer in any market prior to real time) plus the amount of ancillary services purchased by the ISO from that unit (which displaces the amount of energy the unit can bid to sell separately), plus all amounts bid into and/or sold to the CAISO as RT or OOM energy. Note this analysis, by design, does not distinguish between physical withholding, where a generator simply decided not to operate when it could, and economic withholding, in which a generator intentionally bids a price too high to be chosen. The objective was to find the aggregate level of the two forms of withholding without worrying about which of the two a generator chose to employ.

Dr. Reynolds elected to do this analysis only for the five large in-state thermal sellers for a variety of reasons. First, these generators all had large portfolios and thus large market shares, making them likely candidates for profitable withholding. Second, these generators did not have hydroelectric storage dams, which could have introduced questions as to whether to sell at RT in an hour or hold back the water to sell during a future hour (i.e., opportunity costs). For thermal generators, selling in the RT market is clearly the final opportunity to sell one's capacity, so there is no ordinary incentive other than market power to hold back capacity that could be profitably sold.[43]

For these sellers, Dr. Reynolds took a number of additional precautions.[44] First, he assumed all declared plant outages and reserve shutdowns by sellers were legitimate and not withholding;[45] second, he eliminated hours in which start-up costs may have prompted units to remain offline; third, he incorporated limits on how quickly units could change their output ("ramping limits"); fourth, he used conservative measures of the capacity of plants; fifth, he accounted for dispatch instructions from the ISO that may have caused units to turn off; and sixth, he used conservative estimates and conducted sensitivity studies for the cost of nitrogen oxide

42. When the RT price cap was replaced by a "soft cap" in March, 2001 there was no price limit imposed in the definition.

43. Dr. Reynolds specifically excluded combustion turbines from his sample because these units often had a maximum number of hours they were allowed to run under their air emissions permits. The resulting large thermal units he examined totaled 15,369 MW.

44. Many of these measures were adopted in deference to H&H's criticism of the Joskow-Kahn studies; others were addressed to later criticisms by H&H of Dr. Reynolds' calculation in Exhibit MIR-1, H&H's testimony in Docket No. EL00-95-000, March 3, 2003. Dr. Reynolds responded to these criticisms in detail in his rebuttal testimony, Exhibit CA-352 in the same docket, March 20, 2003.

45. A reserve shutdown, as defined by North American Reliability Corporation (NERC), occurs when a plant is "available for load but is not synchronized due to lack of demand." In other words, a unit is on reserve shutdown due to economic reasons, not due to physical causes such as an equipment failure. When the generators declared to the CAISO that their units were experiencing an outage, the CAISO could not dispatch that unit to meet electricity demand. On the other hand, if a unit is on a reserve shutdown, the CAISO can call the unit to generate power when it is needed.

emissions permits, which generators had to buy to cover their generation, and for the overall marginal costs of units.[46]

With this approach, Dr. Reynolds found that the "Big Five" in-state generators collectively withheld an average of more than 1,000 MW per hour during May–September 2000 on-peak hours. During this period, withholding exceeded 1,000 MW during nearly half (45%) of all peak hours and exceeded 2,000 MW 15% of the time. As shown in Figure 6-9, substantial withholding continued throughout the Crisis period, tapering down during the CERS period, when CERS was purchasing power bilaterally from these generators.[47]

Figure 6-9

Percentage of On-Peak Hours in which Withholding Exceeded 1,000MW Using Generator Reported Forced Outages

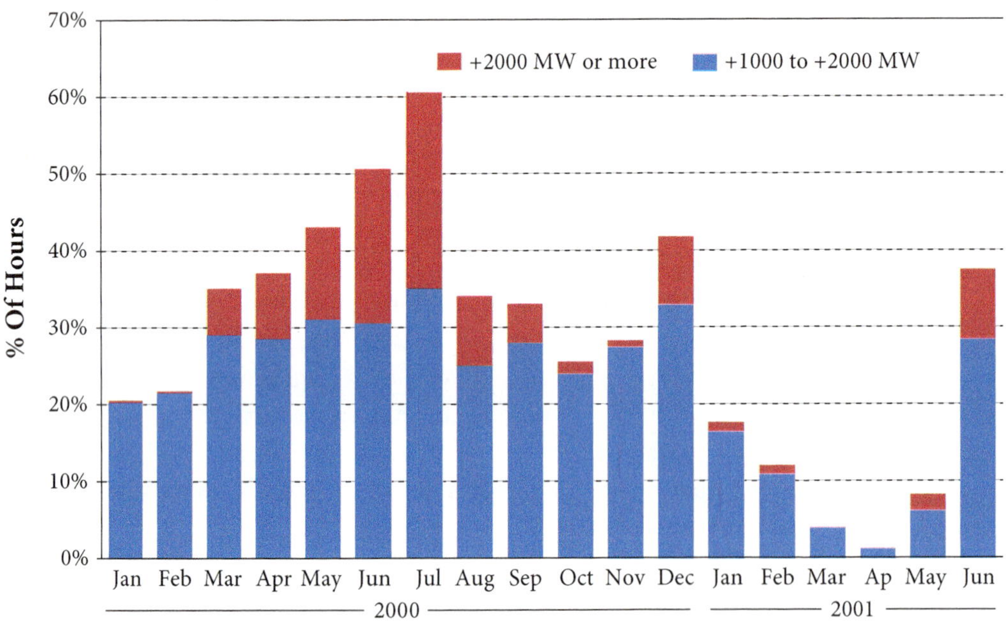

46. These treatments are discussed in Exh. Nos. CA-5 and CA-352 *op cit.*; additional criticisms and Dr. Reynolds' reply to them are summarized in Figure 1 of Exh. No. CA-352.

47. Physical withholding was examined briefly by our colleague Philip Hanser using outage data. In California, the CAISO requires generators to report their plant outages, either a forced, unforced, or reserve shutdown outage in the Scheduling and Logging for ISO of California (SLIC). Typically, a generating unit needs to schedule time out of service for maintenance or its annual checkup for major equipment such as a turbine; this is known as an unforced or planned outage. In contrast, a forced outage occurs unexpectedly due to equipment failures. A reserve shutdown, as defined by North American Reliability Corporation (NERC), occurs when a plant is "available for load but is not synchronized due to lack of demand." In other words, a unit is on reserve shutdown due to economic reasons, not due to physical causes such as an equipment failure. When the generators declared to the CAISO that their units were experiencing an outage, the CAISO could not dispatch that unit to meet electricity demand. On the other hand, if a unit is on a reserve shutdown, the CAISO can call the unit to generate power when it is needed. Mr. Hanser, for example, examined the SLIC data and found some inconsistency in their reports that reduced the CAISO capability to meet its real-time demands. *See Prepared Testimony Philip Hanser, Docket No. EL00-95 et al.*, Exh. Nos. CA-9 and CA-10, February 24, 2003. The Commission never ruled in favor of physical withholding claims, finding them too difficult to evaluate.

Withholding Via High (Anomalous) Bidding

The second approach used to diagnose anticompetitive behavior by sellers was to examine their bids into the PX and CAISO. As mentioned earlier, both organizations' tariffs prohibited "anomalous bidding," defined as "[bidding] behavior that departs significantly from normal behavior in competitive markets."[48] Of course, economists have described and modeled competitive bidding behavior in many market settings, including a handful of research papers centered on power markets.[49] In addition, during the Crisis, economists at the CAISO, who had access to all bidding data on a routine basis, analyzed seller bids and found anticompetitive behavior,[50] but these studies were never acted on by the Commission.[51] However, at one point during the Crisis the Commission did issue an Order giving some guidance, summarized by Dr. Berry as follows:

> The Commission found that "bids that vary with unit output in a way that is unrelated to the known performance characteristics of the unit" such as a 'hockey stick' bid where the last megawatts bid from a unit are bid at an excessively high price relative to the bid(s) on the other capacity from the unit" or a bid from a unit that is at an "excessively high level compared to the remainder of the portfolio, without any apparent performance or input cost basis" were anticompetitive. The Commission also found that bids that "vary over time in a manner that appears unrelated to change in the unit's performance or to changes in the supply environment that would induce additional risks or other adverse shifts in the cost basis" such as "a bid that appears to change only in response to increased demand or reduced reserve margins, particularly if the timing of the bid is related to public announcements of system conditions or to timing of outages in a participant's portfolio" were anticompetitive. [Citing - *San Diego Gas & Elec. Co.*, 95 FERC ¶ 61,115 (2001) ("April 26, 2001 Order") p. 19.]

Dr. Berry used this guidance to assess sellers' anomalous bidding behavior in a series of analyses that stretched across an eight year period.[52] In her first analysis, performed in 2003, she found:

---

48. *CAISO Market Monitoring & Information Protocol, California Independent System Operator Corporation*, FERC Electric Tariff, Original Volume No. III, Aug. 16, 2000 (*CAISO MMIP*) § 2.1.1.

49. For example, Green and Newbery (1992), Cardell *et al.*, (1997), Wolfram (1998) and (1999), Borenstein and Bushnell (1999), Joskow and Kahn (2001), H&H (2001), and Borenstein, Bushnell, Knittel, and Wolfram (2006).

50. Sheffrin (2001) and Hildebrandt (2001).

51. In June 2003 the Commission ordered its own investigation into anomalous bidding by sellers during the Crisis (Docket No. IN03-10-000). The Commission noted that its own Staff investigation of the Crisis concluded that there was no economic justification for bids higher than $250 per MWh, so the Commission directed that Staff examine all bids exceeding this level to determine whether they violated the tariff. The investigation was confidential, however, and was evidently closed without the Commission issuing any further guidance. This behavior by the Commission encouraged sellers to suggest in public that the Commission had, in effect, already concluded on its own that no sellers bid so as to violate the tariff.

52. *See Prepared Direct Testimony Dr. Carolyn A. Berry, Docket No. EL00-95 et al.*, Exhibits CA-7 and CA-8, February 28, 2003 (hereinafter Berry Testimony 2003); *Prepared Direct Testimony of Dr. Carolyn A. Berry, Docket No. EL00-95-248*, CAX-110, August 25, 2011 (hereinafter Berry Testimony 2011).

> . . . overwhelming evidence that in-state generators and importers submitted hockey stick bids, bid spikes (offering all supply at or near the prevailing price cap), bids that varied to exploit expected reserve shortages, bids that were strategically withdrawn, and bids that had no relation to underlying costs. [Exh. No. CAX-112 (providing a copy of the 2003 analysis of bidding in the ISO and PX markets during the Summer Period)].

Although there are many interesting aspects of all her studies, we focus on her 2011 analysis of Summer 2000 bids because it was her most advanced analysis. Her analysis was aimed at a handful of importers remaining in the case at the time. In addition, it is the only one that an ALJ and FERC have formally ruled upon.[53]

In this analysis, Dr. Berry created three classifications for anomalous bids explained in detail in Figure 6-10. "Type I" anomalous bids involved bidding various proportions of the total quantity offered at an "Extremely High Price," which Dr. Berry defined for each hour as $150 per MWh more than the marginal cost of the highest-cost unit dispatched by the ISO in that hour.[54] Dr. Berry noted that the $150 per MWh convention she selected was twice the marginal cost of the highest-cost unit throughout the Summer and seven times the lowest-cost Mitigated Market Clearing Price (MMCP).[55] In simple terms, Dr. Berry labeled bids that had any significant portion at an offer price well above the highest marginal cost estimated by the Commission as meeting the Commission's definition of anomalous.

As indicated in Figure 6-10, Type II anomalous bids were bids placed at prices that were submitted during the same hour that a seller committed one of two market manipulation strategies, False Load or False Export.[56] In contrast to the Type I convention, there was no requirement that the offer price exceed MMCP by $150. Dr. Berry explained that this convention was unnecessary due to the fact that the presence of a manipulation strategy that would profit from a RT price increase placed simultaneously with a bid above marginal cost demonstrated a clear intent to raise prices in the RT market, and that attempts to raise prices in the presence of manipulation violations should be considered anomalous under the tariff definition.

---

53. Philip C. Baten, Presiding Administrative Law Judge, *Initial Decision,* 142 FERC ¶ 63,011, February 2013. *See Opinion No. 536, Order Affirming Factual Findings, Directing Compliance Filing and Ordering Refunds*, 149 FERC ¶ 61,116, November 10, 2014.

54. The MMCP was the cost of the most expensive unit dispatched in the CAISO real-time market. Dr. Joseph Yan estimated the MMCP for Dr. Berry using a detailed methodology established by the Commission in its proceedings directed at calculating the refunds sellers were required to pay buyers in Docket No. EL00-95-000. *See Prepared Director Testimony Dr. Joseph H. Yan, Docket No. EL00-95-248*, Exh. No. CAX-141, August 25, 2011.

55. *See* Berry Testimony 2011, p. 27.

56. These strategies are described in detail in Chapter 7.

Figure 6-10

Dr. Berry's Definitions of Anomalous Bids

Type I

Hockey Stick: 10% or less of total quantity offered at Extremely High Price; the remainder is offered at lower prices

Walking Cane: More than 10% but less than 90% of the total quantity offered at Extremely High Price; the remainder is offered at lower prices.

All-In: More than 90% of total quantity offered at Extremely High Price.

Type II

False Export Anomalous Bids: Any seller bid (a) in which a portion of the bid exceeds that hour's highest market marginal cost; and (b) in that hour, the bidding seller committed a False Export tariff violation.

False Load Anomalous Bids: Any seller bid (a) in which a portion of the bid exceeds that hour's highest market marginal cost; and (b) in that hour, the bidding seller committed a False Load tariff violation.

Type III

Economic Withholding: Any bid submitted to the ISO RT auction in which (a) the offer price exceeded the ISO's market-clearing price; (b) the marginal cost of the seller was less than this price; and (c) the bid was not selected and dispatched by the ISO.[1]

Extremely High Price: An offer price $150 per MWh or more above the MMCP, an hourly price established by the FERC as a proxy for the highest marginal cost of any California market unit required to meet demand in that hour.

1. The ISO occasionally accepted bids above its auction-clearing price to relieve congestion or other system problems. These bids do not set the auction price.

For Type III violations, Dr. Berry used an extremely common definition of economic withholding, i.e., bidding prices above one's own marginal cost and thereby failing to sell at least some supply that would be incrementally profitable were it to have been offered and sold. Although this definition is uncontroversial, it requires an accurate, seller-specific marginal cost as a crucial input. Dr. Berry's analysis exclusively examined importers into California, including some who were purely power traders. In general, Dr. Berry used MMCP as a proxy for these sellers' marginal costs. But for a large hydro-based seller she employed estimates based upon opportunity costs.[57]

Dr. Berry's tests yielded substantial numbers of anomalous bids by her definitions, as shown in Table 6-4. During the summer period with a total of approximately 3,600 hours, over 29,000 Type I bids were identified.[58] Type II False Export and False Load bids occurred in approximately 1,300 and 3,500 hours, respectively, counting each supplier-hour combination separately. Counted similarly, Type III violations occurred in over 9,000 supplier-hours.

Table 6-4

Anomalous Bids Identified by Dr. Berry in 2011 Study

	No. Anomalous Bids	MWh Bid
Type I (Energy and Ancillary Services)	29,214	5,056,372
Type II (False Export/False Load)*	4,749*	4,117,617
Type III*	9,445*	2,515,820

Source: Tables 1-2, 5-6, and 8 of Exh. No. CAX-110 (REVISED).
* Number of hours with anomalous bids. The total hours were not unique hours as they were summed across suppliers being examined.

One additional step in this analysis was an examination of whether each of these anomalous bids had an impact on the auction's actual market-clearing price during each hour. This was made necessary by the Commission's ruling that buyers would receive compensation for tariff violations only if each individual violation could be shown to have an effect on buyers' prices paid. We tested for price impact using a model that simulated the ISO market in each hour, substituting a bid at MMCP for the actual anomalous bid submitted.[59] This was a relatively straightforward market price simulation exercise, and no opposing parties objected to the mechanics of the model. They did object strenuously to the assumption that, absent their

57. Dr. Berry argued that the appropriate standard for sellers who did not have access to hydro storage was the disposal cost of their power if not sold in the RT market. Once power is purchased, marketers' costs are sunk, and the relevant benchmark against which to measure a decision to bid high is the revenue earned from disposing of the power when one's bid is not selected in the CAISO auction. The MMCP was a conservative proxy for disposal cost. *See* Berry Testimony 2011, p. 51.

58. This total counted ancillary services bids separately from supplemental (i.e., RT) energy bids. About three fifths of the bids were in the former market.

59. The price effect test was unique in that it did not attempt to capture the exact magnitude of the price effect, but rather merely to establish that it was greater than zero. In part this was because each tariff violation had to be tested in isolation, omitting any interactions between sellers or other buyers. While artificial, this approach did have the virtue that it incorporated all the markets, fundamentals, i.e., all market scarcity whether real or contrived. While not settling the but-for assumption, this largely mooted the rest of the arguments by sellers that true scarcity explained the level of prices in each hour. *See* Fox-Penner Testimony, Exh. No. CAX-310 (revised March. 28, 2012).

anomalous bids, sellers would have bid MMCP; as explained below, the ALJ ultimately agreed with us. We were able to test for price effects in 8,388 anomalous bidding violations and found that 5,033 violations had some effect on price when treated in isolation.

Separating Undue Market Power from Efficient Scarcity

As experts on behalf of the California Parties, our role with respect to market power was to demonstrate whether sellers had violated the market power provisions of the PX and ISO tariffs. As forensic power market economists, our role was to demonstrate that prices could not be explained solely by true market scarcity, i.e., to isolate the exercise of undue (excessive) market power from scarcity.

As just explained, our overall approach was to first use structural tests to show that the market did not meet the degree of structural competitiveness that the Commission required. We then tested for each stage of two-stage withholding, first by analyzing changes in the DA markets and then by two very different withholding analyses in the RT market—the large-seller estimates from Dr. Reynolds and the identification of anomalous bidding by Dr. Berry.

Sellers' Objections to Our Market Power Tests

Apart from many disagreements over data and technical details, sellers severely criticized this overall approach. First, seller experts argued that essentially all the observed price increases were due to true scarcity, i.e., represented an economically accurate and efficient price signal.[60] While we agreed that scarcity was a factor, we believed that the only way to determine whether market power was significant was to look at the entire picture rather than simply look at comparative absolute supply levels.

As to our tests, sellers' most important criticism reduced to this crucial proposition: we had not, on a seller-specific basis, proven that any seller had willfully and profitably withheld otherwise

60. *See* Hogan Testimony 2011. *See Answering Testimony of Dr. James L. Sweeney, Docket No. EL00-95-248*, October 25, 2011, Exh. No. POW-233, pp. 118-134. In the same proceeding, Dr. Fox-Penner responded to Professor Hogan's and Dr. Sweeney's market fundamental arguments that tight conditions create preconditions for profitable market manipulation and Professor Hogan's exaggerated impacts of market fundamentals on market prices. Dr. Fox-Penner presented inconsistencies in Professor Hogan's market fundamental analysis and concluded that the market fundamentals alone do not explain the sustained high prices during the Crisis Period. *See Dr. Fox-Penner's Prepared Rebuttal Testimony, Docket No. EL00-95-248,* Exh. No. CAX-310, March 2, 2012 pp. 92-112 (hereinafter Fox-Penner Rebuttal 2012).

saleable capacity. Until we did, any scarcity observed in the marketplace had to have been real—and the resulting prices efficient—since withholding is the only way to increase scarcity artificially.[61] Instead, the high prices observed were *entirely* the result of a flawed market design and true scarcity.[62] Professor Hogan and Doctor Harvey epitomized this view in this response:

> At the time there were concerns that high prices were due to a pervasive exercise of market power whereby some market participants would (i) withhold supply from the actual dispatch, thus (ii) raise market clearing prices, and as a result (iii) profit enough from the increase in the price paid for their remaining transactions to overcome the losses on the withheld supply. After many proceedings and intensive investigations of market power allegations, the evidence does not meet the test of demonstrating these three necessary elements of the exercise of market power. If there were any exercise of market power, it was on a scale so small or duration so fleeting that it has not been detected. By contrast, the effects of the combination of a tight market and a flawed market design are plain to see, and well-documented.[63]

We responded to this criticism by making a variety of points.[64] First, we noted that Dr. Reynolds did find substantial withholding, taking care to incorporate all of the market features opposing economists believed were important. Second, we noted that very little withholding was necessary to raise prices in the CAISO RT market with a vertical demand curve, and in bilateral transactions, the threat of withholding was sufficient.[65] Dr. Reynolds pointed out, for example, that in the context of the Crisis withholding could mean diverting supplies out of the California markets, parking the power for use later, or storing the power in hydroelectric reservoirs—all tactics available to generators and in some cases even to marketers as well.[66] Third, we emphasized that while we agreed that there was significant real scarcity during the Crisis, this real scarcity was *necessary* and *complementary* to sellers' acquiring undue market power.[67]

We also noted that sellers' proposed requirement that we prove each seller profited from each individual act of withholding went beyond FERC's requirements. Instead, it was sufficient to show that markets were structurally deficient, bids were far above marginal costs and shaped so as to raise prices, and significant amounts of capacity that should have been profitable to sell

61. These arguments were made most forcefully by Professor Hogan and Dr. Harvey in several filings, such as Hogan Testimony 2011. *See* footnote 60.

62. The design defects of the market were explained in detail in the above-cited testimony, p. 30.

63. Hogan Testimony 2011, p. 7.

64. *See Rebuttal Testimony of Dr. Peter Fox-Penner and Dr. Robert J. Reynolds, Docket No. EL02-71-000,* Exh. No. CLP-125, December 17, 2009, pp. 9-12 (Fox-Penner and Reynolds 2009).

65. Dr. Reynolds developed this line of argument extensively as a "bargaining model" during the CERS period.

66. *See Rebuttal Testimony of Robert J. Reynolds, Docket No. EL02-71-000,* Exh. No. CLP-128, December 17, 2009. This was made to specifically counter assertions that power marketers had no technical ability to withhold power; because they cannot store power, every MWh they purchase must be resold for delivery in the same hour as it is delivered to them. Since purchases must equal sales, it was argued, withholding is impossible.

67. This argument was made in detail in Fox-Penner's Rebuttal 2012, pp. 94-96.

remained unsold, diverted, or stored. In fact, the Commission's seminal Order during the Crisis found that market remedies were necessary and prices were not "just and reasonable," while explicitly finding it unnecessary to prove that individual sellers had exercised market power.[68]

It is worth noting that sellers never filed market power tests of their own, as was common in other FERC proceedings where market power is at issue. Sellers and their experts criticized all our tests but did not file tests showing different results. Indeed, Professor Hogan was often careful to say that he could not completely rule out the exercise of market power, but he doubted that it was large enough to have a significant effect on price.[69]

The second major area of disagreement centered on whether it was appropriate to label seller offers at prices well above estimated marginal costs as an attempt to exercise market power. Professor Hogan and Dr. Harvey argued that the design of the California markets as "energy only" *necessitated* seller bids above marginal cost. The margin between incremental cost and bid price, they argued, was (a) the only means of recouping start-up and no-load costs; and (b) induced by the separation between the energy and ancillary services auctions, run-time, and other generator limitations that created opportunity costs and dispatch constraints.[70] Similar objections to judging above-marginal-cost bids as anomalous were voiced by Dr. Peter Cramton.[71]

Such arguments, however, overlooked the fact that sellers' need to earn revenues higher than their operating costs did not justify bids of the magnitude and shape we observed during the crisis and they ignored completely documentary evidence from supplier business records and communications of their intent through their bidding to elevate RT prices or "protect" their price-taker offerings in the RT market.[72]

Viewing Scarcity From a Long-Term Perspective

One final thread in the debate over undue market power versus true scarcity centered on how power prices over the long term compared to the costs of owning and operating generation. Over the long term, a workably competitive generation market will allow efficient power plant owners to recover their costs including a risk-adjusted return on investment.

68. *See* Fox-Penner and Reynolds 2009, p.12, citing the Commission's November 1, 2000 Order (*see* Chapter 5).

69. One example of this sort of statement is found in Hogan Testimony 2011, p. 87, lines 14-16.

70. *See* Hogan Testimony, 2011, pp. 33-34.

71. *See Answering Testimony of Peter Cramton,* Docket No. EL00-95-248, Exh. No. TRA-1, October 25, 2012.

72. *See, e.g., Prepared Director Testimony of Gerald A. Taylor, Docket No. EL00-95-249,* Exh. No. CAX-001 August 25, 2011, p. 93 (hereinafter Taylor Testimony 2011).

Sellers argued that, prior to the Crisis, energy and ancillary services prices in the CA markets were too low to allow power plants to earn sufficient returns, and that this was one reason why a shortage of generation occurred in the Crisis. When generators' returns from high prices during the Crisis were added to those during the earlier period of prices that were too low, total earnings of an average generator would not be abnormal. This, they argued, proved that prices during the Crisis were not unjust and unreasonable, or out of line with competitive markets. The Crisis was just a "make-up" period to restore generator revenues to proper long-term levels.

To investigate this claim, we estimated the profits of a hypothetical gas combined-cycle power plant selling into the California spot markets from the time they began operating (April, 1998) through the Crisis. We found that such a generator would have recovered between 61% and 93% of its total installed cost during the two years of the Crisis. Ordinarily, generators earn back their investment over an approximately twenty-year period, with some years better than others; this was an unprecedented level of earnings in our experience. Sellers disputed these figures, and the Commission never ruled on whose calculation they believed, but the exercise demonstrated another basis for our conclusion and another useful tool for market analysis.[73]

The FERC's Ruling On Scarcity vs. Market Power

In the early days of the Crisis, the Commission appeared to be sending somewhat conflicting signals as to how they determined the dividing line between beneficial levels of scarcity and excessive levels, perhaps artificially increased by market power. Their most important mid-Crisis Order contained a footnote commenting on its initial investigation of market power, noting that "the Staff report indicated some attempted exercise of market power, if the standard of bidding above marginal cost is used."[74] Obviously, staff was unsure of the Commission's policies at this point. The November 1 Order did not establish any standard for determining market power. "While this record does not support findings of specific exercises of market power, and while we are not able to reach definite conclusions about the actions of individual sellers, there is clear evidence that the California market structure and rules provide the opportunity for sellers to exercise market power when supply is tight, and can result in unjust and unreasonable rates under the FPA." Obviously, Staff was unsure at this point what the Commission's standard for excessive market power was. Later in the same Order, the Commission gave a hint when it explained its increased monitoring of the market:

73. *See* Appendix 6B for more information on this calculation.

74. *See FERC Order Directing Remedies for California Wholesale Electric Markets, 93 FERC ¶ 61, 294, Docket Nos. EL00-95-000 et al.*, December 15, 2000, p. 7.

> In implementing our monitoring, we will rely on several indicators of potential market power, including: the outage rates of the seller's resources, the failure to bid unsold MWs into the ISO's real-time market, and variations in bidding patterns for the same or similar resources (e.g. bidding large blocks of capacity at a low price and a small amount of capacity at a high power price for the purpose of setting the market clearing price for the entire amount).[75]

The Commission announced a conference ". . . to develop a comprehensive and systematic monitoring and mitigation program which incorporates appropriate thresholds and screens and specific mitigation measures if those thresholds and screens are breached."[76] It also rejected a proposal to limit all generator bids to strict marginal costs, saying that this would allow too little room for scarcity signals. Finally, it noted that "we need to distinguish scarcity rents from exercises of market power; however, we disagree that, absent exercises of market power, prices are necessarily just and reasonable."[77] Amidst this somewhat mixed message, one can certainly infer a view that certain forms of bidding represented attempts to exercise market power, and that such attempts could lead to unjust and unreasonable prices.

Nearly all proceedings related to the Crisis settled before the Commission had a chance to clarify what type of analysis would appropriately identify undue market power as distinct from useful scarcity rents.[78] As noted earlier, the Commission adopted a pivotal supplier test as its own approach to limiting generator market power a few years after the Crisis. However, it was not until 2013 that an ALJ's Order ruled clearly on the question of the type of analysis sufficient to support a market power claim.

In a brief order addressing claims against a handful of out-of-state power marketers who had not yet settled, FERC ALJ Phillip Baten found that all three of the types of anomalous bids identified by Dr. Berry violated the ISO's MMIP provision.[79] He did not comment further on the matter of separating scarcity from market power or whether any of the other analyses described in this chapter played a role in his thinking. However, his decision clearly stands for the proposition that it is not necessary to prove that a specific seller withheld power (much less did so profitably) for their bid to be considered anomalous. He thus implicitly acknowledged the importance of inelastic demand, or the ability to raise prices without sacrificing significant sales, in determining undue levels of market power. In addition, by endorsing marginal cost

75. *Id.*, p. 31.

76. *Id.*

77. December 15, 2000 Order, *slip op*, pp. 34-35.

78. Additional signals were sent in one of the most important post-crisis Orders December 19, 2001, when the Commission reaffirmed that it would use MMCP as its measure of what just and reasonable California market prices would have been absent "*market dysfunction*." While not opining specifically on how much of the difference between actual prices and MMCP levels was due to scarcity vs. market power, the Commission rejected claims by sellers that MMCP-level prices were inadequate to collect proper scarcity rents, thus implicitly rejecting the argument that observed prices were due solely to pro-efficient market fundamentals. (Order, Docket No. EL00-95-001, 97FERC ¶ 61,275, *slip op.* December 19, 2001, p.84.)

79. *Initial Decision, Docket No. EL00-95-248, 42FERC ¶ 63,011*, February 15, 2013.

bidding as an implicit standard for competitive pricing, the Judge reaffirmed the Commission's views extending back into the Crisis, when it first adopted MMCP for this purpose. His order was recently affirmed by the FERC in Opinion No. 536.

After thirteen years and thousands of pages of market power analyses, these decisions draw a useful boundary around the crucial question of the limits of scarcity and the diagnosis of market power. Structural tests have improved dramatically since the Crisis, and are used extensively now right up to real-time bid mitigation. Conduct in the form identified by Drs. Reynolds and Berry is of a sufficient magnitude to cross the line from procompetitive to detrimental elevation of prices. In the presence of inelastic demand and the high costs of failing to supply it, bidding designed to elevate prices can become impermissible without having to prove outright profitable withholding—though we continue to believe such withholding did occur during the Crisis.

APPENDIX 6A

Adjustments of Data to Reflect Proper Market Size in Pivotal Supplier Index Tests and an Example

Imports

It is important to point out that during Summer 2000 many suppliers with resources located outside the CAISO balancing authority area (Importers) participated in the CAISO energy imbalance auction market.[80] Their bids were part of the CAISO BEEP Stack. In a given hour, the total amount of MW offered by Importers could exceed the available transmission capacity. We therefore limited the amount of energy bid from Importers to the hourly real-time unused transmission capacity. For example, suppose in Hour 16 of August 4, 2000 import bids reported in the BEEP 2,736 MW; the real-time unused transmission capacity in that hour was 1,600 MW. Import bids allowed in the real-time CAISO market would only be 1,600 MW.[81]

Inclusion of Uninstructed Generation

During Summer 2000, suppliers often generated more than their accepted bids dispatched by the CAISO. This uninstructed generation, which was not reflected in the BEEP and load data, should be included when calculating a total market supply and to examined supplier's supply that served real-time demand.

80. Importers did not directly bid into the CAISO imbalance energy market during the CERS Period.

81. When the unused transmission capacity exceeded total import bids, we did not add any excess import capability to the total supply as we believe that the BEEP stack and the OOM purchases comprised the complete set of supply options.

Inclusion of False Load

Some suppliers submitted "balanced" demand and supply schedules to the CAISO that overstated the real demand of the supplier. In real time, the load actually served was below the supply scheduled and delivered, creating excess supply in the market. Such false load scheduling became known by its Enron designation, "Fat Boy."[82] The amount of excess supply caused by false load or overscheduling load however was not reflected in the BEEP data. For the purpose of the PSI calculation, false load should be included.

Example of PSI Calculation

We demonstrate how the PSI is calculated through a numerical example shown in Table 6A.

On August 4, 2000 for the hour ending 16 (3:00 p.m.–4:00 p.m.) the CAISO real-time energy market had no internal constraints. Local suppliers and importers respectively bid into the CAISO imbalance energy market 2,278 MW [5] and 2,736 MW [6], totaling 5,014 MW. The real-time unused transmission capacity was 1,600 MW. The CAISO also purchased OOM energy in the amount of 1,378 MW [7]. The total uninstructed generation was 200 MW and the False Load was 2,701 MW [3] and [9]. Total Supply in the RT market for this hour was therefore 9,293 MW [11]. CAISO real-time demand was 7,188 MW [4]. With the operating reserve of 7 percent, the CAISO real-time demand plus reserve became 7,691 MW [4b]. The supply margin on this hour [12] was therefore 1,602 (9,293–7,691) MW.

Supplier A is a local generator in the CAISO BAA. It bid into the CAISO energy imbalance market 1,034 MW [13]. It did not have any import bids and did not sell into the CAISO OOM. However, it had uninstructed generation of 181 MW [17] and False Load of 475 MW [18]. Its total supply offered in the real-time market was therefore 1,690 MW [19].

As calculated in [20] of Table 6-A, Supplier A's PSI on August 4, 2000 for HE16 was 1.05. The market needed Supplier A's capacity to meet the CAISO demand. In this instance, Supplier A submitted bids starting at $100 per MWh to $250 per MWh before its last bid of over 300 MW jumped to $499 per MWh, slightly below the price cap of $500. Supplier A's bidding behavior reflected the firm's expectation of having market power to influence the market clearing price. The market clearing price on that hour was $498 per MWh.[83] Supplier A sold 1,390 MW that were presumably economic at or below $250 per MW for $498.

82. *See* the detail discussion of this Enron scheme in Chapter 7.

83. The joint pivotality could be calculated in the same manner. However, the joint pivotal supplier combines bids of the two largest suppliers together, as shown in Table 6-A.

Table 6-A

Example of Unilateral Pivotality Calculation

Date	8/4/2000	Supplier Max Bid	$499
Hour	16	Uni-Fail Max Bid	$499
Seller	A	RT MCP	$498
Zone	NP15		

7% added to Demand	Yes
Market Splitting Threshold	$0.00
Uninstructed Included?	Yes

Total Market		
Metered Load	[1]	19,734
Scheduled Load	[2]	15,247
False Load	[3]	2,701
Real Time Demand	[4a]	7,188
Real Time Demand plus Reserves	[4b] = [1] - [2] + [3]	7,691
BEEP Generation Bids	[5]	2,278
BEEP Import Bids 2,736		
Real Time Unused Transmission 1,600		
BEEP Import Bids Allowed into CA	[6]	2,736
OOM	[7]	1,378
Uninstructed	[8]	200
False Load	[9]	2,701
Path 15/26 Imports	[10]	0
Total Supply	[11] = sum ([5] to [10])	9,293
Total Supply Margin	[12] = [11] - [4b]	1,602
Supplier A		
BEEP taken 319		
BEEP untaken 715		
BEEP bids 1,034		
BEEP Generation Bids	[13]	1,034
BEEP Import Bids 0		
BEEP Import Bids Allowed into CA	[14]	0
OOM	[15]	0
Uninstructed	[17]	181
False Load	[18]	475
Seller Total Supply	[19] = sum ([13] to [18])	1,690
Seller PSI	[20] = [19]/[12]	1.05
Seller Pivotal (1 if yes, 0 if no)		1

APPENDIX 6B

CAPITAL COST RECOVERY AND SCARCITY RENTS

An important factor in evaluating the reasonableness of prices is the ability to recover capital costs during periods of high prices. The California markets included both energy and ancillary services markets that provided sources of revenue to generators. There was no capacity market at the time, and the CERS Period began with no long-term contracts in place, so generators selling to California utilities had to recover their capital costs through their energy and ancillary services sales. To evaluate whether capital recovery opportunities would have been foreclosed by prices used as a benchmark for evaluating the reasonableness of day-ahead energy prices, cumulative margins earned by day-ahead spot price sellers were examined.[84]

Table 6B presents our estimates of cumulative margins a new peaking unit earned from January 18, 2001 to June 20, 2001 at PV and COB. The results indicate that the new combustion turbine entrant would have earned approximately $85/kW when selling at the PV trading hub while it would have earned approximately $340/kW at COB/Mid-C from January 18, 2001 to June 20, 2001. At PV a new entrant during this period would have fully recovered its yearly capital cost, which was estimated by the California generators to be around $80/kW-year.[85] But such an entrant would have earned 4.2 times the annual share of the fixed cost of its peaking unit in the DA market at COB/Mid-C during this period. For the entire two-year period from January 2000 through December 2001, the new entrant would have earned a contribution to its fixed costs of $243/kW and $695/kW (or 3.0 and 8.7 times its annual share of fixed costs) when selling its power at PV and COB/Mid-C, respectively. Recovering the entire fixed cost of a power plant lasting twenty to forty years at the rate earned at COB in a one year period is unprecedented in our experience.[86] A variety of RTOs in the U.S. and around the world calculate price limits or other market design features based on similar conservative assumptions.[87]

---

84. To estimate how much a new entrant operating a peaking unit would have earned for its capital cost recovery during this period, daily differences between prices and short-run marginal operating costs were calculated assuming a new CT entrant has a heat rate of 11,380 btu/kWh and VOM of $6 per MWh.

85. The California generators estimated the annual capital cost of a new combustion turbine unit (CT) to be about $80/kW-year in 2001 dollars. Table 1, Exhibit DYN/WIL-1, Prepared Rebuttal Testimony of William H. Hieronymus, Docket Nos. ER00-95 *et al.*, p. 18.

86. In the Crisis period alone, a CC would have recovered between 61% and 93% of its installed cost.

87. *See Substantive Rule 25.505*, Public Utilities Commission of Texas (2007) for a price cap regime that becomes stricter when cumulative earnings for a hypothetical peaker exceed certain thresholds. For a discussion of Australia's system that triggers a lower price cap if the sum of spot prices over a rolling period of time exceeds a specified threshold, *See Section 3.14*, National Electricity Rules, *available at http://www.aemc.gov.au/pdfs/rules/chapter03.pdf*.

Table 6-B

Cumulative Margins earned above the cost of a new CT peaking unit

	PV Trading Hub	COB Trading Hub
CERS Period (Jan 18, 2001 - Jun 19, 2001)		
Cumulative Sum of Estimated Margins ($/kW-CERS period)	85.3	338.2
Number of Times Above the Annual Fixed Cost of a new CT peaking unit	1.1	4.2
Crisis Period, Pre-CERS period (May 1, 2000 - Jan 17, 2001)		
Cumulative Sum of Estimated Margins ($/kW-Crisis period)	152.1	346.3
Number of Times Above the Annual Fixed Cost of a new CT peaking unit	1.9	4.3
Total Year 2000 & 2001 (Jan 3, 2000 - Dec 31, 2001)		
Cumulative Sum of Estimated Margins ($/kW-year)	242.7	694.6
Number of Times Above the Annual Fixed Cost of a new CT peaking unit	3.0	8.7
Total Year 2001 (Jan 3, 2001 - Dec 31, 2001)		
Cumulative Sum of Estimated Margins ($/kW-year)	90.4	359.2
Number of Times Above the Annual Fixed Cost of a new CT peaking unit	1.1	4.5
Total Year 2000 (Jan 3, 2000 - Dec 31, 2000)		
Cumulative Sum of Estimated Margins ($/kW-year)	152.3 3	35.4
Number of Times Above the Annual Fixed Cost of a new CT peaking unit	1.9	4.2

APPENDIX 6C

AN EXAMPLE OF TWO-STAGE WITHHOLDING

An example of one actual "Supplier A's" behavior on August 1, 2000 hour 17 provides a good illustration of how two-stage withholding was implemented. First, consider Supplier A's bids in the PX day-ahead market for this hour. It offered 990 MW with bid prices spanning from $0 per MWh to $2,500 per MWh and approximately 80 percent of its capacity offers priced above $500 per MWh. As shown in Figure 6-11, Supplier A offered the first 180 MW as a price taker with a bid price of zero, but its incremental bid price of the next 5 MW jumped to almost $495 per MWh. Its bids of additional MWs continued to climb at extraordinary high prices of $520 per MWh, $730 per MWh, $840 per MWh, $1,000 per MWh, $1,487 per MWh, and $2,500 per MWh. These prices did not resemble normal competitive behavior.

Figure 6-11

Supplier A's Bid Curve in the PX Day-Ahead Market August 1, 2000 Hour 17

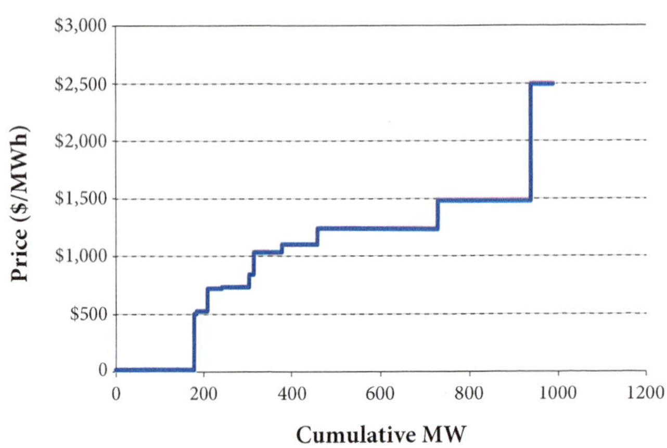

Figure 6-12 presents Supplier A's bid positions (as shown in the pink sections) when combined with total supply in the PX day-ahead market in this hour. The supply curve on this hour was quite inelastic, although over 22,000 MW of bids were offered on a price taker basis, i.e., $0 per MWh. It appears that suppliers other than Supplier A also offered capacity at very high prices. There was supplier willingness to sell at reasonable prices up to around 27,200 MW. Then it appears that suppliers were not willing to sell additional capacity below $400 per MWh.

Above about 32,000 MW there were some bids at $1,500 (three times the RT price cap) with the remainder at the PX price cap of $2500 per MWh. The PX market cleared at $499.96 per MWh and 27,984 MW. Supplier A sold 185 MW, leaving its 805 MW for the real-time market.

Figure 6-12

Total Supply Curve in the PX Day-Ahead Market August 1, 2000 Hour 17

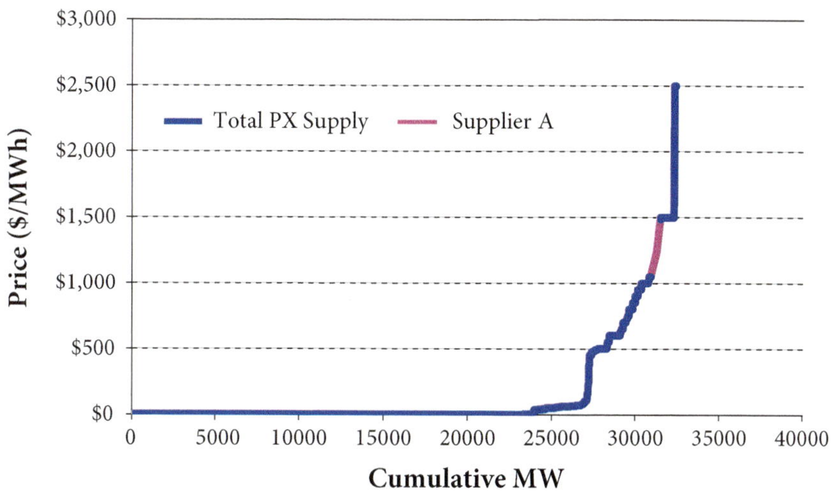

When the real-time market opened, Supplier A offered approximately 1,000 MW in the CAISO imbalance energy market, excluding capacity from its accepted ancillary services bids. It no longer offered power at $0 per MWh. Its real-time bid schedule in this hour was aggressive, as shown in Figure 6-13. It started at $125 per MWh and rose to the price cap level of $500 per MWh. 800 of 1,000 MW (or approximately 80% of its bids) were offered to the CAISO at prices above $400 per MWh.

Figure 6-13

Supplier A's Bid Curve in the CAISO Real-Time Market
August 1, 2000 Hour 17

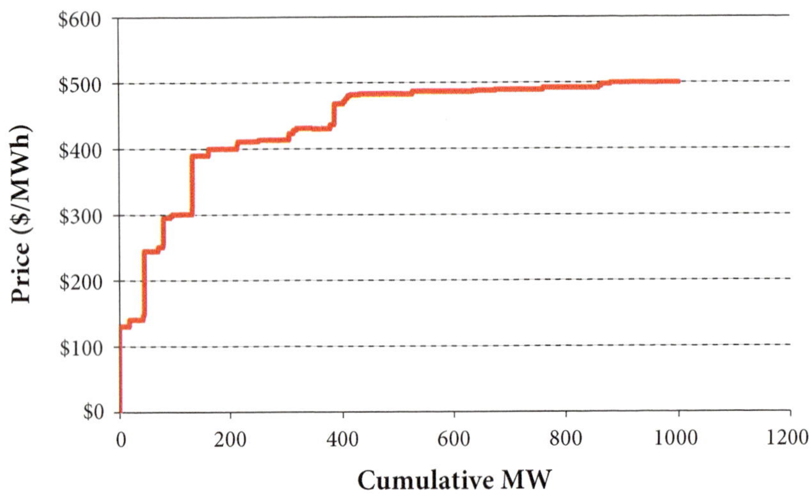

As shown in Figure 6-14, on August 1, 2000 hour 17 most of Supplier A's real-time bids (shown in green) were at the upper end of the supply curve. Although there were over 5,000 MW of price taker bids offered into the RT auction (approximately 3,340 MW from "False Load" transactions), the CAISO total real-time supply offer curve was inelastic where it mattered. Like Supplier A's bids, bids of other suppliers were high and reached $500 per MWh, the price cap level. Some supplier' bids were in the form of Walking Cane bidding strategy,[88] as shown in Figure 6-15. The bid schedule in this graph was composed of only two prices: 1) the first 13 MW at $0 per MWh and 2) the next and also last 110 MW at $500 per MWh.

88. *See* Figure 6-10 for the description of Walking Cane bids.

Figure 6-14

Total Supply Curve in the CAISO Real-Time Market August 1, 2000 Hour 17

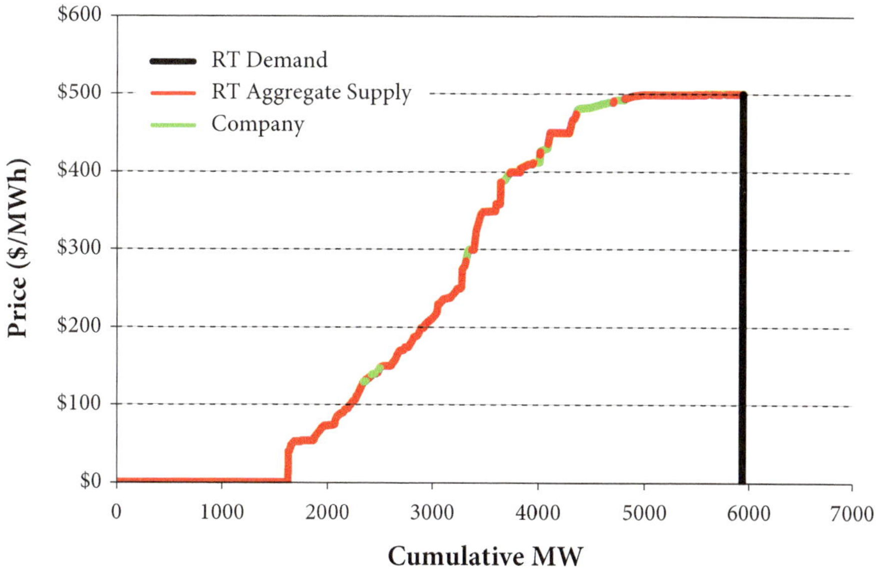

Figure 6-15

Another Supplier's Real-Time Bid Schedule on August 1, 2000 Hour 17

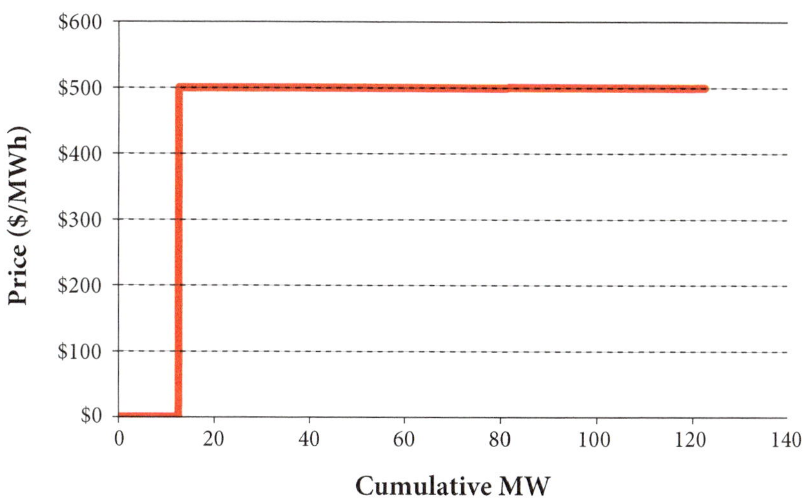

In this hour, the CAISO declared Stage 2 Emergency.[89] The CAISO real-time demand plus reserves totaled more than 13,000 MW when the capacity offered in the BEEP (including "False Load" capacity) was only approximately 9,400 MW. To meet its system demand and maintain reliability, the CAISO purchased approximately 3,350 MW OOM in the bilateral market and shed 1,778 MW of non-firm interruptible load. Our pivotality analyses, described earlier in this chapter, found Supplier A and some other sellers to be unilaterally pivotal suppliers. The CAISO real-time price in this hour was $500 per MWh. Supplier A sold its unsold PX DA quantity plus the additional MW, totaling 1,000 MW in the CAISO real-time market at $500 per MWh.

89. In fact, on this day Stage 1 Emergency was declared by the CAISO at 11:00 a.m. and Stage 2 Emergency at 12:00 p.m. The Stage 2 alert lasted until 7:00 p.m. while the market remained at Stage 1 until 9:00 p.m.

CHAPTER 7

FRAUD-BASED MANIPULATION STRATEGIES DURING THE CRISIS

Enron Manipulation

Enron's fraud-based manipulative strategies fell into three general categories. The activities within each category had similar impacts upon the market and the prices paid by wholesale energy buyers. These were:

- Fraudulent sales of energy in the CAISO Imbalance Energy (or real-time, RT) and ancillary services markets (tariff violations involving false export, false load, and intentionally running generation uninstructed);
- Fraudulent collection of congestion revenues (tariff violations involving false congestion, circular scheduling, withdrawn counterflow schedules, and creating false counterflows through the shifting of false load); and
- Fraudulent sales of goods or services (tariff violations involving the sale of phantom ancillary services and market-priced sales without MBR authority).

Enron also engaged in withholding through anomalous bidding, an exercise of market power, which is discussed in detail in Chapter 6.

Fraudulent Entry into the RT Energy and Ancillary Services Markets

The RT energy market in the CAISO was intended to be a comparatively small balancing market that enabled the CAISO to scale generation up or down quickly in response to fluctuations in load or generation and transmission outages to ensure system reliability in real time.[1] The CAISO tariff makes quite clear that to participate in the RT energy and ancillary services markets, a supplier needed to have immediate physical control of specific resources sold into these

1. It was originally contemplated in the market's design that the RT energy market would only provide about five percent of energy needed to serve load in the CAISO.

markets.[2] In particular, resources committed in these markets had to be capable of responding to CAISO dispatch instructions, and Scheduling Coordinators (SCs) were obligated to respond or to secure a response to CAISO dispatch instructions.[3] Nevertheless, the CAISO Tariff allowed importers to participate in the RT energy and ancillary services markets as long as their schedules identified in each hour where their resources were sourced (e.g., source balancing authority area) and the transmission interface they would utilize for delivery.[4]

Energy purchased in the PX or bilateral contract markets DA or on a longer-term basis was typically not resource-specific, and the amounts were fixed. The buyer had no control over the source of the energy or its dispatch and could not follow an instruction to increase or decrease their output. Thus, marketers, who normally just purchased day-ahead energy in fixed block amounts or energy purchased hourly out of the PX, could not legitimately sell in RT or into the ancillary services auctions under the CAISO tariff. This, of course, is why Enron and other marketers desiring to sell in the RT and ancillary services markets needed to develop schemes to get around the tariff requirements.

One way to circumvent the requirements for RT energy and ancillary services sales was the filing of fraudulent schedules with the CAISO. The evidence shows that this took three forms. The first was the filing of False Export schedules. The False Export scheme falsely "rebranded" energy generated and purchased in California into purported imported energy that could under the CAISO tariff be bid into the ancillary services and RT energy markets. The second form was the filing of False Load schedules. A third strategy for illegal sales in RT was for a firm with generation or rights to dispatch generation to simply defy the tariff and generate beyond the amount they scheduled or that was dispatched ("instructed") by the CAISO. False Load and intentional uninstructed overgeneration created positive imbalances that were settled at the RT *ex-post* price. We explain each of these strategies in detail below.

There were two financial incentives for all this subterfuge. First, the RT prices were frequently higher than the DA prices under certain (generally high-load) conditions, so suppliers could anticipate when buying DA from the PX and selling to the CAISO in RT would make money.[5] The second reason that applied only to False Export was the opportunity to collect twice for each MW sold into the ancillary services markets,[6] once for the capacity and again for the

2. The ISO Tariff included many provisions that were designed to require a supplier to have immediate physical control over the resources it bid into the markets—particularly the bidding provisions, which required a seller to identify specific resources and their capabilities in terms of output and ramp rates. The ISO also had technical requirements for providing ancillary services (ISO § 2.5.6), specified the rules for bidding into the Regulation, Spinning Reserve, Non-spinning Reserve, and Replacement Reserve Auctions (ISO §§ 2.5.14-17) and had rules for submitting Supplemental Energy bids (ISO § 2.5.22.4.2).

3. Dispatch instructions were sent to the SC to increase or decrease output within a timeframe specified in the tariff for each type of generation resource. *See* ISO Tariff §§ 2.2.14.2, 2.5.22.11. SCs also had additional resource control requirements that were set out specifically in the Ancillary Services Requirements Protocol, at 5.6, 5.7, 6.4, April 1998.

4. The power did not need to come from a specified unit but could instead be sourced from "System Resources" in another Control Area. *See* ISO Tariff §§ 2.2.5.22.1.

5. The persistent price differential was largely due to the bidding strategies of suppliers and the major IOU buyers in the PX DA market, which we explain later, and to inelastic demand and supplier withholding in RT.

6. False Exports were typically sold into the Replacement Reserves auction, the least restrictive of the ancillary services markets.

energy if it were dispatched. Early in the Crisis, when the CAISO was having trouble maintaining reserves and the price cap in the CAISO was $750, this meant an opportunity to collect $1,500 per MWh, roughly 30 times the price under normal conditions.

The money was too tempting. When asked why he robbed banks, the notorious thief Willie Sutton reputedly replied, "Because that's where the money is." The President and CEO of Powerex at the time borrowed Mr. Sutton's phrase in succinctly explaining his company's motive for selling into the CAISO RT energy market rather than the PX:

> I'll just say that Powerex has focused most of its energy trading through the CAISO as opposed to the PX for a very simple reason: That's where the money is.[7]

BC Hydro (Powerex's parent company) reaped trading profits of over a billion dollars during the Crisis driven largely by Powerex sales to California. In explaining its success to BC Hydro's Board of Directors, Powerex emphasized its RT sales to the CAISO:

> BC Hydro will earn over one billion dollars in electricity trade income for the fiscal year ending March 31, 2001. Powerex is one of many power marketers and generators that earned substantial profits by selling into the California real-time market. On some hour[s] in June, Powerex sold at the price caps and earned $1,500 per megawatt hour....[8]

Since the price cap for energy was $750 per MWh it is obvious that Powerex was collecting the capped price for both energy and capacity in the ancillary services market.

Ricochet and False Export

Ricochet was the name Enron applied to the "laundering" of the energy it purchased from the PX or from other sources in California by filing a fictitious export schedule with the CAISO, so that it could then be sold in the CAISO RT energy or ancillary services markets. Enron's lawyers described the mechanics of Ricochet as follows:

> Enron buys energy from the PX in the Day Of market, and schedules it for export. The energy is sent out of California to another party, which charges a small fee per MW, and then Enron buys it back to sell the energy in the CAISO real-time market.[9]

The Commission for some reason came to the conclusion that the objective of Ricochet transactions was to evade the CAISO price cap:

---

7. This quote is from a transcript of remarks by Mr. Peterson entitled "Buying and Selling Electric Power in the West," delivered at a gathering of energy executives in Belleview, Washington on January 18-19, 2001.

8. *See* Taylor Testimony 2011, Exh. No. CAX-012, p. 1. We cite this statement only to illustrate the financial incentives at the time by double collection in sales of ancillary services to the ISO, and not as evidence of False Export since Powerex had access to generation and thus could legitimately supply ancillary services.

9. *See* Taylor Testimony 2011, Memorandum to: Richard Sanders, from: Christian Yoder and Stephen Hall (hereinafter Enron Memo), re: Traders' Strategies in the California Wholesale Power Markets/ISO Sanctions, December 6, 2000, Exh. No. CAX-013, pp. 6-7.

> This practice, which is also known as "Ricochet" or "Megawatt Laundering," took advantage of the price differentials that existed between the day-ahead or day-of markets and out-of-market sales in the real-time market. A market participant made arrangements to export power purchased in the California day-ahead or day-of markets to an entity outside the state and to repurchase the power from the out-of-state entity, for which the out-of-state entity received a fee. The "imported" power was then sold in the California real-time market at a price above the cap.[10]

Setting aside the Commission's apparent misunderstanding of "out-of-market" purchases by the CAISO,[11] Enron's own description of the Ricochet strategy clearly indicated that it was intending to sell energy in the CAISO's real-time imbalance market in order to take advantage of the differential between day-ahead prices in the PX and real-time prices in the CAISO. Such sales into the real-time market were clearly subject to the CAISO price cap.

The essence of the Ricochet strategy was fraud: Enron misrepresented the source of energy purchased day-ahead from the PX as coming from outside the CAISO in order to gain access to the real-time energy and ancillary services markets. The misrepresentation was necessary because, as explained previously, requirements of the CAISO Tariff for the sale of energy in the real-time and ancillary services markets, which could not be met with energy purchased from the PX, did not apply to energy imported from outside the CAISO control area. The energy was thus "laundered," like ill-gotten cash, into a product acceptable to the CAISO.

Nevertheless the Commission's thinking about False Import, their term for Ricochet, focused narrowly upon transactions involving sales to the CAISO as OOM energy above the prevailing price cap:

> The reason for creating this fictional import was to take advantage of the fact that the ISO was making out-of-market purchases that were not subject to the price cap during real time whenever there was insufficient supply bid into its market. The ISO buyers responsible for obtaining the energy needed in the real-time market were willing to pay a price above the cap for energy imported from outside of California and accepted offers from sellers engaging in the False Import practice.[12]

This interpretation is inconsistent not only with basic economics[13] and Enron's own documents, but also with the CAISO's efforts to honor the cap even in OOM sales.[14] It had the effect of narrowing the definition to the point of irrelevance.

10. Gaming Order 2003, ¶ 37.

11. As the name implies, out-of-market sales did not occur in the CAISO's real-time auction market, but rather outside of that market in bilateral transactions.

12. Gaming Order 2003, ¶38.

13. Access to the lucrative CAISO RT energy and ancillary services markets provided a more than sufficient economic incentive to violate the relevant tariffs to the detriment of purchasers in the PX and CAISO markets.

14. Prior to December 2000 when the markets were collapsing, the ISO virtually never paid above the applicable price cap in making out-of-market purchases, thus rendering unlikely any Enron intent to sell above the cap.

False Export is our term for transactions that were used to misrepresent energy sourced from California as coming instead from sources outside the CAISO. Unlike energy generated in California, the CAISO tariff did not require identification of the specific source of imported energy beyond the originating balancing (control) area to qualify for sale into the ancillary services markets or the RT imbalance market.[15] Thus, a bid into the Replacement Reserves or other ancillary services auctions had only to indicate that the energy would be coming from a balancing authority area at a particular intertie, from BPA at COB, for example.

This opening in the tariff motivated Enron's Ricochet and other similar strategies. Energy was purchased in California, either DA or HA from the PX or bilaterally from California generators and then scheduled with the CAISO as an export and sold to a recipient in a balancing authority area outside the CAISO. The recipient then resold the energy back to the putative exporter at the same or another interface with the CAISO where it was bid into the ancillary services or RT imbalance energy markets. The buy/resale transaction with the recipient was called "parking," and by parking the energy the recipient became the "sink" for the supposed export and the "source" for the fictitious import that were needed to arrange transmission over the interfaces between the CAISO and adjacent balancing authority areas.[16]

The key to this type of strategy was to misrepresent the ultimate transaction, a purchase of energy in California for resale to the CAISO to serve load within California, as two supposedly independent transactions. It was for this purpose that Enron developed parking and similar activities called control area services.[17] It is also the specific purpose for which parking providers offered their services to potential clients, as was made clear by an excerpt from a marketing presentation by a utility in the Southwest (that we shall call "SWU") that was one of the more prolific parking providers:

---

15. Because they were supposed to be "backed up" by the control area (now called Balancing Authority Areas) on the other side of the interface, the ISO considered imports as reliable and did not require detailed identification of their sources.

16. Scheduling imports and exports over an interface between control areas required a NERC "tag" that identified the time and volume of the electricity flow, the source generation, changes in custody of the energy, the transmission path and the location of the ultimate load served, or sink.

17. Enron promoted the development of parking specifically so that it could emulate Control Area Operators who *could* legitimately sell into the ISO's RT market. This is reflected in a memo from Enron's Sean Crandall to Mary Hain in Enron's legal department:

    There are numerous ways the merchant/wholesale entity can use its control area capability to advantage itself in the whole sale market, including:

    1. Show itself as the source or sink for its wholesale transactions. For example, Washington Water Power may buy power from BC Hydro and either sell this power at the Mid-Columbia or at COB. In either case, Washington Water does not have to show BC Hydro as the ultimate generator, only itself because it is a control area. If a marketer were to undertake a similar transaction, it would have to show the complete path. This is very important for reasons I'll explain later.

    2. Go short or long into the real-time market. A marketer cannot take a long or short position into real time without purchasing this ability from a control area. A marketer has to balance on a preschedule basis. However, a control area can go as long, or as short as it wants into the real-time market.

    * * *

    I believe ultimately the only real approach that mitigates some of the power and influence control areas have is to somehow separate the sending and receiving control areas in a schedule path.

    Separating "the sending and receiving control areas in a schedule path" is the exactly how False Exports accomplished the transformation of California sourced energy into "imports." *See* Taylor Testimony 2011, p. 41; Exh. No. CAX-009.

Two transactions required:

- #1 will show [SWU] as the buyer (sink)
- #2 will show [SWU] as the seller (source)
- The price difference will capture the parking fee.
- Each transaction is treated independently for scheduling, tagging & billing, however each transaction is contingent upon the flow of the other.[18]

An example of how SWU parking could work appears in a submission by one of its parking customers, Customer A, reproduced in Table 7-1. On June 28, 2000, Customer A purchased 400 MWh of Day-Ahead power in California via bilateral contracts. It sold 250 MWh in the PX DA market for $324.39 per MWh and parked the remaining 150 MWh with SWU. Then Customer A sold 125 MWh of the energy it parked into the CAISO's Replacement Reserves market as being sourced from SWU's control area, earning a market clearing price of $740 per MW. The remainder of the parked energy, consisting of 25 MWh, was sold into the HA energy auction market for $610 per MWh, again as a bid of energy imported from SWU's control area. The CAISO also dispatched all 125 MWh of energy from the 125 MW of Replacement Reserves. This means that in addition to the $740 per MW capacity payment, Customer A was paid $725 per MWh for the dispatched energy. Thus, for the 125 MWh portion of the Ricochet transaction that was sold into the CAISO's AS market, Customer A was paid a total of $1,465 per MWh. Overall, Customer A made a profit of over $185 per MWh.

Table 7-1

Reproduced Chart I: Customer A Parked Energy from CAISO OTC

June 28, 2000

Date	Quantity (MWh)	Entity	Wgt. Avg. Price	Cust. A #	P/L
6/28/2000					$74,323
Purchases	400				
Sales	250	PX DA SP 15	$324.39	43,577	
Parked Power	***150***	***SWU Parking***		***43,566 43,567***	
Sales	125 Replacement Ancillary	CANC	$740.00	43,591 43,592	
Sales	125	CAISO	$725.00	43,690	
Sales	25	PX DO	$610.00	46,959	

18. *Prepared Testimony of Gerald A. Taylor,* Docket No. EL03-180-000, Exh. No. CP-001, February 27, 2004, (Exh. No. CP-019, p. 28) (hereinafter Taylor Testimony 2004). This is a presentation slide that was included in the marketing materials of the parking provider.

The high prices and double collection for Replacement Reserves soon led to the lowering of the price cap in the CAISO[19] and eventually to changes in the payment policy for dispatched Replacement Reserves. However, even with these changes traders still employed False Export profitably.

In early December 2000, as conditions in the PX and CAISO were deteriorating rapidly, the CAISO began purchasing OOM at prices above the cap, desperate to avoid the collapse of the power grid. This created a tremendous opportunity to use False Export to purchase out of the PX at low prices and sell at a huge margin to the CAISO in bilateral OOM transactions. This situation was reflected in a power marketers' internal e-mail dated December 6, 2000:

> As Wes describes it:
>
> They (Bill/Rahim/Murray and Wes) are stealing the ISO's lunch and selling it back to them
>
> Buying at 250 at NW1 and wheeling into the NW and sink sourcing it and then Selling it back to NW1 at 1000$/hour
>
> major $[20]

Further details were provided in a review of this company's December trading activities. A presentation slide entitled "Real Time's Best Month EVER" contains the following bullet points:

- Prices are sky high in Mid C, power is tight; we are buying from all over California through the PX market.
- Snohomish acts as Mid C sink and resells us energy for $10 more.
- We wheel it back to the ISO and collect our big fat check![21]

This power marketing company was buying out of the PX at a quasi-capped price of $250 per MWh[22] for export at COB (NW1) to park with Snohomish Public Utility District for a $10 fee and reselling the energy OOM to the CAISO for $1,000 per MWh. The fraudulent misrepresentation of the source energy purchased from the PX is what allowed its sale as OOM energy to the CAISO at a profit of $740 per MWh.

On December 8, the Commission approved an emergency tariff amendment requested by the CAISO that placed a soft cap on PX and CAISO prices at $250 per MWh.[23] The soft cap, which limited auction clearing prices to $250 per MWh, but allowed the PX to take offers above the cap on an as-bid basis, was intended to draw in additional supplies. Instead it merely assured

---

19. The price cap was reduced to $500 per MWh on July 1, 2000 and again to $250 per MWh on August 8, 2000.

20. *See Direct Testimony of Gerald A. Taylor,* EL01-10-085, Exh. No. CAT-041, September 21, 2012, (Exh. No. CAT-055, p. 1) (hereinafter Taylor Testimony 2012).

21. *Id.*, p. 5.

22. At this time the PX price cap was technically $2,500, but because of the $250 cap in the ISO RT market, the PX generally did not clear much above $250.

23. *See* CAISO Emergency Tariff Amendment 33, December 2000. The amendment also required reporting and justification of sales to the PX or ISO at prices above the cap.

that marketers could purchase thousands of MW of energy for (false) export out of the PX at $250 per MWh for resale OOM to the CAISO at huge profits.[24]

After January 17, 2001, CERS stepped in for the CAISO, whose credit position had deteriorated to the point that it could no longer purchase energy. CERS continued to buy energy OOM at the import points into the CAISO to meet the IOUs' net short and the CAISO's RT balancing needs. As volumes purchased in the PX declined,[25] marketers purchased bilaterally in California and continued to play variants of the False Export game to sell OOM to CERS.

There were numerous variants of False Export. Rather than a transaction with a single parking provider, for example, there could be several intermediate parties in the loop from and back into the CAISO. Furthermore, control area operators or certain marketers affiliated with control area operators[26] could park energy themselves with no need to rely upon third parties.[27] Also, in the CERS Period, the profitable laundering of the energy relied less upon differences in DA and CAISO RT prices than upon the differences in prices for energy purchased inside California and what CERS was willing to pay for imports OOM, particularly at COB to supply the northern portion of the CAISO.[28] Thus, exports based upon RT purchases could become the first leg of a profitable False Export transaction. In all cases, however, the essence of these schemes was misrepresentation of the source of the energy in order to sell it in a fashion that otherwise would not have been possible.

False Export Analysis and Evidence

The analysis of False Export transactions proceeded along two paths. First, since the pattern of single-party False Export transactions was straightforward, it was possible simply to compile detailed information on DA and HA export schedules filed with the CAISO and find matches

24. In a series of transactions, a supplier purchased out of the PX and sold to a California municipality at $900 per MWh to $1,000 per MWh. The municipality then simply added $15 per MWh to the price and transferred the energy to the CAISO at the same point it was delivered to them by the supplier. Even during the high-load hours of the Stage III emergency on December 8, this supplier bought more than 1,000 MW out of the PX every hour, in total 22,433 MWh for the day. *See* Taylor Testimony 2012, p. 28, Exh. No. CAT-051.

25. Trading in the PX declined rapidly after the Commission's order of December 15, 2000, which freed the IOUs from having to trade through the PX. By the end of January 2001, the PX ceased to function.

26. Most marketing operations affiliated with control area operators were required to deal with them at arms-length, or not at all. One particular Canadian company, however, was an exception, and while the Commission in granting authority to sell at market-based rates required that it deal with its parent at arms-length in securing transmission on its system, it did not require similar arms-length dealing with the generation arm of the company. Thus the marketing operation could use its parent's system for the sink and source necessary for a False Export transaction.

27. Control area operators could legitimately buy DA from the PX and sell to the ISO in RT or in the AS markets. This could occur where the price in the PX was below the CA operator's marginal generation cost, and the price received by selling energy to the ISO in RT exceeded the marginal cost of its idled generation. Absent these specific economics, however, a CA operator buying from the PX and selling into the ISO was simply using its control area status to engage in False Export.

28. During the CERS Period, NP-15 was frequently deficient in supply. The transmission paths from south-to-north in the CAISO became congested cutting off generation in SP-15. This left the import point at COB the marginal supply option when load was high and the ISO was strapped for reserves. Suppliers there, recognizing the tight spot CERS was in, demanded and got excessively high prices.

to simultaneous sales via import schedules into the CAISO in RT on the same or an interconnected transmission path. The second approach relied upon documentary evidence of multi-party transaction patterns that could then be sought in the relevant parties' transaction data along with the CAISO export schedules and RT purchase data.

Searching for single-party matches, we proceeded first by matching export schedules with RT sales purportedly sourced from imports at the same interface with the CAISO, an export scheduled and a RT sale into the CAISO both at Palo Verde, for example. We then sought matches at different export and import points during hours in which there was no congestion in the CAISO.[29] Adjustments were then made to assure that the exports matched to imported RT energy sales were sourced from generation located within the CAISO.[30]

The results of this analysis merit some general observations. First, while the strategy may have been revealed publicly in the Enron Memos, Enron was eclipsed in its use by many other suppliers. Second, the pattern of False Exports is consistent with the evolution of the Crisis. False Export activity was almost non-existent from January through April of 2000. The heaviest period of False Exports occurred from May through September, when the opportunity to collect twice the price cap on Replacement Reserves created the greatest financial incentive. In the CERS Period, while some players ramped up their use of False Export to make high-priced sales to CERS, the overall number of suppliers engaging in False Export transactions declined markedly because many suppliers, particularly in the Pacific Northwest, would not deal with CERS due to perceived credit concerns and regulatory risk.[31]

An example of the output of the False Export analysis is illustrated in Figure 7-1, which maps the scheduled exports of a marketer in Southern California, "Marketer A," and its sales in the CAISO's ancillary services and Supplemental Energy markets in September 2000. The coincidence of scheduled exports (blue line on the figure) and sales to the CAISO (gray area on the figure) is striking. Marketer A would purchase from the PX or bilaterally in California, schedule an export (generally to a PNW balancing authority area), which would accept and then return the energy for a fee of $5 to $10. Marketer A would bid the energy into the CAISO Replacement Reserves market at an attractive price for the capacity and price-taker (negative cap) bid on the energy, to assure its being taken. If the Reserve Capacity bid was unsuccessful, Marketer A would place a price-taker bid into the Supplemental Energy market (CAISO RT Imbalance energy market) to ensure its "imported" energy was resold.

29. Congestion hours were excluded on the grounds that the Commission believed such movements might relieve congestion and thus provide some benefit to the ISO.

30. Some exports, for example, were part of "wheel-through" transactions where suppliers were merely using ISO operated transmission to move energy from the Southwest through California to the PNW or vice versa.

31. OOM purchases by CERS were often at COB due to the shortfall of generation in NP-15 and frequent constraints on Paths 15 and 26, which cut off supplies from the south. Thus the refusal of many PNW suppliers to deal with CERS increased the bargaining power of the suppliers that would sell to CERS.

Figure 7-1

Marketer A Comparison of Hour-Ahead Exports and Real-Time Imports at Malin September 15, 2000 through September 30, 2000: Peak Hours Only

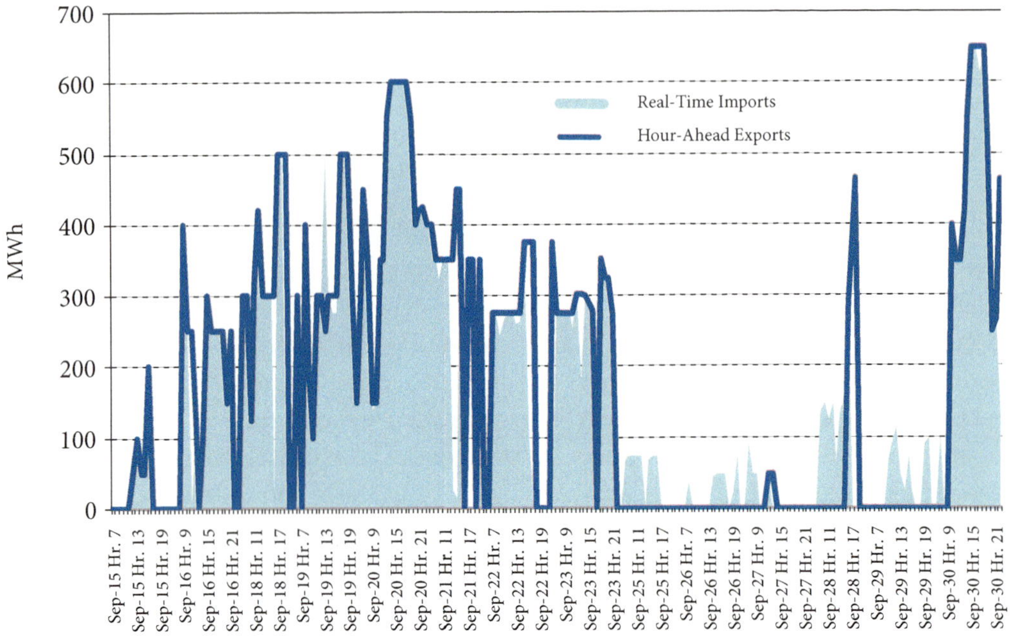

An informative example occurred on September 19, 2000 in HE 9. The arrangement that carried throughout the day was set up for HE 8 in a trader conversation between Marketer A and what we will call the PNW Parking Provider:

Greg: [PNW Parking Provider], Greg.
Ken: Hey Greg, it's Ken at [Marketer A].
Greg: Hey, Ken.
Ken: Hey, next hour would you guys be able to do a buy and sell with us at COB?
Greg: Yeah for $10.
Ken: 10 bucks?
Greg: Uh huh.
Ken: Ok, we have 400 megawatts coming out.
Greg: How many?
Ken: 400.
Greg: Not certain I can do all that, but I think so.
Ken: Give 400 back to us at COB.
Greg: Coming from?
Ken: Coming from the ISO and going back to the ISO at COB.

Greg: Ok[32]

Marketer A had purchased 300 MW in the PX and another 100 MW from another source in California and was sending the 400 MW via a False Export schedule at COB to the PNW Parking Provider, which for $10 would provide a sink and source, returning the energy at COB for sale into the ancillary services and/or Supplemental Energy markets.

The buy/resell was repeated the next hour at a smaller volume. Marketer A purchased 100 MW from the PX and another 100 MW bilaterally and scheduled the 200 MW for export via COB to the PNW Parking Provider, which for $10 would nominally return the energy at COB:

Greg: [PNW Parking Provider], Greg.
Walter: Hi it's Walter from [Marketer A], how are you doing?
Greg: Good, thanks,
Walter: I was calling to see if we could do that buy resale for next hour.
Greg: We can give it a shot if you think it'll work.
Walter: Yeah, it should work. We get a little more organized at this hour. I think it's going to be 200, hold on one second.

***

Walter: It's 200 megawatts.
Greg: Ok.
Walter: You charging $5 for that?
Greg: $10 on peak.
Walter: Oh, $10 on peak, ok.
Greg: Yeah, I'm showing just $100, $110.
Walter: Ok. Now that's something I think we might want to do for a couple hours, but I'll get back to you and maybe we could just set it up.
Greg: Sounds good.
Walter: Ok, cool.[33]

CAISO records show that the 200 MW was first bid into the Replacement Reserves market at a price of $3 per MW with an energy price of -$250. Of the 200 MW bid in, 193 MW were taken, leaving Marketer A with an excess of 7 MW. These were then bid on a price-taker basis (-$250) into the Supplemental Energy auction, but they were not taken. Left with an extra 7 MW, Marketer A sold them to the PNW Parking Provider at the discounted price of $45 per MW, as reflected in a trader phone conversation:

Greg: [PNW Parking Provider], Greg
Ken: Hey Greg, it's Ken at Marketer A
Greg: Hi Ken.
Ken: Hey, Greg, for next hour, for hour 9 there's only going to be 193 megawatts going to the ISO.

32. *See California Parties' Comments in Opposition to Certification and Approval of Agreement . . .*, November 20, 2003, Exh. No. CP-45 p. 107.

33. *Id.*, pp. 109-110.

Greg: 193.

Ken: Yeah, they just don't want the last 7, but we have 200 megawatts coming out, so I was wondering if you could pick up the other 7?

Greg: I could [do] that, but the best I could do is 45 bucks.

Ken: That's fine.

Greg: We got 193 going to the ISO.

Ken: Right you got 200 coming out of the ISO, 193 going back, and then we're selling you 7 megawatts at $45.

Greg: Right, got it.

Ken: Alright.

Greg: Very good.[34]

The following hour the Marketer A trader repeated the parking transaction with PNW Parking Provider at 100MW and discussed raising the volume in later hours:

Marlon: [PNW Parking Provider], it's Marlon.

Ken: Hey Marlon, it's Ken at Marketer A. We did buy resale with Greg last hour at COB.

Marlon: Ok.

Ken: I was wondering if we could do that for hour 10, 100 megawatts.

Marlon: Hour 10, let me look and see what he's got in there.

***

Marlon: You did the 193 before.

Ken: Right, we did 193 and we had to sell on the other 7, yeah so I guess we only wanted the partial, you know supplemental bid.

Marlon: Ok, and you got how much next hour?

Ken: Just a 100.

Marlon: Ok, we'll put in 100.

Ken: Ok, meanwhile can we do the same price, we sell at the $100 and buy back at $110?

Marlon: Yeah that's fine.

Ken: Quick question for you, for hour 11 we'll probably have a little bit more, closer to 300. Is that going to be a problem?

Marlon: No, not as long as we're doing the buy and sale, it won't be a problem.

Ken: Yeah, that's all we're going to do.

Marlon: Ok, that will be fine as long as it's going in and out.

Ken: Yeah, that's all its' doing. Is there like a maximum that you feel comfortable with?

Marlon: Well, as long as you're doing both ends of it, we don't have a problem. It's just one end goes away or one end goes bad, then we go over our limits on going the other direction [talking over each other]...

34. *Id.*, p. 111.

Ken: No, it's always just going out and coming in. We'll just try and pick up the incremental or if there's a decremental cost. It's just going to go out and come right back in.

Marlon: Ok.

Ken: Alright, thanks a lot.[35]

Indeed, similar transactions appear in CAISO records throughout the rest of the day with Marketer A in many hours realizing revenues in excess of the then applicable $250 CAISO price cap.

This final trader discussion demonstrates the fictitious nature of the False Export schedules. The PNW Parking Provider was indifferent to the volume of the transactions because the export schedule and the sales to the CAISO at COB cancelled out in terms of power flows, resulting in no flow at all. There was no impact upon the PNW Parking Provider's system because the energy generated in the CAISO served load within the CAISO. The only consequence of the charade was that Marketer A was able to gain access improperly into the CAISO markets.

These trader communications point toward a second avenue of analysis of False Export transactions. The matching analysis outlined above was only useful in finding single-party transactions. However, transactions in western power markets during this period often involved multiple title or custody transfers in the course of what was essentially a single overall transaction.[36] Trader conversations (either telephonic or via e-mail) or other written documents occasionally identified trading patterns that could then be sought in the transaction data.

E-mails of another marketer, Marketer B, exemplify this sort of scheme involving a municipal utility in Southern California (that we shall call "SC Muni") with a utility in the PNW (that we call "PNW Utility") providing the sink and source needed for the transaction. A message from a trader for Marketer B to his supervisor set out the details:

> In case you are still on-line, Amyx at CDWR just told me that the ISO is going to start cutting firm customers in HE 24 if they don't find more power. We sold them some at $625.
>
> You are going to love this. I am sending mw up the NOB line on [SC Muni] transmission and selling them to [PNW Utility] for a $100 profit for [SC Muni]. I am then having [PNW Utility] launder the mw through their system and redeliver them to us

35. *Id.*, pp. 112-113.

36. There were numerous reasons for custody transfers. Enron traders often used its affiliate Portland General Electric to implement manipulative trading schemes, but they had to insert an intermediary into such dealings to avoid running afoul of the Commission affiliate abuse rules. Buy/resale agreements were often used as a way of effectively gaining transmission access with the transmission holder buying the energy at one point and selling it back to the original owner at the desired destination. In the CERS Period, "sleeving" was used to deal with credit issues. A sleeving party would accept credit risk by buying from the party unwilling to deal directly with CERS and then reselling the energy to CERS at the same location marked up in price to cover the fee for the service.

at Malin where I am selling them at a $225 profit for [Marketer B] to CDWR. I am pretty sure there is a reserved parking space in Hell waiting for me.[37]

A subsequent e-mail indicates that Marketer B repeated the pattern the next hour, selling to the PNW Utility at NOB for $225 and buying back from them at COB for $350, where it sold the energy to CERS at $550 for a $200 gain. Marketer B had an "alliance" agreement with the SC Muni to engage in various manipulative trading schemes arranged by Marketer B and to split the profits.[38] The energy supplied by the SC Muni could have been self-generated or purchased from Marketer B or another supplier in SP-15. The energy originated in Southern California, either generated or purchased by the SC Muni, and was then moved on its transmission rights to NOB, where it was transferred at a gain of $100 to the PNW Utility system at NOB. The energy was then returned to Marketer B at COB where it was sold to CERS at prices reflecting Marketer B margins of $200 to $225. With this "key" to Marketer B's trading pattern, many similar transactions were uncovered in the trading data. Documents and trader conversations of other sellers provided similar keys to their multi-party False Export transactions.

Fat Boy

The balanced schedule provisions of the CAISO Tariff required that the generation scheduled with the CAISO be equal to the forecast demand (expected "load") of the scheduling entity.[39] Enron's Fat Boy scheme involved the filing of a schedule with the CAISO that falsely overstated the load that it actually expected to serve. Fraudulent overstatement of load meant that in Enron's purportedly "balanced" schedule, the generation it actually delivered in an hour would exceed the actual load Enron was obligated to serve. When that energy actually flowed, this created excess generation, a "positive uninstructed imbalance" in the language of the tariff, for which Enron was compensated under the tariff at the CAISO RT Imbalance Energy RT market price.

We have called this strategy False Load, and it provides an excellent example of how and why fraudulent manipulation strategies propagated rapidly throughout the Crisis-era western power trading community. Enron documents show that in addition to using Fat Boy itself, Enron helped other marketers to do it as well. In order to implement a False Load transaction, an entity needed both to be qualified as a Scheduling Coordinator with the CAISO and to have a load obligation within the CAISO. Enron was an SC and it had an affiliate, Enron Energy Services (EES), which had obligations to serve the loads of its retail customers. As an SC, Enron filed fraudulent load schedules against the EES load not only for itself, but for others as indicated in its famous memo:

37. Email from Carey Morris, to: San Diego Real Time, subject: CDWR Credit Level, dated January 26, 2001. *See* Taylor Testimony 2012, Exh. No. CAT-104.

38. *See* Taylor Testimony 2011, Exh. Nos. CAX-026 and CAX-035.

39. *See ISO Tariff at* 2.2.7.2, 2.2.11.1.1-2, pp. 28-29, 36.

> Two other points bear mentioning. Although Enron may have been the first to use this strategy, others have picked up on it, too.
>
> * * *
>
> ...Enron has performed this service for certain other customers for which it acts as scheduling coordinator. The customers using this service are companies such as [Utility D] and [Utility E], [*sic*] that have generation to sell, but no native California load. Because Enron has native California load through EES, it is able to submit a schedule incorporating the generation of a generator like Utility D and Utility and balance the schedule with "dummied-up" load from EES.[40]

The cooperative relationship between Enron and Utility D continued after Utility D qualified as an SC and obtained the right to schedule to load in the CAISO. Utility D arranged to obtain load in California in a deal with a supplier that was Enron's affiliate, PGES, as reflected in an attachment to an e-mail among Utility D traders dated February 3, 2000:

> We have entered into a deal with PGES. In exchange for us paying T.O. debit charges that PGES incurred this summer and fall (approximately $1 million) PGES will allow us to schedule to their load in NP15 and SP15.
>
> * * *
>
> The advantages of scheduling to load directly are:
>
> 1) ...
>
> 2) We can over or under schedule to load in the day ahead market to arbitrage the DA price against the hour ahead or *ex-post* market.[41]

Because Enron enlisted others in its schemes and executed some of them for others, knowledge of the mechanics of their manipulative strategies spread quickly in the close-knit western power trading community, as did the appreciation of their profitability. The means and motive thus soon became clear, and the California markets provided many opportunities.

The vehicle through which Enron and others used False Load to sell into the RT Energy Imbalance market was a perversion of the balanced schedule provision of the CAISO Tariff that stated:

> A Schedule shall be treated as a Balanced Schedule when aggregate Generation, Inter-Scheduling Coordinator Energy Trades (whether purchases or sales), and imports or exports to or from external Control Areas adjusted for Transmission

40. *See* Taylor Testimony 2011, Exh. No. CAX-013, p. 2.

41. *See* Taylor Testimony 2011. Exh. No. CAX-075, p. 2.

> Losses as appropriate, equals aggregate forecast Demand with respect to all entities for which the Scheduling Coordinator schedules in each Zone.[42]

In FERC proceedings investigating manipulation during the crisis, Utility D witnesses argued that schedules showing generation and loads up to 1,700 MW when its actual loads totaled on the order of 200–300 MW were legitimately balanced because it was predictable that their excess generation would always be taken due to underscheduling in the DA and HA markets.[43] This, they claimed, was true even if the generation did not serve entities for which Utility D acted as Scheduling Coordinator.[44] They also claimed that because "uninstructed imbalance energy" was defined in the tariff, it was appropriate to intentionally use it as an avenue into the RT Imbalance Energy market:

> ...there is nothing improper or fraudulent about a Scheduling Coordinator ("SC") such as [Utility D] seeking to make energy available at the Real Time [*sic*] Imbalance Energy market-clearing price as provided under the CAISO Tariff.[45]

Their defense was, "How could it be fraudulent to follow the letter of the tariff?" The FERC ultimately disagreed, calling this strategy a tariff violation, though it declined to assess penalties for any of these violations.[46] This conflict between rules-based (tariffs) and principles-based approaches to regulating behavior will be discussed in Chapter 8.

Another argument in defense of False Load transactions was that it was legitimate arbitrage. As noted in the Enron memo quoted earlier the intent was "...to arbitrage the DA price against the hour ahead or *ex-post* [*sic*] market." It is true that the scheme was a play of DA vs HA or RT prices, but it was not legitimate arbitrage for several reasons. False Load transactions violated express provisions of the CAISO tariff.[47] Suppliers intentionally falsified information required in schedules and bids submitted to the CAISO pursuant to the operational provisions of the CAISO tariff. This not only involved fraud, but it also undercut reliability in the CAISO as recognized by the Market Surveillance Committee (MSC) of the CAISO:

> Arbitrage trades, if they can be implemented without harming system reliability, can benefit the market and consumers. However, California's market rules make it impossible to execute arbitrage trades without also misrepresenting the state of physical resources being offered. The problems with such trades in California were created not by the arbitrage of prices, per se, but by the fact that such trades took the form of false schedules. The inaccuracy of schedules made it more costly for the ISO to maintain reliability.

---

42. *See* Taylor Testimony 2011, CAISO Tariff, Exh. No. CAX-100 at 2.2.7.2, pp. 28-29.

43. "Underscheduling" is a term reflecting the fact that the volume of generation and load cleared in the PX auction and scheduled by the PX with the CAISO was consistently below the expected load in the CAISO.

44. *See Answering Testimony of Dr. James L. Sweeney*, October 25, 2011, Exh. No. POW-233, p. 137.

45. *See Answering Testimony of Thomas M. Bechard*, October 25, 2011, Exh. No. POW-203, pp. 80-81.

46. *See* Gaming Order 2003, ¶60.

47. ***Id.***

* * *

> Operators cannot tell if the energy schedules submitted by a firm represent production and consumption decisions that it intends to undertake in real time or simply actions necessary to exploit profitable financial arbitrage opportunities across markets. Therefore, operators are often forced to acquire additional reserves or undertake other costly actions in order to reconcile ISO forecasts with the potential distorted schedules of market participants.[48]

In short the "arbitrage" was based upon fraud, and the fraud undercut efficient operation of the CAISO's system.[49]

Analysis of Fat Boy Transactions

The CAISO records contained detailed information on scheduled generation and actual metered loads for each scheduler as well as payments made to suppliers for uninstructed imbalances. Thus, it was necessary only to eliminate imbalances due to inadvertent error to determine when load was intentionally overscheduled. Inadvertent error was addressed in two ways. The first was simply to provide an error band of 10% above actual metered load. Since hour-ahead scheduling allowed adjustments for forecast error and all but last-minute outages, a 10% allowance was reasonable. As a second check, we considered the pattern of load overscheduling to assess whether or not it was intentional. Figure 7-2, which depicts the scheduled and actual metered load of Utility F, shows a pattern consistent with inadvertent error even though imbalances could be well above 10% of load when they did occur.

---

48. *Opinion on Oversight and Investigation Review* (Summary), Market Surveillance Committee of the California ISO, July 22, 2002, pp. 1, 10, *Prepared Rebuttal Testimony of Gerald A. Taylor*, EL00-95-249, Exh. No. CAX-167, March 2, 2012, (Exh. No. CAX-231).

49. False Load was not technically arbitrage, but rather speculation in which the supplier undertook the risk that the RT price would fall below the DA price. The fact that this speculation consistently paid off is a reflection of the fact that the RT price was artificially elevated by withholding activities discussed in Chapter 6. Additionally, the product requirements in DA and RT were different—energy purchased DA generally did not qualify for sale in RT as discussed earlier. This undercuts a basic premise of the arbitrage claim, that the product purchased in one market is legitimately salable in the other. Finally, the structure of the PX and ISO markets was inconsistent with the classical economic treatment of arbitrage. The retail load of the IOUs in California had to be met in the PX or through balancing energy acquired by the ISO in RT. False Load transactions took supply that would have been available to the IOUs from the PX and transferred it to RT, thus reducing the amount of load that could be covered by IOU purchases in the PX. As a result, these transactions, in addition to moving supply into RT, also moved additional demand (load) into RT, inhibiting price equilibration.

Figure 7-2

Utility F Scheduled and Metered Load Patterns Consistent with Random Load Forecast Error

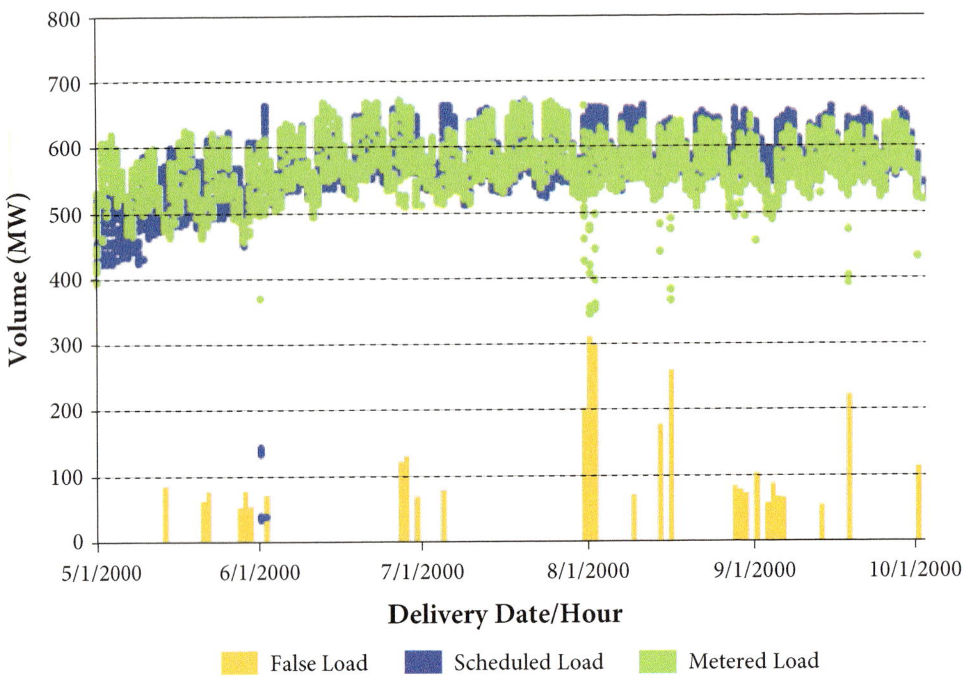

Notes:
[1]: False load is tabulated for hours when false load exceeds 10% of metered load
[2]: False load is calculated as the minimum of DA and HA false load

Utility F's load in the sample period varied from hour to hour over a range of around 150 to 200 MW daily, and generation generally matched as well. Imbalances occurred when metered load fell well below the typical range.

This pattern stands in stark contrast to that seen in Utility D overscheduling, depicted in Figure 7-3. Utility D's load was fixed in peak and off-peak periods as reflected in the straight green lines in the graphic,[50] and thus there is no question of forecast error. Its scheduled generation, however, rarely matched this fixed target and varied wildly, often exceeding the actual load by 400 MW or more. This picture suggests that rather than scheduling generation to meet the load that it expected to serve, Utility D traders "dummied up" load in its CAISO schedules to match the generation it wanted to dump into the RT energy market. This pattern was also seen in the scheduling of Enron and many other marketers.

50. Unlike Utility F, which met varying customer demand, Utility D served fixed loads under contracts with energy service providers. *See* Taylor Testimony 2011, Exh. Nos. CAX-075 and CAX-076.

Figure 7-3

Utility D — Scheduled and Metered Load Patterns Inconsistent with Random Load Forecast Error

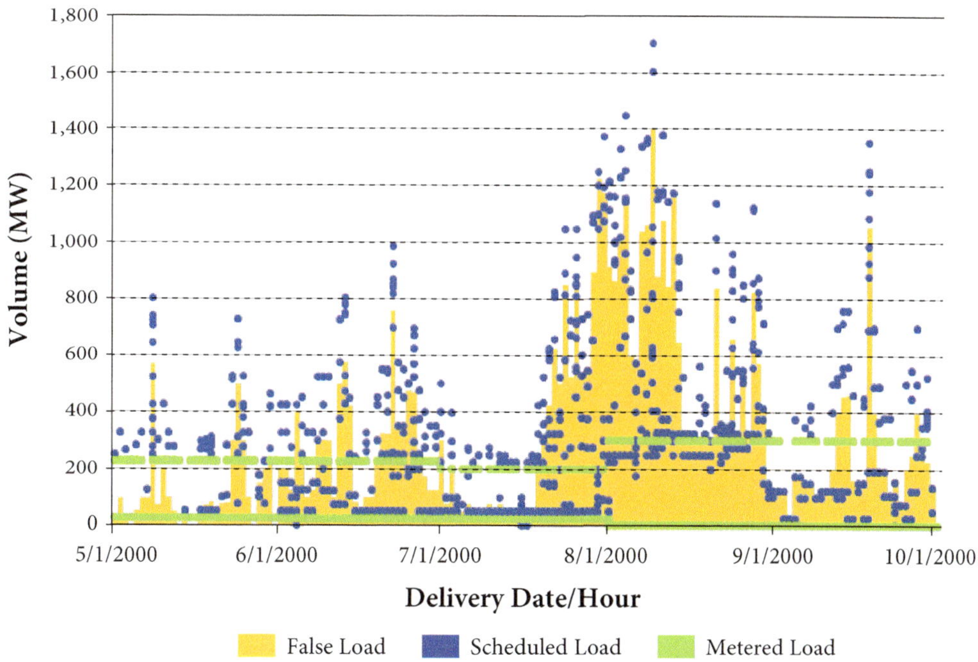

Notes:
[1]: False load is tabulated for hours when false load exceeds 10% of metered load
[2]: False load is calculated as the minimum of DA and HA false load

Another variant was consistently to schedule an amount well above expected load as shown in the trading of a small power marketer, Marketer C, depicted in Figure 7-4. Marketer C's scheduled a fixed amount of generation above the range of the load it actually served, yielding a small but constant stream of positive imbalances.

Figure 7-4

Marketer C — Scheduled and Metered Load Patterns Inconsistent with Random Load Forecast Error

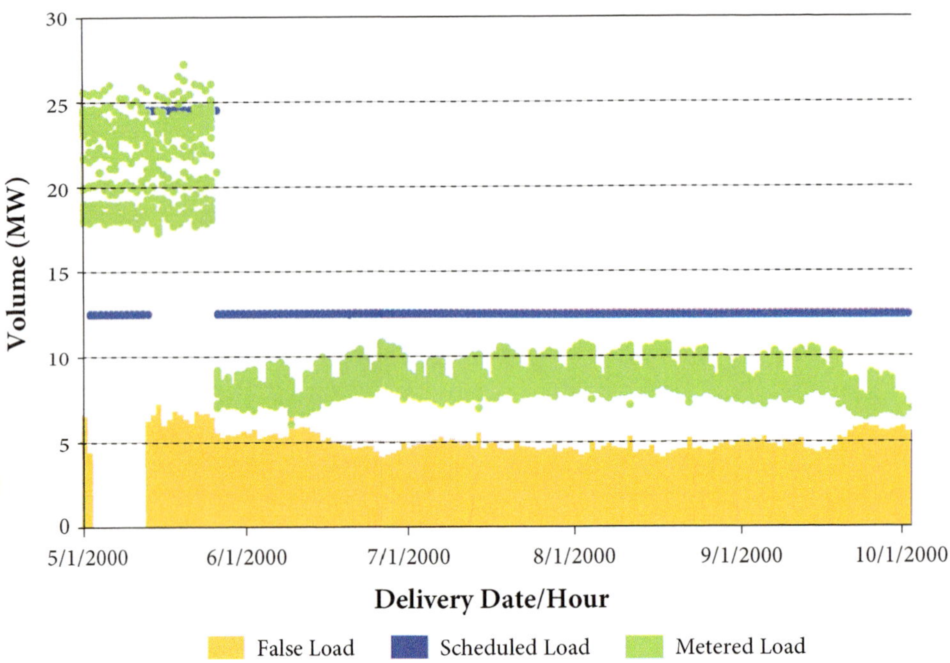

Such patterns allowed us to eliminate the possibility that the overscheduling of load was not the result of intentional misrepresentation in contravention of the tariff. Given the strength of the evidence, it is not surprising that suppliers generally did not deny the practice, but rather sought to justify it as beneficial for the CAISO or as a legitimate response to DA and HA scheduling by the IOUs.[51]

Like other manipulative schemes, the overall pattern of False Load activity is consistent with conditions in the CAISO as the Crisis progressed. False Load activity peaked in the late Summer and Fall as opportunities to double-dip in the ancillary services markets were reined back by changes in the CAISO Tariff. Use of the strategy declined rapidly at the end of 2000 as the deterioration of the CAISO's financial position raised the risk of non-payment, thus reducing the attractiveness of sales to the CAISO.

51. The Commission initially accepted such arguments in the Gaming Order, finding False Load a tariff violation, but choosing not to remedy it because of IOU "underscheduling." When the issue went to hearing, however, the ALJ found that the suppliers had failed to establish that False Load was in fact a response to IOU underscheduling. *See Initial Decision*, Docket No. EL00-95-248, 142 FERC ¶ 63,011, February 15, 2013.

Fraudulent Collection of Congestion Revenues

Because of the distribution of generation and seasonal variations in load, the transmission grid within the CAISO often hit its limits to move power generated in its southern zone to its northern zone where it was needed (or vice versa).[52] Such "congestion" caused prices in the two zones to diverge, and the CAISO established congestion charges for those using the transmission paths into the congested zone from the uncongested zone (i.e., from northern California to southern California when congestion limited southerly power flows). Suppliers creating "counterflows" in the opposite direction of the congestion (i.e., selling power sourced in southern California to northern California) were paid the congestion charge. Such congestion charges and payments were determined at the close of DA and HA scheduling based upon adjustment bids submitted to the CAISO by Scheduling Coordinators.[53]

Enron and other suppliers devised a number of ways to game the CAISO congestion management system to improperly receive congestion-related revenues. Death Star, or Circular Scheduling, is perhaps the most notorious of these fraud-based strategies, which also included Cut Schedules and Load Shift.

Death Star/Circular Scheduling

Death Star, Enron's name for what the Commission called Circular Scheduling, took advantage of power flow characteristics and the fact that the CAISO could only "see" the portions of a transmission path that were within its boundaries. The scheme involved scheduling a flow against congestion (a counterflow) on transmission within the CAISO and then completing a "loop" with a flow scheduled on transmission outside the CAISO. As explained in Enron's description of Death Star, "[t]he net effect of these transactions is that Enron gets paid for moving energy to relieve congestion without actually moving energy or relieving any congestion." In fact, Enron didn't need energy at all since the flows in a loop net to zero—the scheme was entirely a scheduling exercise. The apparent counterflows for which Enron was paid were completely fictitious, the product of fraudulent schedules with the CAISO and a transmission provider outside the CAISO.

52. Congestion occurred as well at the interfaces of the ISO constraining imports.

53. Adjustment bids were price/volume pairs that expressed the willingness of market participants to increase or decrease their generation or load schedules. *See* discussion in Chapter 4.

Figure 7-5

The Forney Perpetual Loop

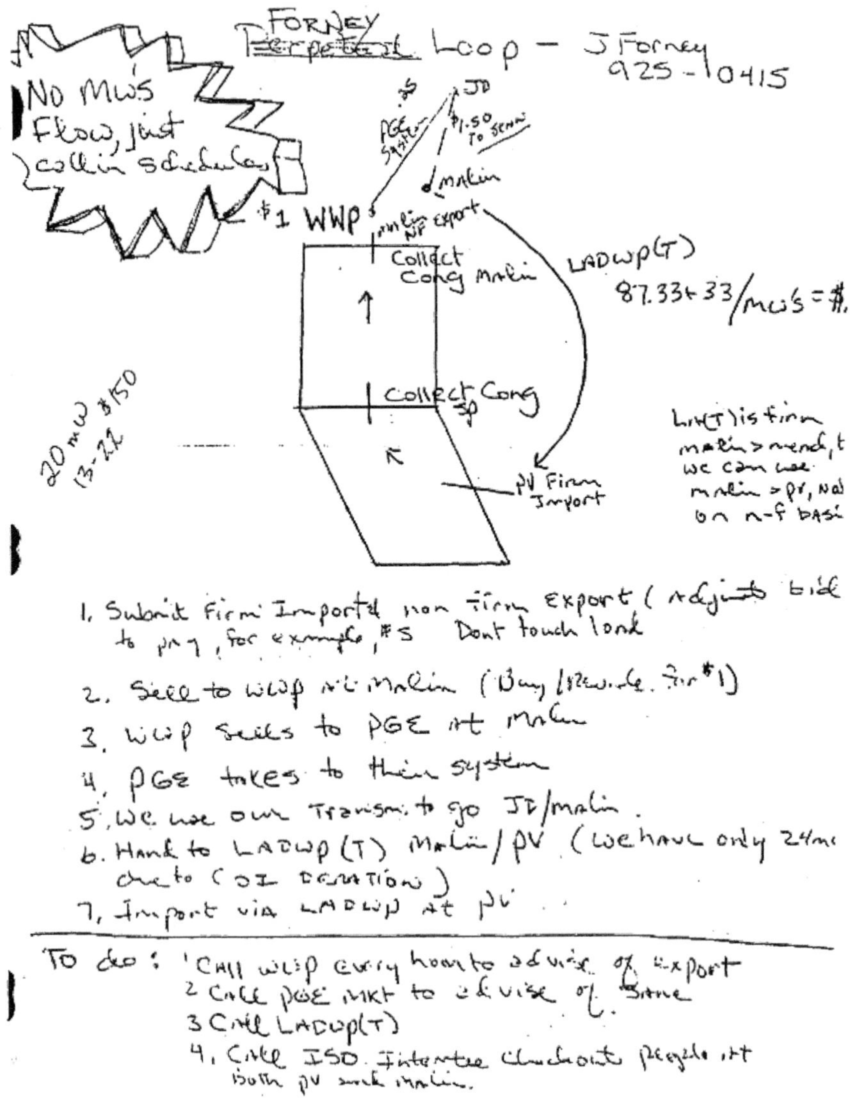

An example of a Death Star transaction is the "Forney Perpetual Loop," which was implemented in early May 2000, just as the Crisis began.[54] As set out in Figure 7-5,[55] Enron first created an apparent flow against north-to-south congestion in the CAISO by scheduling an

54. *See Prepared Direct Testimony of Dr. Peter Fox-Penner,* Docket Nos. EL00-95-000 *et al.,* February 25, 2003, Exh. No. CA-1, (Exh. No. CA-145, pp. 624-25) (hereinafter Fox-Penner Testimony 2003).

55. This is a reproduction of John Forney's hand-written notes on how to execute the Death Star Loop. The authors' interpretation of this difficult to decipher script is provided at the end of this chapter.

import to the CAISO at Palo Verde (PV) and an export at Malin. Enron then did a sale/repurchase transaction with Washington Water and Power (WWP, now Avista), which took the "energy" at Malin and returned it to Enron for a $1 fee at Portland General Electric's (PGE) system.[56] With PGE it did another sale/repurchase at a $.90 differential, receiving the energy at John Day where Enron had transmission back to Malin. From Malin, Enron used LADWP transmission to schedule the energy back to its supposed origin at PV. Mr. Forney's notes on the scheme contain a highlighted entry: "No MW's flow, just call in schedules."[57] Scheduling the transmission did involve some costs, the dollar to Avista, $.90 to PGE, $1.50 for the use of its own transmission rights and $3.50 to $4.50 for the LADWP transmission. As noted in the Enron memo, however, "[b]ecause the congestion charges have been as high as $750/MW,"[58] it would generally be profitable to incur minor costs to collect the congestion payments.

A legacy feature of the CAISO system that facilitated Circular Scheduling was the Existing Transmission Capacity (ETC) held by many municipal utility systems in California. At the formation of the CAISO, many municipal utilities held rights on the PG&E and SCE transmission systems. Even though the IOUs turned over management of their transmission systems to the CAISO upon its formation, the ETCs were retained by the municipal systems and did not fall under CAISO supervision. Thus there were segments of transmission paths that were "outside" the CAISO regardless of the fact that they were physically within CAISO boundaries. These ETC paths were as invisible to the CAISO as transmission outside California, and thus they created opportunities for Circular Schedules that were entirely within CAISO boundaries.

It is thus not surprising that Enron sought alliances with California's many municipal systems to execute Circular Schedules. Like Death Star, these arrangements were often assigned colorful names reflecting Enron's municipal partner. "Red Congo" was the label for the Circular Scheduling strategy Enron arranged with the municipal utility for Redding, California. Its arrangement with the Northern California Power Agency was called "NCPA Cong Catcher." In such arrangements Enron typically secured the transmission on an "as available" basis for a small fee and a share of any profits from the Circular Schedule. Enron's many alliances like these help explain how manipulative schemes became quickly known in the trading community. The easy money made the willingness of many to ally with Enron understandable.

Enron was not the only marketer that grasped the potential of alliances with the municipal utilities. In particular, there is evidence that Marketer B, the trading arm of a major petroleum firm discussed earlier, took advantage of this opportunity through arrangements with the utilities serving California municipalities.

56. PGE was owned by Enron, and the transaction with Avista was necessary to avoid the FERC's prohibition against dealing directly with an affiliate.

57. John Forney was the manager of Enron's West Power Real-Time Trading Desk during the Crisis and involved in many of Enron's manipulative strategies. He was indicted for Wire Fraud and Conspiracy to Commit Wire Fraud for Enron trading schemes including Get Shorty, Death Star, and Ricochet. *See* Taylor Testimony 2011, Exh. No. CAX-106, pp. 1-11.

58. *See* Taylor Testimony 2011, Enron Memo, December 6, 2000, Exh. No. CAX-013, p. 3.

Death Star Analyses

Since Death Star started with a flow scheduled into the CAISO at one point and out at another, the first step in our analysis was to identify wheels through the CAISO that received congestion payments. This was the easy part. The next step was investigating whether or not this was part of a Death Star loop. There were two approaches for verifying the loops. The first was supplier documents. Enron traders kept what were called "inc" sheets for each transaction. These sheets sometimes included labels such as "Death Star" or "Perpetual Loop." Enron transactions were also recorded in a database called *Enpower*, and the comments section of each entry included notations on the type of the transaction, such as "NCPA Cong" or "Project Death Star." Traders also occasionally signaled Death Star transactions in the names they self-assigned to interchange schedules they filed with the CAISO. An Enron interchange ID on an import schedule might be "EPMI_CISO_DEATH" and a simultaneous export schedule in the same amount, "EPMI_CISO_STAR". Examples of these names are shown in Table 7-2. Other suppliers also used descriptive interchange IDs like "SCEM LOOPY" for imports and exports in apparent Death Star transactions.[59]

Table 7-2

Examples of Enron's Interchange IDs Death Star Transactions

			Export Details				Import Details			
Date	Hour	Mkt Type	Tie Point	INTERCHG ID	Energy Type	MW	Tie Point	INTERCHG ID	Energy Type	MW
6/14/2000	14	H	MALIN_5_RNDMTN	EPMI_STAR	NFRM	-19	MEAD_2_WALC	EPMI_DEATH	FIRM	19
6/15/2000	12	H	MALIN_5_RDNMTN	EPMI_DISO_DEATH	NFRM	-20	PVERDE_5_DEVERS	CISO_EPMI_STAR	FIRM	20
7/10/2000	18	H	MALIN_5_RDNMTN	CISO_CISO_ERNIE	NFRM	-35	PVERDE_5_DEVERS	EPMI_CISO_BERT	FIRM	35
7/24/2000	14	H	MALIN_5_RDNMTN	EPMI_CISO_BIRD	NFRM	-10	MEAD_2_WALC	EPMI_CISO_BIG	FIRM	10
7/26/2000	12	H	MALIN_5_RDNMTN	CISO_EPMI_GEORGE	NFRM	-10	PVERDE_5_DEVERS	EPMI_CISO_CURIOUS	FIRM	10
11/5/2000	22	H	FCORNR_5_PSUEDO	EPMI_CISO_FORD	WHEEL	-50	PVERDE_5_DEVERS	EPMI_CISO_FORD	WHEEL	50
12/19/200	13	H	FCORNR_5_PSUEDO	EPMI_CISO_SCOUT	WHEEL	-50	MALIN_5_RNDMTN	EPMI_CISO_SCOUT	WHEEL	50

A second approach involved reviewing transmission data for movements that, when combined with the congestion relieving wheel through the CAISO, completed a loop. During most of the course of our investigation information on transmission use was available only from LADWP and PG&E.[60] Because PG&E scheduled transmission for ETC holders on its system, its transmission data covered the municipal utilities in the north that Enron and others used for Death Star schedules. This allowed identification/verification of such transactions with municipalities.

Many municipal systems in Southern California had rights on the LADWP transmission network. Among these was the SC Muni discussed earlier. This municipal utility had an alliance agreement with Marketer B through which the parties shared the profits from trading

59. *See* Fox-Penner Testimony 2003, Exh. No. CA-2, Appendix E.

60. Information from BPA was obtained late the litigation process, by which time Death Star was no longer relevant either because of the scope of the proceeding or the fact that the Respondents remaining in the proceedings were not alleged to have engaged in the strategy.

activities, one of which appears consistent with Death Star. When LADWP transmission data were linked to the CAISO data on wheels that collected congestion, numerous loops are detected at the Mead and Sylmar interfaces between the LADWP and CAISO systems.[61] While these transactions were generally small in volume, averaging slightly over 20 MW, the congestion revenues collected averaged $136 per MW. After accounting for transmission costs and CAISO charges, Marketer B and the SC Muni would have netted over $100 per MW for doing nothing but scheduling. No generation/energy was even needed.

Cut Schedules

The Cut Schedule strategy simply took advantage of the fact that the CAISO accounting system determined congestion payments based upon DA and HA schedules rather than actual flows of energy. Enron simply scheduled a non-firm export with the CAISO against congestion on a constrained transmission path, waited until the CAISO had determined congestion payments and then cut (rescinded) the export schedule. Since the CAISO accounting system did not go back and adjust for schedule changes after its initial calculation, Enron got paid for relieving congestion, but had no intention of fulfilling the schedule filed with the CAISO. This was a blatant fraud.

Unlike other strategies like Death Star, the Cut Schedule scheme was fairly easy to detect. In August 2000 the CAISO issued a notice specifically prohibiting this practice, and Enron along with other generators ceased using it. We have included it only to illustrate how tariffs and system architecture and operation can create opportunities for manipulation that are open to almost any supplier in the market. Market power is not required. One needs only the willingness to engage in simple but carefully crafted deception.

Load Shift

In the Load Shift Scheme, the supplier used False Load either to create congestion or to create the appearance of counterflows to relieve congestion. The description Load Shift in the Enron Memos actually included both of these approaches. Because False Load was completely fictitious, it could be located or moved arbitrarily to the supplier's benefit. If a supplier had load points in NP15 and in SP15, it could manipulate False Load schedules to affect congestion. If there were north-to-south congestion, for example, a supplier could overschedule to load in

61. *Declaration of Gerald A. Taylor Re: Proposed Settlement with Coral Power L.L.C.* Docket No. EL03-151-000 and Docket No. EL03-186-000, December 4, 2003, Attachment C, Table 2.

SP15 and increase congestion. If the supplier had Firm Transmission Rights (FTRs), it would receive congestion payments for them.[62]

The supplier could also "shift" load by reducing load overscheduled in SP15 and at the same time overscheduling or increasing an overschedule in NP15. This shifting of imaginary loads created a fictitious counterflow that would be awarded congestion revenues. The supplier could lower and raise its load arbitrarily in this fashion without consequence because the originally-scheduled amount in SP15 was far in excess of what was needed to serve that load point. Thus, there was no load that went unserved by the change in schedules. The only difference to anyone in this example (other than the collection of congestion revenues) would be that the imbalance created by the False Load would show up in NP15 rather than SP15.[63] Another version of this variant was simply to schedule generation or an import in the congested zone to serve false load in the uncongested zone.[64] With north-to-south congestion, one would simply schedule a generation source in SP15 to serve false load in NP15.

The gaming that was undertaken through shifting False Load is amply illustrated by an excerpt from communication among Utility D traders:

> Overscheduled at NP15 and SP15 as attached. All overschedule from system is coming in via NOB. . . Splits throughout the day today.
>
> We are heavily overscheduled in SP, congestion NP to SP. You could try and reduce load in NP and take up load in SP in hours that they are likely to split (HD 14, 16-18) for less than $200 bucks and capture the higher BEEP in the South or, if congestion prices remain really high, then perhaps reduce your SP load and send it north to grab some of that juicy congestion.[65]

Utility D had filed False Load schedules in both SP15 and NP15, but predominantly the former. It was expecting the Path 15 to become constrained north-to-south, thus splitting the CAISO into two differently-priced zones, and creating higher prices in the SP15 zone. If the difference in the RT prices was greater than congestion charges over Path 15, Utility D intended to shift more false load from NP15 to SP15 to take advantage of the RT price differential. If congestion prices remained high (that is, higher than the NP/SP price differential), then Utility D would lower its overschedule in SP15 and increase its overschedule in NP15, creating a fictitious flow

62. FTRs hedged the holder against congestion charges by paying the holder the congestion charge for each MW of FTR. Thus, when the FTR holder took advantage of the FTR to schedule into the congested zone, the congestion charges incurred for the MW scheduled in were covered by the FTR payment. When the holder did not schedule into the congested zone, it nevertheless received the congestion payments. Thus, the holder of 1000 MW of FTRs that scheduled 200 MW into the congested zone (thus increasing congestion) netted congestion payments on 800 MW of FTRs.

63. The imbalance would thus garner the NP-15 *ex-post* imbalance energy price rather than that for SP15.

64. As discussed later in Chapter 8, the Commission for some reason failed to recognize the second variant of Load Shift. Thus its definition required the ownership of FTRs, and it missed the much more prevalent version that required no FTRs.

65. Utility D Notes to Real time for Tuesday, July 22, 2000, *See* Taylor Testimony 2011, Exh. No. CAX-024. "BEEP" refers to the formal names for RT prices, the Balancing *Ex-Post* Energy Price.

against congestion that would capture the "juicy" congestion price.[66] Because the loads were not really there, they could be changed arbitrarily to suit Utility D's interests. All this shifting, of course, meant that the CAISO was getting unreliable signals as to what to expect in managing California's transmission system. The cavalier trader attitude toward these schedules upon which the CAISO was relying underscores their entirely fictitious, fraudulent character.

The second variant on Load Shift, scheduling generation in the congested zone across a congested interface to False Load in the uncongested zone, was explained in a document outlining possible profitable strategies that Marketer B could pursue with its alliance partner, SC Muni:

> ...Inside the ISO, you can take [SC Muni] supplied power via an SC-to-SC transfer in South Path, move it to North Path (against congestion) and park it on a [Marketer B] Load ID. [SC Muni] would earn the congestion payment and any gain (or loss) on the power from being paid the Decremental Price in NP15.

Here Marketer B takes energy generated by SC Muni via an SC to SC trade in SP15, and then Marketer B schedules it against congestion to False Load at a point in NP15 where Marketer B is qualified to serve load. The false "counterflow" collects a congestion payment, and the resulting False Load overscheduled in NP15 collects the RT *ex-post* (decremental) price for NP15.

Analysis of Load Shift

Detailed CAISO data on schedules, metered load, and congestion payments for counterflows and FTRs permitted analysis of cases in which a supplier used False Load to increase congestion in order to increase the payments to its unused FTRs or create false counterflows that would reap congestion payments. The signature of a FTR benefit strategy was the scheduling of false load in the congested zone into which the scheduler held FTRs. Alternatively, the signature of a congestion-garnering false counterflow was scheduling or increasing False Load in the uncongested zone and scheduling generation or decreasing False Load in the congested zone. Consequently, we reviewed CAISO schedule and congestion data for these signatures.

Enron, consistent with the description in the Enron Memos, used both of these approaches, sometimes in combination. It appears that Enron employed versions of Load Shift in 1998 and 1999, but used it most heavily over the period May through December of 2000, after which the CAISO could not be counted upon to make congestion payments due to its precarious financial state. Other suppliers that appear to have engaged in Load Shift transactions were Marketer B and Utility D.

Our analysis revealed possible Load Shift transactions by Utility D and Marketer B consistent with the descriptions in their documents quoted earlier. The data indicate that Utility D gained over $10 million shifting more than 98,000 MW of False Load generally south-to-north

66. When advance power schedules are changed, the difference between the flows under the old and new schedules was treated by the ISO as a new flow of power entitled to congestion payments.

against congestion from May through September of 2000.[67] Similarly, Marketer B appears to have received payments of about $1.9 million by scheduling 18,285 MW of generation in SP15 to load falsely overscheduled in NP15 against congestion in July, August, and September 2000.[68] These schemes appear to have netted more than $100 per MW by doing nothing but shifting the location of their fictitious load.

Fraudulent Sales of Ancillary Services/Get Shorty

We have already discussed improper entry into the ancillary services markets using False Export. There were other avenues to game the ancillary services market through misrepresentation. An ancillary services sale is very like the sale of an option. In the two part ancillary services bid, the capacity price is analogous to the option price with the energy price as the strike price. If the capacity bid were taken, the offer to deliver the energy might or might not be exercised. If the energy portion of the bid was then "exercised" by the CAISO, the supplier with capacity would simply generate the requisite electricity for delivery.[69]

The manipulation consisted of Enron submitting bids to make capacity available when it had no available generation, similar to a short sale (hence, Enron's name for this strategy: Get Shorty).[70] If the bid was selected by the CAISO, Enron looked for a way to cover its commitment to generate energy by quickly covering its "short" position.

An Enron email dated January 11, 2000 outlines the approach:

> As of last Friday Enron has decided to undertake a more aggressive strategy in <u>bidding spin</u>. Currently are employing this strategy with [SC Muni] only, but this might change going forward. The strategy is as follows:
>
> Enron is essentially going short spin by bidding volumes into the day-ahead market which [*sic*] [SC Muni] does not necessarily have. We are doing so at a high <u>capacity price</u>. If we get awarded we will look to fill the short in one of three ways:
>
> 1. Go to [SC Muni] and see if they can absorb the short (this can be done by reallocating their Hoover allocation—they probably can absorb up to 15 MW)
> 2. Purchase spin from LA for $5 (this is the going rate no matter what is going on in the ISO).
> 3. Buy back the AS from the ISO in the hour-ahead market—This is usually the best option after [SC Muni] absorbs what it can. The reason for this is that the Hour

67. *See* Taylor Testimony 2011, Exh. No. CAX-001, Table V-10, p. 132.
68. *Id.*, Table V-11, p. 137.
69. Typically the energy portion of the bid would cover their marginal costs of supplying the energy.
70. This strategy was also called "Phantom Ancillary Services" or "Paper Trading."

> Ahead market has been noticeably dilapidated (this is a John Forney word) versus the day ahead price and hence there should be an arbitrage opportunity.[71]

When its bid was taken and it needed to supply energy, Enron could seek coverage from its alliance partner, SC Muni, purchase spin bilaterally from LADWP, or it could purchase spinning reserves in the HA ancillary services market. Ancillary services prices in the HA market were typically below those in the DA market ("dilapidated"), so this provided an often profitable gamble.

There were also other options for addressing short sales. Since calls on energy from Replacement Reserves obligations allowed an hour to make delivery, the short seller, instead of purchasing capacity to cover its obligation, could use the hour to make arrangements for energy.[72] Communications among Utility D traders provide an example:

> I oversold by 50 MW our replacement [reserves] schedule at Mead. Please either cut or try to re-supply the 25 MW we are short at Mead. The other 25 MW can come from our overschedule at Mead that Michelle is having put in HE 1-24.[73] [Material in brackets added.]

Here 25 MW of the 50 MW sold short could be covered by redirecting energy already scheduled to False Load that was being supplied via an import through the CAISO interface at Mead. That left 25 MW to be found to bring Utility D back in line with its obligations.

Of course, when the CAISO did not call, Enron did nothing and kept the capacity payment—it had succeeded in "going naked" on an option. The risk of going naked on short sales in this fashion was reduced by putting a high price on the energy component of the ancillary service bid. This type of price management is reflected in a Utility D trader message:

> Replacement Reserves at COB, NOB, PV, Mead and Cascade in some hours. Energy price is at $500 (no price taker), see attached, except for HE 15-17 at -500 to get hit. We already have a partial dispatch from CALPX in these hours.
>
> Note that we are overscheduled on our PV TX [transmission] if we get hit for the energy on the repl. [replacement reserve] schedules at PV HE 14-16. Therefore do not reduce price of energy in these hours, unless you are confident you can resupply in those hours via other sources.[74] [Material in brackets added.]

---

71. *See* Taylor Testimony 2004, Exh. No. CP-8, p. 2; *Testimony of Paul G.Scheuerman*, September 2, 2003, Exh. No. GLN-16.

72. This ploy was not feasible with spinning and non-spinning reserves commitments because these required that energy be deliverable within ten minutes of being called upon.

73. [Utility D] Notes to Real Time for September 18, 2000, *see* Taylor Testimony 2011, Exh. No. CAX-024, p. 10.

74. [Utility D] Notes to Real Time for July 12, 2000, *see* Taylor Testimony 2011, Exh. No. CAX-024, p. 2.

The bids at the then applicable price cap of $500 were obviously intended to discourage the CAISO from using the energy. Conversely, the negative cap bids of -$500 were price-taker bids that would almost certainly be taken (hit) by the CAISO.[75]

Such short sales are the antithesis of the reliable capacity commitments the CAISO was seeking and the CAISO tariff required in ancillary services transactions. The CAISO needed capacity reserves that would meet WSPP reliability standards, not mere contractual commitments to supply energy on short notice. Thus it was nothing short of fraud to bid into the CAISO's ancillary services markets without capacity procured in advance and available with a high degree of certainty, as required by the tariff.

The CAISO recognized that Paper Trading was a tariff violation with a negative impact on its ability to manage system reliability and costs:

> By reducing the ISO's ability to reliably manage the grid, it clearly constitutes taking unfair advantage of the rules and procedures set forth in the ISO tariff in a manner that may have the effect of, or potential for, undermining the efficiency, workability and reliability of the ISO Markets. ISO Tariff MMIP 2.3.23 (description of anomalous behavior subject to sanctions including fines or suspensions).[76]

Analysis of Fraudulent Ancillary Services Sales

The CAISO provided data on DA and HA sales into the ancillary services markets. Comparison of DA and HA sales indicated when suppliers had substituted another supplier for the DA ancillary services commitment by buying in the HA market.[77] This allowed assessment of the pattern of buybacks to see if they were consistent with a conscious buy-back strategy. One can determine whether or not a supplier consistently buys back its DA ancillary services commitments or whether or not its behavior when it buys back its commitments differs markedly from periods when it does not make such buybacks.

In the period leading up to the Crisis, Enron appears to be the only supplier engaging in Get Shorty transactions, buying back over 50 percent of its DA ancillary services commitments. From May through September of 2000 Enron appears to have been joined by Marketer A and Marketer B in buying back a large percentage of DA commitments in a significant number of hours. In the period from the beginning of October 2000 running through January 17, 2001, when CERS stepped into the picture, Marketer B and Marketer A were the principal short

75. Utility D and other suppliers wanted to avoid the impression that they did not really intend to supply on their ancillary services bids, so they ensured that their bids were occasionally taken.

76. *Request for Rehearing and/or Clarification of the California Independent System Operator Corporation,* Docket No. EL03-137-000, *et al.*, July 25, 2003, p. 17 ("ISO Rehearing").

77. HA bids were then checked to ensure that the AS buy-backs were intentional rather than the result of some unforeseen condition on the transmission system.

sellers of ancillary services, with Enron buying back a low percentage of its commitments in only a few hours.

During this later period, Marketer B bought back literally all of its DA ancillary services commitments. This seems incredible enough to call into question the validity of our interpretation of Marketer B's intent in making the capacity bids. However, conversations among Marketer B's traders leave little doubt about what they intended and that they were incredulous about being able to get away with selling capacity they did not have. This is evident in a recording dated April 8, 2000:

Tobin:	We probably made a...made about a quarter million today.
Female Voice:	Again!
Tobin:	Yeah, so we're up about—we're up—
Female Voice:	Is this the million we—
Tobin:	Same thing, no, same lead.
Female Voice:	Buying—
Tobin:	Buying the hour ahead—selling the day ahead, going short, and then buying back the hour that's—
Female Voice:	Is like—ISO know all this or...
Tobin:	It's candy from a baby. I don't know—I don't know—
Female Voice:	I mean—
Tobin:	It's funny like that isn't it?
Female Voice:	It is funny. It's like ISO—I mean, don't they get what we're doing or—
Tobin:	Well—
Female Voice:	—are they like just don't care?
	***
Tobin:	So, you know, when you think about it, if we're buying back even anything, we're giving them money back and short—and giving them back money for something that they didn't need as badly as they thought, so—
Female Voice:	Yeah, but—yeah, but that doesn't tell them, like, maybe we don't have this shit?
Tobin:	Who cares?
Female Voice:	Who cares?
Tobin:	That doesn't matter.
Female Voice:	Cool.[78]

Although bemused, the Marketer B traders appeared not to care that they were essentially committing fraud.

78. This conversation, recorded on a Marketer B line the afternoon of April 8, 2000. The written transcript does not convey the dismay in the female traders' voice. *See* Taylor Testimony 2011, Exh. No. CAX-067, pp. 9-11.

APPENDIX 7-1

Figure 7-6
The Forney Perpetual Loop

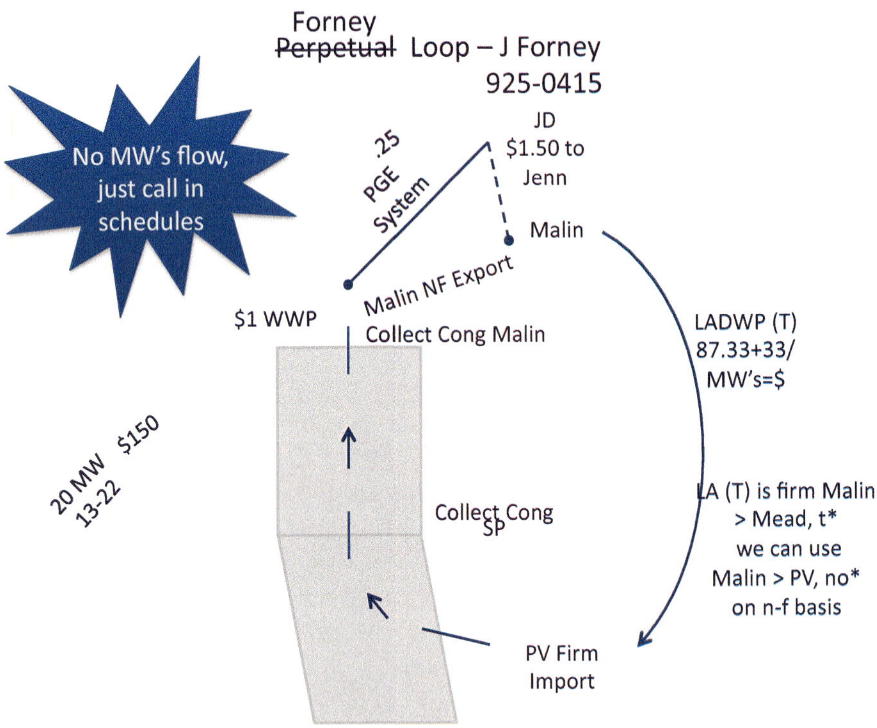

1. Submit firm import & non firm export (adjust bid to pay, for example, $5 don't touch load
2. Sell to WWP at Malin (buy/resale for $1)
3. WWP sells to PGE at Malin
4. PGE takes to their system
5. We use our transmi to go JD/Malin
6. Hand to LADWP (T) Malin/PV (we have only 24 MW due to COI deration)
7. Import via LADWP at PV

To do: 1. Call WWP every hour to advise of export
2. Call PGE mkt to advise of same
3. Call LADWP (T)
4. Call ISO Intertie check out people at both PV and Malin

**words cut off on original image.*

CHAPTER 8

REGULATORY HANDICAPS THEN AND NOW

Chapter 4's recounting of the Commission's efforts to deal with the Crisis in the western power markets reveals that it faced numerous challenges. Some of these were simply the product of the time. California's bold experiment in deregulation was just that, an initial stab at a very complex endeavor. It was on the bleeding edge. The market design was a political compromise that forced the IOUs to buy and sell in the PX and CAISO, which became susceptible to manipulation and lacked price mitigation mechanisms. The Commission had not prepared itself to monitor markets closely or to address rapidly escalating and damaging market dysfunction. It had not progressed beyond market power concepts to develop an appreciation for other types of manipulative behavior that could destabilize electric power systems. There were mixed signals, with many indicia pointing to scarcity and poor market design as the causes of the Crisis, and the Commission needed to be cautious about moving hastily and too zealously against suppliers lest they recoil from further investment in needed generation facilities.

In the decade since the Crisis, we have gained much valuable experience, and many of these problems have been addressed and corrected. There have also been developments that improve the situation such as better market designs with automatic price mitigation procedures, expanded authority and remedial power for the FERC and other agencies to address manipulation, and dedicated monitoring and enforcement resources. However, even today, it appears the Commission may be handicapped in ways reminiscent of its situation at the time of the Crisis. These handicaps are worth considering as a prelude to discussing how best to move forward now with approaches for constraining manipulation in electric power and other commodity markets. For example, as discussed in Chapter 3 and borne out in the recent flurry of enforcement actions, electric power and natural gas markets remain quite vulnerable to manipulation. Here we address other potential problems.

Vagueness: Manipulation versus Pornography

Some concepts are difficult to pin down. Justice Potter Stewart once famously declined to define hard-core pornography precisely but observed: "But I know it when I see it."[1] The FERC found itself in somewhat similar territory in responding to the revelations in the Enron memos regarding manipulative strategies. The provisions upon which the FERC relied in concluding that Enron-type manipulations violated the PX and CAISO Tariffs, identified as "practices subject to scrutiny" both "anomalous market behavior" and "gaming" are set out in the sidebar.

Anomalous market behavior was defined as any behavior departing significantly from that observed in normal, competitive markets, and a list of five examples was provided. Of these, three, withholding of generation, unusual redeclarations of generation, and excessive bidding (or pricing) all deal with traditional market power. The other two examples were "*unusual* trades" and, "*unusual* activity...relating to imports from or exports to other markets...." So, aside from traditional exercises of market power, "unusual" was the standard for proscribed behavior. As a legal standard, unfortunately, "unusual," like "beauty," is often in the eyes of the beholder.

Gaming, according to the tariff, was taking unfair advantage of tariff rules, or transmission constraints when they are binding or other system conditions that may render the markets vulnerable to price manipulation to the detriment of market efficiency. But the argument of many suppliers was that strategies like Load Shift, Fat Boy, and Get Shorty were *promoting* efficient operation of the system by arbitraging price differences, thus driving the energy and ancillary services markets toward equilibrium.

Rather than giving more clarity to these definitions, the Commission chose instead to judge whether or not the specific strategies described in the Enron memos violated the MMIP. Even though it recognized consistently that a critical element of many of the Enron practices it condemned was making false representations to the CAISO to gain advantage, the Commission declined to state this as a guiding principle in defining proscribed behavior. This left the Commission clinging to technical distinctions devoid of any economic logic. For example, California energy "ricocheted" off a third party and sold to the CAISO misrepresented as an import would not be considered a False Import violation by the Commission unless it were sold at a price above the CAISO price cap. However, bouncing energy off another control area to gain a fallacious import designation was highly profitable when the eventual sale simply garnered the artificially inflated real-time price, regardless of whether or not that price had reached the cap. Enron's own description of the strategy unequivocally identifies that a sale at the real-time price was the stratagem's objective, as explained in Chapter 7. Gaining improper access to the RT and ancillary services through fraud was the essence of the violation.

1. *Jacobellis v. Ohio*, 378 U.S. 184 (1964). *See* Justice Potter Stewart's concurring opinion regarding possible obscenity in a motion picture.

MMIP 2.1.1 Anomalous Market Behavior

Anomalous market behavior, which is defined as behavior that departs significantly from the normal behavior in competitive markets that do not require continuing regulation or as behavior leading to unusual or unexplained market outcomes. Evidence of such behavior may be derived from a number of circumstances, including:

- **MMIP 2.1.1.1** withholding of Generation capacity under circumstances in which it would normally be offered in a competitive market;
- **MMIP 2.1.1.2** unexplained or unusual redeclarations of availability by Generators;
- **MMIP 2.1.1.3** unusual trades or transactions;
- **MMIP 2.1.1.4** pricing and bidding patterns that are inconsistent with prevailing supply and demand conditions, e.g., prices and bids that appear consistently excessive for or otherwise inconsistent with such conditions; and
- **MMIP 2.1.1.5** unusual activity or circumstances relating to imports from or exports to other markets or exchanges.

MMIP 2.1.3 Gaming

"Gaming," or taking unfair advantage of the rules and procedures set forth in the PX or ISO Tariffs, Protocols or Activity Rules, or of transmission constraints in periods in which exist substantial Congestion, to the detriment of the efficiency of, and of consumers in, the ISO Markets. "Gaming" may also include taking undue advantage of other conditions that may affect the availability of transmission and generation capacity, such as loop flow, facility outages, level of hydropower output or seasonal limits on energy imports from out-of-state, or actions or behaviors that may otherwise render the system and the ISO Markets vulnerable to price manipulation to the detriment of their efficiency.

A similar, overly narrow view shows up in the FERC's treatment of Enron's Load Shift, for which it required seller gains to be derived from revenues to unused FTRs when the documents show that congestion revenues from falsely scheduled counterflows were profitable even without the seller owning FTRs, as also previously discussed.

The narrowness of these definitions, however, was only part of the problem caused by reliance upon the Enron memos as the guide to manipulative activity. Also of concern is behavior that was *not addressed in the memos at all.* The memos do not discuss, for example, congestion plays like the "Silver Peak" incident on May 24, 1999. In this episode Enron scheduled a flow of 2,900 MW over an import point with a capacity of only 15 MW in order to force the CAISO to implement congestion management procedures that ultimately raised prices in the PX. Other suppliers employed similar strategies, for instance, intentionally overloading the CAISO's transmission links in the north leaving the CAISO with no choice but to take their high-priced generation offered at CAISO interfaces in the south. As with the Silver Peak gambit, there was no intention of ever executing the initially scheduled flow that created congestion; it was done specifically to support a beneficial outcome at another interface with the CAISO. Because the Commission had no clear, guiding theory of manipulation, such behavior was not scrutinized. Manipulative schemes took many forms and were developed by numerous suppliers. Enron had no monopoly on manipulation, and the Commission's reliance upon the Enron memos as its road map left many potentially fruitful investigative routes untraveled.

Tariffs vs General Prescriptions

The rules and rates that traditionally governed transactions between a regulated utility company and its customers were set out in detailed tariffs that were oriented toward restraining market power in franchised monopoly markets. Tariffs describe in detail procedures for operations and for dealing with customers and regulators and the types of services offered and their prices. They are understood to put the utility on notice very specifically as to what it can and cannot do. The FERC-approved CAISO Tariff and its associated protocols at the time of the Crisis totaled nearly 1,500 pages.

Anti-manipulation provisions in the law, on the other hand, can typically be set out on a single page and make no attempt comprehensively to enumerate proscribed behaviors. They focus instead upon the fraudulent nature and elements of undesirable activities. The anomalous market behavior and gaming provisions of the MMIP of the PX and CAISO tariffs had this sort of orientation.

These two approaches, one arising from regulated monopolies and the other from presumably competitive markets, do not necessarily merge comfortably in hybrid, liberalized electricity and natural gas markets. Suppliers, in fact, argued that the MMIP was too vague to give them fair notice of what behaviors would justify the Commission ordering them to disgorge their profits.[2] Although the Commission rejected this argument, the conflict between specific tariff provisions and the general descriptions of the MMIP continued to spur debate throughout the Crisis-related proceedings.

2. Federal Energy Regulatory Commission (FERC). *Order to Show Cause Concerning Gaming and/or Anomalous Market Behavior, Docket No. EL03-137-000, et al.*, June 2003, ¶ 21.

As discussed earlier,[3] this type of conflict arose over the "balanced schedule" provision at the heart of the False Load scheme. Utility D traders testified that by submitting schedules to the CAISO that had equal amounts of generation and load they were complying with the very specific scheduling requirements of the tariff. In contrast, the anomalous market behavior and gaming provisions of the MMIP were vague—too vague, they claimed—to be the basis for any remedial action.[4]

Trader attitudes toward generalized values of right and wrong were candidly explained by the CEO of Utility D:

> All of our traders are incented to make money. They look for opportunities. Some call it gaming; we say it's playing by the rules as they're laid out.
>
> ***
>
> There's obviously an expectation that all players are going to abide by the written rules. But there's also kind of an expectation that some form of unwritten rules governing behavior will also apply, that people won't take advantage of money lying on the table, but somehow, by nature of being good citizens, bid their incremental costs as opposed to bidding what the market will bear.[5]

Following this direction, Utility D traders played only by their interpretation of the rules. They would honor the letter of the tariff, but, "good luck" to you, if you expected traders to let some vague, "good citizen" standard stand in the way of making a buck. Obviously, the Utility D interpretation of CAISO tariff provisions could be quite self-serving.[6] That the load entries in their CAISO schedules were wildly overstated did not seem to bother Utility D traders, as reflected in the sentiments of the Utility D head trader:

> Overscheduling [False Load] was just another way to execute a power sale. In this case it is a price taker. It was taken in context with the daily decision to make any power sales anywhere on the grid that we were making that next day or the current day.[7] [Material in brackets added.]

---

3. *See* the discussion of Fat Boy in Chapter 7.
4. This position was also argued by Dr. Craig Pirrong, *see Answering Testimony of Dr. Craig Pirrong, EL00-95-248*, Exhibit No. POW-257, pp. 21-22.
5. *See* Taylor Testimony 2011, Exh. No. CAX-006, pp. 17-18.
6. As discussed previously in Chapter 7, Utility D traders conveniently ignored the plain language of the tariff that limited the load that SCs could schedule to that they were obligated to serve.
7. *See* Taylor Testimony 2011, Exh. No. CAX-007.

Furthermore, Utility D witnesses pointed to the fact that uninstructed over-generation was defined in the tariff and paid for by the CAISO at the *ex-post* RT price as proof that False Load was an acceptable practice.[8]

These attitudes regarding tariff compliance were bolstered by the feeling that scheduling False Load was beneficial to the CAISO, as reflected in the treatment of False Load in the Enron Memos:

> Interestingly, the strategy appears to benefit the reliability of the ISO's grid. It is well known the California IOUs have systematically underscheduled their load in the PX's Day-Ahead market.
>
> * * *
>
> By deliberately overscheduling load, Enron has been offsetting the ISO's real-time energy deficit by supplying extra energy that the ISO needs.[9]

In justifying manipulative activities, the two themes of following the strict letter of the tariff and providing assistance to the CAISO in dealing with operational challenges arose frequently. Suppliers argued that the entities ultimately receiving the energy in False Export, for example, were the IOUs that underscheduled their load.[10] In another example, a rationale for Get Shorty sales was found in provisions of the CAISO tariff:

> The ISO tariff does provide for situations where a scheduling coordinator sells ancillary services in the day-ahead market, and then reduces them in the day-of market. Under these circumstances, the tariff simply requires that the scheduling coordinator replace the capacity in the hour-ahead market. ISO Tariff, SBP 5.3, *Buy Back of Ancillary Services.*[11]

Where such justifications can be found in the tariff or because of the tariff, restraining trader behavior through vague standards of conduct is an uphill battle.

---

8. *See* the earlier discussion in Chapter 7.

9. Enron Memo of December 6, 2000, pp. 2-3. During the long course of the Crisis-related proceedings before the Commission, the so called underscheduling by the ISOs was shown to be a red herring. The fact that the market clearing load and generation scheduled through the PX DA and HA auctions was significantly less than that required to meet load in the ISO proved to be the result of suppliers reducing the amount of generation bid into the PX market. *See Prepared Rebuttal Testimony of Dr. Gary A. Stern on Behalf of the California Parties, Docket No. EL00-95-248*, Exh. No. CAX-350, March 2, 2012, pp. 9-22.

10. *Id.* p. 7.

11. *Id.* p. 6.

Weaknesses in Statutory Authority

At the time of the Crisis, the FERC's oversight authority came from the Federal Power Act as implemented through relevant tariffs—in this case, the PX and CAISO Tariffs, the WSPP Agreement that governed transactions in the PNW, and the MBR authorization that was required of every supplier participating in liberalized markets, whether organized like the PX and CAISO, or bilateral, which was the model in the PNW. None of these even contained the word manipulation during this period or addressed the concept in any way except for the vague, backhanded treatment of gaming and anomalous behavior in the MMIP.

To a large extent this occurred because, in the United States, electric market liberalization was done incrementally under a statute that was never designed to allow for, much less provide oversight of, competitive processes. The Federal Power Act declares unlawful any rate that is "unjust, unreasonable, unduly discriminatory, or preferentia."[12] The FPA was passed to prevent the exercise of market power and discrimination in wholesale market transactions that were subject to *ex-ante* price regulation. The use of markets was not contemplated anywhere in the statute. Given that the whole point of the law was to create a process that guaranteed just and reasonable prices in advance, there was no conceivable reason why the statute would contain any provisions defining or controlling market manipulation. Manipulation, as distinct from the exercise of market power, was not its target.

The FERC's granting of "market-based rates"—its workaround for allowing deregulated prices under the FPA—was intended to work by testing each supplier for market power prior to granting MBR authorization (i.e., the ability to sell at prices determined by free bilateral negotiation or approved auction processes) and then monitoring for the exercise of market power thereafter.[13] But there was no treatment or discussion of manipulation in the Commission's oversight of market-based rates prior to the Crisis. When faced with evidence of Enron's fraudulent schemes, it took the position that a presumption against fraud, deception, and misrepresentation was "implicit in Commission orders granting market-based rates", and relied in part upon violation of this prohibition and the resulting manipulated CAISO prices and excessive congestion fees in revoking Enron's MBR authorization.[14]

Despite this determination that Enron's manipulative schemes based upon fraud violated the requirements of its MBR grants sufficiently to justify their revocation, the Commission apparently found such manipulation an insufficient basis for remedial action more generally. As discussed previously, much later, in response to a remand from the Ninth Circuit, the Commission warned litigants of limitations upon its authority to address manipulation: "at the time

12. Federal Power Act § 206 (a), 16 U.S. Code, Chapter 12, Subchapter II, § 824e.

13. *See Order on Remand*, Docket No. EL02-71-004, March 21, 2008, ¶ 10. Unfortunately, the Commission did little monitoring until the Crisis was in full swing, and only then discovered that the data they had been collecting for years for this purpose was insufficient for the task. *See* the discussion in Chapter 5.

14. Enron MBR Revocation Order, ¶¶ 52-54.

of the crisis, neither the Commission's regulations nor its grants of market-based rate authority contained market behavior rules prohibiting market manipulation or defining prohibited market manipulation."[15]

The perception of limited authority also constrained the Commission's response to the Crisis in other ways. The Commission's initial order of refunds related to the Crisis was limited to the period beginning on October 2, 2000 because of its interpretation of the procedure under § 206 of the FPA for establishing the Refund Effective Date.[16] The remedies available to the FERC, legacies from the bygone era of vertically integrated, franchised monopolies, also proved problematic in the context of liberalized auction and bilateral markets. With a single monopoly supplier, resetting rates to just and reasonable levels or requiring the offending supplier to disgorge excess profits worked well because this deprived the supplier of ill-gotten gains and compensated customers for illicit overcharges.

In markets with numerous suppliers such remedies are much less well suited. Since the costs of supplying electricity and gas vary substantially from one supplier to another, resetting the price to a just and reasonable level in a single price auction market like the PX and CAISO may leave some suppliers unable to recover their actual incurred costs. This concern motivated the Commission to undertake a complex and extended process intended to allow suppliers to recover their costs. However, because costs claimed by many sellers were themselves artificially elevated by the market dysfunction created by widespread gaming, and because the Commission relief did not address claims against upstream suppliers (the so called "ripple claims"), the FERC's cost recovery procedure guaranteed that refunds would fall far short of the overcharges suffered by buyers in the PX and CAISO markets and that many suppliers would enjoy prices above just and reasonable levels. Requiring disgorgement of profits of only those suppliers proven to have engaged in manipulative behavior can have the same effect because other non-offending suppliers may have enjoyed prices elevated through the influence of manipulation upon the market.

A limitation of another sort arose in the Commission's handling of claims in the PNW outside of the PX and CAISO markets. Its reading of the *Morgan Stanley* decision to mandate application of the *Mobile-Sierra Doctrine* to spot transactions in bilateral markets was a significant expansion of the doctrine's reach. The origins of the doctrine in long-term contract cases and its raison d'etre, the public's interest in arrangements that provide price stability, have little to do with the short-term transactions that dominate bilateral spot markets that operate throughout the country as alternatives to the organized auction markets. While the *Morgan Stanley* court went to great lengths to make the point that the *Mobile-Sierra Doctrine* did not create separate

15. *Order on Remand, Puget Sound Energy, Inc., Docket No. EL01-10-026*, 137 FERC ¶ 61,001, October 3, 2011, ¶ 17. *See* the discussion in Chapter 5.

16. *See CPUC Order on Remand*, 129 FERC ¶ 61,147, ¶¶ 7, 9-12, November 19, 2009. This order was issued in response to a Ninth Circuit decision finding that the Commission had erred in disallowing relief for the period prior to October 2, 2000 on the basis of § 309 of the FPA.

just and reasonable and public interest standards, it is evident that the Commission sees the burden of proof faced by buyers seeking relief from an onerous contract as much higher, if not nearly insurmountable, where the *Mobile-Sierra* just and reasonable presumption applies. Given the volumes traded in bilateral spot markets, this could be a significant limitation upon the Commission's oversight capability going forward.

Current Challenges

Many of the problems faced by the Commission in dealing with the Crisis have been addressed in the past decade. Automatic price mitigation mechanisms in most RTOs operate to reduce economic withholding, inadvertent or otherwise. As noted in Chapter 2, the FERC has now been given explicit authority over manipulation in its jurisdictional markets. MBR grants have been modified to prohibit manipulation and to allow the Commission to reach back to the date of any violation. Remedies have been further expanded to permit the Commission to levy substantial penalties upon offending suppliers. Nevertheless, there are concerns that some of the handicaps that plagued Crisis-era enforcement could hamper future efforts to curb manipulative activities in electricity and other energy markets.

The many recent enforcement actions involving electric power and natural gas markets reflect the unfortunate fact that they remain quite vulnerable to manipulation. The dynamism and complexity of electric power markets keep traders a step or two ahead of regulators in fashioning manipulative schemes. Temporary illiquidity caused by temporal and physical constraints continues to plague electricity markets and natural gas price index mechanisms. Derivatives and indexed instruments facilitate high levels of leverage that make profitable even small manipulation-induced price movements.

Despite considerable progress, a clear articulation of what behavior should, as a matter of policy, be considered manipulation subject to sanction remains elusive. Most of the enforcement actions by the FERC and CFTC to date have concluded with settlements that, while somewhat instructive, neither provide a comprehensive treatment of the concept of manipulation nor have the force of precedent. Clarity is important for both regulators and market participants, and thus is critical in assuring the vitality of the markets. We hope to contribute to greater clarity in the later chapters of this book.

Incompatibilities between rules-based tariffs and principles-based manipulation approaches are to some degree inevitable and are likely to continue to bedevil regulators and market participants as boundaries are established.[17] We argue below that economic efficiency principles

17. For a recent discussion of this tension by a sitting FERC Commissioner, *see* Clark and Meidhof (2014).

may be helpful in resolving such conflicts. If under the tariff design, behavior fully compliant with the tariff that has the indicia of manipulation nonetheless enhances market efficiency in the primary market by moving prices to convergence or improves market or system performance as contemplated in the market design underlying the tariff, then we submit that as a matter of policy, enforcement is likely not merited. In other words, if the tariff provides incentives for market participants to act in a manner that by design benefits overall market or system performance, then behavior compliant with the tariff consistent with those incentives should not be prosecuted as fraudulent even though it may be considered uneconomic in the primary market.

When it comes to weaknesses or gaps in the Commission's authority to address manipulative behavior, a significant one appears to be jurisdictional limitations. Manipulative schemes, as laid out in the chapters that follow, often involve a payoff on leverage provided in financial, non-physical instruments, which fall within the jurisdiction of the CFTC. This problem was showcased in the *Amaranth* case, in which the Commission ordered a $30 million civil penalty against Brian Hunter, the trader behind the alleged scheme, for driving down prices for NYMEX natural gas futures prices to benefit related swap and option positions. On appeal of the order, the court found that FERC lacked jurisdiction over these transactions, rejecting the Commission's argument that they affected natural gas prices in its jurisdictional physical gas markets.[18] Of even greater concern is a jurisdictional challenge now pending in the *Barclay's* case, in which prices in physical power markets were allegedly influenced to benefit financial positions. This is likely to be the most common manipulative pattern, so a loss on this issue would severely limit the Commission's reach.

Another arguable weakness in the Commission's anti-manipulation enforcement scheme is the prohibition of private actions.[19] Except for the Enron Memos,[20] virtually the entire evidentiary record regarding manipulation of the PX and CAISO markets by suppliers was developed by private parties seeking redress for the excessive prices that resulted from widespread manipulative behavior. Their efforts led to a significant expansion of the scope and depth of the investigation and to increases in the compensation paid to consumers of literally billions of dollars. Without the resources the private litigants brought to bear, the manipulators would have escaped with most of their ill-gotten gains, and the opportunity to develop an understanding of the true nature of the manipulative activities that brought down the markets would have been minimized. While there are obvious concerns about spurious, willy-nilly complaints for every increase in prices, and the Commission Staff's investigative powers have been considerably enhanced, the loss of firepower, informed expertise, and hence, deterrence, resulting from the prohibition against private actions is not inconsequential.

18. *See* the discussion of this case in Chapter 10.

19. The EPAct of 2005, expressly prohibits private actions. *See* 16 USC §824v.

20. And even these were not obtained through the Commission's investigative efforts.

An interesting question that has yet to be resolved is whether the gap created by the prohibition in private actions might be plugged using the FERC's traditional authority to remedy unjust and unreasonable rates. The earlier discussion of the Enron MBR Revocation order points out that the Commission concluded therein that Enron's fraud-based manipulation in the PX and CAISO resulted in prices that were unjust and unreasonable. This being the case, parties aggrieved by the unjust and unreasonable prices should have an avenue to seek relief via FPA §§ 206 and 309 as they did in the cases relating to the Crisis. According to Ninth Circuit precedent set in the course of the Crisis-related proceedings, this right is independent of any action the Commission may choose to initiate on its own authority. The Commission in interpreting the Ninth Circuit also found that the Commission's investigation and enforcement proceeding does not preclude a civil proceeding instituted by a third party complaint. Specifically, the Ninth Circuit stated:

> 'A party's valid request for relief cannot be denied purely on the basis that the agency is considering its own enforcement action that may impart a portion of the relief sought. If an aggrieved party tenders sufficient evidence that tariffs have been violated, then it is entitled to have FERC adjudicate whether the tariff has been violated and what relief is appropriate.'[21]

In this line of attack the *Mobile-Sierra Doctrine* might again be argued to apply a presumption of just and reasonable rates in transactions outside the context of organized CAISO auction markets.[22] However, the *Morgan Stanley* decision held that the presumption should not apply in cases where fraud or manipulation by one of the parties affected the formation of the sale agreement. Thus, pursuit of redress by aggrieved parties seems possible despite the specific prohibition in EPAct. This would still leave complainants with the considerable challenge of establishing the degree to which prices were impacted by manipulative behavior—a challenge we now turn to in Part III.

21. *Order on Requests for Rehearing and Clarification and Motions to Dismiss*, 135 FERC ¶ 61,183, Docket No. EL00-95-236, May 26, 2011, ¶16, quoting *Pub. Util. Com'n of the State of Cal. v. FERC*, 462 F.3d 1027 (9th Cir. 2006) (CPUC Decision) at 1051.

22. The *Mobile-Sierra Doctrine* has not yet been extended to energy purchases and sales effected through organized auction markets.

Part III: New Developments in Market Manipulation

CHAPTER 9

MARKET POWER AND MANIPULATION: A NEW CONCEPTUAL FRAMEWORK

The diagnostic framework we introduce in this book is a useful way of expanding the traditional physical-goods market power conceptual model into one that more naturally incorporates the role of short-term information and financial products. Importantly, this framework is based on a definition of market manipulation that is broader than market power. Market power, as explained in Chapter 2, is merely one method to execute a manipulation. The framework accounts for the incentives created by linkages between product markets, whether created by the short-term inflexibilities of electric supply and demand, by financial contracts developed specifically to hedge against or speculate on market outcomes, or other connections linked by time, function, or use. It is designed to allow for an accurate diagnosis of market manipulation in both energy and non-energy markets consistent across all products, statutes, and agencies relevant to the implementation and enforcement of market manipulation rules.[1]

The framework also helps resolve a tension in the literature, often noted by economic experts such as Professor Pirrong, between market-power-based and fraud-based manipulations.[2] While we agree that analyzing these two types of manipulation require somewhat different quantitative and qualitative exercises, the framework provides a conceptual structure in which both types of manipulation can be organized, understood, and diagnosed.

The framework is constructed around three elements that involve two or more related markets that are linked together by a particular outcome. Figure 9-1 identifies the three elements of the framework.

1. Additional general discussions of the diagnostic framework can be found in Ledgerwood and Harris (2012); Ledgerwood and Pfeifenberger (2013); Ledgerwood (2013); Ledgerwood and Carpenter (2012); Ledgerwood, S. *et al.* (2011); and Ledgerwood (2010).

2. *See* Pirrong (1994 and 2010).

Figure 9-1:

A Conceptual Framework for Analyzing Market Manipulation

The first element, the *trigger*, is an act or omission intended to ultimately bias a price, quantity, or other market outcome—i.e., change or influence the outcome in a predictable manner. In more precise neoclassical language, the trigger causes (or attempts to cause) a market to operate in a manner inconsistent with competition.[3] As explained in more detail below, there are three primary types of *triggers*: (a) *the exercise of market power*, typically executed through an act of withholding or threatening to withhold; (b) *outright fraud*, such as knowingly filing a fraudulent report or failing to divulge a material fact; or (c) *intentional uneconomic (i.e., unprofitable) trading*, that is, incurring a loss by trading excessive quantities in the market in order to bias a market outcome. Behavior that does not fall into one of these three categories generally serves a stand-alone legitimate business purpose and thus deserves the presumption that it is not manipulation. Triggers that involve the exercise of market power—primarily by physical or economic withholding—have been amply discussed in the literature and are examined in Chapter 2. The use of false information or outright fraud as a trigger is also fairly well-documented. The use of uneconomic trading as a trigger is, however, a relatively new topic to the literature and is therefore discussed in more detail below.

The *nexus* of a manipulation can be any market-related mechanism that can be systemically affected by the manipulation trigger, such as a market price or quantity traded. In conventional antitrust economics—and in conventional neoclassical theory—the trigger and the nexus are typically not discussed in detail as distinct elements because the desired impact of the price change is limited to the primary market in which the withholding occurs. By comparison, in the manipulation framework, the desired impact of the act of withholding in the primary market (a trigger) is in a separate market or markets linked to the primary market through its price (the nexus). Accordingly, in a comprehensive framework, these two elements are identified distinctly.

The third element of the framework is the *target*. The manipulation's *target* is one or more assets—financial derivatives, securities, or price-indexed physical positions—or other sources of payments that are positioned to benefit from the biased nexus. In conventional antitrust economics, the "target" that benefits from the manipulation derives from the trade of the units

3. The latter statement is more precise than may first be apparent. As we demonstrate below, competitive markets for private goods with small externalities maximize economic surplus; manipulation causes market outcomes that do not maximize surplus and in this way are inconsistent with competitive outcomes.

not withheld by a seller in the primary market at the upwardly-biased market price. However, market manipulation cases consider the impact of the biased nexus on linked positions *outside of the primary market*. For example, a trader may publish false information concerning expected prices in the spot market for natural gas (a trigger). This information may affect trading in the spot market and affect the resulting price of spot gas (the nexus). The targets in this example could then be anything linked to this price, such as financial derivatives, indexed contracts, or options contracts.

Proof of a manipulation therefore requires the demonstration that the manipulator intentionally acted in a manner designed to cause (trigger) a change in some market mechanism (nexus) to alter the value of one or more positions (target) that benefit from the change. Whether evaluated under a fraud-based or artificial price standard, the framework provides a uniform approach to assessing intent in a way that is logically consistent and that melds the use of economic evidence with more objective indicia of intent (e.g., emails, IMs, voice recordings, and whistleblower testimony). All anti-manipulation enforcement actions that have been brought by the FERC, CFTC, or SEC can be analyzed using this framework, as they ultimately follow an equivalent logic of cause and effect.

The framework's elements provide an additional dimension treated only narrowly in market power models but that is much broader and is highly relevant to the treatment of market manipulation. Specifically, for manipulation to be successful, the revenues derived from the target of the behavior must exceed any losses incurred in the primary market, a condition we refer to as having sufficient *financial leverage*. In the case of an exercise of market power, where the manipulation target is confined to the primary market, an act of withholding (trigger) is sufficiently financially leveraged only if at the biased price (nexus), the sales revenues from the units not withheld in the primary market (target) more than cover the revenues lost on the units withheld. In such cases, conventional antitrust principles—and the economic tools used to support them—are sufficient to analyze the behavior because the trigger, nexus, and target are all within the same market. However, if one or more of the targets of the behavior lies outside of the primary market, traditional economic tools are less useful. This is because the financial leverage provided by those linked markets amplifies the profitability derived from the biased market outcome, thus reducing the need for the manipulator to possess the attributes associated with traditional market power (e.g., large market share). Leverage in markets other than the primary market also creates another distinction from traditional market power analyses. Because instruments providing leverage can benefit from either upward or downward price movements, a seller can potentially benefit as much from depressing prices as from increasing them in the primary market.

Before turning to a discussion of the elements of the framework in more detail, there are two more terms that need to be defined: *liquidity*, and *market depth*. A definition of liquidity is "the degree to which an asset or security can be bought or sold in the market without affecting the asset's price."[4] From a market perspective, liquidity is defined as "a market's ability to facilitate

4. *See http://www.investopedia.com/terms/l/liquidity.asp.*

an asset being sold *quickly* without having to reduce its price very much (or even at all)."[5] The element of speed has been used to distinguish liquidity from the concept of *market depth*, which allows for *larger* orders to be executed without much price movement.[6] Both of these tie closely with the more familiar concept of *elasticity*, for the reactivity of product's quantity exchanged to a change in price (or conversely the degree to which price responds to a change in the quantity exchanged) is a function of both the liquidity and depth of a market.

Manipulation Triggers

Market Power—Extensions Outside of the Primary Market

As discussed above, the exercise of market power typically works through an act of withholding, either by a seller (monopoly power) or a buyer (monopsony power). The amount of withholding needed to maximize gains as well as the size of the gain for any level of withholding are functions of the elasticities of supply and demand, with lower demand elasticities (monopoly) or higher supply elasticities (monopsony) conferring greater potential gains. The cases of the monopolist and monopsonist are illustrated below in Figure 9-2 A and B, respectively.

Figure 9-2 A and B

The Exercise of Market Power through Withholding

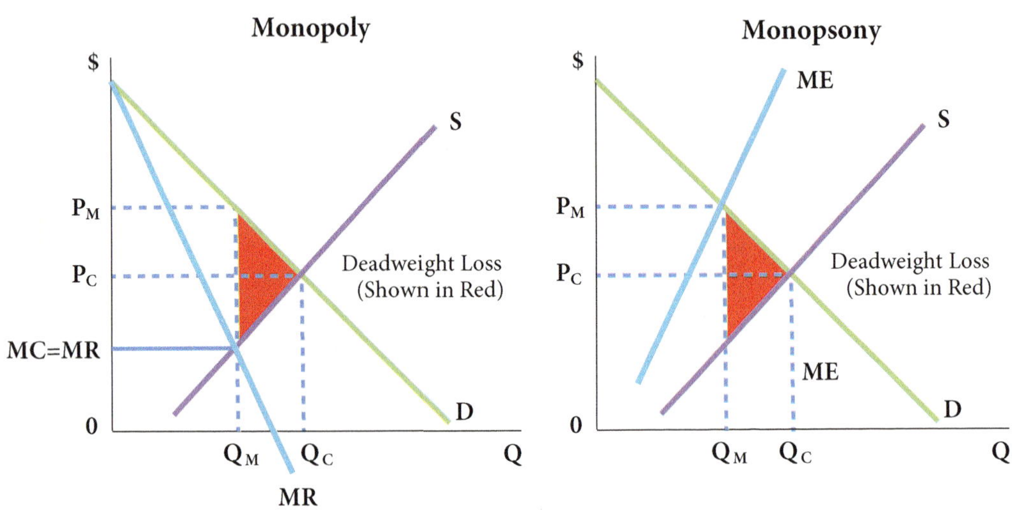

5. *See http://en.wikipedia.org/wiki/Market_liquidity.*

6. *See http://www.investopedia.com/terms/m/marketdepth.asp.*

Figure 9-2 A shows an example of the exercise of market power by a monopolist. The market begins at a competitive equilibrium at the intersection of supply and demand, clearing at the price "P_C" with the market quantity traded "Q_C." To maximize its profits, the monopolist restricts (withholds) output until its marginal revenues equal its marginal costs, the latter of which is equal to supply under competitive market conditions. Reducing its output to the quantity "Q_M" allows the monopolist to raise the price charged for the remaining units traded to "P_M" such that the gain made on those units more than offsets the loss incurred from the units withheld and not sold. Because the units withheld from the market are never traded, the welfare gain from the production and exchange of those units is foregone. For this reason, monopoly incurs a deadweight loss to society relative to the competitive equilibrium, shown by the shaded region of Figure 9-2 A.

Figure 9-2 B likewise shows the exercise of market power by a monopsonist.[7] The market begins at a competitive equilibrium at the price "P_C" and quantity traded "Q_C." The monopsonist will then restrict (withhold) its quantity purchased until its marginal expenditures equal its demand (willingness to pay), thus reducing the market quantity traded to "Q_M" and allowing the monopsonist to force sellers to reduce the price charged for those units to "P_M." This behavior profits the monopsonist on a stand-alone basis, for the savings on the units purchased more than offset any benefits that would derive from purchasing the units not traded. Like the example involving the monopolist, the act of withholding incurs a deadweight loss to society relative to the competitive equilibrium, shown by the shaded region of Figure 9-2 B.

Upon first glance, the reader might ask whether the behavior described above could be thought of as market manipulation. From this perspective, the act of withholding could be viewed as an intentional sacrifice of profit on the untraded units (a form of intentional, seemingly uneconomic behavior as the trigger) to cause a price change (the nexus) to benefit the profitability of the remaining units purchased or sold (the target). However, as we discussed above, such behavior is better analyzed using traditional antitrust tools, for they are best designed to evaluate the cause and effect of market power when its scope is confined to the primary market. Further, as we will discuss below when considering uneconomic trading, withholding produces a price change that benefits the actor on a stand-alone basis in the primary market, *thus inducing an immediate competitive response from other participants on the same side of that market.*[8] By comparison, uneconomic acts that move prices in a direction that injure the actor cannot be thwarted by other participants on the same side of that market, and are only encouraged by market participants on the other side as they directly benefit from the behavior.

---

7. The monopsony model presented here is often used to describe labor markets dominated by a single, large employer. *See*, for example, Walter Nicholson and Christopher Snyder, *Microeconomic Theory: Basic Principles and Extensions*, 10th ed., Eagan, MN: South-Western Publishing Co., 2008, pp. 584-586.

8. The exercise of market power is therefore unsustainable in the absence of entry barriers or other types of exclusory behavior, for natural competitive forces otherwise thwart the price movement that is necessary for the behavior to succeed.

Traditional (or Outright) Fraud—Recognized in Common Law

The second mechanism to trigger market manipulation is the commission of outright fraud, either by injecting false information into the market or by the omission of material information. This is the traditional basis for the anti-manipulation enforcement actions brought by the SEC under its fraud-based Rule 10b-5, upon which the FERC's Rule 1c and CFTC's Rule 180.1 are based. For example, traders in "pump and dump" schemes buy stock positions in advance of disseminating false information to induce others to buy the stock, which then triggers the upward price movement that benefits the manipulator's sales of the stock after the price increase.[9] Similarly, "wash trades" may be executed to convey false information as to perceptions of volumetric trade (either of the trader or the asset traded) or price.[10] Under European market manipulation law, inside information about system events (such as unplanned outages) can likewise be used to trigger manipulations, such as through the front-running of trades before the information is made public.[11]

The essence of a manipulation claim based on outright fraud parallels the equivalent concept of fraud in broader contract law—e.g., where a party intentionally provides false information to a counterparty, who then contracts in reliance on that misinformation. Indeed, in schemes that involve derivatives manipulations, it is the manipulator's ability to dupe its counterparty into the belief that the contract's expected (pre-manipulation) price is a correct indication of value that allows for the subsequent manipulation to pay off. In electricity markets, outright fraud can take several other forms, such as selling services that cannot be provided or setting false baselines to garner payments from market mechanisms that are benchmarked against them.[12]

Uneconomic Trading—Can Be Seen as "Transactional Fraud"

While market power and outright fraud are recognized means by which to manipulate markets, a third type of behavior less discussed in the literature nevertheless has served as the trigger in many recent market manipulation cases brought by the FERC: *uneconomic trading*, or intentional below-market sales (or above-market purchases). Concerns about uneconomic trades are heightened if the trades are used as an integral part of a "price-making" process that is used to value other instruments, such as by contributing to the formation of an index or auction clearing price. If so, given the right market conditions (such as when system constraints

9. Intentional dissemination of false information is specifically prohibited by Sections 9a-2 through 9a-4 of the Exchange Act. *See also* the complaint filed in *SEC v. Pawel Dynkowski et al.*, Case No. 09-361 (May 20, 2009), which is available online at *http://www.sec.gov/litigation/complaints/2009/comp21053.pdf*. Note that uneconomic transactions can also accompany pump and dump schemes if the manipulator purchases stock to help fuel the buying frenzy.

10. Wash trades are specifically prohibited under Section 9a-1 of the Securities Act.

11. Specifically, the EU Commission has nested an insider trading provision within the list of abusive market practices in the Regulation of the European Parliament and of the Council on Energy Market Integrity and Transparency, better known as "REMIT." *See* Council Regulation (EU) No. 1227/2011, On Wholesale Energy Market Integrity and Transparency, at art. 2(4)(a), 2011 O.J. (L326) 1. By comparison, legitimate hedging based on knowledge of outages or other system events is allowed under U.S. market manipulation rules.

12. It is possible for acts of fraud to be committed that do not constitute a manipulation, particularly those that are akin to direct theft.

are binding and market liquidity is lacking), market participants with small market shares can cause a significant price bias by placing uneconomic trades strategically to maximize their directional impact on the benchmark price, to the benefit of financially leveraged price-taking positions that are tied to that price.[13]

In contrast to acts of withholding, uneconomic trading triggers a manipulation by causing the market (properly defined) to *be oversupplied.* The price movement caused by withholding benefits the actor on a stand-alone basis in the primary market, allowing it to buy or sell the units not withheld for a profit—i.e., by either "buying low" or "selling high." By comparison, the price movement caused by uneconomic trading can only injure the actor in the primary market by causing it to intentionally incur a loss on the units bought or sold to produce the desired effect. By necessity, for a manipulation to be profitable, the benefits from uneconomic trading *must* then derive from targets positioned in markets other than the primary market that are nevertheless linked to the primary market by a common nexus. Whereas traditional antitrust economics is best at evaluating the cause and effect of behavior arising within the boundaries of the primary market, the economics of market manipulation—as described through our framework—provides a better platform for evaluating the effects of behavior extending beyond those boundaries.

The market impact of uneconomic trading is illustrated for a seller and buyer in Figure 9-3 A and B respectively.

Figure 9-3 A and B

The Effect of Uneconomic Trading

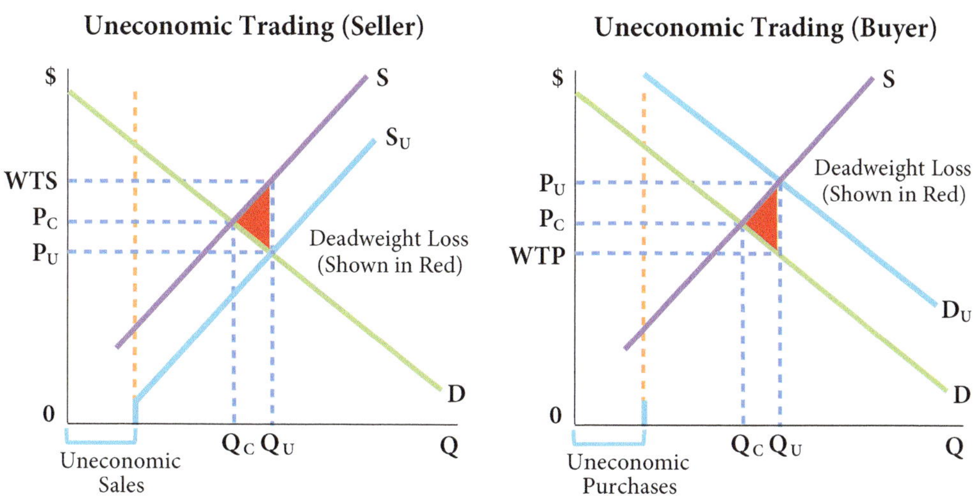

13. The greater the financial leverage, the smaller the price movement necessary for the manipulation to be profitable.

Figure 9-3 A demonstrates the effect of uneconomic sales. The market begins at a competitive equilibrium at the intersection of supply and demand, clearing at the price "P_C" with the market quantity traded "Q_C". The manipulative seller then injects sales into the market, causing a rightward shift in market supply to "S_U."[14] This forces output to the quantity "Q_U" and the market price down to "P_U." Because the actual cost of producing these units is "WTS" (a profit-seeking seller's true willingness to sell), the seller loses money on these sales. Although consumers benefit from the lower prices, the net welfare effect is a deadweight loss to society relative to the competitive equilibrium, shown by the shaded region of Figure 9-3 A.

Figure 9-3 B shows the effect of uneconomic purchases. Assuming the market again begins at a competitive equilibrium at the price "P_C" and quantity traded "Q_C," the manipulative buyer bids to make purchases into the market at a price far enough above market to assure their execution. This causes a rightward shift in market Demand to "D_U," which increases market output to "Q_U" and forces the market price up to "P_U." Because the buyer's true willingness to pay ("WTP") for the product alone is below this new price, it willingly loses money on these purchases. Sellers benefit from the higher price, but the net welfare effect is again a deadweight loss to society relative to the competitive equilibrium, shown by the shaded region of Figure 9-3 B.

A defining aspect of uneconomic trading is the response that such behavior induces from participants on the same side of the market. To explain this, consider first an act of withholding by a seller. The resulting price increase will face resistance by other sellers who are incented to compete away the profit opportunity, thus pressuring the price to return to competitive levels. A successful market-power-triggered manipulation therefore requires that the seller must have the ability to thwart these competitive pressures to prevent this participation from occurring, such as by taking advantage of size, entry barriers, or through implementing other restraints of trade—the hallmarks of traditional monopoly power.

Contrast this with the seller who dumps uneconomic volumes of product into the market at sub-competitive prices. Absent arbitrage opportunities, which would require that other accessible markets exist where the price effects of the uneconomic behavior are not felt,[15] other sellers are not positioned to stop this behavior and may be driven out of business if it is allowed to persist.[16] Whereas the exercise of market power requires (and is in part defined by) the ability to prevent other sellers from participating in the market and thus thwart the effect of the exercise on the price, the reaction of other sellers to uneconomic trading faces no such immediate resistance. This means that successful manipulations triggered by uneconomic trading can be executed by firms with much smaller market concentrations than traditional antitrust eco-

14. The supply curve is shown as shifting to the right, which is equivalent to assuming that uneconomic supply is injected into the market at a price of zero. However, the seller can inject the uneconomic supply at any price far enough below market to enable a profitable manipulation, which need not be (and in practice is usually not) zero.

15. This assumes that the arbitrageur could buy the product from the lower-priced market, then transport or store product for resale in the higher-priced market. This is typically difficult in electricity markets due to the absence of storage and the lack of transmission options when constraints are binding.

16. Ledgerwood and Heath (2012), pp. 509-568.

nomics would deem relevant. The ability to make such sales profitably is not a function of market power, but rather of the willingness of the actor to absorb losses in the primary market,[17] as well as its ability to build financial leverage through targets positioned in other linked markets.

One historic manipulation case prosecuted by the CFTC demonstrates these principles. Consider the case of the copper market corner executed by Sumitomo Corporation trader Yasuo Hamanaka in the mid-1990s.[18] Through Sumitomo, Mr. Hamanaka controlled less than five percent of the world's physical copper supply, earning him the nickname "Mr. Five Percent."[19] However, by focusing uneconomic purchases of copper at a single location (trigger), Mr. Hamanaka was able to corner and squeeze the London Metals Exchange copper market, artificially increasing global prices for copper (nexus) to the benefit of Sumitomo's other related physical positions (targets). Through concentrated, uneconomic trades at an illiquid trading point in a market with binding delivery constraints, Sumitomo provides a microcosm of the many facets of manipulation that we have discussed thus far.

Although concentrated trading could be (and has been) thought of as exercising a type of "market power," Sumitomo demonstrates that the traditional measures of market power such as market share and industry concentration calculations used in antitrust applications are not as relevant in evaluating manipulations triggered by uneconomic behavior. Intentional uneconomic trading is better explained as a form of transactional fraud. Consider this example: an electricity trader holds derivatives contracts that are long to an end-of-day spot electricity price, purchased earlier in the day at a price of $30/MWh. Now consider two alternative scenarios:

Scenario One:	The trader releases to the market a false report of an unplanned system outage just before the end of the trading day, driving up the spot price to $60/MWh.
Scenario Two:	The trader makes no statements whatsoever, but uneconomically purchases electricity in the spot market near the end of the trading day in quantities sufficient to drive the end-of-day spot price to $60/MWh.

17. Many legitimate reasons might underlie a trader's willingness to incur losses on specific transactions, ranging from pure unintended error to the need for immediate liquidation (or procurement) of the asset traded. However, the trader's willingness to incur such losses on a repeated or anomalous basis brings into question whether the motivation for the behavior was legitimate on a stand-alone basis. As we discuss, one purpose of the manipulation framework we present is to describe and help identify behavior that could give rise to loss-based opportunism. This behavior is often confused with traditional market power, especially on the buyer side. For examples where concerns about uneconomic entry have led to the mitigation of buyer market power in electricity capacity markets, *see Order on Proposed Revisions to In-City Buyer-Side Mitigation Measures*, 133 FERC ¶ 61,178, 2010; *Order Accepting Proposed Tariff Revisions Subject to Conditions, and Addressing Related Complaint*, 135 FERC ¶ 61,022, 2011; and *Order on Paper Hearing and Order on Rehearing*, 135 FERC ¶ 61,029, 2011, note 57.

18. *See In the Matter of Sumitomo Corporation*, as referenced in CFTC Press Release #4144-98 and available at *http://www.cftc.gov/ogc/oporders98/ogcfsumitomo.htm* (May 11, 1998).

19. *See* Andrew Beattie, "Who is Mr. Copper?" available at: *http://www.investopedia.com/ask/answers/ 08/mr-copper-sumitomo-hamanaka.asp.*

The effect of the trader's actions is identical in both scenarios: the derivatives contracts rise in value as the price rises from $30 to $60. Scenario One is an example of a manipulation executed by outright fraud, assuming, of course, that the requisite legal elements of intent are satisfied. If equivalent evidence of intent can be shown as the reason for the trader's uneconomic trades in Scenario Two, why should that behavior be treated any differently?[20]

If the purpose of the uneconomic trades (the trigger) is to bias the market price (the nexus) to increase the value of the derivatives (the target), the trades inject *fraudulent* information into the market no less effectively than did the false report. Indeed, moving the market by actual trades may be more effective than the pure use of information (albeit more costly), as suggested by the long-standing slang-phrase "money talks."

From an economic standpoint, the key difference between "outright fraud" and "transactional fraud" is who bears the loss on the losing trades that trigger the manipulation. Market participants other than the manipulator bear the entire loss in strategies relying on outright fraud, whereas the manipulator bears some (but likely not all) of the primary market losses with uneconomic trades. As the prior discussion demonstrates, the ability of a trader to trigger a manipulation using uneconomic trades does not depend on market power per se, but rather on (1) the liquidity and market depth provided by the side of the market that benefits from the transactions, and (2) the amount of financial leverage the trader holds through possessing one or more manipulation targets. Whereas the first element ties closely with the elasticity concept that is relevant to antitrust and other analyses of competition,[21] the concept of leverage has received little attention. For this reason, we now discuss potential manipulation targets which may provide the source for this financial leverage.

Manipulation Targets

Whereas manipulation triggers are designed to create a market bias, manipulation targets are designed to benefit from the bias created. A misconception exists that manipulation targets must be cross-market positions, such as financial derivatives or other types of related physical products that tie to the manipulated outcome. While it is certainly true that cross-market positions can be gamed in this manner, the example of Sumitomo's corner of the copper market demonstrates that this need not be the case. Indeed, the linked market(s) containing the potential targets can be in the same product market, but separated temporally. Though we

20. The skeptic may immediately assert that there is no amount of proof that can definitively demonstrate that open market trades were placed for fraudulent purposes. As we will discuss in the chapters to come, the analytical framework presented above is helpful in distinguishing whether such trades are deserving of higher scrutiny. If so, then a review of more objective evidence of intent is warranted, as is the practice of the enforcement agencies tasked with anti-manipulation mandates.

21. For example, relating back to the examples of Scenarios One and Two, neither manipulation would be possible if the bid stack (i.e., demand) had been sufficiently deep (i.e., elastic) such that the market could absorb the directional trades with little or no price effect.

consider several target examples in this section, the reader should keep in mind that no list can be exhaustive.

Financial Derivatives Contracts

As the 2008 Financial Crisis demonstrated, a key source of leverage used by market participants to hedge against or speculate on market outcomes is financial derivatives contracts, often referred to simply as derivatives. Derivatives "derive" their value from prices set by the trading of some underlying commodity. A good example of derivatives contracts used widely in electricity markets are financial transmission rights, commonly referred to as "FTRs."[22]

FTRs pay their holders the difference in congestion prices between two nodes on the electric grid, with the holder paying the congestion price at the FTR source and receiving the congestion price at its sink. FTRs provide load serving entities with a financial hedge against the cost of physical congestion that arises over transmission paths the entities use for power flows. Other market participants purchase FTRs as speculative investments, thus benefitting from congestion over the affected path in the "long" direction. By taking actions to deliberately increase congestion on the FTR paths they hold, such as by placing intentionally uneconomic virtual or physical bids or offers, market participants can use these positions as the target of a manipulative scheme.

Other types of electric market derivatives are available through the RTOs, as well as through the CFTC-jurisdictional InterContinental Exchange (ICE), CME, and Nodal Exchange. These may tie to prices at particular nodes, hubs, zones, interties, constraints, or across an entire RTO. Some tie to different temporal markets (e.g., day-ahead versus real-time), to complimentary products such as electricity and natural gas (i.e., heat rate swaps), or even fundamental market factors such as weather. Others are written as options contracts, or as contracts that trade exposure to a stream of prices over time against a single, discrete price. While the bulk of the oversight responsibility for derivatives falls on the CFTC, the FERC retains primary oversight responsibility for FTRs and other RTO-traded derivative instruments, and (at present) has access to CFTC data through a Memorandum of Understanding executed between the two agencies.[23]

Derivative contracts can be written to tie to any provable market price or set of prices, including a market basket of prices from several goods or a series of prices determined over time. Further, because derivatives are financially settled (i.e., there is no physical delivery associated with the contract's settlement), they can be written in large quantities limited only by the willingness of counterparties to take the risk position associated with the other side of the transaction. These combined attributes provide the ability of potential manipulators to accumulate

22. The nomenclature for these instruments varies by RTO, with the CAISO trading "congestion revenue rights" (CRRs) and the NYISO trading "transmission congestion credits" (TCCs).

23. *Memorandum of Understanding between the Federal Energy Regulatory Commission and the Commodity Futures Trading Commission*, available at: *http://www.cftc.gov/ucm/groups/public/ @newsroom/documents/file/cftcfercjmou2014.pdf.*

large, financially leveraged positions that can serve as targets and that may be difficult to identify. Such leverage allows the manipulator to profit by triggering relatively small biases in market prices that may be indistinguishable from the noise of other trading in the marketplace.[24]

Physical Positions "Traded at Settlement" or "at Index"

While derivatives are often used as targets of manipulation schemes, physical positions are also used with great frequency. For example, futures contracts will settle each day up to the final settlement date when physical delivery obligations attach. A trader holding such positions has the incentive to enter the daily settlement period to execute trades in volumes designed to bias the final daily price. Because the positions are marked-to-market based on this settlement price, the trader's account may benefit as a result.[25] If the manipulator is able to sustain the manipulation over time, as did Sumitomo with world copper prices in the 1990s, it is possible that the manipulation can distort the value of futures contracts "out the curve" such that the manipulator can profit from positions held for delivery in later months. This same logic applies to the manipulation of forward contracts, which may be even more susceptible to gaming because there is typically less liquidity in the markets for such non-standardized products.

Other types of physical contracts have unique pricing terms that make them especially useful for serving as the targets of manipulation schemes. A prime example is physical contracts that are "Traded at Settlement" ("TAS") also known as contracts traded "at index." These contracts trade at a price that is to be determined by fixed-price trades in some later settlement period, so that they play no role in current market price formation.[26] Because the holder of a large position "at index" would directly benefit from movement of that index in one direction or the other, it has the incentive to trade during the settlement period to create a directional price

24. The derivatives-related components of Dodd-Frank reduce traders' ability to amplify the effects of small uneconomic trades via large derivative positions. Title VII of the Act requires derivatives contracts to be cleared through and reported on a central exchange, thereby standardizing certain swaps and promoting transparency—as noted by former CFTC Chairman Gary Gensler below—which in turn significantly reduces the ability of market participants to accumulate hidden positions tied to uncertain benchmarks.

    "On the dealer community . . . the business conduct standards would protect against fraud, manipulation, and other abuses. The recordkeeping and reporting, importantly, would allow the regulators to see a complete picture and aggregate this picture. In addition, I do believe, though, we need to regulate the markets as well. This is a complementary regime to bring the standardized products, those products that can be brought into clearing and brought onto exchanges, further lowers risk. Clearing has the attribute that no longer would the financial system be so interconnected. . . . Regulated exchanges and transparent regulated trading facilities or trading platforms bring additional transparency . . . there would be a real-time reporting of those transactions of the standardized products. So the full market could see on a real-time basis, as they do in the corporate bond market and they do in the securities market, the pricing of the products as clearly as they can. (Committee on Agriculture, Nutrition, and Forestry, United States Senate, 2009. "Statement of Gary Gensler, Chairman, Commodity Futures Trading Commission, Washington, DC." *Hearing, Regulatory Reform and the Derivatives Market*, S.HRG. 111-246. (June 4, 2009)."

25. Another concerning outcome is that the affected counterparties are then forced to post margin to cover the gains paid to the manipulator. A counterparty unable to post this margin risks having its positions liquidated to cover the deficiency.

26. Indexed contracts are particularly favored by firms that are subject to state regulation where rates are subject to review under a "just and reasonable" standard. Such firms that engage in market trades to secure competitive supplies may find that the profits from "winning" trades are simply passed through to ratepayers, while losses from "losing" trades are viewed as unwise speculations that should reduce the payments to shareholders. By trading at index, the firm thus absolves itself of responsibility for the rate paid, since the ultimate price it pays for those supplies is determined through a transparent market process.

bias. Interestingly, the trader can use surplus physical index positions as the source for these price-setting trades. For example, assume a regulated electricity provider needs to buy 8,000 MWh from the wholesale market to serve native load. It first buys 10,000 MWh at index, leaving it financially short to the index price (i.e., benefitting from a lower price), but physically long 2,000 MWh above that needed to serve its load. It then waits until the index settlement period, where it sells the extra 2,000 MWh at uneconomically low prices to suppress the index price. The firm incurs a loss on these 2,000 MWh equal to the difference in the price of the low-price sales and the index price, but then benefits from a lower index price on the 8,000 MWh it needed to purchase in the first place.[27]

Options on physical contracts can provide unique targets for manipulation, due to the variety of types and terms of such contracts. For example, "barrier" option contracts can be written that tie to a spot market, such that a single spot market trade posted at a price at or outside of the strike price set by the contract triggers the option. This gives the holder of the contracts the incentive to inject concentrated, uneconomic trades into the market to cause a price spike sufficiently large to hit the strike and thus trigger the option. Once struck, the manipulator stops its uneconomic trades, allowing the price to revert toward its original levels and thus increasing the value of the physical units obtained from the option. Options on standard futures and derivatives contracts also provide creative opportunities for gaming due to their price-taking nature and resulting payoffs equivalent to those of the contracts to which they tie.

Other Positions

Despite best efforts on the part of regulators to require the reporting of an array of derivatives and other contracts, many potential manipulation targets are simply impossible to track. This is often because no quantifiable benefit can be measured as an outcome from the behavior. For example, predation (uneconomic sales) by a seller can negatively impact its rivals and may deter future entry given the seller's reputation as a fearsome competitor, but the antitrust laws provide almost no protection against this behavior unless quantifiable proof of harm is shown through the seller's later ability to charge supracompetitive prices.[28] Similarly, uneconomic power purchases made in future periods could potentially be used to manipulate perceptions as to the future value of power, to the benefit of a power generator looking to divest some portion of its fleet. A regulator could not be expected to connect the dots and perform the

27. Readers may recognize that if this behavior occurred though supply bids into a single-price capacity auction by buyers that were net short capacity, the FERC would consider this a type of "buyer market power." *See* PJM Power Providers Group v. PJM Interconnection, L.L.C., *Order on Compliance Filing, Rehearing, and Technical Conference*, 137 FERC ¶ 61,145, November 17, 2011, p. 244.

28. Ledgerwood and Heath (2012), p. 512.

discounted cash flow analyses needed to prove this out in the normal course of its surveillance function.[29]

Because the universe of potential targets cannot be known absent legal discovery that extends outside of the normal process of data reporting, regulators must recognize that manipulation can be effectuated through sources of financial leverage that are invisible to most traditional market surveillance processes. As such, it is plausible that a regulator might investigate sufficiently suspicious behavior that could serve as a manipulation trigger, even without proof of financial leverage at the outset of the inquiry. Because such proof must ultimately be shown for an enforcement action to be justified, and because due process requires that reasonable cause be shown to serve discovery on the suspected manipulator concerning its extra-jurisdictional positions, the regulator must therefore ascertain and establish the causal linkage between the evidence of the trigger detected and any potential targets its perceives that could be at play—i.e., the nexus of the manipulation.

Manipulation Nexuses

As the frameworks suggests, any market mechanism that provides a linkage between a triggering act (or omission) in the primary market and a manipulation target could serve as the nexus for a manipulation. This could be a market process, as was used by several market participants in ISO-NE to allegedly set false load baselines to receive demand response payments.[30] It can be a market quantity, as was used by a market participant selling power into the CAISO to artificially relieve congestion at the Palo Verde intertie, thus allowing it to artificially increase its sales to the state.[31] However, the quintessential manipulation nexus is a market-based price that is referenced by one or more other price-taking positions to determine their value. Indeed, the CFTC's first anti-manipulation rule required proof that the behavior prosecuted created an "artificial price," thus exempting non-price manipulations from scrutiny.[32] Many of the most recently pursued manipulation cases concern prices indexed to information provided at a specific time or over some discrete period in which the index settles. This is true of cases involving the LIBOR (calculated as the average of the 10 median quotes of 18 quotes taken at 4 p.m. GMT), FOREX (average of trades 30 seconds before and after the 4 p.m. London "fix"),

29. Indeed this nuance could be thought of as differentiating the roles of market monitoring from market surveillance, where surveillance focuses on the specifics of the trading data and monitoring focuses on more broad issues related to the industry. As of the time of this writing, the FERC has separated these functions through separate Divisions of Market Oversight and of Analytics and Surveillance.

30. For example, *see* Rumford Paper Company, *Order Approving Stipulation and Consent Agreement*, 142 FERC ¶ 61,218, March 22, 2013.

31. Gila River Power, LLC, *Order Approving Stipulation and Consent Agreement*, 141 FERC ¶ 61,136, November 19, 2012.

32. This authority was granted through the Commodity Futures Trading Commission Act of 1974, P.L. 93-463, October 23, 1974. The reader should note that the CFTC retained this artificial price statute following the passage of Dodd-Frank under section 6(c)(3) of the revised Commodity Exchange Act, adopted by the Commission as Rule 180.2. This is available in addition to the CFTC's new fraud-based provision added through CEA section 6(c)(1), adopted by the Commission as Rule 180.1.

"Platt's Window" (average of trades in the last 30-to-45 minutes for dated Brent crude), and other energy-related cases that we will discuss in Chapter 11.

The types of indices that can serve as a manipulation nexus are as wide and varied as the physical and financial instruments that could reference them, can vary widely across products, and can even vary within the same contract. For example, monthly natural gas futures contracts traded on NYMEX for delivery at the Henry Hub settle daily based on the Volume-Weighted Average Price (VWAP) of trades executed in the last two minutes of the trading day, while the final value of the contract is settled by the VWAP in the last 30 minutes of trading for the contract prior to expiry. By comparison, the indexing of monthly natural gas contracts delivered at many regional hubs ties to the VWAP of trades placed during the last five days of trading, commonly known as "bidweek." Electricity-related physical and financial contracts in RTOs usually tie to one or more hourly auction prices, while those outside of the organized markets index to a span of peak or off-peak hourly prices. Electricity and natural gas also trade in "spot" markets, the prices of which can likewise be used as a reference. Some contracts tie to multiple prices across time or products. For example, heat rate swaps tie to electricity and natural gas prices, whereas natural gas swing swaps tie to monthly and daily gas prices.

As discussed above, a primary market attribute that enables the manipulation of prices is a lack of market liquidity and market depth in the price-making mechanism. This is true irrespective of the process through which the reference price is formed, e.g., by index, auction, end-of-day mark, or spot. In fact, *any* price can serve as the nexus for a manipulation if a valid target can be established and there is insufficient market participation to thwart the behavior.

Given that scarce regulatory resources cannot possibly foresee all possible linkages between all potential triggers and targets, the hope of proactively deterring manipulation through market monitoring and surveillance may seem an impossible task. However, as screening methods improve and become more efficient with time, tools can evolve to improve results. The framework can be helpful to this process, as we will discuss in the next chapter.

Market Features That Affect the Incentive to Manipulate

Proof that a market actor controlled and operated (or attempted to operate) the three framework components to its benefit is necessary to demonstrate the manipulation's cause and effect, but is not dispositive proof of the actor's manipulative intent.[33] Under a fraud-based statute, such as those which govern the anti-manipulation enforcement efforts of the FERC, CFTC,

33. We introduced the necessity of proving intent under the main manipulation statutes in Chapter 2 above and discuss implementation practicalities in the Chapter following.

SEC, and FTC, proof of intent requires a showing of additional evidence to demonstrate that the alleged manipulator acted with requisite scienter—i.e., *fraudulent intent*.[34]

When using the framework to search for intentional market manipulation, it is useful to understand how it helps explain the incentive to manipulate that we have defined as the linked market. More concretely, the framework helps decompose the payoff a willful manipulator expects to earn from the manipulation. The overall total payoff of a manipulation is the combination of: (1) the gains or losses incurred in the primary market by the triggering act; (2) the effect of the trigger on the nexus to the linked market(s); (3) the response of the terms of trade in the specific targeted instruments in the linked market(s) to the change in the nexus; and (4) the number of these targeted instruments in the trader's position in the linked market(s). A comparison of the latter three elements on this list combined with any losses incurred in the first is the basis of the concept of financial leverage, which was introduced earlier in this chapter.

The analysis of financial leverage introduces several interesting practical issues that we will turn to in the next chapter. For example, the greater the sensitivity of the nexus to the triggering action, the greater the effect on the trader's overall payoff. If, for example, withholding a very small amount of spot power would raise spot prices substantially, and the price of spot power was the nexus for a manipulation of a futures contract, this would tend to incentivize manipulation of those contracts (or other derivatives tied to them). Similarly, if the terms of trade magnify the effect of the spot price changes relative to the futures price, then the manipulation has higher expected profits. For example, if the manipulator holds a derivative security (e.g., shares of a "leveraged" ETF) that pays a profit of $3 for every $1 of profit on a generic futures contract, the expected payoff is increased. Finally, and more obviously, the larger the number of these targets held by the manipulator, the higher the expected payoff. As noted above, the profits produced from the combined effect of these three factors must exceed any losses incurred in the trigger for financial leverage to exist, thus making the manipulation profitable overall.

In the primary market, the profits and losses from manipulation depend on the type of trigger and can be analyzed using conventional economic tools and trading records. In the next chapter we discuss a number of implementation challenges, but at the conceptual level the method of measuring the net gains or losses from any of the three types of triggers is straightforward. For trading involving the exercise of market power, the analysis follows the familiar charts shown in Figure 9-2 above; for uneconomic trading, the analysis is illustrated in Figure 9-3; for outright fraud, the analysis will focus on the effects of the fraud on other actors in the primary market.

34. By comparison, proof of manipulation under an artificial price statute requires demonstration that the alleged manipulator caused (or, for attempted manipulation, attempted to cause) the creation of an "artificial" price. Since an "artificial" price is effectively a mechanism to trigger a fraud on the market, manipulations triggered by uneconomic trading are equivalently prosecutable under either a fraud-based or artificial price statute.

Avoiding False Positives and the Presumption of Legitimate Trading

The absence of ready-made microeconomic models designed to evaluate cross-market linkages means that the economic analysis of almost every manipulation case is somewhat unique. As a result, investigations of suspected manipulative behavior expend substantial internal or agency resources and can subject suspected traders and their firms to millions of dollars in lost productivity and legal fees, sometimes irrespective of whether the behavior in question is ultimately determined to be manipulative. The possibility that legitimate trading behavior is erroneously identified and investigated as manipulative—known in economic terms as a "false positive"—thus presents a huge concern for market participants, so much so that traders may forego some (or many) legitimate trading opportunities for fear of tripping a regulator's screens. This robs the market of liquidity and depth, paradoxically making the markets only more susceptible to manipulation over time by strengthening the nexuses between potential manipulation triggers and targets.

A more reasonable approach to the analysis of manipulative behavior—not to mention adherence to the principle of the presumption of innocence—would recognize that a presumption of transactional legitimacy must follow all open market trades in a free economic system. The assemblage and movement of the framework's three components is a necessary, but not sufficient, requirement for overcoming this presumption and proving a market manipulation. To fulfill the additional requirement of proof of intent, regulators typically provide economic evidence of a pattern of behavior over time designed to generate profits from the manipulative scheme, combined with more objective evidence of intent—e.g., emails, IMs, or tape recorded conversations. We discuss this in more detail in the next chapter.

We close this chapter and introduce the practical issues associated with implementing the framework with an example that illustrates many of the concepts just discussed. Consider, for example, a trader who owns a 100 MW FTR position over a transmission path, who repeatedly makes power sales of 50 MW over the path at a loss. A curious regulator may sense a manipulation afoot, for the uneconomic power trades could be designed to create congestion over the path to benefit the value of the FTR. However, this makes many assumptions that need to be vetted before a market manipulation claim should proceed. Why were the "uneconomic" power sales made? Perhaps the trader was required to deliver the power under a contract obligation, such that the loss was economically unavoidable. Alternatively, the power may come from a renewable resource, thus making the sales profitable when combined with the underlying tax credits. Either of these cases would justify the sales as serving a stand-alone legitimate business purpose, thus invalidating the trigger of the alleged manipulation.

But now assume that there is no valid reason shown for the uneconomic trades. Given apparent leverage in the target (the 100 MW FTR) relative to the trigger (the losing 50 MW power sales), is a clear manipulation case now proven? No, because this *apparent leverage* may not in practice confer sufficient *actual financial leverage* to make the manipulation profitable overall. This is an issue of stability of the nexus in preserving the linkage between the trigger and target. If there indeed was congestion over the transmission path when the losing power flows occurred, then the power flows exacerbated that congestion to the benefit of the FTR. However, if there was no congestion on the line at those times, the nexus of the manipulation was ineffective and no profit could arise. Variations of this example can be devised to show that different strengths of the nexus affect the relative power of the trigger on the target, with the resulting interpretation of financial leverage casting the FTR as either a hedge for the losing power trades or as a speculative position designed to act as a valid manipulation target.

CHAPTER 10

Implementation of the Framework in Practice

In the language of the framework, nearly every instrument traded in markets jurisdictional to electric regulators is either primary to or linked with another market—in fact, some instruments can simultaneously serve as a trigger in one market and a target in another.[1] In primary markets, almost every bid or offer that deviates from perceived competitive benchmarks could potentially be interpreted by a regulator as being worthy of scrutiny as potentially manipulative. If such scrutiny were costless, there would be little reason for concern. Of course, nothing could be further from the truth. Regulatory investigations make substantial use of scarce agency resources and can subject suspected traders and their firms to millions of dollars in lost productivity and legal fees, irrespective of whether or not their behavior is ultimately determined to be manipulative.[2] Accordingly, in this chapter we discuss how the framework can be used to assist the detection, investigation, and proof (or disproof) of manipulative behavior in energy markets, focusing pragmatically on how to maximize the efficient use of oversight resources and simultaneously avoid false positives.

---

1. For example, virtual trades affect the auction price settlement in the day-ahead (potentially primary) market, but then can act as a price-taking instrument in the real-time (potentially linked) market.

2. This is one reason why the "innocent until proven guilty" principle is important, and the efficiency criterion is important when judging tariff-compliant behavior in the primary market.

The Proof (or Disproof) of Suspected Manipulative Behavior

A process for applying the framework to assist the proof of manipulative behavior is shown below in Figure 10-1. Proof of manipulation can be met by developing economic evidence establishing each successive element of the framework along with intent at the relevant legal standard of proof.[3] Because each element is necessary it is efficient to consider them sequentially as shown in Figure 10-1.

Figure 10-1

Use of the Framework to Prove (or Disprove) Manipulation

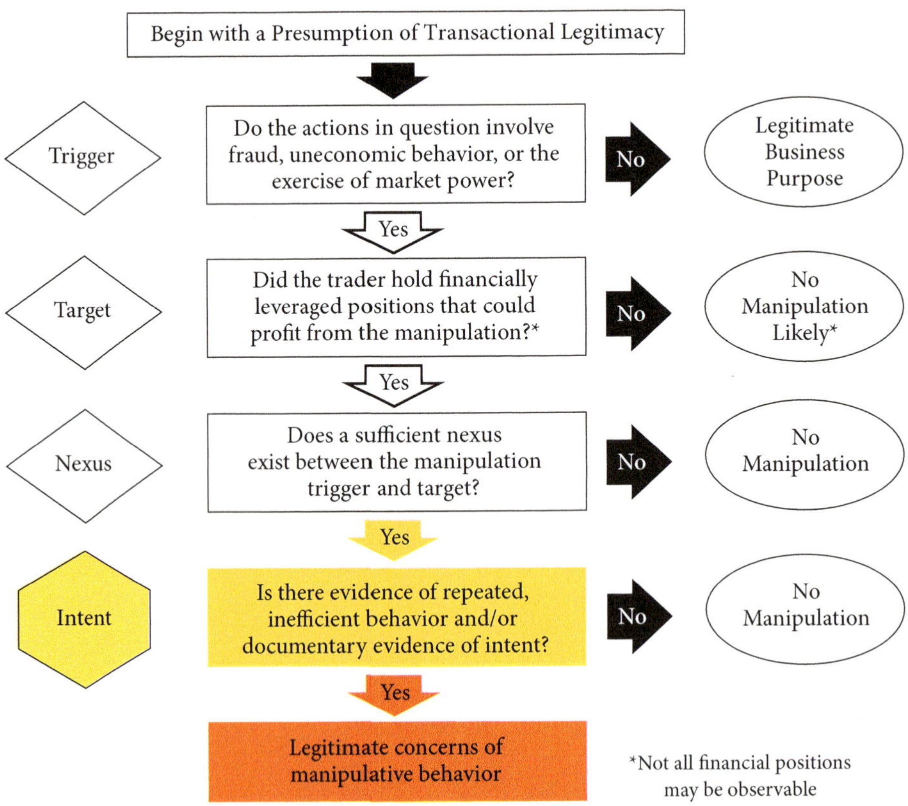
Begin with a Presumption of Transactional Legitimacy
Trigger
Do the actions in question involve fraud, uneconomic behavior, or the exercise of market power?
No
Legitimate Business Purpose
Yes
Target
Did the trader hold financially leveraged positions that could profit from the manipulation?*
No
No Manipulation Likely*
Yes
Nexus
Does a sufficient nexus exist between the manipulation trigger and target?
No
No Manipulation
Yes
Intent
Is there evidence of repeated, inefficient behavior and/or documentary evidence of intent?
No
No Manipulation
Yes
Legitimate concerns of manipulative behavior
*Not all financial positions may be observable

3. Because the manipulation rules are civil statutes, the requisite level of proof would normally be based on a "preponderance of the evidence," meaning more likely than not. However, because the basis of liability under the FERC's anti-manipulation rule is fraud, it may need to satisfy the higher burden of proof associated with "clear and convincing evidence," meaning that it is substantially more likely than not that its allegations are true. Note that neither of these standards is as stringent as the "beyond a reasonable doubt" burden of proof afforded to defendants in criminal cases. For discussion, *see http://courts.uslegal.com/burden-of-proof/clear-and-convincing-evidence/*.

As Figure 10-1 shows, the logical first question to address is whether there is convincing evidence of behavior that could serve as the manipulation's trigger (i.e., the *cause* of the manipulation)—uneconomic trading, outright fraud, or the exercise of market power. In the absence of such evidence, the analysis ends because the behavior alleged to have triggered the manipulation served a stand-alone legitimate business purpose that retains the presumption of transactional legitimacy.

As we have discussed extensively in Chapters 3 and 6, there are a number of well-established means of determining whether market power was exercised as a trigger. If the alleged trigger is uneconomic trading, the trigger can be established by evidence of repeated and/or anomalous losses measured relative to the trader's opportunity costs. The construction of antitrust-based structural indices such as HHIs will typically not provide useful information because they are not designed to evaluate uneconomic behavior. Similarly, if the alleged trigger is outright fraud, the proof centers on whether the false information—by an act of commission or omission—was in fact willfully (or recklessly) conveyed and relied upon.

The second step of the proof involves establishing the presence of a target. If evidence of a valid trigger is shown, the logical next step is to establish is whether one or more manipulation targets were in place to benefit from the manipulation (i.e., the *effect* of the manipulation). As noted in Figure 10-1, if the trader did not hold positions that *could* profit from the alleged manipulation, the proof fails. As we discussed in Chapter 9, if uneconomic trading is used as the trigger, this second step requires additional evidence that the financial leverage provided by the target(s) was sufficient to make the manipulation profitable overall. Evidence of such financial leverage differentiates legitimate trading strategies designed to hedge against losses from price movements in the primary market on the one hand from manipulative strategies designed to profit from such movements on the other.

If a target exists, the next step is to determine whether there is a nexus that provides a causal link between the trigger and target. The nature of the evidence needed to establish a nexus varies widely across different markets and instruments. In some cases the nexus is indisputably determined by the specific terms of the target, such as when the price of a derivative is set entirely by the clearing price in another market in which the triggering act occurred. However, in more complex cases, it may be necessary to create an economic model of the linkage between the markets involved in order to provide empirical proof that the nexus was quantitatively relevant. A wide variety of approaches can be used for these types of analyses.

The Evaluation of Intent

If economic evidence establishes the framework's three elements, the final step required to prove a manipulation and overcome the presumption of transactional legitimacy is the proof of intent. As introduced in Chapter 2 and mentioned at the end of Chapter 9, there are two types of evidence used to prove intent in manipulation cases: documentary evidence and economic evidence. These are usually combined—in proportions sometimes dictated by the evidence available—to portray the trader's knowledge of the manipulative scheme as well as the intent to employ it.

Documentary evidence can include statements, emails, and/or other forms of communication by the implicated traders that show, to the finder of fact, whether intent existed to work the framework's components in a fraudulent manner (or, alternatively, in a manner designed to create an "artificial" price). While economists can help interpret this information and relate it to the available economic evidence, there is no formal economic analysis involved. Such "objective" evidence of intent is often preferred by enforcement authorities due to less subjectivity in interpretation.

Despite this preference, economic evidence is increasingly relied on to establish intent in market manipulation cases, particularly when uneconomic trading is used as the trigger.[4] The approach used to develop this sort of evidence typically examines whether the behavior of the trader took a form that *would not be rationally profit-increasing but for the manipulative scheme*. Obviously, evidence of this nature requires an economic exercise that demonstrates the expected profitability of the potential triggering behavior without the alleged manipulation. If this analysis shows that one specific action or trade could not rationally have been expected to be profitable, a demonstration of intent requires the further showing that the action was not inadvertent. Practically speaking, this is demonstrated by showing that this or other similar actions were taken repeatedly to accomplish the same overall effect, or that the outcome was so anomalous that a finding of manipulative intent is warranted.[5]

As noted in Chapters 7 and 8, participants in electricity markets trade subject to complex tariffs that establish the rules for trading the various products authorized for each market. These may create interesting wrinkles in inferring manipulative intent from patterns of apparent uneconomic behavior. Tariffs may, by design, seek to motivate what appears to be uneconomic behavior on the part of market participants in order to enhance the overall performance of the electric power system. An example of such behavior in the context of the CAISO Tariff during the Crisis

4. The works of Dr. Craig Pirrong were seminal in advancing this notion. *See* Pirrong (1996) for one of the original arguments.

5. Ledgerwood and Carpenter (2012), p. 255, fn. 2. Most of the cases discussed in Chapter 11 allege some type of sustained or repeated behavior over time as proof of intent, especially when uneconomic trading is allegedly used as the trigger. However, one key economic act can be the foundation for a manipulation claim if supported by additional evidence. *See U.S. v. KeySpan Corporation, Complaint,* Case 1:10-cv-01415 (SDNY, February 22, 2010) (execution of a swap designed to build financial leverage in advance of an act of withholding alleged to be manipulative).

would be the scheduling of a flow from a high-priced zone to a low-priced zone when transmission between the zones was congested. The scheduled flow would be uneconomic, effectively passing up the higher price for the lower price. Furthermore under the tariff, the flow would garner a payment in a linked market, the congestion market, which would likely make the entire transaction profitable. Thus the behavior presents the signature of a manipulative transaction implemented through uneconomic trading. However, this is precisely the congestion-relieving behavior contemplated in the market design and intentionally motivated by the tariff.

In this context we posit that market or system efficiency should be an important criterion in evaluating the actions of traders if uneconomic behavior is used to establish manipulative intent. Where the actions of the trader are compliant with the relevant tariff and act to enhance the efficiency of the market or electric power system, as contemplated in the market design and implemented in the tariff, then such actions should not be treated as markers of intent to manipulate, regardless of whether they are repeated. Behavior compliant with the tariff that is beneficial to market efficiency, such as acts that move day-ahead and real-time prices toward convergence, should not be targeted for enforcement actions. Conversely, uneconomic behavior that harms market efficiency, such as by causing day-ahead and real-time prices to diverge or by creating an "artificial" price, warrants investigation even where facially consistent with the tariff. Such principles should guide agency enforcement efforts so as not to deter behavior promoted in tariffs to improve market/system performance.

The Detection of Potentially Manipulative Behavior

Before manipulation can be proven or disproven in any formal context, some sort of investigative process must occur. Purely for discussion purposes, the options for these processes may be categorized into the matrix of possibilities shown in Table 10-1.

Table 10-1

Categories of Manipulation Inquiries

	Inquiries Initialized by Specific Allegations	"Clean-Sheet" Processes for Screening Transactions
Internal Inquiries	Internal Investigation	Trade Surveillance
Inquiries by Agencies	Agency Investigation	Market Surveillance
Third Party Inquiries	Claims Investigation	-

The first key dimension of these possibilities is whether the inquiry is internal, performed by an agency with jurisdiction over the behavior or performed externally by other market participants, such as by plaintiffs seeking to verify a potential manipulation claim. This dimension greatly affects the initial information set available to the analyst. The second dimension is how the process is initialized: by specific allegations brought forward, or by a broader compliance-based motivation to screen transactions for evidence of manipulative behavior. In the remainder of this chapter, we explain how our framework may be used, albeit with some practical differences in application, in all five of the categories presented in Table 10-1.

Informational Asymmetries and Challenges

There is an inherent informational asymmetry that separates the information accessible to internal parties (e.g., compliance personnel within trading houses or the like) versus external parties such as regulatory agencies, market monitors, or third parties affected by market outcomes. Internal parties have the ability to see all internal trades and positions, but without the benefit of trade data for the broader market against which to benchmark. Conversely, a market monitor or regulatory agency can evaluate a suspected manipulation using trading and position data for all market participants under its purview, giving it superior ability to compare any behavior of concern against historical and contemporaneous benchmarks; however, the monitor will not be able to "see" trades or positions outside of its jurisdictional reach. Third parties are in the worst position to evaluate suspected manipulative behavior, for they lack both the proprietary data available to the suspected manipulator and the market data available to regulatory authorities. Combined with the complex array of products, trading instruments, market rules, and regulations that are endemic to electricity markets, the limited information set raises the costs of searching for manipulation for regulators and market participants alike.

These information differences evolve when regulatory agencies begin formal investigations of suspected manipulative behavior. Regulatory agencies typically begin with better access to the data needed to evaluate a suspected manipulator's behavior relative to that of the rest of the market, and may take advantage of compulsory (and sometimes invasive) discovery tools that can probe for the evidence needed to assemble proof of the framework's three elements and of the trader's intent.[6] In the same adversarial context, defendants/respondents begin with superior information concerning their own trading behavior, including detailed records of their trades as well as extensive records of internal communications by traders in a variety of forms, but may not learn of other relevant information until the case proceeds through discovery.[7] If

6. Indeed, is it asserted by some that the FERC's manipulation investigation process inherently lacks due process protections that would be afforded in other equivalent proceedings before other government or administrative bodies. *See* Scherman (2014), p. 101.

7. Ideally, these should allow for a relatively rapid assessment of the viability of manipulation claims asserted against them. However, a lack of internal surveillance systems often leaves companies scrambling to assemble this data in the wake of a flurry of data requests after the opening of an investigation by regulators.

the governing statutes allow actions by third-party plaintiffs, they begin with the least relevant information of all and are left to initially diagnose potential manipulations via their own trading records and whatever public data they can locate.[8] If this analysis is sufficient to survive a motion to dismiss, plaintiffs too receive the benefit of discovery, giving them greater ability to support their case.[9]

Another challenge to all investigations is the interpretation of data presented from trade-capture systems, which are often a mix of legacy systems that were not designed to produce data in formats that would assist forensic analysis. Anyone who has spoken with a trader about the mechanics of what they do may find themselves rapidly drowning in a mixture of jargon, with discussions of a dizzying array of "long" and "short" physical and financial positions traded across multiple locations, times, products, and exchanges. The independent analysis of raw trading data presents difficult challenges and must generally be undertaken without the benefit of the trader to explain what it reflects and how it all fits together. A most vexing issue is that none of what is presented in isolation seems that difficult. While most everyone can understand buy vs. sell, long vs. short, node vs. hub, and prompt-month vs. prompt-next, the interactions of all such actions in combination can seem impenetrable.

Yet another complicating factor is the determination of accurate benchmarks against which the trading data is compared to determine if there is evidence of anomalous behavior. Any traded market is subject to fluctuations in price and volumes traded, such that comparisons of suspicious trading behavior against the "normal noise" of the market—i.e., normal variances in prices and flows—may make distinguishing legitimate signals from anomalous ones quite difficult. This can often be made worse at times when constraints bind, such that the variance of prices trading volumes increases and what is "normal" becomes much less relevant. Cross-product comparisons across time (e.g., spot vs. futures), locations, products (e.g., physical vs. financial), or inputs (e.g., natural gas prices vs. electricity prices) can be helpful, but they too can be subject to decoupling under abnormal market conditions.

Using the Framework to Investigate Specific Allegations

When a specific allegation of market manipulation is brought forward to relevant investigators, whether internal or external, our framework provides a useful guide to analyzing the allegation. By definition, the allegation will identify at least one element of the framework. For example, if a whistleblower alleges that a trader is engaging in suspicious, repeated, loss-making trades, it is clear that the allegation refers to uneconomic trading as a trigger.

8. The manipulation statutes under which the FERC prosecutes electric and gas market manipulations do not allow third party actions.
9. Pragmatically, this is why plaintiff claims of market manipulation are typically filed only in the wake of public investigations by regulatory agencies.

Conversely, if an automated screening tool identifies an unusually large derivatives position that is tied to a particular price, it is possible that the position could represent a potential manipulation target.

The specific next steps of the investigation depend on the information available to the analyst, but the goal is ultimately the same: to determine whether all the remaining elements of the framework are present, and, if so, whether there is evidence of intent. If the inquiry is internal, analysis of the communications of the trader (searching for intent) and examination of trading positions to see whether there exists a target that has a link (nexus) to the alleged trigger actions are an efficient way to proceed. External investigators receiving the allegation should have the same specific objectives, but will have to work around the information available to them. In short, when specific allegations initialize the investigation, these are used as a starting point to search for the remaining elements of the framework.

Using the Framework as "Clean-Sheet" Processes to Detect Potentially Manipulative Behavior

How do compliance personnel establish a system to screen for and evaluate trading data for manipulation in a manner that is efficient but mindful of the possibly legitimate purposes those offers might serve? More importantly, as market conditions, products, and trading instruments evolve over time, how can this system adapt and provide an effective screen against potentially manipulative behavior while being flexible enough to allow for legitimate, profitable trading to thrive? An answer lies in the establishment of an adaptive, information-based compliance loop based on our framework.

As an initial matter, it is useful to distinguish between two market oversight functions we label *monitoring* and *surveillance*. Monitoring is the ongoing observation of high-level market data to evaluate anomalies relative to economic or physical system condition and events. Monitoring, which relies heavily on the institutional and technical knowledge of market experts, is an "early warning system" to market regulators, alerting them to problems that include potential episodes of manipulation, but also emergencies, institutional failures, market design problems, the effects of particular structural transactions (such as mergers), and potential market improvements.

The term surveillance refers to the specific review of data concerning the trading activities of specific traders in the market. In contrast to market monitoring, surveillance is conducted by internal units within trading organizations or by entities within or chartered by regulators.[10]

10. The difference in these functions is highlighted by the fact that the FERC houses these functions in separate divisions within its Office of Enforcement.

Our framework is well-suited to assist internal or external surveillance efforts, as we explain using Figure 10-2.

Figure 10-2

Use of the Framework in Surveillance to Detect Potential Manipulation

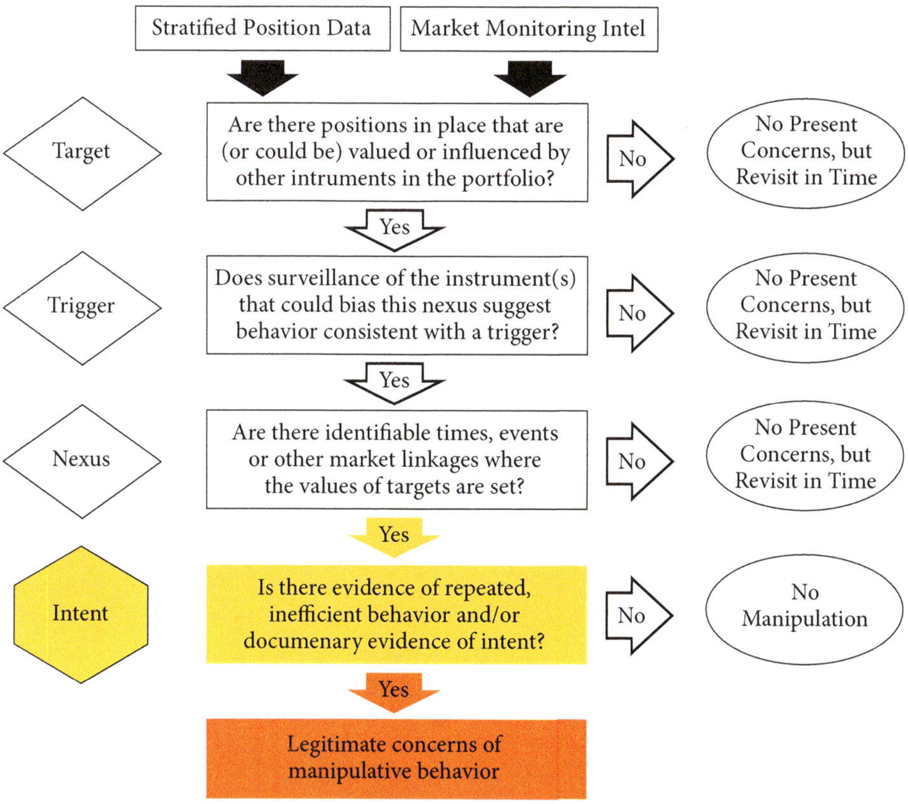
Stratified Position Data
Market Monitoring Intel
Target
Are there positions in place that are (or could be) valued or influenced by other intruments in the portfolio?
No
No Present Concerns, but Revisit in Time
Yes
Trigger
Does surveillance of the instrument(s) that could bias this nexus suggest behavior consistent with a trigger?
No
No Present Concerns, but Revisit in Time
Yes
Nexus
Are there identifiable times, events or other market linkages where the values of targets are set?
No
No Present Concerns, but Revisit in Time
Yes
Intent
Is there evidence of repeated, inefficient behavior and/or documenary evidence of intent?
No
No Manipulation
Yes
Legitimate concerns of manipulative behavior

The use of our framework for surveillance begins with two key sources of information: data concerning the accumulation, liquidation, and settlement of the various instruments in the trader's portfolio over time, which we refer to as "rolled up" transactions data, and intelligence as to the market and system mechanisms that influence (or are influenced by) the trading of those instruments. A somewhat surprising reality of many electricity trading firms is their lack of ability to "roll up" their complete trading data into position reports for forensic analysis. This often results from legacy trade-capture systems designed to provide instantaneous position reports to traders during the trading day,[11] but which typically do not archive

11. A further complicating factor is that most modern trading companies were formed through a series of mergers and acquisitions, meaning that many firms continue to operate several such legacy systems independently and without integration.

transaction-level data in a format useful to assist later analyses.[12] Indeed, firms often have been averse to archiving such data for fear of making regulators' jobs easier, or of exposing the firm to questions as to why compliance personnel failed to find and report suspected manipulative activity. However, the increased threat of trade-based surveillance now in place at the agencies can expose behavior that can lead to massive civil and criminal liability, meaning that there is considerable risk in avoiding proactive internal surveillance efforts.

Stratification of the Rolled-Up Trading Data

Armed with rolled-up trade data, the next step in the screening application of the framework is to create two subdivisions of the rolled-up trading portfolio: a longer list of potential targets and a shorter list of potential triggers. The surveillance analyst should presume that each rolled-up position is a potential target, unless this possibility can be easily ruled out. A position is a target if it is possible that the same trading entity could take a position (or influence a process) in any market where the outcome might have a connection to the value of the potential target. Although there may be exceptions that warrant removing a position as a potential target, it may be simpler as a preliminary matter for the analyst to presume that all positions could serve as potential manipulation targets, then screen for their nexus to triggers, as explained below.

The next step is to review the rolled-up position data to identify and separate the instruments in the portfolio that through their trading could serve as potential triggers. If the trades associated with a position have (or will have) no measurable impact on a market outcome or processes, such as the creation of a price, the trades and associated position should be presumed benign. In other words, if one can rule out the trades associated with a position as having any potential impact on the outcomes that influence other markets, these positions should not be able to serve as triggers in a manipulation.

Application of the Framework to the Stratified Triggers and Targets

The next step of the surveillance process is to search for a nexus between the lists of potential triggers and targets. At this point, knowledge of the interactions between the markets in which the positions are established becomes critical, and the knowledge acquired by market monitors as well as other analysts, traders, and experts is very useful. Monitoring intelligence can then inform which of these instruments are the most likely to interact through a common nexus, informed by knowledge of actual system operations and constraints and the history of past

12. An exception is the creation of high-level, end-of-day profit and loss statements that are used by risk managers to evaluate individual traders' limits for subsequent trading. Unfortunately, these reports usually say little about the profitability of the individual instruments in the traders' portfolios.

enforcement cases that have focused on specific manipulative activity—e.g., using virtual bids to manipulate the value of FTRs. Effectively, this inquiry simplifies the surveillance analyst's task by limiting the scope of the analysis to the examination of those relationships amongst the data that are the most likely to be exploited by the traders associated with the portfolio under scrutiny. If either a trigger or target is missing on either side of the nexus in a given market and time period, there is no further need to explore the nexus in this iteration of the surveillance process.

Once the key nexuses of concern are identified, targeted instruments that tie to a given nexus—such as a price set in a specific market at specific location and time—should be combined to determine the trader's net exposure to that nexus. This is critical, as an isolated position that appears to provide a leveraged manipulation target (or a harmless hedge) may be significantly less (or more) concerning when combined with other positions that offset (or enhance) the exposure. Once determined, the analysis should then focus narrowly on the subset of trades that could trigger the manipulation of the nexus and associated targets identified. If all pieces of the framework are in place—and, thus, a manipulation is suspected—the surveillance team should examine evidence concerning the trader's intent, such as by examining contemporaneous voice recordings, IMs, emails, or by questioning the trader directly concerning the suspected conduct.

A primary concern for firms considering the implementation of internal surveillance programs is the cost associated with a large number of complex and computationally intense market manipulation screens. Firms can partly alleviate these costs by employing the process we have outlined for screening transactions. Over time, application of this overall screening process will eventually reveal the nexuses of the greatest concern for a particular firm's typical transactions and help build screens designed to detect specific behavior at times and locations most relevant to the firm's chief market-based activities and instruments traded.

As these screens are vetted, improved, and automated, surveillance efforts can turn to evaluating new nexuses using the knowledge obtained from prior experience. If successful, a "compliance loop" is created wherein monitoring, surveillance, and compliance personnel develop scale economies in processing information and implementing new screening methodologies. Ideally, this system will develop the ability to detect new, innovative forms of manipulation while maximizing the amount of legitimate trading that can take place.

CHAPTER 11

Recent Enforcement Actions and Their Links to The Framework

As we discussed earlier in Chapter 8, the FERC's anti-manipulation enforcement efforts have grown substantially in the wake of Enron and following EPAct 2005 and Order 670, which adopted the FERC's fraud-based anti-manipulation Rule 1c. Of lesser fanfare, but perhaps of equal concern to electricity market participants, the CFTC has also exercised its anti-manipulation authority in cases involving electricity markets, both prior to and following the provision of its fraud-based anti-manipulation rule through Dodd-Frank.[1] Indeed, although the CFTC has issued an order generally exempting instruments issued by and traded in organized electricity markets (ISOs/RTOs) from its broader jurisdiction,[2] the order specifically states that these instruments are not excluded from its anti-manipulation authority.[3] The increase in enforcement activity in electricity, other commodity, and financial markets has garnered fines and restitution that are increasingly measured in the hundreds of millions or billions of dollars, is summarized for the FERC and CFTC in Figure 11-1.

1. *See* the discussion of the CFTC's authority under the CEA in Chapter 2.

2. *Final Order in Response to a Petition from Certain Independent System Operators and Regional Transmission Organizations to Exempt Specified Transactions Authorized by a Tariff or Protocol Approved by the Federal Energy Regulatory Commission or the Public Utility Commission of Texas from Certain Provisions of the Commodity Exchange Act Pursuant to the Authority Provided in Section 4(c)(6) of the Act*, available at *http://www.cftc.gov/ucm/groups/public/@newsroom/ documents/file/federalregister032813b.pdf* (March 23, 2013).

3. *Id.*, p. 101 *et seq.*

Figure 11-1

Fines and Restitution Garnered By FERC and CFTC Anti-Manipulation Enforcement Actions (Millions of Dollars)[4]

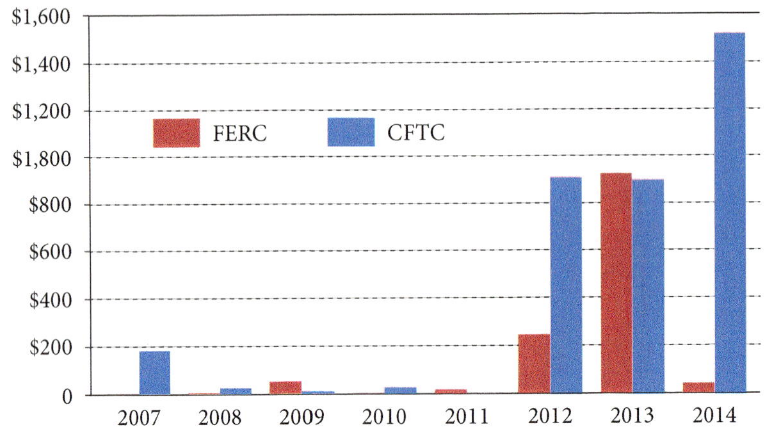

The sharp increase in fines levied by the agencies corresponds with their willingness and ability to prosecute behavior considered to be in violation of their new fraud-based authority—schemes involving not only uneconomic behavior, but also fraudulent acts used to generate revenue/profit where no value has been provided. Indeed, many of the schemes alleged are very similar to those used by Enron and others during the Crisis.[5] To tie the past, present, and future of market manipulation enforcement together, it is helpful to compare and contrast several of these recent cases using our framework. We will group the discussion based on the type of trigger employed, discussing in order uneconomic behavior, the exercise of market power, and outright fraud.

In this chapter, we describe several market manipulation enforcement actions that were brought by the FERC and CFTC, as well as a few cases brought by other regulatory bodies in the U.S. and the European Union. A key issue relevant to all of these cases is the detrimental effect the alleged behavior had on market efficiency, such as through the intentional creation of price distortions or price divergence, the inefficient dispatch of generation units out of merit, the release of payments from reliability, demand response, or other out-of-market mechanisms through the gaming of market rules, and/or the exercise of market power to benefit swaps or affiliated companies. Although several of these cases involve energy commodities other than electricity, understanding the breadth of the behavior involved is helpful to understanding the types of behavior that merit serious regulatory scrutiny. *We must also stress that with the exception of DiPlacido, E.ON Energy, and Gila River, the cases discussed are either* _*still*_

4. Fines and Restitutions data collected from the FERC Enforcement website (*see https://www.ferc.gov/enforcement/civil-penalties/civil-penalty-action.asp*), and the CFTC lists of enforcement actions (*see http://www.cftc.gov/LawRegulation/Enforcement/EnforcementActions/index.htm*).

5. We discuss Enron's Gaming strategies in Chapter 7.

being litigated or are settlements where the accused has neither admitted nor denied the behavior alleged. In all settled cases, we clarify that the allegations of manipulation remain just that, and we refer to them as such.

Uneconomic Trading

Here, we examine 9 examples of alleged uneconomic behavior used to trigger manipulative schemes. These cases, but for *DiPlacido*, remain to be litigated or resulted in settlements between the government and the accused manipulator(s), meaning that the outcomes, while instructive, do not provide legal precedent. As you read these cases, keep in mind some key questions. Would the trades allegedly used to trigger each scheme have been placed but for the benefits gained from the manipulation's target? What is the effect of those trades on market efficiency? Is public policy better served by deterring the challenged types of trades, or by allowing them so as to boost liquidity?

Index Manipulations

An almost ubiquitous feature of the contracts that trade in commodity and financial markets is their reliance upon an "index" determined by a subset of trades, usually executed over a specific time period and at a particular location or on particular exchange, to establish the contract price. The typical pricing mechanism uses the volume-weighted average price ("VWAP") of eligible trades made during the period, which can span time frames as short as a minute or as long as a week. The period itself can be referred to by many generalized names—including the "settlement period," "window," or "fix"—or by more colloquial names unique to the commodity traded—e.g., "bidweek" for natural gas, or "the ring" for precious metals. Irrespective of these conventions, the ultimate result is a rather narrowly established *index*, from which the value of a much broader set of physical and financial contracts is determined.

Because the prices of a relatively small number of transactions set the value of a much greater universe of positions, the potential impact of influencing the index on large, financially leveraged positions can motivate traders to place substantial, uneconomic trades so as to directionally bias the index up or down. As we discussed in Chapter 9, the fragility of the index price depends on the depth and liquidity of the market at the time the price-making trades are executed. Even the timing of the trades during the settlement period can be critical. For example, a concentrated burst of trades at the beginning of the settlement period (known as "framing the open") can bias the expectations of other market participants such that subsequent trades are "poisoned" by the behavior. Conversely, the manipulator can focus the burst of uneconomic trades at the end of the settlement period (called "banging the close") so as to register trades at artificial prices without giving participants on the other side of the market time to react to the price change. Several examples of these phenomena are described below.

Amaranth Advisors LLC (Amaranth) and Brian Hunter

Amaranth Advisors LLC (Amaranth) was a hedge fund management company based in the United States. By 2005, the majority of the company's investments were tied to speculative positions in energy markets, mainly New York Mercantile Exchange (NYMEX) monthly natural gas futures contracts and associated 'look-alike' swap contracts traded on NYMEX ClearPort and the InterContinental Exchange (ICE).[6] Led by trader Brian Hunter, the energy trading segment of Amaranth made big profits in the fall of 2005 from the placement of large, net long speculative positions in advance of Hurricanes Katrina and Rita. The profits drove additional capital into Amaranth, allegedly emboldening Mr. Hunter to try an "experiment" starting in February 2006.[7]

Mr. Hunter entered February 24, 2006, the last day of trading for the March 2006 NYMEX Natural Gas Futures Contract, short 1,729 contracts.[8] As a hedge fund, Amaranth could neither take nor deliver natural gas, meaning that its end-of-day position would have to be zero. During the trading day, but before the final 30 minutes of trading during which the price of the March contract would be set, Mr. Hunter allegedly purchased about 5,000 futures contracts to swing long approximately 3,000 contracts.[9] By itself, this behavior was not price-making, but was used to accumulate the position that would trigger the manipulation. Mr. Hunter's representative was then alleged to have entered the trading pit where open outcry bids and offers were placed, and proceeded rapidly to sell the 3,000 contracts at the beginning of the 30 minute settlement period, thus biasing the index price down. The result on the market price is shown below in Figure 11-2. This alleged behavior was clearly uneconomic, given that the 5,000 contracts were bought during the trading day at prices generally greater than \$7.30, while the contracts liquidated in the settlement period were continuously sold well-below that price.[10]

6. NYMEX ClearPort (now CME Group) and ICE are electronic exchanges which provide for the trading of physical and financial energy contracts. In many cases, physical futures contracts are traded in parallel with "look-alike" contracts which bear identical financial terms but settle financially (i.e., without any obligations to take or make physical delivery of the underlying commodity).
7. Amaranth Advisors L.L.C., *Order to Show Cause and Notice of Proposed Penalties*, ("Amaranth OSC") 120 FERC ¶ 61,085, July 26, 2007, ¶ 2.
8. *Id.*, ¶ 70.
9. *Id.*
10. Further, Mr. Hunter's behavior was found to be fraudulent outright because his trader's liquidation by the open outcry process was alleged to have been designed to induce other traders to further the downward pricing momentum by selling for fear of a price collapse.

Figure 11-2

Alleged Manipulation of NYMEX Natural Gas Futures by Amaranth Trader Brian Hunter (Trading for the March 2006 Contract on February 24, 2006)[11]

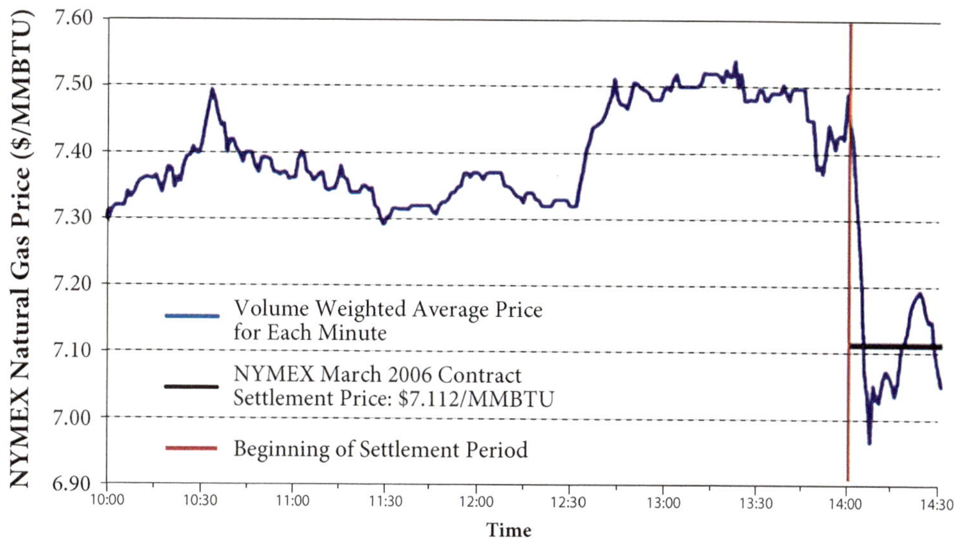

Later agency analysis revealed that Hunter had a large position in financial swaps and options, equivalent to approximately 16,613.25 NYMEX contracts that were short to the settlement price of the March contract.[12] Given the uneconomic liquidation of about 3,000 contracts (the trigger) to bias the final settlement price of the March 2006 contract (the nexus), Mr. Hunter therefore held financial leverage of about 5-to-1 in these swap and option contracts (the targets). The FERC found evidence of similar behavior for the April and May 2006 NYMEX contracts[13] and used this repeated behavior, and Mr. Hunter's IMs, as its evidence regarding proof of intent.[14]

Perhaps the most interesting aspect of this case is its highly unusual outcome. After settling with Amaranth and other parties,[15] the FERC proceeded against Mr. Hunter in an action before an agency Administrative Law Judge ("ALJ"). The result was a civil penalty of $30 million,[16] which was later affirmed by the Commission.[17] This was challenged on jurisdictional grounds by the

11. Amaranth OSC, ¶ 41.
12. *Id.*, at ¶ 78.
13. *Id.*, at ¶¶ 85-106.
14. *Id.*, at ¶¶ 67-75.
15. Amaranth Advisors L.L.C., *Order Approving Uncontested Settlement*, 128 FERC ¶ 61,154, August 12, 2009.
16. Brian Hunter, *Initial Decision*, 130 FERC ¶ 63,004, January 22, 2010.
17. Brian Hunter, *Order Affirming Initial Decision and Ordering Payment of Civil Penalty*, 135 FERC ¶ 61,054, April 21, 2011.

CFTC,[18] which had also brought an enforcement action against Mr. Hunter and Amaranth[19] and had settled all claims against the latter.[20] At issue was the fact that jurisdiction over the trigger, nexus, and target of the manipulation rested exclusively with the CFTC. The FERC's only jurisdictional claim was that the manipulative behavior affected the value of physical natural gas contracts, and thus was used "in connection with" transactions that were FERC-jurisdictional.[21] The appellate court disagreed with FERC and dismissed the case,[22] thus nullifying the agency's first formal finding of market manipulation. The CFTC then settled its case against Mr. Hunter on September 14, 2014 for $750,000, with him neither admitting nor denying the behavior. Thus, one U.S. agency spent taxpayer funds to sue another for the rights to sue an already proven manipulator, only to settle the case for over $29 million less than the original judgment and to remove the verdict against him.

The reason for the CFTC's settlement is the legal rule used to prosecute the behavior. The acts occurred in 2006, after the FERC had its fraud-based anti-manipulation rule under EPAct 2005, but before the CFTC had its fraud-based rule under Dodd-Frank. The FERC could levy a $30 million penalty under its fraud-based rule because it did not require proof of any harm to the market. By comparison, the CFTC was left to prosecute the behavior under its old "artificial price" rule, which required a showing of harm. Since the CFTC could not show harm by establishing an "artificial" price, it makes sense that the CFTC had to settle the case for almost nothing relative to the penalties handed down by the FERC.

This lesson is highly relevant to European regulators, who are about to enforce their own market manipulation rules under REMIT. Like Dodd-Frank, REMIT includes anti-manipulation rules based on fraud and artificial price. However, the framework discussed above is equally useful for analyzing manipulation under either type of rule, especially in cases involving intentional uneconomic trading. Specifically, because the behavior used to cause the manipulation will simultaneously inject fraudulent information into the marketplace and cause (or attempt to cause) an artificial price, the economic analysis required to prove (or disprove) liability for the behavior under either rule is identical.

18. *Hunter v. Federal Energy Regulatory Commission*, (DC Cir 2013). The CFTC participated in this case as an Intervenor.

19. *United States Commodity Futures Exchange Commission v. Amaranth Advisors, L.L.C., Amaranth Advisors (Calgary) ULC, and Brian Hunter*, 07 Civ. 6682 (DC) (SDNY, May 21, 2007).

20. *Consent Order of Permanent Injunction, Civil Monetary Penalty and Other Relief as to Defendants Amaranth Advisors, L.L.C. and Amaranth Advisors (Calgary) ULC, United States Commodity Futures Exchange Commission v. Amaranth Advisors, L.L.C., et al.*, 07 Civ. 6682 (DC) (SDNY, August 12, 2009).

21. This claim ties to language contained in § 4A of the Natural Gas Act, 15 U.S.C. § 717c-1, as amended by EPAct 2005. *See Order Affirming Initial Decision and Ordering Payment of Civil Penalty*, p. 2.

22. *Hunter v. Federal Energy Regulatory Commission*, 11-1477, U.S. Court of Appeals for the District of Columbia (Washington) (Decided March 15, 2013).

Barclays Bank PLC, et al. (Barclays)

The FERC is also active in pursuing index manipulations in electricity markets. On point, the FERC issued an Order to Show Cause against Barclays Bank, PLC and four individual traders in 2012, alleging they engaged in loss-generating trading of next-day fixed-price physical electricity over-the-counter (OTC) contracts on ICE for delivery at the western locations of Mid-Columbia, Palo Verde, South Path 15, and North Path 15 to benefit Barclays' financial swap positions in those markets.[23] The alleged manipulation involved building significant swap positions at the four trading hubs that were directionally long or short to daily indices on ICE, acquiring monthly physical index positions that were directionally opposite to the price exposure of the swaps positions, then liquidating the physical index positions uneconomically (the trigger) in the daily market to bias the index (the nexus) to benefit the swaps' values (the target).[24] The Order to Show Cause sought $469.9 million in civil penalties and disgorgement (plus interest) from Barclays, as well as $18 million from the four individual traders.[25] The FERC upheld this result.[26] The case awaits resolution in federal district court at the time of this writing.[27]

The Barclays case raises several interesting aspects of how a manipulative scheme can work, in particular the mechanism used to trigger the alleged scheme. Physical index positions are usually thought of as price-taking instruments that can serve as a manipulation's target. However, because the price that is ultimately paid for the position is the index price, the position can be used as the source for uneconomic physical fixed-price trades placed during the period when the index is formed, thus biasing the index in a direction that makes the physical index position cheaper to acquire.[28] As the example provided in Chapter 9 demonstrates, if sufficiently-leveraged financial targets (such as derivatives or additional physical index positions) are then directionally aligned to benefit from the biased index price, a successful manipulation may result.

The evidence of intent presented by the FERC against Barclays rested on the pattern of behavior manifested over a 35-month span, including the repeated assemblage of the pieces necessary

---

23. Barclays Bank PLC, Daniel Brin, Scott Connelly, Karen Levine, and Ryan Smith, *Order to Show Cause and Notice of Proposed Penalty*, 141 FERC ¶ 61,084, October 31, 2012, ¶ 2.

24. *Id.*, Enforcement Staff Report and Recommendation, pp. 11-35.

25. *Id.*, ¶ 1.

26. Barclays Bank PLC, Daniel Brin, Scott Connelly, Karen Levine, and Ryan Smith, *Order Assessing Civil Penalties* ("Barclays Order"), 144 FERC ¶ 61,041, July 16, 2013.

27. *FERC v. Barclays Bank PLC*, No. 2:13-cv-02093, E.D. Cal., October 9, 2013. Defendants to Rule 1c enforcement cases brought under the Federal Power Act have the option to elect a trial either by a FERC ALJ or in federal court. By comparison, cases brought under the Natural Gas Act must be heard before a FERC ALJ.

28. Interestingly, if the fixed price trades are 100% of those setting the index's value, the fixed price trades must by definition break even. Whether these trades could then be viewed as "uneconomic" is an open question. This conundrum was first posited by Mr. Matthew L. Hunter, former Senior Advisor of the FERC's Office of Enforcement and presently Deputy Director, Division of Market Oversight, Surveillance Branch of the CFTC.

to execute the manipulation, the change in the traders' behavior during those 35 months relative to other months, Barclays' willingness to incur continual losses in the daily trades that triggered the alleged manipulation, often colorful emails and IMs amongst the traders describing the scheme, and the implausibility of the defenses raised by the traders and company to justify the legitimate business purpose of the alleged behavior.[29]

Barclays also raises an interesting jurisdictional issue in the wake of the *Brian Hunter* decision: the wholesale physical power trades that served to trigger the alleged manipulation are FERC jurisdictional, but the financial derivatives targets are CFTC jurisdictional. *Barclays et al.* asserted that the FERC therefore lacked jurisdiction over the case because a critical component of the manipulation lay within the exclusive jurisdiction of the CFTC.[30] The FERC countered that it retained jurisdiction given its dominion over the trigger, as well as a CFTC acknowledgement of the FERC's jurisdiction in the matter.[31]

BP America Inc., et al. (BP)

Another manipulation case in process at the time of this writing is the FERC's case against BP America, Inc. *et al.*[32] BP's "Texas Team" traded physical natural gas at Katy Hub and Houston Ship Channel ("HSC"), and controlled physical pipeline capacity to flow gas from Katy to HSC. Going into mid-September 2008, BP held a HSC-Henry Hub spread position that was short to the Gas Daily index at HSC and long to the price at the Henry Hub, on which the FERC alleges BP's Texas Team was losing money.[33] However, the approach of Hurricane Ike prompted industrial plant closures in Houston, resulting in a surplus of natural gas that tanked the *Gas Daily* HSC Index, thus making BP's spread position profitable by $2 million.[34] FERC alleged that this profit motivated the Texas Team to amplify and prolong the profits through uneconomic sales of gas from Katy to HSC from September 18, 2008 through the end of November 2008 (the trigger), designed to bias downward the *Gas Daily* HSC Index (the nexus) to benefit its financial swaps that were short to that price (the target).[35] The Order to Show Cause sought $28.8 million in civil penalties and disgorgement (plus interest).[36] The Commission set the case for hearing before a FERC ALJ.[37] The case is pending at the time of this writing.

29. Barclays Order, ¶ 32.

30. *Notice of Motion and Motion to Dismiss*, FERC v. Barclays Bank PLC, No. 2:13-cv-02093, E.D. Cal. December, 16, 2013.

31. *Petitioner's Opposition to Respondents' Motion*, FERC v. Barclays Bank PLC, No. 2:13-cv-02093, E.D. Cal. February 14, 2013.

32. BP America Inc., *et al.*, *Order to Show Cause and Notice of Proposed Penalty* ("BP OSC"), 144 FERC ¶ 61,100, August 5, 2013, p. 2.

33. *Id.*, Enforcement Staff Report and Recommendation, p. 48.

34. *Id.*

35. *Id.*, pp. 1-2.

36. *Id.*, ¶ 1.

37. BP America Inc., *Order Establishing Hearing*, 147 FERC ¶ 61,130, May 15, 2014.

As compared to the other manipulation cases brought by the FERC, the allegations in the BP case rely less upon documentary evidence—which consists predominantly of a single recorded telephone conversation (and the company's internal reactions thereto)[38]—but rather more heavily upon economic evidence for the proof of intent.[39] Much of the FERC's case is built around the observation that the Texas Team's behavior during the period at issue significantly deviated from its past behavior, as shown in Figure 11-3.

Figure 11-3

Alleged Manipulation of HSC Natural Gas Prices at HSC by BP's Texas Team[40]

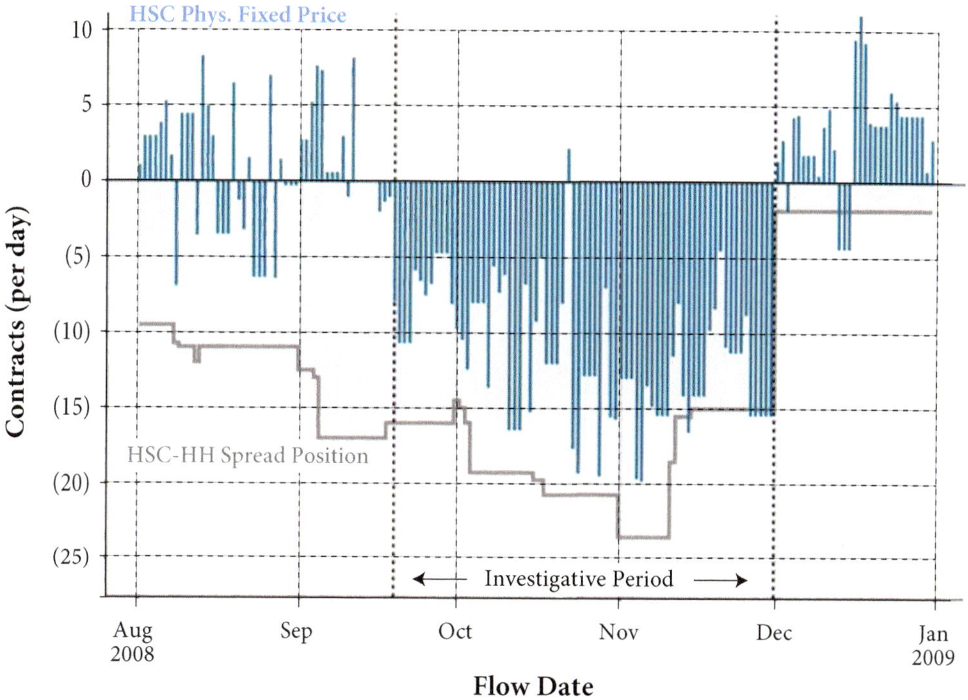

The FERC noted that while BP historically both bought and sold gas at HSC, it almost exclusively sold gas during the period of interest,[41] making atypically full use of its pipeline capacity

38. BP OSC, Enforcement Staff Report and Recommendation, pp. 4-16. The conversation in question prompted the company to perform an internal investigation of the behavior, the result of which found no behavior of concern. *Id.*, pp. 63-67.

39. *Id.*, pp. 16-67.

40. *Id.*, p. 24, Figure 4.

41. *Id.*, pp. 28-29.

from Katy in the process.[42] Further, BP expanded its derivatives positions that were short to the index at HSC,[43] thus increasing the amount of financial leverage in the alleged target.

Two aspects of the FERC's analysis of the Texas Team's alleged uneconomic trades are notable relative to the other cases discussed herein. First, the sales that FERC alleged were uneconomic did not lose money on an accounting basis, but instead were asserted to be below BP's opportunity costs of prevailing daily prices that were otherwise available at HSC or at Katy.[44] This was deemed inconsistent with the "arbitrage strategy" that the Texas Team normally pursued between these trading hubs prior to the period at issue.[45] Second, the traders used these allegedly uneconomic sales heavily at the beginning of each trading day in an effort to "mark the open" at a lower price, thus tending to bias any later trades towards also executing at lower prices given the misinformation inserted into the market.[46]

Optiver US, LLC, et al. (Optiver)

Optiver traded commodity futures on the New York Mercantile Exchange (NYMEX). On five days in March 2007, several of the company's traders were alleged to have engaged in a strategy designed to manipulate the prices of the April 2007 NYMEX contracts for Light Sweet Crude Oil, New York Harbor Heating Oil, and New York Harbor Reformulated Gasoline Blendstock.[47] The traders allegedly accumulated net long or net short physical index (also known as "Trade at Settlement" or "TAS") positions prior to the two minute settlement period at the end of each trading day. The traders then executed an algorithmic program called "the Hammer," which placed a concentrated burst of purchases or sales of futures contracts in the daily "pre-close" and closing period to bias the VWAP to benefit to their net TAS positions.[48] This illustrates how concentrated, uneconomic trades (the potential trigger) might be used to bias settlement prices (the nexus) to benefit the value of physical index positions (the targets).

The CFTC filed a complaint against Optiver and its traders in July 2008, alleging manipulation (or attempted manipulation) in violation of the CEA's artificial price rule.[49] The most salient evidence of intent presented by the agency was a series of emails in which the traders vividly described their scheme and use of "the Hammer." A $14 million settlement was approved in April 2012 ($13 million in civil penalties and $1 million in disgorgement), with the involved

42. *Id.*, pp. 23-24.

43. *Id.*, pp. 17-20.

44. *Id.*, pp. 39-41.

45. *Id.*, pp. 41-45.

46. *Id.*, pp. 31-34.

47. CFTC v. Optiver US, LLC, *et al.*, *Complaint for Injunctive and Other Equitable Relief and Civil Monetary Penalties under the Commodity Exchange Act*, ("Optiver Complaint") 08 Civ. 6560, SDNY, July 24, 2008, p. 1.

48. Case Background Information, CFTC Press Release re: CFTC v. Optiver US, LLC, *et al.*, July 24, 2008.

49. Optiver Complaint, p. 1.

traders banned from trading between 2-8 years.[50] *Optiver* should serve as a reminder to traders that nothing better serves as objective evidence of manipulative intent than detailed IMs, emails, or voice recordings describing in detail the scheme attempted, especially using provocative names such as "Death Star," "Get Shorty," "Ricochet," "Fat Boy," or "the Hammer."

Energy Transfer Partners, L.P., et al. (ETP)

From 2003-2005, ETP was a large physical natural gas supplier in Texas and was a large net buyer of natural gas at Houston Ship Channel ("HSC"), where it supplied its industrial and other customers. ETP typically bought the gas used to serve these customers at prices set by the *Inside FERC* HSC Monthly Natural Gas Index ("IFERC Index"). The IFERC Index was set by the VWAP of fixed-price trades of physical gas and physical basis transactions made during the last five days of the trading month at HSC, commonly referred to as "bidweek."[51] ETP and its affiliates owned the physical pipeline capacity needed to ship gas from Waha (the West Texas production area) to Katy Hub (an interstate trading hub north of Houston), and then on to HSC.[52] The alleged manipulation took place across 17 months from December 2003 through December 2005.[53] Because this predated the passage of EPAct 2005, the case was pursued under the FERC's untested Market Behavior Rule 2.[54]

The alleged manipulation involved ETP's building of large derivatives positions that were short to the IFERC Index price, as well as physical index positions in excess of those needed to serve its customers at HSC.[55] ETP was alleged to have uneconomically sold its excess physical index position during bidweek (the trigger) to suppress the IFERC Index price (the nexus) to the benefit of its remaining physical index purchases and derivatives positions (the targets). ETP's allegedly uneconomic sales were so prevalent over the period that they were observed to drive other sellers out of the market, supported by the fact that ETP's trades comprised all or almost all of the index's volume in many months.[56]

50. CFTC v. Optiver US, LLC *et al.*, *Final Consent Order of Permanent Injunction, Civil Monetary Penalty and Other Relief*, 08 Civ. 6560, SDNY, April 19, 2012, pp. 5, 8-10.

51. Energy Transfer Partners, L.P., *et al.*, *Order to Show Cause and Notice of Proposed Penalties* ("ETP OSC"), 120 FERC ¶ 61,086, July 26, 2007, ¶ 5.

52. *Id.*, ¶¶ 23-24.

53. Although the OSC listed only 10 months of interest, staff later expanded the number to 17. Energy Transfer Partners, L.P., *et al.*, *Order Approving Uncontested Settlement* ("ETP Settlement"), 128 FERC ¶ 61,269, September 21, 2009, ¶ 6.

54. ETP OSC, ¶¶ 34-35.

55. *Id.*, ¶¶ 5-6.

56. *Id.*, ¶¶ 39, 55-57. The case was opened based on a phone call made to the FERC Enforcement Hotline by one of ETP's competitors, complaining that prices at HSC were being manipulated downward. *Id.*, ¶ 4. Whereas the complaining party in ETP received no direct remuneration for its tip, new whistleblower statutes are being put in place to elicit third-party information concerning manipulative schemes. *See*, for example, the CFTC's whistleblower statute contained in 7 U.S.C. 2, 5, 12a(5) and 26, as amended by Title VII of the Dodd-Frank Wall Street Reform and Consumer Protection Act, Pub. L. 111–203, 124 Stat. 1376, July 16, 2010.

The leverage held by ETP in its derivatives positions at HSC became apparent in September 2005 in the wake of Hurricanes Katrina and Rita. Damage from these storms effectively stranded gas at the Houston Ship Channel because Henry Hub, the key natural gas distribution hub used to set the price of NYMEX natural gas futures contracts, flooded—literally went underwater—and could not transit gas from Houston to demand centers in the Northern U.S. As prices dropped dramatically at HSC due to the huge surplus of stranded gas and rose dramatically at the Henry Hub due to the inability to receive gas, ETP reported trading profits of $40 million for a single day, suggesting an extremely large short position at HSC and long position at the Henry Hub.[57]

As with the case against BP discussed above, enforcement staff based its assertions of ETP's uneconomic trades on opportunity cost measurements, comparing ETP's trades at HSC to fixed-price sales by other parties at HSC and to the prices garnered at other nearby gas hubs.[58] Intent was shown by the pattern of the behavior over time, conjoined with various voice recordings instructing traders to "push Ship Down."[59] The case settled in September 2009 for $25 million in civil penalties and $5 million in disgorgement.[60]

In the Matter of Anthony DiPlacido (DiPlacido)

Interestingly, the CFTC's only successful prosecution of market manipulation under its artificial price rule involved physical electricity markets.[61] Trader DiPlacido was found on five days in 1998 to have engaged in a variety of uneconomic trades (triggers) to affect the daily settlement prices of the NYMEX Palo Verde and COB electricity futures contracts (nexuses) to benefit the values of over-the-counter derivatives that would profit from the futures price movements (targets).[62] The economic evidence presented showed instances of intentional purchases above and sales below prevailing market prices, "entering into noncompetitive trades" and "placing large orders… without legitimate, economic reasons or considerations."[63] Objective evidence to confirm intent was also provided, including transcribed voice recordings and testimony from third parties. The ALJ hearing the case ruled for the agency and imposed a 20-year trading ban, revocation of trading credentials, and $500,000 civil penalty on Mr. DiPlacido.[64] The CFTC later increased the civil penalty to $1 million, but this was reduced to

57. ETP OSC, ¶ 7.
58. ETP OSC, ¶¶ 58-62.
59. *Id.*, ¶ 52.
60. ETP Settlement, ¶ 11.
61. *In re DiPlacido, et al.*, [2000-2002 Transfer Binder] Comm. Fut. 1. Rep. (CCH) ~ 28,625, CFTC August 21, 2001.
62. *In re DiPlacido*, Comm. Fut. L. Rep. (CCH) ¶ 30,970, CFTC November 5, 2008, pp. 5-7.
63. *Id.*, p. 6.
64. *Id.*, p. 2.

$680,000 by the appellate court, which otherwise affirmed the outcome.[65] The overwhelming evidence needed to prove this case prompted a lament by one CFTC commissioner concerning the inadequacy of the Commission's artificial price statute.[66] This perceived weakness was soon addressed by the passage of Dodd-Frank, which added a fraud-based anti-manipulation rule to the CFTC's anti-manipulation arsenal.

Auction Manipulations

While the values of futures contracts and derivatives instruments traded in CFTC-jurisdictional markets are almost always tied to an index, similar electric market instruments that are traded within the RTOs typically tie to prices determined by one or more RTO-administered auctions. For example, all day-ahead energy and ancillary services products that trade in hourly RTO auctions are contracts of standardized quantity and quality for a price agreed upon today with delivery and payment occurring the next day—i.e., futures contracts—tied to RTO auction prices. As discussed in Chapter 9, FTRs pay their holders congestion charges or the difference in day-ahead congestion prices between two locations over a period of time and thus are effectively price-taking derivatives. Virtual transactions are derivatives that take their value from the difference of the hourly day-ahead and real-time auction LMPs;[67] however, as we will discuss, virtual bids and offers can also be used as price-making instruments that can bias auction outcomes to benefit other positions.

Constellation Energy Commodities Group, Inc. (Constellation)

Constellation was accused of using uneconomic virtual and physical trades (the triggers) to bias day-ahead and real-time energy auction prices (the nexuses) to benefit the value of its FTRs and other financial derivatives positions within and across multiple RTOs in the U.S. and Canada (the targets).[68] The scale and scope of the alleged behavior, coupled with the sixteen-month period from September 2007 through December 2008 when the behavior was alleged,

---

65. *DiPlacido v. CFTC*, 2009 U.S. App., 2d Cir. 2009, p. 10.

66. As then Commissioner Bart Chilton stated in remarks made on March 23, 2010 to the Metals Market Investors group in Washington, D.C."...in 35 years, there has been only one successful prosecution for manipulation" by the CFTC under its artificial price rule.

67. Traders use virtual demand bids (also known as "decremental bids" or "DECs") and virtual supply offers (also known as "incremental bids" or "INCs") to arbitrage expected differences between day-ahead and real-time prices. A distinguishing characteristic of a virtual trade is that the quantity of megawatts bought or sold by the trader in the day-ahead is exactly offset by a sale or purchase of an identical quantity in the real-time, such that the net effect on the physical market quantity traded is zero. In essence, the trader uses the day-ahead market to buy from or sell to itself in the future real-time market such that the net effect is that of a purely "financial" transaction. For further discussion, *see* Ledgerwood and Pfeifenberger (2013), pp. 11-13.

68. Constellation Energy Commodities Group, Inc., *Order Approving Stipulation and Consent Agreement*, 138 FERC ¶ 61,168, March 9, 2012.

suggested that the civil penalties associated with the case could top $1 billion, especially if the maximum fine of $1 million per incident, per day applied. However, a settlement of $245 million was reached with the FERC, consisting of $135 million in civil penalties and $110 million in disgorgement paid to the NYISO, ISO-NE, and PJM, with several traders' licenses revoked.[69] The relatively low penalty relative to the initial alleged damages may have also reflected the difficulties of proving intent and harm within the highly complicated production optimization models that are used to determine the outcomes of energy market auctions. That said, a later case brought by the FERC against Louis Dreyfus Energy Services for similar behavior settled in early 2014 for $8.1 million, involving the alleged manipulation of a single node in the MISO for a three-month period.[70]

Despite this complexity, a relatively straightforward approach to understanding the mechanics of the manipulation alleged was developed by the authors and was used by the FERC in formulating its case against Constellation.[71] The approach begins by describing the trader's decision to place virtual bids on a stand-alone basis, then examines how the addition of FTRs at the same location affects the trader's behavior. The payment from the FTR motivates the trader to increase the size of its virtual bids beyond what it would otherwise place, causing the trader to sacrifice gains on the virtual bids to pursue payments from the FTR. As the size of the trader's FTR position grows—and the amount of financial leverage created by the manipulation of its value increases—the trader is ultimately driven to intentionally lose money on the virtual bids to obtain even larger profits on the FTR.

The virtual/FTR example raises an economic conundrum. Profitable virtual bids benefit market efficiency by promoting convergence between day-ahead and real-time prices, meaning that power plants are optimally dispatched in the day-ahead market to exactly meet the actual demand presented in real-time. If the trader sacrifices some (but not all) profits on his virtual bids to increase the value of his FTR, the result *improves* market efficiency in the primary market by converging day-ahead and real-time prices. In fact, perfect convergence results only if the trader makes *nothing* on his virtual bids. However, a trader intentionally placing virtual bids at this quantity risks being accused of market manipulation, because those trades are uneconomic relative to the trader's opportunity costs—i.e., the profits the trader would have made had he placed virtual bids in quantities designed to maximize their stand-alone profitability without the FTR. This raises the efficiency issue discussed in the previous chapter but which has yet to be addressed in this relatively new field involving uneconomic behavior: *how can behavior that benefits market efficiency through the use of trading instruments in a manner laid out in the tariff that is fully consistent with the intent of the market design be prosecuted as fraudulent?*

---

69. *Id.*, p. 1.

70. MISO Virtual and FTR Trading, *Order Approving Stipulation and Consent Agreement*, 146 FERC ¶ 61,072, February 7, 2014.

71. The refined version of this model is presented by Ledgerwood and Pfeifenberger (2013).

At the time of this writing, the authors are involved in several market manipulation cases before the FERC where this issue is at play. There is no question that the act of intentionally incurring true stand-alone losses on virtual bids to favor related positions can be investigated as a market manipulation, justified by the inefficiency the act interjects into the market when it forces divergence of day-ahead and real-time prices and the inefficient dispatch that results. However, we contend that an enforcement action is inappropriate where the trader seeking to enhance the value of his FTR portfolio actively practiced restraint in his virtual bidding activity to assure that his actions would only promote price convergence. Behavior promoted by the tariff to improve efficient market or system operation should not be targeted as manipulative as long as it yields better market performance. Indeed, if electricity markets were perfectly competitive, the market would tend toward convergence (and drive the profitability of all virtuals to zero) irrespective of the trader's actions. Whereas aggressive manipulation enforcement to deter inefficient activity promotes market integrity over time, the prosecution of efficient behavior does the opposite, leading to uncertainty, reduced market participation and illiquidity—factors that make markets only easier to manipulate over time.

Deutsche Bank Energy Trading (DBET)

DBET was accused by the FERC of executing uneconomic trades at the Silver Peak intertie of the CAISO (the trigger) to benefit the value of its Congestion Revenue Rights ("CRRs") position (the target) that was long to the congestion price at that grid location (the nexus).[72] Silver Peak is a 13-17 MW transmission line made famous from Enron's notorious scheduling of 2,900 MW to flow over the line in order to create congestion and alter market clearing prices to benefit other positions in its portfolio.[73] The FERC alleged that DBET's exports of physical power from Silver Peak "were entered into without regard to their economics or supply and demand fundamentals," but rather "to increase the value of Silver Peak CRRs by altering congestion at Silver Peak."[74] The most interesting feature of this case is that DBET *admitted* that the purpose of its actions was to remove the "phantom congestion" created by a CAISO derate of the line to enhance the value of its CRRs.[75] However, DBET defended its behavior by arguing that its physical power trades were in fact seeking legitimate profit opportunities on a stand-alone basis, and thus could not be considered manipulative because they were intended to be profitable.[76]

72. Deutsche Bank Energy Trading, LLC, *Order to Show Cause and Notice of Proposed Penalties* ("DBET OSC"), 140 FERC ¶ 61,178, September 5, 2012.

73. *See* Enron Power Marketing, Inc., *et al.*, *Prepared Supplemental Testimony of Robert F. McCullough on Behalf of Public Utility District No. 1 of Snohomish County, Washington*, filed in Docket No. EL03-180-000, pp. 26:17-32:4.

74. DBET OSC, Enforcement Staff Report and Recommendation, p. 3.

75. Deutsche Bank Energy Trading, LLC, *Answer of DB Energy Trading LLC to Order to Show Cause* ("DBET Answer"), p. 2.

76. *Id.*, pp. 2-5.

In January 2010, DBET owned about 50 MW of CRRs at the Silver Peak intertie of the CAISO.[77] On January 19, 2010, the CAISO derated Silver Peak, meaning that no imports into California would be allowed over the tie. As a result, the congestion component of the power price at Silver Peak fell, causing DBET's CRRs to lose money. The CAISO explained the low price as the result of a "degenerate" solution, shown conceptually in Figure 11-4.

Figure 11-4 A and B:

Degenerate Pricing Solution at Silver Peak (January 19, 2010)[78]

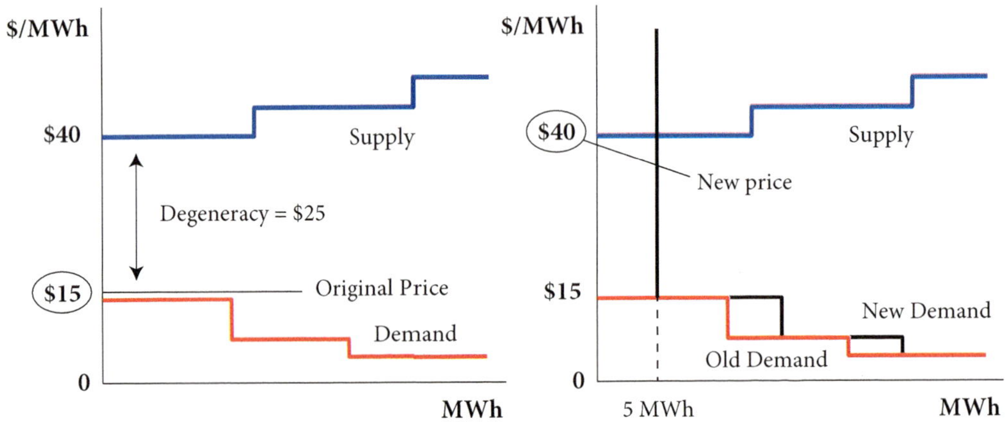

Figure 11-4 A shows the supply and demand of power exports from the CAISO through Silver Peak, as affected by the derating of the line. The equilibrium normally would occur to the left of the vertical axis, corresponding with importing power into the CAISO. However, the derate precluded imports, causing supply and demand to overlap over the range from $15 to $40/MWh. This "degeneracy" could be solved by any price within the range, yet the CAISO's market rules forced the price to its lowest possible outcome of $15, thus inflicting the worst possible losses on DBET's CRRs. DBET protested this result to the CAISO and attempted to divest itself of the losing CRRs, but remained saddled with CRR positions destined to lose money for the life of the derate.

To alleviate this congestion, DBET traders devised an "Export Strategy" by creating an allegedly circular schedule flowing power out of Silver Peak through Nevada to the CAISO's Summit intertie, then wheeling the power back through California.[79] The effect of this behavior at Silver Peak is shown in Figure 11-4 B. DBET began by exporting 5 MWh from Silver Peak to

77. DBET OSC, Enforcement Staff Report and Recommendation, p. 6.

78. Adapted from Deutsche Bank Energy Trading, LLC, *Answer of DB Energy Trading LLC to Order to Show Cause* ("DBET Answer"), Exhibit P: Affidavit of William W. Hogan, Ph.D., p. 20, Figure 7.

79. DBET OSC, Enforcement Staff Report and Recommendation, p. 3. In addition to asserting that these transactions were uneconomic, FERC enforcement staff alleged that the wheel-through transaction was mistagged and thus fraudulent. DBET OSC, ¶ 2.

Summit, submitted to the auction as price-taking bids thus guaranteeing they would clear.[80] This broke the degeneracy by shifting the demand curve to the right and raising the congestion price at Silver Peak to make DBET's CRRs profitable again. Over a 44-day period, DBET continued this strategy, ultimately increasing the size of its CRR position and the volume of its exports to the 13 MW limit of the tie.[81] The magnitude of the penalties and damages sought by FERC for the activity was notable for its small size relative to a large, multinational bank: $1,500,000 in civil penalties, with disgorgement of only $123,198.[82]

Despite (or, perhaps, because of) this relatively minor exposure, DBET filed an 89-page answering brief supported by 665 pages of documents and testimony, admitting that the intent of the Export Strategy was to restore the value of the CRRs, but that said intent was irrelevant because the physical exports pursued a stand-alone legitimate business purpose. Some of the key arguments raised were: that the physical exports appeared profitable given the degenerate (low) price at Silver Peak; that DBET's failure to discover that the trades were unprofitable resulted from poor billing records provided by the CAISO, which gave an unclear depiction of DBET's actual transmission costs; and that DBET tried to improve the profitability (or reduce the losses) of the Export Strategy by increasing its volume of trades over time.[83] To evaluate these claims, we analyzed the data provided in DBET's Answer, and the results are shown below in Figure 11-5.

80. DBET OSC, Enforcement Staff Report and Recommendation, p. 10.

81. *Id.*, pp. 11-12.

82. DBET OSC, ¶ 1.

83. DBET Answer, pp. 46-56.

Figure 11-5

Analysis of Deutsche Bank Spreads vs. an Assumed $5/MW Transmission Cost[84]

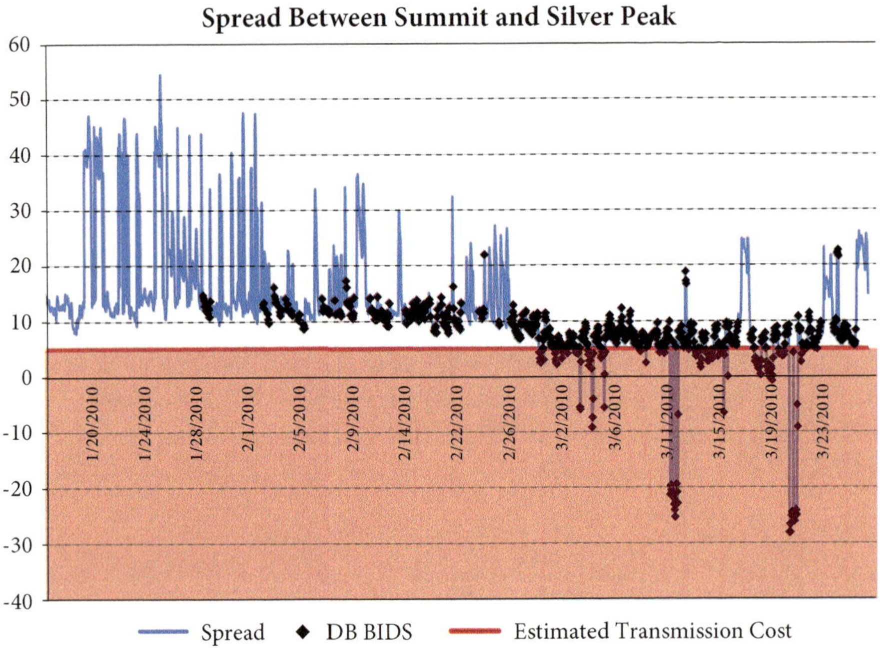

The blue line reflects the Silver Peak-to-Summit congestion LMP spreads from January 1, 2010 through March 31, 2010. This shows the effect of the pricing degeneracy at Silver Peak, which increased the congestion spread from its historical norm of $10-$15 per MWh to over $40 per MWh. These values suggest that the Export Strategy could be profitable if the traders' assumed cost of transmission at $5 per MW (shown in red) was correct. The black dots represent the hours when DBET executed the Export Strategy. As intended, these scheduled flows eliminated the degeneracy at Silver Peak in benefit to DBET's CRRs, reducing the Silver Peak/Summit spread back to historical levels. Further, given the market data available to them through late February, DBET's traders could reasonably infer the profitability of these transactions absent sufficiently accurate billing detail from the CAISO. The effects of these trades are shown in blue in Figure 11-6.

84. Sources: LMP data is taken from the CAISO website; DBET exports are taken from DBET Exhibit A, pp. 22-23; assumed $5/MW transmission cost is taken from DBET Exhibit O, p. 24, ¶ 39.

Figure 11-6

Graphic of DBET's Physical Export Strategy[85]

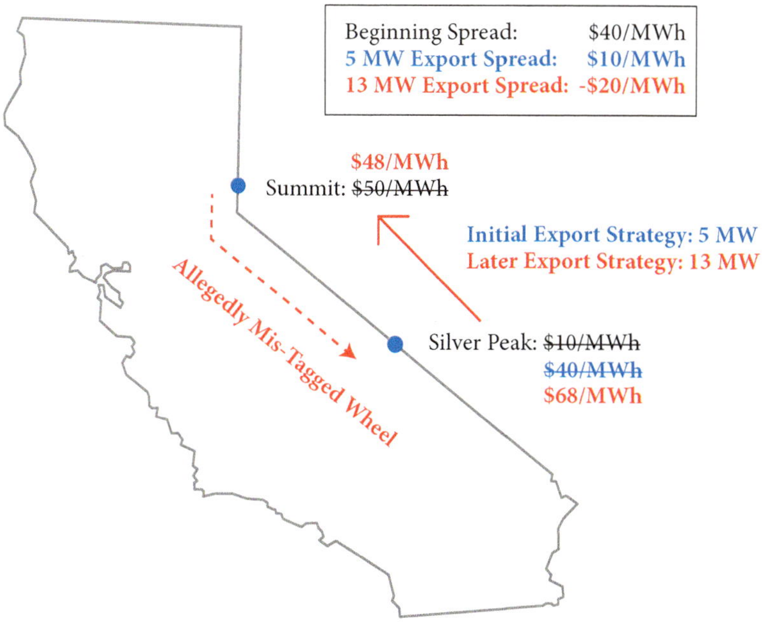

However, conditions changed toward the end of February when DBET began to increase the size of its Export Strategy, as well as the size of its March CRR position. The increased size of DBET's physical trades pushed the Silver Peak/Summit spread below its historical norms, in some hours creating a negative spread indicative of the *creation of congestion* on the Silver Peak-to-Summit transmission path and divergence of the prices between the two hubs. This is shown by the sharp downward spikes in Figure 11-5 and by the red text in Figure 11-6.[86] Given that DBET's traders would have seen these LMP's after the day-ahead awards were posted, arguments that the trades were intended to be economic or that larger exports could reduce transmission costs became less credible. Faced with such evidence, as well as an admission of guilt by another market participant that rendered suspect the propriety of DBET's wheel through the CAISO,[87] the company settled the charges against it for $1,672,645.[88]

85. Adapted from DBET Answer, Appendix O-6, p. 2.

86. This figure suggests that DBET had resurrected Enron's Death Star strategy by creating a circular schedule.

87. Gila River Power, LLC, *Order Approving Stipulation and Consent Agreement*, 141 FERC ¶ 61,136, November 19, 2012.

88. Deutsche Bank Energy Trading, LLC, *Order Approving Stipulation and Consent Agreement*, 142 FERC ¶ 61,056, January 22, 2013.

Inefficient Dispatch: J.P. Morgan Ventures Energy Corp. (JPM)

The J.P. Morgan case involved twelve alleged schemes using uneconomic offers of power plants (triggers) to take advantage of various market rules (nexuses) to receive various types of out-of-market payments from the CAISO and MISO (targets). The FERC aggressively pursued evidence regarding the behavior, first issuing an Order to Show Cause[89] and later suspending JPM's market-based rate authority in response to the firm's perceived lack of cooperation with the investigation.[90] The first description of the alleged behavior appeared in a Commission Notice of Alleged Violations,[91] followed the next day by a settlement for $410 million.[92] JPM stipulated to the facts but neither admitted nor denied liability, and no penalties were assessed against any of the individual traders or managers involved. This drew criticism from two U.S. Senators, resulting in further probes by the U.S. Department of Justice and Federal Bureau of Investigation.[93]

One alleged strategy took advantage of the CAISO's deference to the ramp rates of dispatched units. JPM's units in the CAISO were gas boilers, which are slow to ramp up or down between different levels of output. These units were uneconomically "self-scheduled" to guarantee they would run at high outputs every third hour, with high prices offered in the intervening hours. Because the units could not ramp offline quickly enough, the CAISO dispatched them in the intervening hours, paying them between $73 to $98/MWh when the average day-ahead prices were in the range of $30 to $35/MWh.[94] A similar scheme placed uneconomic bids in hour ending 24 of the CAISO day-ahead market to assure the units were running going into the next day, then bid the units in at $999/MWh for hours ending 1 and 2 for the next day.[95] Because the units' ramp rates would not allow them to be switched off entirely, the CAISO was forced to keep the plants online and pay JPM $999/MWh for their energy.

Two of JMP's other alleged schemes made use of uneconomic day-ahead offers of "regulation down," an ancillary service that helps grid operators respond to immediate, small downward changes in total demand on the system. The first matched these regulation bids with high-priced offers of energy; because the regulation-down bids were always accepted, CAISO would pay JPM for the value of its energy used to supply the service, priced at the unit's high energy bids.[96] The second scheme was even more creative. In addition to price-taking

89. J.P. Morgan Ventures Energy Corporation, *Order to Show Cause*, 140 FERC ¶ 61,227, September 20, 2012.

90. J.P. Morgan Ventures Energy Corporation, *Order Suspending Market-Based Rate Authority*, 141 FERC ¶ 61,131, November 14, 2012.

91. *Staff Notice of Alleged Violations*, July 29, 2013.

92. In Re Make-Whole Payments and Related Bidding Strategies, *Order Approving Stipulation and Consent Agreement* ("JPM Settlement"), 144 FERC ¶ 61,068, July 30, 2013, ¶ 3. This included $285 million in civil penalties and $125 million in disgorgement.

93. Emily Flitter, "Exclusive: JPMorgan subject of obstruction probe in energy case," Reuters, 9/4/13, available at: *http://www.reuters.com/article/2013/09/04/us-jpm-ferc-doj-idUSBRE9830QM20130904*.

94. *Id.*, ¶¶ 53-54.

95. *Id.*, ¶¶ 57-58. JPM continued this behavior into 2012. *Id.*, ¶ 68(a).

96. *Id.*, ¶¶ 55-56.

($1/MWh) regulation-down bids, JPM would bid energy from the units into the real-time market at $999/MWh, the market cap.[97] Because the units were accepted to provide regulation-down, the CAISO would dispatch them to be online and operating at levels of output sufficiently above minimum generation levels in order to provide the service. However, the high real-time offers incented the CAISO to ramp the units down, creating a paradox. This problem was reconciled through "exceptional dispatch" orders, which kept the units running at the higher output, and paid $999/MWh for the resulting energy.[98]

Would-be defenders of these types of behavior might point to the fact that none of the activities alleged by FERC technically violated any specific CAISO or MISO market rules. However this perspective ignores the destruction left in the wake of Enron, and hence the purpose of the Commission's anti-manipulation Rule 1c—to deter *fraud* in FERC's jurisdictional markets. As we have discussed throughout this section of the book, under our analysis the intentional use of uneconomic transactions injects fraudulent information into the marketplace to the detriment of market efficiency and the counterparties who must pay for the wealth transfer that results. Actions to dispatch old, inefficient power plants out of merit to game market rules and garner unjustified payments from ratepayers epitomize this phenomenon and underscore the need for an effective anti-manipulation enforcement program to detect and deter such behavior.

Manipulation Triggered by the Exercise of Market Power

In contrast with the uneconomic trading cases, the cases that follow involve acts of withholding by sellers in their primary markets to trigger benefits derived from markets or processes linked thereto. Thus, the higher market price and (typically) lower market output that is caused by the withholding (or threat of withholding) simultaneously serve as a source of profits from the traditional exercise of monopoly power and as potential triggers for a market manipulation. As we discussed in Chapter 9, such actions affecting only targets contained within the confines of the primary market are unlikely to be prosecutable using the anti-manipulation rules because the price and output movements associated with the nexus serve a stand-alone legitimate business purpose—i.e., higher profits by the act of withholding. However, if the nexus extends to linked markets, manipulation claims can attach.

97. *Id.*, ¶¶ 59-60.

98. *Id.* JPM was also alleged to have increased its prices when it learned units were to be exceptionally dispatched, as well as to bid unreasonably high prices in hours where it thought that exceptional dispatch orders were likely. *Id.*, ¶¶ 68(c) and 68(d).

KeySpan-Ravenswood, et al. (KeySpan)

In 2007, several market participants filed a complaint with the FERC that KeySpan, Astoria Generating Company Acquisitions, LLC ("Astoria") and Morgan Stanley Capital Group Inc. ("Morgan Stanley") manipulated the New York City Installed Capacity ("ICAP") market in 2006.[99] KeySpan and Astoria were two large owners of generation capacity serving New York City.[100] From 2003 to 2005, KeySpan consistently bid its generation into the ICAP market at its bid cap, usually with some capacity not accepted.[101] The result was that the majority of KeySpan's 2,250 MW of capacity cleared at the bid cap, suggesting that it had successfully engaged in economic withholding during this period.[102]

In early 2006, 1,000 MW of new generation was positioned to enter the ICAP market.[103] According to the allegations, this additional capacity would have required KeySpan to withhold a much larger amount of capacity from the market to keep the price at its bid cap, leaving an insufficient amount to clear at the cap to make the withholding profitable overall.[104] An example of this is depicted in Figure 11-7 A and B.[105] Assuming the 2006 ICAP auction cleared competitively with all capacity made available, Figure 11-7 A shows that the auction would clear at a price of $6/kW-month, resulting in auction revenues of $162 million paid to KeySpan.[106] If KeySpan were to economically withhold 1,250 MW of this generation, Figure 11-7 B shows that it could raise the market clearing price up to its bid cap of approximately $12/kW-month, but would then earn revenues of only $144 million on the 1,000 MW cleared.[107] KeySpan's profit-maximizing choice therefore would be to bid all of its capacity competitively into the auction, as this would increase its expected revenues by $18 million.

99. FERC Enforcement Staff Report, *Findings of a Non-Public Investigation of Potential Market Manipulation by Suppliers in the New York City Capacity Market* ("FERC KeySpan Report"), filed in Docket Nos. IN08-2-000 & EL07-39-000 (February 28, 2008), p. 2.

100. *Id.*, p. 4.

101. U.S. v. KeySpan Corporation, *Complaint*, Case 1:10-cv-01415 (SDNY, February 22, 2010), ¶ 20; U.S. v. KeySpan Corporation, *Memorandum & Order*, Case 1:10-cv-01415 (SDNY, February 2, 2011), p. 3.

102. In comparison to physical withholding, where a seller would simply choose not make some capacity available to the auction, economic withholding involves the seller making all capacity available at a price sufficiently high to be marginal, thus leaving some MW of capacity to not clear in the auction. As discussed in Chapters 2 and 9, this is a profitable strategy if the gains made on the MW that clear at the higher price more than offset the losses incurred on the MW withheld.

103. FERC KeySpan Report, p. 9.

104. U.S. v. KeySpan Corporation, *Memorandum & Order*, p. 3.

105. While this example is designed to be illustrative of KeySpan's decision making, it is not intended to accurately replicate the results of the 2006 ICAP auction, nor to provide an exact measurement of KeySpan's actual revenues derived therefrom.

106. FERC KeySpan Report, p. 9, quoting NYISO, *Proposed Revisions to Services Tariff, Attachment II: Affidavit of David B. Patton, Ph.D.*, Docket No. ER07-360-000 (Dec. 22, 2006), pp. 3-5. Revenues are calculated as $6/kW-month * 2,250,000 kW * 12 months, equaling $162 million.

107. *Id.* Revenues are calculated as $12/kW-month * 1,000,000 kW * 12 months, equaling $144 million.

Figure 11-7 A and B:

Example of Unprofitable Withholding in Primary Market

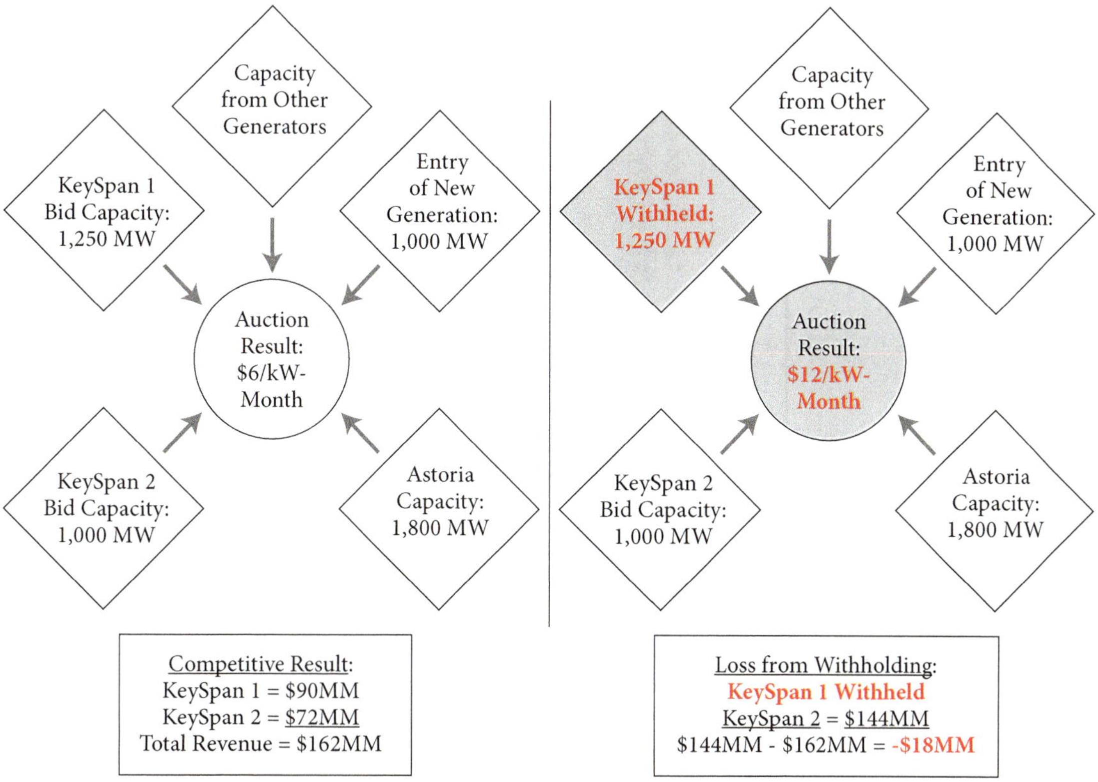

To obtain additional leverage, KeySpan considered acquiring the assets of Astoria to maintain the profitability of its strategy. After determining that this would raise too many market power issues,[108] KeySpan entered into an agreement, brokered through Morgan Stanley, to acquire a financial interest in Astoria's 1,800 MW fleet of generators that were eligible to participate in the 2006 ICAP auction.[109] Under the terms of this "KeySpan Swap," KeySpan paid Morgan Stanley a fixed fee of $7.57/kW-month for a floating financial interest in 1,800 MW of capacity paid at the cleared 2006 ICAP auction price.[110] This gave KeySpan the financial leverage[111] to profitably withhold the larger volume of MW from the auction (the trigger) necessary to keep the market clearing price at the bid cap (the nexus).

108. *Id.*

109. *Id.*, pp. 3-4; FERC KeySpan Report, pp. 10-12.

110. Morgan Stanley then executed the "Astoria Hedge," which paid Astoria a fixed price of $7.07 per kW-month for its 1,800 MW of capacity in return for the profits it made from the ICAP auction. This left Morgan Stanley perfectly hedged in its exposure to KeySpan—with a transactional profit of $0.50 per kW-month—and provided Astoria with a relatively high fixed payment for its capacity relative to a potentially much lower payment it could receive if the auction were to clear competitively given the entry of new capacity. *Id.*; U.S. v. KeySpan Corporation, *Complaint*, ¶¶ 26-29.

111. After the swap, KeySpan would benefit from a price increase not only on the volume of its own MW cleared in the auction (target in the primary market) but also on its 1,800 MW financial position (target in the linked market).

Figure 11-8 A and B show an example of how this worked.[112] Figure 11-8 A shows the revenues that would flow to KeySpan if the auction cleared at the competitive price of $6/kW-month, resulting in auction revenues of $291.6 million paid to KeySpan through its 2,250 MW of capacity in the primary market and 1,800 MW of financial exposure gained through the KeySpan Swap.[113] Conversely, if KeySpan economically withheld 1,250 MW of its physical capacity to raise the market clearing price to $12/kW-month, Figure 11-8 B shows that KeySpan could increase its revenues by another $111.6 million due to the additional leverage provided by the swap.[114]

Figure 11-8 A and B

"KeySpan Swap" Made Alleged Withholding Profitable

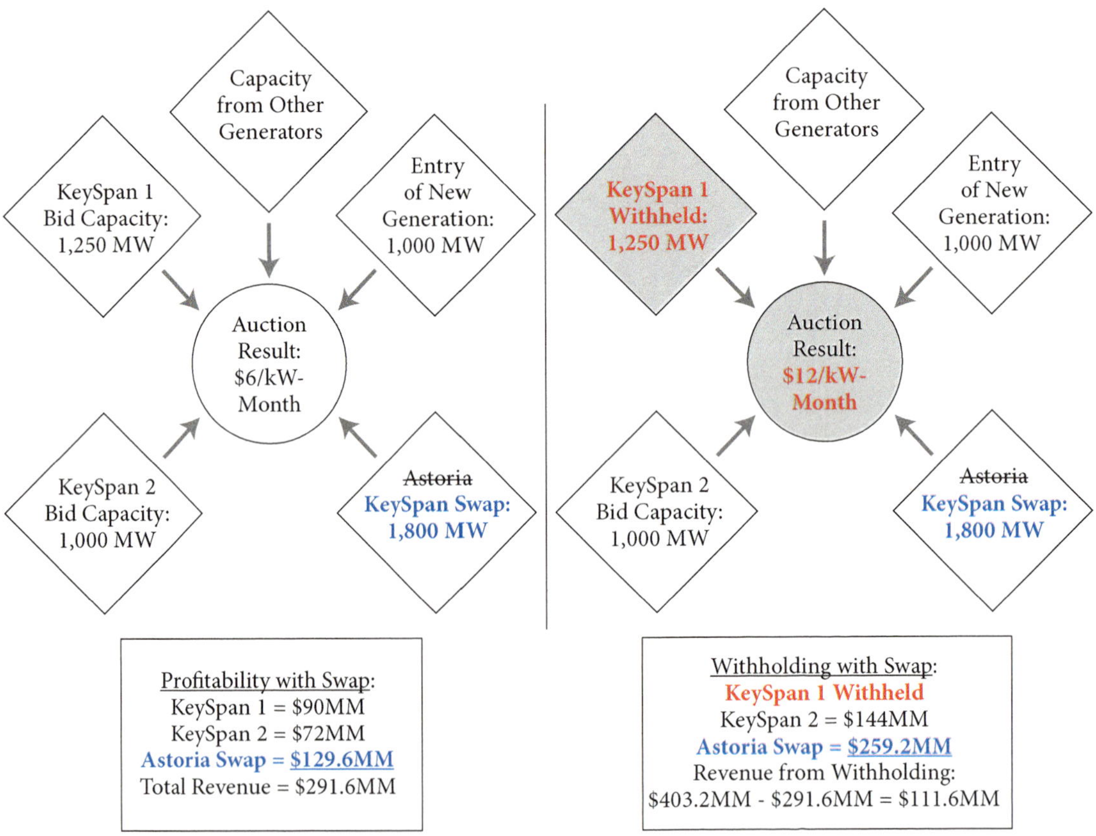

112. While this example is designed to be illustrative of KeySpan's decision making, it is not intended to accurately replicate the results of the 2006 ICAP auction, nor to provide an exact measurement of KeySpan's actual revenues derived therefrom.

113. Revenues equal $6/kW-month * 4,050,000 kW * 12 months, equaling $291.6 million.

114. Revenues are calculated as $12/kW-month * 2,800,000 kW * 12 months, equaling $403.2 million.

Because the entry of new generation did not lower the clearing price of the 2006 ICAP auction, the NYISO Independent Market Monitor and other market participants complained to the FERC that KeySpan had engaged in market manipulation.[115] Although the Commission investigated the behavior, the investigation was closed because FERC Enforcement staff found that KeySpan's bidding behavior pursued a *legitimate business purpose* in a manner that was consistent with its authority granted under NYISO and FERC-approved market power mitigation rules.[116] Notably, staff concluded that:

> There is a difference between engaging in (1) market manipulation in violation of section 1c.2, which includes fraud or deceit as discussed above and (2) a party exercising market power. Of course, an exercise of market power may be a factor to consider in examining whether Part 1c was violated. However, it is not the only relevant factor.[117]

Staff's comments underscore a key point that we first addressed in Chapter 2: that the exercise of market power is not, in and of itself, a fraudulent act in violation of the Commission's anti-manipulations rule.[118] This is logical assuming the act is profit maximizing on a stand-alone basis, which we have stressed means *within the confines of the primary market*. However, Staff's analysis incorrectly overlooked the effects of this market power on the linked market:

> Thus, the swap did not provide KeySpan with an independent incentive to change its offering behavior in the physical market (i.e., artificially increase capacity prices) to benefit its derivative position. Rather, KeySpan's offering behavior in the physical market was based on its goal to maximize revenue, while limiting risk, in that single market.[119]

Staff failed to perceive that the swap *did* alter KeySpan's behavior. Figures 11-8 and 11-9 show that but for the leverage provided through the financial swap, KeySpan would in fact have been better off by *not withholding* in the primary market. The focus on KeySpan's act of withholding from one auction to the next focused only on the manipulation's trigger, without recognizing the financial swap as a separate target linked to the primary market through the auction price nexus. Following staff's recommendation that "the appropriate rules to mitigate the exercise of market power, will be addressed by the Commission upon review of the NYISO's proposal to strengthen its market mitigation rules applicable to the in-city ICAP market,"[120] the Commission closed the KeySpan investigation, without ever ruling on the merits of the case.

---

115. FERC KeySpan Report, pp. 9-10.

116. FERC KeySpan Report, p. 3.

117. *Id.*, p. 17.

118. Likewise, there is nothing "artificial" about the exercise of market power when it is profit maximizing on a stand-alone basis.

119. FERC KeySpan Report, p. 21.

120. *Id.*, p. 17.

The FERC's inaction opened a door that is usually foreclosed under the filed rate doctrine: to pursue the case on antitrust grounds.[121] The U.S. Attorney General filed a complaint against KeySpan alleging that its agreement with Morgan Stanley violated Sherman Act § 1, which prohibits agreements that unreasonably restrain competition.[122] However, in the Memorandum and Order settling the case, the court construed the act as a *market manipulation* and ordered KeySpan to pay *disgorgement* of $12 million.[123]

This outcome presents a sobering reality for market participants that trade across linked markets: even without specific anti-manipulation authority governing the products traded or action by the regulator with primary jurisdiction over those products, market participants can nevertheless be pursued for manipulative behavior under the antitrust laws. This ancillary authority thus could pursue claims of manipulative activity triggered by acts of withholding in a primary market that are profitable due to the financial leverage provided by positions in other markets.

Parnon Energy Inc., et al. (Parnon)

Parnon and its parent co-defendants traded oil futures on the NYMEX, physical oil priced at Calendar Merc Average ("CMA"), and related derivatives contracts on NYMEX and ICE.[124] The case alleged the use of two different types of triggers—physical withholding and uneconomic sales—to manipulate the value of targets tied to two different points in time. On twelve days in January and March 2008, Parnon's traders allegedly purchased large physical futures positions for near-month delivery in quantities at or near the maximum physical delivery capacity available to the market and in excess of their commercial needs.[125] Parnon was also alleged to have assembled large "calendar spread" positions that were long to the "near-month" NYMEX futures price and short to the "next-month" NYMEX futures price, meaning that the derivatives would benefit from actions that increased oil prices before the "near-month" settlement and from actions that suppressed prices afterwards.[126]

The CFTC's complaint alleged that Parnon began the manipulation by building and ultimately withholding the physical oil associated with its futures positions through the settlement

121. This common law doctrine preserves regulatory authority by precluding lawsuits for claims arising from "filed" rates established by tariff. By failing to rule on KeySpan's behavior, the filed rate doctrine did not attach, allowing for a lawsuit on antitrust grounds.

122. U.S. v. KeySpan Corporation, *Complaint*, p. 1.

123. U.S. v. KeySpan Corporation, *Memorandum & Order*, p. 15. This case represents the first time that disgorgement, which requires a party who profits from illegal or wrongful acts to give up those profits, has been used to assess damages in an antitrust claim. *Id.*, p. 7 *et seq.* This is the same remedy used by the FERC in remedying harm under its anti-manipulation rule. Note that Morgan Stanley paid $4.8 million in a separate Sherman Act § 1 case for its role in the alleged manipulation.

124. CFTC vs. Parnon Energy, Inc. *et al.*, *Complaint for Injunctive and Other Equitable Relief and Civil Monetary Penalties Under the Commodity Exchange Act* ("Parnon Complaint"), Case No. 11-cv-3543, SDNY May 24, 2011, ¶¶ 15-22.

125. *Id.*, ¶ 3.

126. *Id.*

period of the near-month contract (market power as the first trigger), thus driving up the near-month settlement price (the first nexus) in benefit to the company's long calendar spread position (the target).[127] Parnon was alleged to have expanded the size of its targeted calendar swaps position after the withholding, so as to provide even greater leverage for the subsequent manipulation of the next-month futures price.[128] Following the settlement of the near-month contract, Parnon then liquidated its physical oil into the market (uneconomic trading as the second trigger), thus suppressing the next-month contract price (second nexus) in benefit to the company's short calendar spread positions (target).[129] The case was settled for a $13 million civil penalty, with Parnon and other associated parties neither admitting nor denying responsibility.[130]

Given the difficulties associated with proceeding under its pre-Dodd-Frank artificial price rule, the CFTC faced serious proof problems with this case, as application of the framework demonstrates. Specifically, there were problems with both of the nexuses alleged. For the first nexus, the CFTC would need to show that Parnon's physical futures trades made *before* the settlement period of the near-month contract, some of which were physical index (i.e., price-taking) positions, had the effect of increasing the near-month NYMEX futures settlement price. For the second, the CFTC would need to show that Parnon's alleged uneconomic sales into the market almost a month in advance of the next-month NYMEX futures settlement meaningfully impacted that price. Thus, proof of the manipulation in court may have proven quite challenging.

E.ON SE (E.ON)

In Germany, the European Electricity Exchange (EEX) determines an hourly auction price for power, with the price set by the marginal unit. E.ON had a significant infra-marginal nuclear, hydro, and coal capacity in Germany that all sold power into the EEX, and thus had sufficient leverage to potentially benefit from capacity withholding. As the transmission system operator (TSO), E.ON also was responsible for purchasing ancillary services for balancing the grid.

Based upon concerns as to E.ON's behavior, the European Commission (EC) launched two antitrust inquiries against E.ON for the period 2002-2007.[131] First, the EC was concerned that E.ON may have carried out short-term capacity withholding of an inframarginal generator,

127. *Id.*

128. *Id.*

129. *Id.*

130. CFTC Press Release, "Federal Court Orders $13 Million Fine in CFTC Crude Oil Manipulation Action against Parnon Energy Inc., Arcadia Petroleum Ltd., and Arcadia Energy (Suisse) SA, and Crude Oil Traders James Dyer and Nicholas Wildgoose," August 4, 2014, available at *http://www.cftc.gov/ PressRoom/PressReleases/pr6971-14.*

131. Official Journal of the European Union, *Commission Decision of 26 November 2008*, Cases COMP 39.388 and 39.389, November 26, 2008.

which benefitted E.ON's remaining fleet through higher energy prices.[132] The investigation further found that E.ON's behavior may have intentionally deterred investments in generation by third parties.[133] Second, there was concern that as a TSO, E.ON carried out a strategy to favor its own supply affiliate for ancillary services, thus raising costs for consumers.[134] E.ON settled both allegations by agreeing to a commitment decision that required the company to divest 5,000 MW of generation capacity, as well as its high-voltage transmission grid.[135]

The E.ON case provides an example of the value of market manipulation rules as an adjunct to more traditional antitrust law. It is appropriate to think of the EC's first claim against E.ON as an antitrust claim, for the benefit of withholding in the primary market caused prices on the EEX to rise, to the benefit of E.ON's remaining fleet in that same market. However, the second claim might better be thought of as a form of market manipulation. E.ON used its act of withholding in one market (trigger) to create energy imbalances (nexus) designed to benefit the provision of ancillary services from its affiliate (target). In the future, with the passage of REMIT, such behavior can more easily be prosecuted as attempted manipulation under the EU's fraud-based rule.

Manipulation Triggered by Outright Fraud

If compared to the challenges of proving manipulations triggered by uneconomic trading or the exercise of market power, demonstrating the use of outright fraud as a manipulation trigger would seem to be a relatively straightforward exercise because economic evidence is typically less essential to the proof of manipulative intent. This is not to say that economic evidence is irrelevant to such cases, for proof that the behavior occurred and had an economic impact only strengthens an enforcement action and remains a requirement for the computation of damages. Studying the many types of behavior that can be construed as "fraudulent" in this context is an interesting and relevant exercise, for while most manipulative conduct has at its core some element of fraud, not all cases of fraud are necessarily manipulative.

132. *Id.*, ¶¶ 28-40.

133. *Id.*, ¶¶ 41-45.

134. *Id.*, ¶¶ 50-55.

135. EU Commission Press Release, "Antitrust: Commission opens German electricity market to competition", November 26, 2008, available at *http://europa.eu/rapid/press-release_IP-08-1774_en.htm?locale=en.*

Demand Response Manipulation: Rumford Paper Company (Rumford) and Others

The Commission's Order to Show Cause against Rumford[136] was filed in parallel with three other Show Cause orders[137] targeting similar behavior in the ISO-NE "Day-Ahead Load Response Program" (DALRP). To participate in the DALRP, a resource would need to set a "baseline" to establish a "normal" load against which demand response would be measured. The initial baseline was set by a simple average of the resource's hourly demand, measured over a five workday period from 7:00 p.m. to 6:00 p.m. The program specified that the baseline would be adjusted over time based on subsequent actual load, but not on days when the resource was used by the system for demand response.[138] The minimum price at which a resource could bid into the day-ahead market was restricted to $50/MWh.[139]

Rumford owned and operated a large lumber mill in Maine that had a 95 MW load that operated 24 hours per day during the workweek.[140] This load was typically served entirely by a 110 MW on-site generator that was economic at power prices above $45/MWh.[141] After enrolling in the DALRP, the FERC alleged that Rumford purposely ramped its generator down by 30-40 MW during the times when its baseline was being set, resulting in approximately 40 MW of phantom load being made eligible for demand response payments.[142] The pattern of behavior cited by Enforcement staff is shown below in Figure 11-9, which shows Rumford's normal load of around 10 MW in hours at times outside the benchmarking period and increased load of 40-50 MW when the baseline was being set.

136. Rumford Paper Company, *Order to Show Cause and Notice of Proposed Penalty* ("Rumford OSC"), 140 FERC ¶ 61,030, July 17, 2012.

137. Lincoln Paper and Tissue, LLC, *Order to Show Cause and Notice of Proposed Penalty*, 140 FERC ¶ 61,031, July 17, 2012; Competitive Energy Services, LLC, *Order to Show Cause and Notice of Proposed Penalty*, 140 FERC ¶ 61,032, July 17, 2012; and Richard Silkman, *Order to Show Cause and Notice of Proposed Penalty*, 140 FERC ¶ 61,033, July 17, 2012.

138. Rumford OSC, Enforcement Staff Report and Recommendations, pp. 4-5.

139. *Id.*, p. 6.

140. *Id.*, pp. 2-3.

141. *Id.*, pp. 2-3, 24.

142. *Id.*, pp. 11-14.

Figure 11-9

Rumford's Load during the Baseline Period[143]

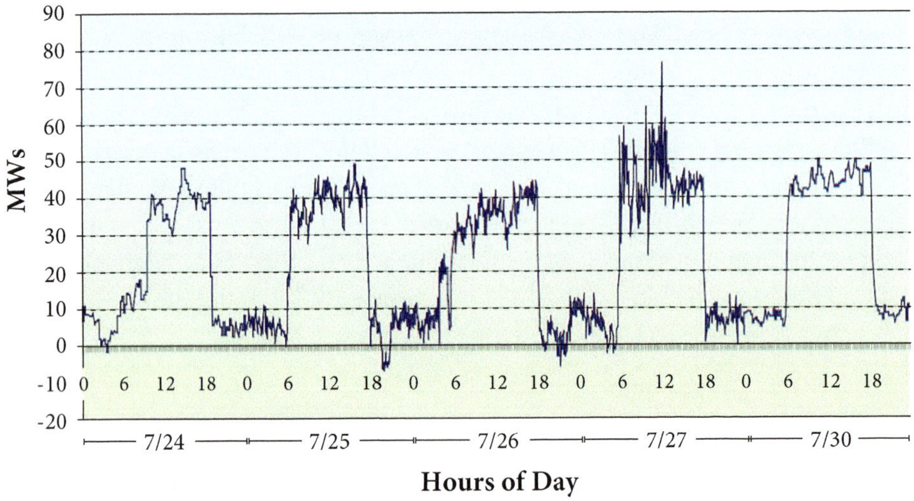

Once established, Rumford maintained this allegedly false baseline by continually offering the unit for demand response into the day-ahead market at the floor of $50/MWh, which typically cleared given the prevailing market prices.[144] By doing so, Rumford was continually picked up and paid for demand response that the FERC contends did not exist, as well as preventing its baseline from being adjusted later when normal operations resumed.[145]

The FERC's primary argument rested on the basis of outright fraud, where Rumford's intentional misreporting of its eligible load to the ISO (the trigger) altered and perpetuated its baseline (the nexus) to garner demand response payments from the DALRP (the target). The Order to Show Cause stated that "fraudulent intent is a fact-specific inquiry, not a matter of general economic principles."[146] It is interesting, however, that the OSC nevertheless made extensive use of economic evidence to support its case, corroborated by "objective" statements by the implicated parties involved in the alleged manipulation. Further, it is noteworthy that the OSC alleged that Rumford's choice to buy $120,000 of replacement power during the setting of its initial baseline was *uneconomic* relative to production out of its own generator. This is consistent with the view that behavior that is intentionally uneconomic is best considered a form of fraud. Rumford settled the case for $10 million in civil penalties and $2 million in

143. *Id.*, p. 12.

144. *Id.*, p. 13.

145. *Id.*, pp. 13-14.

146. *Id.*, p. 20.

disgorgement;[147] the cases against the other three participants alleged to have manipulated the DALRP are pending.[148]

Circular Scheduling: Gila River Power, LLC (Gila River)

Gila River owned and operated a 2,220 MW plant southwest of Phoenix, AZ.[149] The company preferred to sell the plant's energy into the CAISO through the Palo Verde intertie ("PV"), but congestion at the node limited its imports to less than 3,000 MWh per day and resulted in low prices. Gila River devised two strategies to relieve this congestion. The first, referred to as the "Standalone Wheel Strategy," scheduled a "wheel-through" transaction by buying power at an uncongested node in the CAISO and exporting it through the CAISO PV tie point. Gila River then scheduled power and transmission outside of the CAISO from PV back to the uncongested node on another transmission path, thus creating a circular schedule.[150] No power flowed as a result of this scheme, but congestion at PV was reduced, thus allowing Gila River to sell greater amounts of power into the state.

Gila River's second scheme, known as the "Adjustment Wheel Strategy," would schedule a day-ahead wheel-though export transaction to raise prices at the source node and reduce import congestion at an intertie, then simultaneously would schedule a day-ahead flow from the plant to that same intertie.[151] The firm would then schedule imports from the plant into the CAISO in the hour-ahead market, buying back its day-ahead schedules so that the power was redirected from the plant over the intertie directly to the original source.

Gila River settled with the FERC for $2.5 million in civil penalties and $911,553 in disgorgement.[152] The company also *admitted* that its behavior was manipulative, which may have played a role in Deutsche Bank's decision, discussed above, to settle its action with the FERC[153] and in the Commission's subsequent decision to formally ban circular scheduling in the CAISO.[154]

---

147. Rumford Paper Company, *Order Approving Stipulation and Consent Agreement*, 142 FERC ¶ 61,218, Mar. 22, 2013, p. 1. Note that only $1 million in civil penalties were actually assessed due to Rumford's bankruptcy.

148. Lincoln Paper and Tissue, LLC, *Petition for an Order Affirming the Federal Energy Regulatory Commission's August 29, 2013 Orders Assessing Civil Penalties against Lincoln Paper and Tissue, LLC*, D. Mass. 12/02/13; Richard Silkman and Competitive Energy Services, LLC, *Petition for an Order Affirming the Federal Energy Regulatory Commission's August 29, 2013 Orders Assessing Civil Penalties against Richard Silkman and Competitive Energy Services, LLC*, D. Mass. 12/02/13.

149. Gila River Power, LLC, *Order Approving Stipulation and Consent Agreement*, 141 FERC ¶ 61,136, November 19, 2012, ¶ 2.

150. *Id.*, ¶ 6.

151. *Id.*, ¶¶ 8-10.

152. *Id.*, ¶ 1.

153. Specifically, Deutsche Bank's "Export Strategy," used in conjunction with its allegedly mistagged wheel-through transaction, looks optically very similar to the "Standalone Wheel Strategy" employed by Gila River.

154. California Independent System Operator Corporation, *Order on Proposed Tariff Revisions*, 142 FERC ¶ 61,072, January 29, 2013.

CHAPTER 12

CONCLUSION

Market pricing of energy products is a relatively recent phenomenon. Although the process of deregulating natural gas prices began in the late 1970s, they were not fully determined by the market until 1993 with the implementation of the Natural Gas Wellhead Decontrol Act.[1] Crude oil prices were effectively controlled until the late 1970s either by the Texas Railroad Commission or through federal price control programs, and crude oil futures prices only began trading on the NYMEX in 1983. Electricity was not bought and sold competitively until the late 1990s, as California and Texas established market platforms respectively in the CAISO, as discussed earlier, and in ERCOT.[2]

In addition to being new, electricity markets are quite dynamic and complex due to their network features, multiple cross-market linkages, and their inherent price volatility. Thus it was understood that regulators would face a difficult challenge in keeping up with market developments and trader behavior. Dr. Paul Joskow of MIT explained the challenge in Senate committee hearings on the California Crisis:

> It is impossible to get it right the first time around. Electricity markets with good performance attributes do not create themselves and do not fix themselves.
>
> Ongoing market reforms and regulatory "mitigation" initiatives designed to remedy serious market performance problems should be an expected feature of the process of creating efficient competitive wholesale electricity markets.[3]

As set out in the previous chapters, the FERC was poorly prepared for the California Crisis. Its approach to constraining market power was woefully antiquated, and it had failed to collect the data necessary to understand what was going on in the markets. The concept of fraud-based manipulation had not even entered the Commission's thinking. It had no workable model of manipulative behavior, no analytic approach for diagnosing it, and no remedial tools to deter it or compensate consumers for any consequential damage. As a result of its inability to detect and deal quickly with manipulation of the sort Enron conceived and disseminated into the marketplace, a massive wealth transfer, estimated at $40 billion, occurred in just fourteen months. A decade of litigation and millions of dollars in costs have afforded recovery of only a fraction of this loss.

---

1. *See http://naturalgas.org/regulation/history/.*

2. The Electric Reliability Council of Texas (ERCOT), which covers most of the State of Texas, became the first ISO in the U.S. in 1996 after the Texas legislature voted to deregulate wholesale electricity generation. Like the CAISO, ERCOT operated an energy-only wholesale market. Unlike the CAISO, it was and remains only weakly linked to electric systems and markets outside the state.

3. Statement of Dr. Paul L. Joskow before the Committee on Governmental Affairs, United States Senate, June 13, 2001.

The Crisis spurred considerable reform, and the Commission is now much better equipped to deal with market dysfunction, whatever its cause. Through legislation it has been granted clear authority to address manipulation, and it has gained experience in identifying manipulative behavior based upon fraudulent uneconomic trading. It has the ability to levy penalties that can act as a real deterrent. The Commission's thinking on market power has evolved as well to reflect the fact that market conditions can confer market power to certain suppliers for periods that are short by traditional antitrust standards, but are sufficiently anticompetitive and burdensome to warrant prevention and/or *ex-post* remediation.

Nonetheless, in the ever-evolving electricity markets, the regulator will always be one or two steps behind the ingenuity of traders who gain an almost organic appreciation of market dynamics and relationships through their observation of market movements on a daily, if not hourly, basis.[4] And, as we have stated repeatedly, the features of electricity markets and pricing make them particularly vulnerable to manipulation. The regulator's challenge remains daunting not only because identifying and effectively addressing manipulation are difficult, but also because overly aggressive regulation can undermine markets and cause as much damage in the long run as manipulation itself. As was the case when it first confronted the Crisis, the Commission must walk the fine line between too much and too little enforcement.

In this book we have laid out approaches our experience has shown to be effective in diagnosing—that is, identifying and gauging the extent of—market power and market manipulation more generally. These approaches are guided by a conceptual framework, depicted in Figure 12-1, that includes both market power and fraud linked by uneconomic trading. Pure market power is distinguished from manipulation based on uneconomic behavior in that it occurs in a single market and is profit maximizing in that market. This distinction is lost when an exercise of market power (withholding) is combined with a position in a second, linked market. Fraud differs from uneconomic trading when misinformation is injected into the market through misleading statements or omissions rather than through misleading trading activity. By encompassing market power, uneconomic trading, and fraud, the framework could be of assistance in selecting the appropriate statutory basis and regulatory jurisdiction through which to pursue enforcement actions.

4. A particular trader will typically deal with a few types of trades in a relatively narrow set of markets. Thus, he or she can develop a very deep understanding of how these perform and react to various trading practices the trader may try or see others trying over time. The regulator, however, is trying to cover all the bases all the time—an immense undertaking.

Figure 12-1

Manipulation Framework

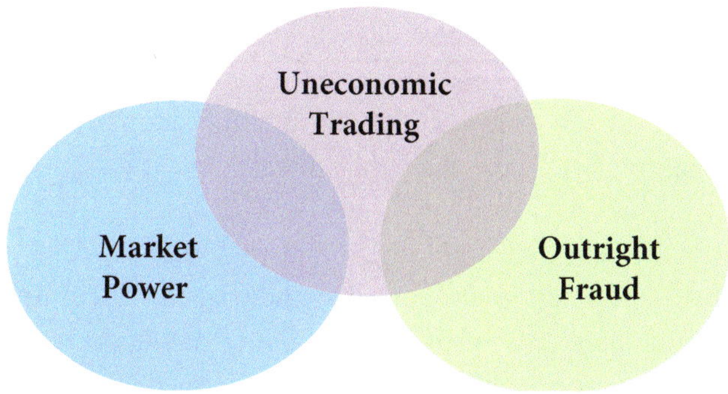

We have also laid out processes for applying the framework in monitoring activities and in enforcement actions. It is hoped that this will be helpful both to regulators in overseeing markets and to market participants engaged in trading—either for hedging the business risks they face in energy markets or those engaged in speculative risk-taking of the sort that provides liquidity in the markets.[5] The key to an effective regulatory regime is an understanding, shared by regulators and market participants, as to the behaviors that are and are not acceptable in the marketplace. Clarity is the foundation of a sound regulatory edifice. Without this, regulators will forever be charged with arbitrary overreach and traders discouraged from potentially legitimate, efficiency-enhancing activity.

In addition to laying out a framework we hope will be helpful, we have identified some problems that may hamper effective regulation of manipulative activity and, thus, perhaps, merit remedial action. The first of these, the disputed sharing of enforcement authority between the FERC and the CFTC cannot help but handicap efforts to curb manipulative activity that will frequently involve both physical and financial positions. The agencies have drafted Memoranda of Understanding, but these deal for the most part with information sharing and have done little to resolve jurisdictional issues. It would be beneficial to reach some of sort of arrangement that reflects the realities of the marketplace and takes advantage of the agencies' respective areas of expertise.

A second issue is the prohibition against private actions. As amply illustrated in the litigation over the Crisis, affected parties bring to the table first-hand knowledge of markets and events, expertise in industry practices, and resources to pursue and analyze market data. If the stakes are high, such resources can dwarf those available to the Commission. Because this prohibition is part of the statutory foundation of the FERC's anti-manipulation rule, Congressional action will be required to make private causes of action possible.

5. Although our discussion of the framework has focused largely on the electricity markets, it is, as we have explained, applicable as well to other commodity and financial markets.

Finally, the Commission's interpretation of the *Morgan Stanley* decision as to applying the *Mobile-Sierra Doctrine* to spot price contracts amplifies the conflict between fraud-based and tariff-based regulatory regimes. What is the import of a manipulation claim relating to a price deemed just and reasonable due to a *Mobile-Sierra* presumption? This question alone could lead to another decade of litigation. Unlike its use in the protection of long-term contracts, we argue that extension of the *Mobile-Sierra Doctrine* to spot transactions is unwise from a regulatory perspective and that it fails to serve the public interest.

Although economics is thought by some to be the dismal science, it is evolving regardless. Regulation and enforcement practices developed in the past that focus upon competition in specific, individual markets are now insufficient to police activity across the multi-dimensional physical and financial energy markets that have developed over the last few decades. In this environment, divining a trader's intent involves looking at his or her activity across markets. We hope that through this book we can advance the use of economic tools suited to this multi-dimensional world. The challenge is difficult, and the stakes are high. Efficient use of our energy resources now extends beyond minimizing the costs of running our refrigerators and iPads to expanding our use of renewable resources and reducing our impact upon the planet. If we are to rely upon market prices to allocate resources efficiently in these efforts, we must be able to trust the signals the markets provide to guide our behavior. We hope that this volume furthers the development of that trust.

GLOSSARY OF TERMS

TERM	DEFINITION
ABA	American Bar Association
actus reus	An unlawful act.
AES	Allegheny Energy Supply
Algorithm	The maximum allowed price that was lowered twice during Summer 2000;[1] the algorithm for setting the clearing price was changed substantially in Fall 2000.
ALJ	Administrative Law Judge, the official who adjudicates at Federal Energy Regulatory Commission hearings and issues the initial ruling.
Amaranth	Amaranth Advisors LLC
Ancillary Services	Electrical products other than basic electrical energy sold by large suppliers to ISOs to help them operate the grid. In the CAISO, the most important ancillary services were reserves.
Anomalous Bidding	A description of seller or buyer bidding behavior in California's power markets prohibited by the California ISO's FERC tariff. Described in the tariff as bidding behavior that departs significantly from normal behavior in competitive markets.
Assembly Bill (AB 1X)	A state law enacted at the height of the crisis that created CERS and gave it the authority to purchase all electricity needed to supply California's three IOUs.
Assembly Bill (AB) 1890	The Electric Utility Industry Restructuring Act, which deregulated the generation of electricity in California. Enacted September 23, 1996.
Astoria	Astoria Generating Company Acquisitions, LLC, an independent power producer located in New York City.
Avista	Avista Corp. and Avista Energy, collectively.
Avista Corp.	Avista Corporation (f/k/a Washington Water Power).
Avista Energy	Avista Energy, Inc.
BAA	Balancing Authority Area, the collection of generation, transmission, and loads within the metered boundaries of the Balancing Authority. The Balancing Authority maintains load-resource balance within this area.
Back to Back (B2B)	"Back-to-back" transactions in which Coral allegedly bought power and then immediately resold the same quantity of power to CERS at the same location.
Balancing Authority	The responsible entity that integrates resource plans ahead of time, maintains load-interchange-generation balance within a Balancing Authority Area, and supports Interconnection frequency in real-time.
Barclays	Barclays Bank PLC

1. *See* Chapters 4 and 7 for more detail.

"Base Load" Units	A type of power plant designed to operate at full output continuously except during maintenance periods or unplanned outages. Typical baseload units include coal-fired and nuclear power plants.
BEEP stack	Balancing Energy Ex-Post Price Stack. The set of offers to sell power in the California's Imbalance Energy market for any single hour. Essentially equivalent to the hourly real-time market supply curve.
BFM	Block Forward Market. A market operated briefly by the California Power Exchange. Block forward products were contracts to deliver fixed quantity of power at a specified location during peak hours for one calendar month.
BP	BP America, Inc.
BPA	The Bonneville Power Administration
Buy-Side Market Power	Market power held by a buyer in the market, i.e., the ability to force sellers to lower their price by withholding demand. Also known as *monopsony power.*
CAISO	California Independent System Operator
California buyers	The California buyers include Southern California Edison (SCE), Pacific Gas and Electric (PG&E), San Diego Gas & Electric (SDG&E) and other load serving entities in California (collectively the California Parties).
California Crisis (or Crisis)	The period from May 1, 2000 through June 20, 2001, during which California's deregulated electricity markets experienced sustained high prices as the result of, among other things, market manipulation and tariff violations by multiple sellers. The Crisis spread throughout the Western United States.
CalParties	The California Parties. At various times, this group has included the California Attorney General, the California Public Utilities Commission, the California Electricity Oversight Board, Pacific Gas and Electric, Southern California Edison and San Diego Gas and Electric.
CDWR	California Department of Water Resources
CEA	Commodities Exchange Act
CEC	California Energy Commission
CERS	The California Energy Resources Scheduling division of the California Department of Water Resources, acting solely under the authority and powers created by California Assembly Bill 1 (2001).
CERS Period	The period from January 17, 2001 through June 20, 2001, during which CERS was primarily responsible for buying California's power.
CFTC	Commodity Futures Trading Commission
Chief Judge	The Chief Administrative Law Judge for the Commission's Office of Administrative Law Judges and Dispute Resolution.
Circular Scheduling	A violation of the California ISO tariff in which power is scheduled on a circular path. Referred to by Enron traders as "Death Star."

CMA	Calendar MERC Average. Physical oil priced at CMA is priced ratably at the average of each day's near month settlement price during the month of delivery.
CME	NYMEX ClearPort (now CME Group). Firm that owns and operates U.S. futures and trading exchanges.
COB	The California-Oregon Border interface with the CAISO, a trading hub approximately located at the physical border of the two states at which brokers trade physical and financial electricity products.
Commission or FERC	The Federal Energy Regulatory Commission or its predecessor, the Federal Power Commission (FPC).
Commission Staff	Commission Staff refers to all staff members employed by the Commission other than trial staff. The term "Staff" is defined below and refers only to trial staff.
Constellation	Constellation Energy Commodities Group, Inc.
Coral	Coral Power LLC (n/k/a Shell Energy North America). References to either Shell Energy or Coral are to the same entity.
Counterflows	A power sale that creates a flow on the power grid that goes in the opposite direction as pre-existing flows. The counterflows and pre-existing flows cancel each other out electrically if they are the same size and travel the same path. More commonly, counterflows reduce but do not eliminate existing flows.
CPUC	The California Public Utilities Commission
CRRs	Congestion Revenue Rights, financial instruments issued by electric market operators that entitle the owner to receive the revenues collected by operators to allay congestion over a transmission path on the power grid. Also see *FTR* in this glossary.
CTC	Competitive Transition Charge
D.C. Circuit	The United States Court of Appeals for the District of Columbia Circuit.
DALRP	day-ahead Load Response Program. A program in which California utilities asked customers to reduce their power use the following day and paid rewards to customers who complied.
Day-Ahead (DA)	A term used to describe energy transactions in which product delivery occurs during the 24-hour time period following the trading day, or, in the case of weekends, the two or three days following the trading day.
Day-Of (DO)	A term used to describe both real-time and hour-ahead energy transactions.
DBET	Deutsche Bank Energy Trading

Death Star	Enron's trader's name for a strategy in which a series of power sales are scheduled over a series of transmission paths that, in total, represent a full circle. Each transaction is unwittingly treated by market operators as a separate trade and paid congestion fees and all other applicable payments. However, when the power system's operating software integrates the full schedule, no power actually flows because the software understands that the same power has been simply sent around in a circle. Also see Circular scheduling.
DEC (Physical)	Decremental bid, a price or prices at which a Scheduling Coordinator would be willing to increase its demand in the CAISO Imbalance Energy Market.
DEC (Virtual)	Decremental bid, a.k.a. virtual load. An offer to buy energy in the Day-ahead market and sell an equivalent amount in the Real-time.
DiPlacido	In the Matter of Anthony DiPlacido, a complaint brought by the CFTC in 2001.
DMA	Department of Market Analysis
Dodd-Frank	Dodd-Frank Wall Street Reform and Consumer Protection Act
DOJ/FTC	Department of Justice and Federal Trade Commission
DPT	Delivered Price Test, a test employed by the FERC to determine whether a proposed merger increases market concentration.
Duke	Duke Energy Corporation
Dynegy	Dynegy Inc.
E.ON Energy	German utility company
EC	European Commission
EES	Enron Energy Services
EEX	European Electric Exchange, an electronic trading platform for electric power.
EISA	Energy Independence and Security Act
Enron	Enron Corporation (including Enron Power Marketing, Inc. and Enron Energy Services, Inc.).
EOL	Enron's electronic trading platform, known as the Enron Online.
EPAct	Energy Policy Act of 2005, 42 USC § 15801.
ERCOT	Electric Reliability Council of Texas
ETF	Exchange-traded fund
ETP	Energy Transfer Partners, L.P.
EU	European Union
False Export	A tariff violation in which a seller misrepresented a transaction to the ISO or CERS by selling power to an entity located outside of California so as to be able to falsely represent that it was importing the power into California for sale in real-time. Also see *Ricochet* in this glossary.

False Load	A type of violation of the CAISO tariff in which a schedule coordinator willingly submits a schedule with larger customer loads than the scheduler believes will be required. Also referred to as "overscheduling load" (or simply "overscheduling") and by the name given to this trading strategy by Enron traders, "Fat Boy."
Fat Boy	See False Load.
FERC	The Federal Energy Regulatory Commission
FERC or Commission	See Commission or FERC.
Final Joint Statement of Issues	Final Joint Statement of Issues, Docket No. EL01-10-085 (Aug. 23, 2013).
Firm	Firm services and products are sales or transmission of electric energy that are essentially guaranteed to be delivered under all but emergency circumstances. When power supplies or transmission are limited, firm services have priority. Non-Firm services and products are curtailed or interrupted before any Firm services are reduced. The WSPP Agreement and most other firm power sales agreements require that Firm power must be backed by a seller's capacity reserves.
First Circuit	The United States Court of Appeals for the First Circuit.
FOREX	Foreign Exchange
Forney Perpetual Loop	One particular type of Circular Scheduling (or "Death Star") transaction implemented in early May 2000, just as the Crisis began. See Death Star and Circular Scheduling.
FPA	The Federal Power Act
FPA Section 201	16 U.S.C. § 824 (2006): Declaration of policy; application of subchapter.
FPA Section 205	16 U.S.C. § 824d (2006): Rates and charges; schedules; suspension of new rates; automatic adjustment clauses.
FPA Section 206	16 U.S.C. § 824e (2006): Power of Commission to fix rates and charges; determination of cost of production or transmission.
FTC	Federal Trade Commission
FTR	Firm Transmission Rights, financial instruments that entitle the owner to receive the congestion revenues collected by a market operator over a specific transmission interface. This allows the owner of the FTR to hedge the cost for transmitting power over the same interface. FTRs can also be held or traded as speculative investments. In the CAISO, FTRs are referred to as "Congestion Revenue Rights" or CRRs. See http://www.caiso.com/Documents/Chapter5_Inter-ZonalCongestionManagementMarkets.pdf (1/19/15).
Gaming order	A FERC Order issued in 2003, requiring 49 suppliers to show cause why they should not be found to have engaged in Enron-type manipulation strategies in violation of specified sections of the MMIP of the CAISO Tariff. (Order to Show Cause Concerning Gaming and/or Anomalous Behavior, Docket No. EL03-137-000 et al., June 25, 2003).

"Gaming Provisions"	The Market Monitoring and Information Protocol (MMIP) provisions of the PX and CAISO tariffs. These tariff sections, commonly referred to as the "gaming provisions," set forth in somewhat vague language the trading strategies that were prohibiting in the California ISO and PX markets.
Gila River	Gila River Power, LLC
HE	Hour ending, a convention for labeling the hour in which power is scheduled or delivered.
Hedging	A trading strategy designed to reduce risk and/or mitigate losses.
HHI	Herfindahl-Hirschman Index, an index for measuring the degree of concentration of sellers in a market.
Hour-Ahead or HA	The hour-ahead market for energy operated by the California PX. This market accepted sales offers from sellers up to approximately 3 hours prior to the hour of delivery each hour of each day.
HSC	Houston Ship Channel
Hub-and-Spoke test	Prior to 2001, the test used by the FERC to determine whether a power seller would not have undue market power and therefore would be allowed to sell power at deregulated prices.
ICAP	Abbreviation for Installed Capacity. Typically refers to a market for units of generating capability provided by power plants and other similar power supply resources. The New York ISO operates an ICAP market.
ICE	InterContinental Exchange, an electronic trading platform.
ID	*Puget Sound Energy, Inc.*, Initial Decision, 146 FERC ¶ 63,028 (2014) (as amended).
IFERC Index	Inside FERC Houston Ship Channel Monthly Natural Gas Index, a pricing benchmark for natural gas.
Imbalance Energy	Same as "real-time" energy. Energy offered into or purchased by the ISO in the imbalance energy or real-time market (also known in California as the "BEEP stack"). Imbalance energy is used only by the CAISO to perform real-time balancing of the grid.
Imbalance Energy Market	Also referred to as the real-time market. The market for imbalance or real-time energy operated by the California ISO. A separate auction with a separate "market-clearing price" was generated for each hour of every day in each zone of the CAISO.
INC (Physical)	Incremental bid, a price or prices at which a Scheduling Coordinator would be willing to increase its supply in the CAISO Imbalance Energy Market.
INC (Virtual)	Incremental bid, a.k.a. a virtual supply offer. An offer to sell energy in the day-ahead market and buy an equivalent amount in the real-time.
Incremental Cost	Sometimes used interchangeably with marginal or operating costs. Incremental costs represent the additional cost incurred by a seller when generating one more unit of power.
Interlocutory Order	*Puget Sound Energy, Inc.*, 141 FERC ¶ 61,248 (2012).

Into Cinergy	A former trading point on the power grid in the Midwestern U.S. roughly equal to the borders of the transmission grid leading into Cincinnati, Ohio.
IOUs	Investor-Owned Utilities (as distinct from utilities owned by municipalities or cooperatives). In the context of the California Energy Crisis, California's investor-owned utilities: Pacific Gas and Electric Company; Southern California Edison Company; and San Diego Gas & Electric Company, collectively.
ISO	Independent System Operator, a nonprofit corporation that operates but does not own the transmission system in a large area and also operates short-term markets for power and ancillary services.
ISO Tariff	The Commission-approved tariff containing the terms and conditions under which an ISO operates and under which sellers and buyers may transact in the markets operated.
JMP	J.P. Morgan Ventures Energy Corporation
Joint Procedural History	Joint Procedural History, Docket No. EL01-10-085 (August 12, 2013).
Katy Hub	An interstate natural gas trading hub north of Houston.
KET	Koch Energy Trading
KeySpan	KeySpan-Ravenswood
LADWP	The Los Angeles Department of Water and Power, a city-owned utility serving LA.
Lerner Index	A measure of one firm's market power determined by a ratio of the difference between that firm's sales price and its marginal cost to firm's sale price.
LIBOR	London Interbank Offered Rate, an interest rate used for transactions between banks and as an index for other commercial transactions.
LMP	Locational Marginal Price. The price of electrical energy sold or bought at one pricing point on an electrical grid in markets operated by system operators. LMPs are typically reset for each point every five minutes to one hour based on offers from electric generators and purchase bids from power buyers. LMPs may be set in either day-ahead, hour-ahead, or real-time markets.
Load	Physical demand for electricity by all electricity-using customers within a specified area.
M&A	Mergers and acquisitions
Marginal Unit	This is the last unit that is dispatched to satisfy the last incremental unit of load, at a given dispatch interval.
MBRs	Market-Based Rates, the FERC's term for wholesale power prices that are freely negotiated by buyers and sellers within its rules. Loosely referred to as "deregulated prices."
MC	Marginal Cost, the cost of supplying one additional unit of output. Approximately equivalent to incremental cost.
Mid-C	The Mid-Columbia trading hub, located in Washington State, at which brokers trade physical and financial electricity products.

MISO	Midcontinental Independent System Operator, a nonprofit ISO that operates the transmission system and spot power markets in much of the middle portion of the U.S.
MMBtu	One million British thermal units, one common unit of measure for natural gas.
MMC	Market Monitoring Committee, a committee of economic experts created by many ISOs to provide analysis and recommendations regarding its operation.
MMCP	Mitigated Market Clearing Price. A calculated set of hourly prices in the California PX and ISO markets directed by the FERC as its proxy for what appropriate competitive prices would have been in the absence of the California Crisis. Roughly described as the estimated marginal cost of the highest-cost power generator required to meet total demand in any hour of the crisis. The Commission adopted this methodology in its July 25, 2001 Order in *San Diego Gas & Elec. Co.*, 96 FERC ¶ 61,120 (2001).
MMIP	Market Monitoring and Information Protocol provisions of the CAISO and PX Tariffs. These protocols held the language of trading activities that were not allowed by sellers or buyers in the markets operated by the ISO and PX.
Mobile-Sierra (MS) or *Mobile-Sierra* doctrine	A legal doctrine adopted by the FERC that stands for the proposition that contracts freely negotiated by buyers and sellers in deregulated power markets should not have their prices reset by action of the FERC after the fact simply because either buyers or sellers find the outcome uneconomical for them. Instead, the Commission can overturn contract prices retroactively only if such action can be shown to be in the overall public interest, except in cases of fraud, duress, or market manipulation. See *United Gas Pipe Line Co. v. Mobile Gas Serv. Corp.*, 350 U.S. 332 (1956); *FPC v. Sierra Pac. Power Co.*, 350 U.S. 348 (1956).
MSC	Market Surveillance Committee. A committee roughly equivalent to a Market Monitoring Committee created by the California ISO in 1997 and which continued to operate through the Crisis.
MSU	Market Surveillance Unit
MW	Megawatt, one million electrical watts.
MWh	Megawatt-hour, one million electrical watts delivered continuously for one hour.
NCAA	National Collegiate Athletic Association v. Board of Regents of University of Oklahoma, 468 U.S. 85 (1984).
NCPA	Northern California Power Agency
NCPA Cong Catcher	Particular type of Circular Scheduling transaction arranged by Enron using transmission rights owned by the municipal utility for Redding California.
NERC	North American Reliability Corporation, the electric industry's self-regulatory agency that administered reliability rules and standards.
NGA	The Natural Gas Act, 15 U.S.C. Chapter 15B.

Ninth Circuit	The United States Court of Appeals for the Ninth Circuit.
NOB	The Nevada-Oregon Border trading hub for physical and financial electricity products flowing over an 850 mile long DC transmission line starting in Celilo in northern Oregon and ending in Sylmar, California.
Nodal Exchange	A commodities exchange dedicated to offering locational (nodal) futures contracts and related services to participants in the organized North American power markets.
Non-Firm	Non-Firm services or products are subject to curtailment or interruption. The service has lower priorty than firm services; thus, Non-Firm is less valuable, less reliable, and has lower priority than Firm. See Firm in this glossary.
Non-spinning Reserves	A type of Ancillary Service purchased by the California ISO, representing electric generating capacity that can be fully operational and ready to deliver power within 10 minutes of a request by the CAISO. See http://www.caiso.com/market/Pages/ProductsServices/Default.aspx (1/19/2015).
NOx	The set of several nitrogen/oxygen compounds emitted by fossil-fueled electric power plants. Typically these compounds are regulated as a group rather than as individual compounds.
NP15	Northern market area of the CAISO, roughly the portion of California that lies north of Monterrey.
NYISO	New York Independent System Operator
NYMEX	New York Mercantile Exchange
Oligopoly	A market structure characterized by relatively few sellers whose pricing and output decisions are interdependent.
OOM	Out-of-Market transactions, or transactions that were not conducted in the ISO or PX regular auction markets. Instead, when these markets did not have sufficient supplies, the CAISO would initiate immediate short-term emergency purchases bilaterally by contacting suppliers and entering into short-term purchases with them.
Optiver	Optiver US, LLC
OSC	Order to Show Cause
OTC	Over-the-counter, a term used to describe trading of an instrument that does not occur on organized exchanges.
Parnon	Parnon Energy, Inc.

Partnership Order	On June 25, 2003 the Commission issued four orders based upon the Staff investigation and the 100 Days Evidence submitted by participants in the Crisis-related proceedings. The first, the so called Gaming Order, required various suppliers to show cause why they should not be found to have engaged in Enron-type manipulation strategies in violation of specified sections of the MMIP of the CAISO Tariff.[2] The second, referred to as the *Partnership Order*, demanded that named parties show cause why they should not be found to have been in league with Enron in executing its manipulative schemes.
Peakers or Peaking Units	Power plants which tend to operate only during periods of very high power demand, typically only a few dozen of the hottest hours of the year.
PG&E	Pacific Gas and Electric Company, a California IOU and one of the California Parties.
PGES or PGEES	Portland General (Electric) Electric Supply
Phase I	The liability phase of *Puget Sound Energy, Inc.*, Order Confirming Rulings from Sept. 6, 2012 Prehearing Conference at P 15, Docket No. EL01-10-085 (September 13, 2012).
Phase II	The phase addressing issues other than liability, including the appropriate remedy, in *Puget Sound Energy, Inc.*, Order Confirming Rulings from September 6, 2012 Prehearing Conference at P 15, Docket No. EL01-10-085 (September 13, 2012).
Pivotal Supplier Index (PSI)	Pivotal Supplier Index. A seller-specific metric for determining whether one or more individual sellers in a market has market power. According to FERC, a seller with a PSI greater than one is presumed to have market power.
Pivotal Supplier tests	Pivotal Supplier Index tests. Tests that measure the PSI for a seller to determine whether that seller has an ability to exercise market power.
Pivotal Unit	A power generator who "fails" the pivotal supplier test and is thereby found to have market power. Casually referred to as "pivotality."
"Platt's Window" Oil Prices	Average of reported prices of trades in last 30-to-45 minutes for dated Brent crude oil.
PJM	PJM Interconnection LLC, the independent system operator for Mid-Atlantic region of the U.S.
PNW	The Pacific Northwest. For the purpose of litigation involving the California Crisis, the FERC adopted the definition of the region in the Northwest Power Planning Act: "the area consisting of the States of Oregon, Washington, and Idaho, the portion of the State of Montana west of the Continental Divide, and such portions of the States of Nevada, Utah, and Wyoming as are within the Columbia River drainage basin and any contiguous areas, which are a part of the service area of a rural electric cooperative customer served by the Administrator of BPA on December 5, 1990, and which has a distribution system from which it serves both within and without such region."

2. *See Order to Show Cause Concerning Gaming and/or Anomalous Market Behavior* (hereinafter Gaming Order 2003), 103 FERC ¶61,345, June 25, 2003.

Portland General	Portland General Electric Company, an Oregon utility that was owned by Enron from 1997 until 2006.
Powerex-CalParties Settlement	Joint Offer of Settlement and Motion for Procedural Relief for Purposes of Disposition of the Settlement and for Expedited Comments and Expedited Action, Docket No. EL00-95-273 (Aug. 16, 2013).
PPOA	The Power Pool of Alberta
Price Inelastic Demand Curve	A demand curve in which the buyer or buyers in a market do not reduce their purchases much or at all as prices increase. *Cf.* "price-elastic" demand curves, where buyers buy significantly less of a product as its price increases. Electric demand curves are considered price-inelastic, especially demand curves reflecting the real-time purchases by ISOs.
Prima facie	Based on the first impression; accepted as correct until proved otherwise.
Puget	Puget Sound Energy, Inc. a utility serving the Seattle area. Also refers to a proceeding involving the California Crisis in which buyers of power in the Pacific Northwest sought refunds from sellers, *Puget Sound Energy, Inc.*, 137 FERC ¶ 61,001 (2011).
PV	Palo Verde Trading Hub
PX	The California Power Exchange, an electronic day-ahead power market operated by a nonprofit corporation of the same name in California from 1997 to early 2001. Dismantled by the FERC as part of the attempt to control the California Crisis.
PX Tariff	The Commission-approved tariff containing the terms and conditions under which the PX operated its markets.
Q	Abbreviation for Quantity of electric power; often refers to the "market-clearing" quantity, or the quantity of power at which the price paid by buyers produces the same quantity of power supplied by sellers.
QFs	Qualifying Facilities, a term for a particular type of non-utility power generator exempted from traditional price regulation by the Public Utilities Regulatory Policy Act of 1978 (PURPA). QFs are typically cogeneration or renewable energy power generators.
Real-Time (RT)	Generally refers to the period within one hour or less prior to operation. When referring to a specific energy product or market, the energy purchased by the ISO in the Imbalance Energy Market.
Regional Transmission Operators (RTOs)	See Independent System Operators.
Regulation	One type of Ancillary Service purchased by ISOs and RTOs. Selling Regulation to an ISO is allowing the ISO's operators and computers to directly and instantly control a power generator's output within a small output band around a pre-existing set point. The size of the adjustment range is the quantity of Regulation provided.
Reliant	Reliant Energy Company
Remand Order	*Puget Sound Energy, Inc.*, 137 FERC ¶ 61,001 (2011).

Remand Rehearing Order	*Puget Sound Energy, Inc.*, 143 FERC ¶ 61,020 (2013).
REPA	Regulation Energy Payment Adjustment. An adjustment made by an ISO or RTO to payment for the provision of the ancillary service known as Regulation.
Replacement Reserves	A form of Ancillary Services purchased by the CAISO during the period before and during the Crisis, but which is no longer used in this form by the CAISO via a market. Electric generating capacity able to deliver power to the grid within one hour of receiving a request from the CAISO.
Residual Supplier Index (RSI)	Residual Supplier Index. An index conceptually very similar to the Pivotal Supplier Index.
Respondents	In FERC complaint proceedings, the name given to parties responding to the complaint. In the California Crisis proceedings, most complaints were brought by buyers, so most Respondents are specific named power generators or marketers.
"Ricochet"	Also referred to as "False Export." A trading strategy named by Enron's traders in which energy is scheduled to be exported and sold at a trading point outside the California ISO and then re-imported and resold within the ISO. The "export" sale was typically conducted in the day-ahead market and the "import" sale was conducted in the real-time market. The two trades cancel each other out and the electrical energy never actually leaves the California ISO.
Ripple Claims	When a buyer makes a refund claim against a seller, that seller may have purchased the energy subject to the claim from another seller. If the named seller might then make a claim against the seller from whom it purchased the energy named in the claim, the second claim is referred to as a ripple claim.
RMR	Reliability Must-Run. A designation given to a power generator by an ISO or RTO that dictates that the generator must produce power regardless of whether it submits offers into the ISO's markets and regardless of the price set in those markets.
Rumford	Rumford Paper Company
Scarcity Rents	The profits earned by sellers due to the fact that buyers are demanding more supply than the market can provide at the moment. Formally, the level of profits earned by sellers above competitive levels of risk-adjusted return on investment.
SCE	Southern California Edison, a California IOU and one of the California Parties.
Scheduling Coordinators (SCs)	The entities responsible for submitting generation and load schedules to the California ISO for all power bought and sold in the CAISO. Many generators served as their own SCs, but some gave this responsibility to firms acting as their agent. By Summer 2000, there were approximately 100 Scheduling Coordinators in the CAISO markets.
Scienter	Intent to deceive, manipulate or defraud.

SDG&E	San Diego Gas and Electric Company, a California IOU and one of the California Parties.
SEC	Securities Exchange Commission
Sell-side market power	The ability of an individual supplier or group of suppliers to profitably maintain prices above competitive levels for a significant period of time.
Senate Bill 7X	The Senate bill counterpart to Assembly Bill 1X.
Sherman Act	Sherman Antitrust Act
SLIC	Scheduling and Logging of ISO of California. The logbooks kept by the operators of the California ISO while on duty in the control room indicating, among other things, instructions issued to power generators.
SMA	Supply Margin Assessment. A term used by the FERC to describe one particular form of Pivotal Supplier Test proposed as the basis for Market-Based Rates. Originally proposed in 2001 and adopted in 2004; see 107 FERC ¶ 61,018.
Soft Cap	Price limits that were set during the California Crisis by the FERC, not set at a fixed numerical level but rather by formula. The formula set the maximum price at which the CAISO real-time market price could be set. However, sellers could offer to sell power at a price above the Soft Cap by providing proof to the ISO that their costs were higher than the then-current Soft Cap level. Soft Caps were set monthly based on a formula promulgated by the FERC.
SP15	Southern market area, roughly the portion of California south of Monterrey, excluding Los Angeles and some portions of the Imperial Valley.
Spinning Reserves	One type of Ancillary Service purchased by the CAISO via a market. "Spinning reserve is the portion of unloaded capacity from units already connected or synchronized to the grid and that can deliver their energy in 10 minutes." http://www.caiso.com/market/Pages/ProductsServices/Default.aspx (1/19/2015).
Staff	Staff employed by the FERC dedicated specifically to representing the Commission as a party in litigated matters. As used in this volume, Staff does not refer to the remainder of the Commission Staff, which does not participate as a party in Commission litigation.
SWU	Acronym for a Utility in the Southwestern U.S.
TAS	Trade at Settlement, a trading term that indicates that the price of a trade will be determined by the average price determined at the contract's settlement.
TCCs	Transmission Congestion Credits. These are the credits given to the holders of Firm Transmission Rights, effectively as the payments from the governing ISO for actual congestion that has occurred. See Financial Transmission Rights.
The State	The State of California
TransAlta	TransAlta Energy Marketing (U.S.) Inc. and TransAlta Energy Marketing (California) Inc.

TransCanada	TransCanada Energy Ltd.
TSO	Transmission System Operator. A firm that operates but does not own the transmission system in an area. This is a general term that could refer to an ISO or RTO, which are nonprofit, FERC-regulated grid operators, but could also refer to a for-profit firm contracted to operate a transmission system it does not own. The U.S. has only ISOs and RTOs as approved by FERC, but TSOs are somewhat common in other parts of the world.
UMCP	Uncongested market clearing price. The day-ahead zonal price calculated by the California ISO for each hour prior to the ISO running its congestion management software.
VWAP	Volume Weighted Average Price
Waha	The West Texas natural gas production area
WECC	Western Electricity Coordinating Council. The self-regulatory council that is the regional unit of NERC charged with overseeing each electric market participant's adherence to voluntary reliability standards and rules.
West	The Western portion of the United States of America, including California and the Pacific Northwest.
WSPP	Western Systems Power Pool. A nonprofit association of Western electric market participants who have all entered in a special multilateral power trading contract approved by the FERC. This contract enabled short-term sales between approved sellers and buyers throughout the Western U.S. at freely-negotiated ("deregulated") prices with a minimum of paperwork.
WSPP Agreement	A Commission-jurisdictional, standardized form agreement for the sale and purchase of electric power that was widely used during the CERS Period by members of the WSPP, both jurisdictional and non-jurisdictional, for transactions in the Western United States, including the PNW.
WWP	Washington Water and Power, a Washington State IOU affiliated with Avista.

BIBLIOGRAPHY

AEP Power Marketing, Inc., et al. *Order on Triennial Market Power Updates and Announcing New, Interim Generation Market Power Screen and Mitigation Policy,* Docket No. ER96-2495-015 et al., 97 FERC ¶ 61,219 (November 20, 2001).

__________ et al., *Order on Rehearing and Modifying Interim Generation Market Power Analysis and Mitigation Policy*, Docket No. ER96-2495-016 *et al.*, 107 FERC ¶ 61,018, (April 14, 2004).

Aggarwal, R.K. and G. Wu. "Stock Market Manipulation - Theory and Evidence." Paper presented at the 64th Annual Meeting of the American Finance Association, Washington, DC, March 11, 2003.

Allen, F. and D. Gale. "Stock-Price Manipulation." *Review of Financial Studies* 5 (1992): 503-529.

Amaranth Advisors L.L.C., et al., *Order Approving Uncontested Settlement*, 128 FERC ¶ 61,154, August 12, 2009.

__________, *Order to Show Cause and Notice of Proposed Penalties*, 120 FERC ¶ 61,085 (July 26, 2007).

American Electric Power Service Corporation, et al. *Request for Rehearing and/or Clarification of the California Independent System Operator Corporation*, Docket No. EL03-137-000 et al., (July 25, 2003).

Anthony J. DiPlacido, Comm. Fut. L. Rep. (CCH) ¶ 30,970 (CFTC Docket No. 01-23, Nov. 5, 2008).

Areeda P.E., H. Hovenkamp, and J.L. Solow. *Antitrust Law: An Analysis of Antitrust Principles and Their Application*. New York: Aspen Publishers, (1995).

Aspen Skiing Co. v. Aspen Highlands Skiing Corp, 472 U.S. 585 (1985).

Attari, M., A.S. Mello, and M.E. Ruckes. "Arbitraging Arbitrageurs." *Journal of Finance* 60 (October 2005): 2471-2511.

Ballard, James S. *Prepared Direct and Answering Testimony,* Docket No. EL00-95-248, Exh. S-0, January 2012.

Barclays Bank PLC, Daniel Brin, Scott Connelly, Karen Levine, and Ryan Smith, *Order to Show Cause and Notice of Proposed Penalty*, 141 FERC ¶ 61,084 (October 31, 2012).

__________. *Order Assessing Civil Penalties*, 144 FERC ¶ 61,041 (July 16, 2013).

Beattie, Andrew. "Who is Mr. Copper?" http://www.investopedia.com/ask/answers/08/mr-copper-sumitomo-hamanaka.asp.

Bechard, Thomas M., *Answering Testimony*, Docket No. EL00-95-248, Exh. POW-203, October 25, 2011.

Berry, Carolyn, *Prepared Direct Testimony*, Docket No. EL00-95 et al., Exh. CA-7 and Exh. CA-8, February 28, 2003.

__________, *Prepared Direct Testimony*, Docket No. EL00-95-248, Exh. CAX-110, August 2011.

Blumstein, Carl, L.S. Friedman, and R.J. Green. "The History of Electricity Restructuring in California." *CSEM Working Paper Series*, CSEM WP 103 (August 2002).

Borenstein, S. "The Trouble with Electricity Markets: Understanding California's Restructuring Disaster." *Journal of Economic Perspectives*, 16 (Winter 2002): 191-211.

__________ and J. Bushnell. "An Empirical Analysis of the Potential for Market Power in California's Electricity Industry." *Journal of Industrial Economics* 47 (September 1999): 285-323.

__________. "Electricity Restructuring: Deregulation or Reregulation?" *Regulation* 23 (2000): 46-52.

__________, J. Bushnell, and F. Wolak. "Diagnosing Market Power in California's Restructured Wholesale Electricity Market." *POWER Working Paper Series*, PWP-064, (July 1999).

__________. "Measuring Market inefficiencies in California's Restructured Wholesale Electricity Market." *American Economic Review* 92 (December 2002): 1376-1405.

__________, Bushnell, C.R. Knittel, and C. Wolfram. "Inefficiencies and Market Power in Financial Arbitrage: A Study of California's Electricity Markets." *Journal of Industrial Economics* 56 (June 2008): 347-378.

__________, J.B. Bushnell, and S. Stoft. "The Competitive Effects of Transmission Capacity in a Deregulated Electricity Industry." *RAND Journal of Economics* 31 (Summer 2000): 294-325.

BP America Inc., et al. *Order to Show Cause and Notice of Proposed Penalty,* Docket No. IN13-15-000, 144 FERC ¶ 61,100 (August 5, 2013).

__________, *Order Establishing Hearing,* Docket No. IN13-15-000, 147 FERC ¶ 61,130 (May 15, 2014).

Brian Hunter, *Initial Decision,* Docket No. IN07-26-004, 130 FERC ¶ 63,004 (January 22, 2010).

__________, *Order Affirming Initial Decision and Ordering Payment of Civil Penalty,* 1 Docket No. IN07-26-004, 35 FERC ¶ 61,054 (April 21, 2011).

"California's Electricity Crisis: A Market Apart?" *Center for the Study of Energy Markets (CSEM) Working Paper Series,* University of California Berkeley (November 2003).

Cabral, L.M.B. "Chapter 9 - Market Structure and Market Power." *Introduction to Industrial Organization,* Cambridge, MA: MIT Press, 2000.

California Energy Commission Electricity Analysis Office and Energy Information & Analysis Division. *Market Clearing Prices Under Alternative Resource Scenarios 2000-2010* (February 2000).

California Independent System Operator Market Surveillance Unit. *Annual Report on Market Issues and Performance* (June 1999).

California Independent System Operator. *FERC Electric Tariff: Ancillary Services Requirement Protocol* (April 1988).

__________. *Market Monitoring and Information Protocol* (June 1998).

__________. *FERC Electric Tariff: Market Monitoring & Information Protocol* (August 2000).

__________. *ERC Electric Tariff, Third Revised Volume No. 1* (August 2000).

__________. *FERC Electric Tariff: Second Revised Sheet No. 42* (September 2000).

__________. *Emergency Tariff Amendment 33* (December 2000).

__________. *Limited Motion For Clarification Of The California Independent System Operator Corporation And Answer To The California Power Exchange's Motion For Emergency Expedited Modification of Amendment 33.* Docket No. ER01-607 (December 12, 2000).

__________. *CAISO 2001 Summer Assessment, Version 1.0* (March 22, 2001).

__________. *FERC Electric Tariff, Amended and Restated Third Replacement Volume No. 1,* 2007. http://www.caiso.com/Documents/CombinedPDFFile-September12_2007ConformedTariff.pdf.

__________. *Opinion on Oversight and Investigation Review* (July 22, 2002).

__________. *Order on Proposed Tariff Revisions,* Docket No. ER13-449-000, 142 FERC ¶ 61,072 (January 29, 2013).

California Power Exchange Corporation Market Compliance Unit. *Price Movements in California Electricity Markets: Analysis of Price Activity: May-June 2000* (September 29, 2000).

__________. *Cal PX Primer, The Basics: How the California Power Exchange Works, Version 6* (December 1999).

Cardell, Judith B., Carrie Cullen Hitt, and William H. Hogan. "Market Power and Strategic Interaction in Electricity Networks." *Resource and Energy Economics* 19(12) (March 1997): 109-137.

Carlton, Dennis W. "Market Definition: Use and Abuse." U.S. Department of Justice Economic Analysis Group Discussion Paper (April 2007).

Casey, Keith, *Prepared Direct Testimony*, Docket No. ER06-615-000, Exh. ISO-6, February 7, 2006.

Chandley, J. D., S. M. Harvey, and W. W. Hogan. "Electricity Market Reform in California" (November 22, 2000). http://www.hks.harvard.edu/fs/whogan/chhferc_ca_112200.pdf.

Church, J. and R. Ware. "Chapter 8 - Classical Models of Oligopoly," in *Industrial Organization a Strategic Approach*. Boston, MA: McGraw-Hill, 2000.

Cicchetti, C.J., J.A. Dubin, and C.M. Long. *The California Electricity Crisis: What, Why, and What's Next*. Norwell, MA: Kluwer Academic Publishers, 2004.

Citizens Power & Light Corporation, *Order Noting Intervention, Accepting in Part and Denying in Part Request for Waivers, and Conditionally Accepting Rate Schedules*. Docket No. ER89-401-000 (August 8, 1989).

Clark, Tony and Robin Z. Meidhof. "Ensuring Reliability and a Fair Energy Marketplace." *Energy and Environment Literature Review* 25(2) (2014): 340-355.

Commodity Exchange Act, 7 U.S.C. § 13(a) et seq. (2009).

Commodity Futures Trading Commission, *Transmission Organizations to Exempt Specified Transactions and by a Tariff or Protocol Approved by the Federal Energy Regulatory Commission or the Public Utility Commission of Texas from Certain Provisions of the Commodity Exchange Act Pursuant to the Authority Provided in Section 4(c)(6) of the Act* (March 23, 2013).

Commodity Futures Trading Commission Act of 1974, P.L. 93-463 (October 23, 1974).

Commodity Futures Trading Commission v. Amaranth Advisors, L.L.C., et al., *Consent Order of Permanent Injunction, Civil Monetary Penalty and Other Relief as to Defendants Amaranth Advisors, L.L.C. and Amaranth Advisors (Calgary) ULC*, 07 Civ. 6682 (DC) (SDNY 2009).

CFTC v. Enron Corp. and Hunter Shively, Civil Action No. H-03-909 (SDTX 2004).

CFTC Factsheet. "*Anti-Manipulation and Anti-Fraud Final Rules*." (2011).

CFTC v. Optiver US, LLC, et al., *Complaint for Injunctive and Other Equitable Relief and Civil Monetary Penalties under the Commodity Exchange Act*, 08 Civ. 6560 (SDNY 2008).

__________, *Final Consent Order of Permanent Injunction, Civil Monetary Penalty and Other Relief*, 08 Civ. 6560 (SDNY 2012).

CFTC vs. Parnon Energy, Inc. et al., *Complaint for Injunctive and Other Equitable Relief and Civil Monetary Penalties Under the Commodity Exchange Act*, Case No. 11-cv-3543 (SDNY 2011).

CFTC Press Release. "In the Matter of Sumitomo Corporation: Order Instituting Proceedings Pursuant to Sections 6(c) And 6(d) of the Commodity Exchange Act and Findings and Order Imposing Remedial Sanctions" (May 11, 1998).

__________. "Case Background Information, CFTC v. Optiver US, LLC, et al." (July 24, 2008).

__________. "Federal Court Orders $14 Million in Fines and Disgorgement Stemming from CFTC Charges against Optiver and Others for Manipulation of NYMEX Crude Oil, Heating Oil, and Gasoline Futures Contracts and Making False Statements" (April 19, 2012).

__________. "CFTC Releases Enforcement Division's Annual Results" (October 24, 2013).

__________. "Memorandum of Understanding between the Federal Energy Regulatory Commission and the Commodity Futures Trading Commission" (January 2, 2014).

__________. "Federal Court Orders $13 Million Fine in CFTC Crude Oil Manipulation Action against Parnon Energy Inc., Arcadia Petroleum Ltd., and Arcadia Energy (Suisse) SA, and Crude Oil Traders James Dyer and Nicholas Wildgoose" (August 4, 2014).

CFTC Whistleblower Statute, 7 U.S.C. 2, 5, 12a(5) and 26 (July 21, 2010).

Competitive Energy Services, LLC, *Order to Show Cause and Notice of Proposed Penalty*, Docket No. IN12-12-000, 140 FERC ¶ 61,032 (July 17, 2012).

Constellation Energy Commodities Group, Inc., *Order Approving Stipulation and Consent Agreement*, Docket No. IN12-7-000, 138 FERC ¶ 61,168 (March 9, 2012).

Coral Power, L.L.C., *Letter Order Accepting Market Based Rate Schedule*, Docket No. ER96-25-000 (December 9, 1995).

Council Regulation (EU) No 1227/2011, On Wholesale Energy Market Integrity and Transparency, at art. 2(4)(a), 2011 O.J. (L326).

Cramton, Peter, *Answering Testimony*, Docket No. EL00-95-248, Exh. No. TRA-1, October 25, 2012.

Deutsche Bank Energy Trading, LLC., *Order to Show Cause and Notice of Proposed Penalties*, Docket No. IN12-4-000, 140 FERC ¶ 61,178 (September 5, 2012).

__________, *Answer of DB Energy Trading LLC to Order to Show Cause*, filed in Docket No. IN12-4-000 (November 5, 2012).

__________, *Order Approving Stipulation and Consent Agreement*, Docket No. IN12-4-000, 142 FERC ¶ 61,056 (January 22, 2013).

DiPlacido, et al., [2000-2002 Transfer Binder] Comm. Fut. 1. Rep. (CCH) ~ 28,625 (CFTC Docket No. 01-23, August. 21, 2001).

DiPlacido v. CFTC, 2009 U.S. App. (2d Cir. 2009).

Dodd-Frank Wall Street Reform and Consumer Protection Act, Pub. L. 111–203, 124 Stat. 1376 (July 21, 2010).

Electric Reliability Council of Texas. *ERCOT Texas Nodal Protocols Section 3: Management Activities for the ERCOT System* (November 1, 2007).

Energy Policy Act of 2005, 42 U.S.C. § 13201 (2005).

Energy Transfer Partners, L.P., et al., *Order Approving Uncontested Settlement*, Docket No. IN06-03-003, 128 FERC ¶ 61,269 (September 21, 2009).

EnerNOC, Inc., *Order Approving Stipulation and Consent Agreement*, Docket No. IN13-6-000, 141 FERC ¶ 61,211 (December 17, 2012).

Enerwise Global Technologies, Inc., *Order Approving Stipulation and Consent Agreement*, Docket No. IN12-15-000, 143 FERC ¶ 61,218 (June 7, 2013).

Enron Power Marketing Inc. and Enron Energy Services, Inc., *Order Revoking Market-Based Rate Authorities and Terminating Blanket Marketing Certificates*, Docket No. EL03-77-000 et al. 103 FERC ¶ 61,343, (June 25, 2003).

__________, *Order to Show Cause Concerning Gaming and/or Anomalous Market Behavior*, Docket Nos. EL03-137-000, et al., (June 25, 2003).

Ernst & Ernst v. Hochfelder, 425 U.S. 185 (1976).

EU Commission Press Release, "Antitrust: Commission opens German electricity market to competition" (November 26, 2008).

FERC v. Barclays Bank PLC, No. 2:13-cv-02093 (E.D. Cal. 2013).

__________, *Notice of Motion and Motion to Dismiss*, No. 2:13-cv-02093 (E.D. Cal. 2013).

__________, *Petitioner's Opposition to Respondents' Motion*, No. 2:13-cv-02093 (E.D. Cal. 2013).

Federal Energy Regulatory Commission. "Guide to Market Oversight – Glossary." http://www.ferc.gov/market-oversight/guide/glossary.asp.

__________. *Inquiry Concerning the Commission's Merger Policy Under the Federal Power Act: Policy Statement*, Order No. 592, 61 Fed. Reg. 68,595 (1996), FERC Statutes and Regulations ¶ 31,044 (1996).

__________. *Merger Policy Statement. Order No. 592-A*, 62 Fed. Reg. 33,341 (1997), 79 FERC ¶ 61,321 (1997).

__________. Order Directing Staff Investigation, 98 FERC ¶ 61,165 (February 13, 2002).

__________. FPA Section 203 Supplemental Policy Statement, 72 Fed. Reg. 42,277 (August 2, 2007).

__________. *Order Reaffirming Commission Policy and Terminating Proceeding*, Docket No. RM11-14-000, 138 FERC ¶ 61,109 (February 6, 2012).

__________. *Order Requiring Demonstration That Certain Bids Did Not Constitute Anomalous Market Behavior*, Docket No. IN03-10-000, 103 FERC ¶ 61,347 (June 25, 2003).

__________. *Order Revoking Market-Based Rate Authorities and Terminating Blanket Marketing Certificates*, Docket No. EL03-77-000, 103 FERC ¶ 61,343 (June 25, 2003).

__________. *Staff Notice of Alleged Violations* [JP Morgan Ventures Energy Corporation] (July 29, 2013).

FERC Order No. 670, *Prohibition of Energy Market Manipulation*, Docket RM06-3-000 (January 1, 2006).

__________. 745 *Demand Response Compensation in Organized Wholesale Energy Markets*, 134 FERC ¶ 61,187 (March 15, 2011).

__________, Enforcement Staff Report. "Findings of a Non-Public Investigation of Potential Market Manipulation by Suppliers in the New York City Capacity Market," filed in Docket Nos. IN08-2-000 & EL07-39-000 (February 28, 2008).

__________. "2010 Report on Enforcement" Docket No. AD07-13-003 (November 18, 2010).

__________. "2011 Report on Enforcement" Docket No. AD07-13-004 (November 15, 2011).

__________. "2012 Report on Enforcement" Docket No. AD07-13-005 (November 15, 2012).

__________. "2013 Report on Enforcement" Docket No. AD07-13-006 (November 21, 2013).

__________. "2013 Assessment of Demand Response & Advanced Metering" (October 2013).

__________. *Initial Report on Company-Specific Separate Proceeding and Generic Reevaluations; Published Natural Gas Price Data; and Enron Trading Strategies: Fact-Finding Investigation of Potential Manipulation of Electric and Natural Gas Prices.* Docket No. PA02-2-000, August 2002.

__________. *Staff Report to the Federal Energy Regulatory Commission on Western Markets and the Causes of the Summer 2000 Price Abnormalities*, November 1, 2000.

Federal Power Act, 16 U.S.C. Chapter 12 (2005).

Federal Trade Commission, "16 .FR Part 317 Prohibitions on Market Manipulation; Final Rule." *Federal Register Notice*, 74:40686-40706 (August 12, 2009).

Fischel, D.R. and D.J. Ross. "Should the Law Prohibit 'Manipulation' in Financial Markets?" *Harvard Law Review* 105 (December 1991): 505-553.

Fortner Enterprises, Inc. V. United States Steel Corp., 394 U. S. 495 (1969).

Fox-Penner, P., G. Taylor, R. Broehm, and J. Bohn. "Competition in Wholesale Electric Power Markets." *Energy Law Journal* 23 (2002): 281-348.

__________, *Prepared Testimony*, Docket No. EL00-95-000, Exh. CA-001, February 25, 2003.

__________, *Prepared Rebuttal Testimony*, Docket No. EL00-95-248, Exh. CAX-310, March 2, 2012.

__________ and Robert J. Reynolds, *Rebuttal Testimony*, Docket No. EL02-71-000, Exh. CLP-125, December 17, 2009.

__________ and W. P. Zarakas. "Analysis of Benefits: PSE&G's Energy Strong Program." A study performed on behalf of Public Service Electric & Gas (October 7, 2013).

Frey v. Commodity Future Trading Commission, 931 F.2d 1171 (7th Cir. 1991).

Florio, Michael Peter, *Direct Testimony*, Docket No. EL01-10-85, Exh. CAT-001, September 21, 2012.

Gelinas, Donald J. *Letter, FERC Office of Markets, Tariffs and Rates, to: All Jurisdictional Sellers and Non-Jurisdictional Sellers in the West*, Docket No. PA02-2-000, March 5, 2002.

Gensler, Gary, "*Hearing, Regulatory Reform and the Derivatives Market*," Chairman, Commodity Futures Trading Commission, Washington, DC. S.HRG, 111-246, June 4, 2009.

Gerard, B. and V. Nanda. "Trading and Manipulation Around Seasoned Equity Offerings." *Review of Economic Studies* 48 (March 1993): 213-245.

Gila River Power, LLC, *Order Approving Stipulation and Consent Agreement*, Docket No. IN12-8-000, 141 FERC ¶ 61,136 (November 19, 2012).

Gilbert, R.J., K. Neuhoff and D.M. Newbery. "Mediating Market Power in Electricity Networks." *Rand Journal of Economics*. 35(4) (Winter 2004): 691-711.

Goldstein, I. and A. Guembel. "Manipulation and the Allocational Role of Prices." *Review of Economic Studies* 75 (January 2008): 133-164.

Green, Richard J. and David M. Newbery. "Competition in the British Electricity Spot Market." *Journal of Political Economy* 100(5) (1992): 929-953.

Hanser, Philip, *Prepared Direct Testimony*, Docket No. EL00-95 et al., Exh. CA-9 and Exh. CA-10, March 2002.

Harvey, Scott M., and William W. Hogan, *Prepared Direct Testimony*, Docket No. EL00-95-075, Exh. MIR-1, March 3, 2003.

__________, *Affidavit*, Docket No. EL00-95-000, August 4, 2009.

__________. "Issues in the Analysis of Market Power in California" (October 27, 2000). http://www.hks.harvard.edu/fs/whogan/HHMktPwr_1027.pdf.

__________. "On the Exercise of Market Power through Strategic Withholding in California." Center for Business and Government, John F. Kennedy School of Government, Harvard University (April 24, 2001).

__________. "Further analysis of the Exercise of Market Power in the California Electricity Market." Center for Business and Government, John F. Kennedy School of Government, Harvard University (November 21, 2001).

__________. "Identifying the Exercise of Market Power in California." Center for Business and Government, John F. Kennedy School of Government, Harvard University (December 28, 2001).

__________. "Market Power and Market Simulations" (July 16, 2002). http://www.hks.harvard.edu/hepg/Papers/Hogan_Harvey_Market_Power&Simulations_071602.pdf.

Hay, G.A. "Market Power in Antitrust." *Antitrust Law Journal*. 60 (1991-1992): 807-827.

Hieronymus, William H., *Prepared Rebuttal Testimony*, Docket Nos. ER00-95-075 et al., Exh DYN/WIL-1, March 20, 2003.

Hildebrandt, Eric. "Further Analyses of the Exercise and Cost Impacts of Market Power in California's Wholesale Energy Market," Department of Market Analysis, California Independent System Operator, March 2001.

__________, *Declaration on Behalf of the California Independent System Operator Corporation*, United States Bankruptcy Court, Northern District of California, Case No. 01-30923-DM, Chapter 11, July 2001.

Hogan, William W., *Answering Testimony*, Docket No. EL95-00-248, Exh. CSG-1, October 25, 2011.

Hunter v. Federal Energy Regulatory Commission, 11-1477, U.S. Court of Appeals for the District of Columbia (Washington) (Decided March 15, 2013).

In the Matter of Sumitomo Corporation, an order referenced in CFTC Press Release #4144-98, May 11, 1998. http://www.cftc.gov/ogc/oporders98/ogcfsumitomo.htm.

ISO New England Inc., *et al.*, *Order Granting RTO Status Subject to Fulfillment of Requirements and Establishing Hearing and Settlement Judge Procedures*, Docket No. RT04-2-000 *et al.*, (March 24, 2004).

ISO New England, Inc. FERC Electric Tariff No. 3 (April 21, 2006). http://www.vermonttransco.com/library/document/download-migrated/SCHEDULE%2021-VTTRANSCO.pdf.

ISO New England, Inc. and New England Power Pool Participants Committee *et al.*, *Order on Paper Hearing and Order on Rehearing*, Docket Nos. ER10-787-000 *et al.*, 135 FERC ¶61,029 (April 13, 2011).

J.P. Morgan Ventures Energy Corporation, *Order to Show Cause*, 140 FERC ¶ 61,227 (September 20, 2012).

__________, *Order Suspending Market-Based Rate Authority*, Docket No. EL12-103-000, 141 FERC ¶ 61,131 (November 14, 2012).

Jacobellis v. State of Ohio, 378 U.S. 184 (1964).

Jarrow, R.A. "Derivative Security Markets, Market Manipulation, and Option Pricing Theory." *Journal of Financial and Quantitative Analysis* 29 (1994): 241-261.

Jefferson Parish Hosp. Dist. No. 2 v. Hyde, 466 U.S. 2 (1984).

Joskow, Paul. L. "California's Electricity Crisis." *Oxford Review of Economic Policy* 17 (2001): 365-388.

__________. *Statement, before the Committee on Governmental Affairs, United States Senate*. (June 13, 2001).

__________. "A Quantitative Analysis of Pricing Behavior in California's Wholesale Electricity Market During Summer 2000." *The Energy Journal* 23 (2002): 1-36.

__________. "Competitive Electricity Markets and Investment in New Generating Capacity." MIT Working Paper, June 12, 2006.

__________ and J. Tirole. "Transmission Rights and Market Power on Electric Power Networks." *RAND Journal of Economics* 31 (Autumn 2000): 450-487.

Kalt, Joseph P., *Summary of Prepared Testimony*, Docket No. EL00-95-248, Exh. MI-1, October 25, 2011.

Kaplow, L. "Market Share Thresholds: On the Conflation of Empirical Assessments and Legal Policy Judgment." *Journal of Competition Law & Economics* 7 (May 2011): 243-276.

__________. "Why (Ever) Define Markets?" *Harvard Law Review* 124 (December 2010): 437-517.

Kumar, P. and D. J. Seppi. "Futures Manipulation with 'Cash Settlement.'" *Journal of Finance* 47 (September 1992): 1485-1502.

Kyle, A.S. and S. Viswanathan. "How to Define Illegal Price Manipulation." *American Economic Review* 98 (May 2008): 274-279.

Lambert, J.D. *Energy Companies and Market Reform: How Deregulation Went Wrong*. Tulsa, OK: PennWell Books, September 2006.

Landes, W.M. and R.A. Posner. "Market Power in Antitrust Cases." *Harvard Law Review* 94 (March 1981): 937-996.

Ledgerwood, S. "Screens for the Detection of Manipulative Intent." Available on SSRN (December 2010).

__________. "Uneconomic Trading and Market Manipulation." *Energy Risk Magazine* (July 2013): 33-37.

__________ and D. Harris, "A Comparison of Anti-Manipulation Rules in U.S. and EU Electricity and Natural Gas Markets: A Proposal for a Common Standard." *Energy Law Journal* 33 (April 2012): 1-40.

__________ and H. Pfeifenberger. "Using Virtual Bids to Manipulate the Value of Financial Transmission Rights." *The Electricity Journal* 26 (November 2013): 9-25.

__________ and P. Carpenter, "A Framework for Analyzing Market Manipulation." *Review of Law & Economics*. 8 (September 2012): 253-295.

__________ et al. "Losing Money to Increase Profits: A Proposed Framework for Defining Market Manipulation." The Brattle Group Discussion Paper (March 2011).

__________ et al. "Defining Market Manipulation in a Post-REMIT World." The Brattle Group Discussion Paper (June 2011).

__________ and Wesley Heath. "Rummaging through the Bottom of Pandora's Box: Funding Predatory Pricing through Contemporaneous Recoupment." *Virginia Law and Business Review* 6(3) (April 2012): 509-568.

Lewis, Michael. *Flash Boys: A Wall Street Revolt*, New York: W. W. Norton & Company, March 31, 2014.

Lincoln Paper and Tissue, LLC, *Order to Show Cause and Notice of Proposed Penalty*, Docket No. IN12-10-000, 140 FERC ¶ 61,031 (July 17, 2012).

__________, *Petition for an Order Affirming the Federal Energy Regulatory Commission's August 29, 2013 Orders Assessing Civil Penalties against Lincoln Paper and Tissue, LLC* (D. Mass. December 2, 2013).

"List of State Anti-Price Gouging Laws." Knowledge Problem (November 3, 2012). http://knowledgeproblem.com/2012/11/03/list-of-price-gouging-laws/.

Make-Whole Payments and Related Bidding Strategies, *Order Approving Stipulation and Consent Agreement*, Docket Nos. IN11-800 and IN13-5-000, 144 FERC ¶ 61,068 (July 30, 2013).

Marcoux, J.M. "Canaries in the Coal Mine: Facts from Securities Fraud Private Civil Actions Can Identify Intent to Manipulate Energy Market." *Energy Law Journal* 29 (2008): 141-156.

Market Power Handbook: Competition Law and Economic Foundations. American Bar Association (ABA) Section of Antitrust Law. Chicago, IL: ABA Publishing, 2005.

Massa, M. and Z. Rehman. "Information Flows within Financial Conglomerates: Evidence from the Banks-Mutual Funds Relation." *Journal of Financial Economics* 89 (2008): 288-306.

McCullough, Robert F., *Prepared Supplemental Testimony*, Docket No. EL03-180-000, Exh. SNO 710.

McNamara, W. *The California Energy Crisis: Lessons for a Deregulating Industry*. Tulsa, OK: PennWell Books, 2002.

Memorandum from Christian Yoder and Stephen Hall to Richards Sanders, Re: Traders' Strategies in the California Wholesale Power Markets/ISO Sanctions (Enron Memo), December 6, 2000.

Midwest Independent System Operator. *Business Practices Manual for Market Monitoring and Mitigation* (August 8, 2005).

MISO Virtual and FTR Trading, *Order Approving Stipulation and Consent Agreement*, Docket No. IN12-6-000, 146 FERC ¶ 61,072 (February 7, 2014).

Morgan Stanley Capital Group, Inc. v. Pub. Util. Dist. No. 1 of Snohomish County *et al.*, 554 U.S. 527 (2008).

Moss, D. L. and P. Fox-Penner. *Network Access, Regulation and Antitrust*. New York: Routledge, 2005.

Nat'l Collegiate Athletic Ass'n v. Bd. of Regents of Univ. of Oklahoma, 468 U.S. 85 (1984).

NERC. "GADS Data Reporting Instructions." http://www.nerc.com/pub/sys/all_updl/gads/dri/sec3.pdf.

Newbery, D. M. "Power Markets and Market Power." *The Energy Journal* 16 (1995): 39-66.

New York Independent System Operator, Inc., *Order on Proposed Revisions to In-City Buyer-Side Mitigation Measures*, Docket No. ER10-3043-000, 133 FERC ¶ 61,178 (November 26, 2010).

Nicholson, Walter and Christopher Snyder. *Microeconomic Theory: Basic Principles and Extensions, 10th ed.* Eagan, MN: South-Western Publishers, 2008.

Official Journal of the European Union, *Commission Decision of 26 November 2008*, Cases COMP 39.388 and 39.389 (November 26, 2008).

Oren, S.S. "Economic Inefficiency of Passive Transmission Rights in Congested Electricity Systems with Competitive Generation." *The Energy Journal* 18(1) (1997): 63-83.

Osipovich, Alexander. "GDF Suez faces CFTC market manipulation probe." *Energy Risk*, (June 24, 2014).

Panther Energy Trading LLC and Michael J. Coscia, *Order Instituting Proceedings Pursuant to Sections 6(C) and 6(D) of the Commodity Exchange Act, as Amended, Making Findings and Imposing Remedial Sanctions*, CFTC Docket No. 13-26 (July 22, 2013).

Pirrong, Craig, "Manipulation of the Commodity Futures Price Delivery Process." *Journal of Business* 66 (July 1993): 335-369.

__________. "Commodity Market Manipulation Law: A (Very) Critical Analysis and a Proposed Alternative." *Washington and Lee Law Review* 51 (1994): 945-1014.

__________. "Detecting Manipulation in Futures Markets: The Feruzzi Soybean Episode." *American Law and Economics Review* 6 (Spring 2004): 28-71.

__________. "Energy Market Manipulation: Definition, Diagnosis, and Deterrence." *Energy Law Journal* 31 (2010): 1-20.

__________. *Answering Testimony*, Docket No. EL00-95-248, Exh. POW-257, October 24, 2011.

PJM Interconnection, L.L.C., *Order Accepting Proposed Tariff Revisions Subject to Conditions, and Addressing Related Complaint*, Docket No. ER11-2875-000, 135 FERC ¶ 61,022 (April 12, 2011).

PJM Market Monitoring Unit. "Analysis of the Three Pivotal Supplier Test: March 1 through December 31, 2006," (May 7, 2007).

PJM Power Providers Group v. PJM Interconnection, L.L.C., *Order on Compliance Filing, Rehearing, and Technical Conference*, Docket Nos. ER11-2875-001 *et al.*, 137 FERC ¶ 61,145 (November 17, 2011).

"Prohibition of Market Manipulation." *Federal Register* 75:212 (November 3, 2010): 67657-67662.

Prohibition on the Employment, or Attempted Employment, of Manipulative and Deceptive Devices - Prohibition on Price Manipulation, 17 C.F.R. Part 180 (August 15, 2011).

Puget Sound Energy, Inc. *Order Granting Rehearing, Denying Request to Withdraw Complaint and Terminating Proceeding, Puget Sound Energy, Inc. v. All Jurisdictional Sellers of Energy and/or Capacity at Wholesale into Electric Energy and/or Capacity Markets in the Pacific Northwest*, Docket No. EL01-10-000, et al., 103 FERC ¶ 61,348 (June 25, 2003).

__________, *Order Denying Rehearing, Puget Sound Energy, Inc. v. All Jurisdictional Sellers of Energy and/or Capacity at Wholesale into Electric Energy and/or Capacity Markets in the Pacific Northwest*, Docket No. EL01-10-011, 105 FERC ¶ 61,183 (November 10, 2003).

__________, *Order on Remand,* Docket No. EL91-10-026, 137 FERC ¶ 61,001 (October 3, 2011).

__________, *Order on Rehearing*, Docket No. EL01-10-076, 143 FERC ¶ 61,020 (April 5, 2013).

__________, *Initial Decision,* Docket No. EL 01-10-085, 146 FERC ¶ 63,028, (March 28, 2014).

Pub. Util. Com'n of the State of Cal. v. FERC, 462 F.3d 1027 (9th Cir. 2006).

__________, Slip op. No. 01-71051 (Apr. 15, 2009).

Public Utilities Commission of Texas. *Substantive Rule 25.505* (2007).

Reynolds, Robert J., *Prepared Testimony*, op cit.; additional criticisms, Docket No. EL00-95-000 et al., Exh. CA-5 (February 27, 2003) and Exh. CA-352 (March 18, 2003).

__________, *Prepared Rebuttal Testimony*, Docket No. EL00-95 et al., Exh. CA-352 and CA-353, March 18, 2003.

Richard Silkman, *Order to Show Cause and Notice of Proposed Penalty*, Docket No. IN12-13-000, 140 FERC ¶ 61,033 (July 17, 2012).

__________ and Competitive Energy Services, LLC, *Petition for an Order Affirming the Federal Energy Regulatory Commission's August 29, 2013 Orders Assessing Civil Penalties against Richard Silkman and Competitive Energy Services, LLC* (D. Mass. December 2, 2013).

Rumford Paper Company, *Order Approving Stipulation and Consent Agreement*, Docket No. IN-12-11-000, 142 FERC ¶ 61,218 (March 22, 2013).

__________, *Order to Show Cause and Notice of Proposed Penalty*, Docket No. IN-12-11-000, 140 FERC ¶ 61,030 (July 17, 2012).

San Diego Gas & Electric Company, et al. *Order Initiating Hearing Proceedings to Investigate Justness and Reasonableness of Rates of Public Utility Sellers in California ISO and PX Markets, San Diego Gas & Electric Company v. Sellers of Energy and Ancillary Services Into Markets Operated by the California Independent System Operator and the California Power Exchange*, Docket No. EL00-95-000, 92 FERC ¶ 61,172 (August 23, 2000).

__________, *Market Order Proposing Remedies for California Wholesale Electrics*, Docket No. EL00-95-000, 93 FERC ¶ 61,121 (November 1, 2000).

__________, *Order Directing Remedies for California Wholesale Electric Markets*, Docket No. EL00-95-000, 93 FERC ¶ 61,294 (December 15, 2000).

__________, *Order Establishing Prospective Mitigation and Monitoring Plan for the California Wholesale Electric Markets and Establishing an Investigation of Public Utility Rates in Wholesale Western Energy Markets*, Docket No. EL00-95-012, et al., 95 FERC ¶61,115, (April 26, 2001).

__________, *Order on Clarification and Rehearing*, Docket Nos., EL00-95-000 et al. 97 FERC ¶ 61,275 (December 19, 2001).

__________, *Order on Motion for Discovery Order*, Docket No. EL00-95-000, 101 FERC ¶ 61,186, (November 20, 2002).

__________, *Order on Remand*, Docket No. EL00-95-184, 129 FERC ¶ 61,147 (November 19, 2009).

__________, *Opinion No. 512, Order Affirming Initial Decision*, Docket No. EL02-71- 017, 135 FERC ¶61,113, (May 4, 2011).

__________, *Order on Requests for Rehearing and Clarification and Motions to Dismiss*, 135 FERC ¶ 61,183, Docket No. EL00-95-236 (May 26, 2011).

__________, *Initial Decision*, Docket No. EL00-95-248, 142 FERC ¶ 63,011, (February 15, 2013).

__________, *Opinion No. 536, Order Affirming Factual Findings, Directing Compliance Filing and Ordering Refunds*, Docket No. EL00-95-248, 149 FERC ¶ 61,116, (November 10, 2014).

Savitski, David, *Prepared Answering Testimony*, Docket No. EL01-10-085, Exh. S-13, February 5, 2013.

Scherman, William S., Brandon C. Johnson, and Jason J. Fleischer. "The FERC Enforcement Process: Time for Structural Due Process and Substantive Reforms." *The Energy Law Journal* 35(101) (May 2014): 101-145.

Scheuerman, Paul G., *Direct Testimony*, Docket No. EL03-180-000, *et al.*, Exh. GLN-16, September 2, 2003.

Schmalensee, R. and B.W. Golub. "Estimating Effective Concentration in Deregulated Wholesale Electricity Markets." *RAND Journal of Economics* 15 (Spring 1984): 12-26.

Securities and Exchange Commission. "Investor Information - Market Manipulation." http://www.sec.gov/answers/tmanipul.htm.

Securities Exchange Act of 1934, 15 U.S.C. § 78a (2012).

Securities and Exchange Commission Anti-Manipulation Rule, 17 CF.R. § 240.10-5 (1951).

SEC v. Pawel Dynkowski *et al.*, Case No. 09-361 (Del. 2009).

Senator Jeff Bingaman. "Restoring American Financial Stability Act of 2010." *Congressional Record - Senate* (May 18, 2010): S3881.

Senator Maria Cantwell. "Energy Policy Act of 2003." *Congressional Record - Senate* (July 30, 2003): S10175.

__________. "Creating Long-Term Energy Alternatives for the Nation Act of 2007." *Congressional Record - Senate* (June 13, 2007): S7588.

Sheffrin, A. "Anjali Sheffrin to Market Issues/ADR Committee of the California ISO, Memorandum." *Market Analysis Report* (June 9, 2000).

__________. "Empirical Evidence of Strategic Bidding in California ISO Real Time Market." California Independent System Operator (March 21, 2001).

Stern, Gary A., *Direct Testimony,* Docket No. EL00-95-000 et al., Exh. CA-3 and Exh. CA-4, March 2002.

__________, *Prepared Rebuttal Testimony,* Docket No. EL00-95-248, Exh. CAX-350, March 2, 2012.

Stoft, S. "Financial Transmission Rights Meet Cournot: How TCCs Curb Market Power." *The Energy Journal.* 20 (January 1999): 1-23.

Sweeney, J.L. *The California Electricity Crisis.* Stanford, CA: Hoover Institution Press, 2002.

__________, *Answering Testimony,* Docket No. EL00-95-248, Ex. POW-233, October 25, 2011.

Taylor, Gerald A., *Declaration,* Docket No. EL03-151-000 and Docket No. EL03-186-000, December 4, 2003.

__________, *Prepared Direct Testimony*, EL03-180-000 et al., February 27, 2004, Exh. CP-01, (Exh. CP-8).

__________, *Prepared Direct Testimony*, Docket No. EL00-95-249, Exh. CAX-001 August 25, 2011. (Exh. CAX-006, Exh. CAX-009,CAX-013, CAX-024, CAX-075 and CAX-100).

__________, *Prepared Rebuttal Testimony*, Docket No. EL00-95-249, Exh. CAX-167, March 2, 2012, (Exh. CAX-231).

__________, *Prepared Direct Testimony,* Docket No. EL01-10-085, Exh. CAT-041, September 21, 2012 (Exh. CAT-051 and Exh. CAT-055).

Reitzes, James D., et al. *Review of PJM's Market Power Mitigation Practices in Comparison to Other Organized Electricity Markets.* A report for PJM Interconnection, LLC (September 14, 2007).

State of California, *ex rel.* Bill Lockyer, Attorney General of the State of California, *Order on Rehearing and Clarification*, Docket No. EL02-71-010 125 FERC ¶ 61,016 (October 6, 2008).

__________, *Order Affirming Initial Decision*, Docket No. EL02-71-017, 135 FERC ¶61,113 (May 4, 2011).

Sempra Energy Trading Corporation, et al., *The California Parties' Comments In Opposition To Certification And Approval Of Agreement And Stipulation Concerning Sempra Energy Trading Corporation And Exhibits Showing Genuine Issues Of Material Fact*, EL03-173-000 et al., (November 2003), Exh. No. CP-45.

The California Public Utility Commission (CPUC), *Order Instituting Rulemaking on the Commission's Proposed Policies Governing Restructuring California's Electric Services Industry and Reforming Regulation.* Decision 95-12-063, December 20, 1995 and Decision 96-01-009, January 10, 1996.

Tirole, Jean. *The Theory of Industrial Organization.* Cambridge, MA: MIT Press, 1988.

Tranen, Jeffrey, *Testimony,* Docket No. EL00-95-248, Exh.SNA-3, October 25, 2011.

U.S. Department of Justice. "Oil Pipelines Deregulation Report" (May 1986).

U.S. Department of Justice and Federal Trade Commission. "Horizontal Merger Guidelines, Revised" (April 8, 1997).

__________. "Horizontal Merger Guidelines" (August 19, 2010).

United States v. KeySpan Corporation, *Complaint*, Case 1:10-cv-01415 (SDNY 2010).

__________, *Memorandum & Order*, Case 1:10-cv-01415 (SDNY 2011).

United States Commodity Futures Exchange Commission v. Amaranth Advisors, L.L.C., Amaranth Advisors (Calgary) ULC, and Brian Hunter, 07 Civ. 6682 (DC) (SDNY 2007).

United States Steel Corp. v. Fortner Enterprises, 429 U.S. 610 (1977).

United States v. E.I. du Pont de Nemours & Co, 351 U.S. 377 (1956).

Volkart Brothers, Inc. v. Freeman, 311 F.2d 52 (5th Cir. 1962).

Weare, C. *The California Electricity Crisis: Causes and Policy Options*. San Francisco, CA: Public Policy Institute of California, 2003.

Werden, G.J. "Demand Elasticities in Antitrust Analysis." *Antitrust Law Journal* 66 (1998): 363-414.

Wolak, F.A. "Report on Redesign of California Real-Time Energy and Ancillary Services Markets." Market Surveillance Committee of California Independent System Operator (October 18, 1999).

__________. "An Empirical Analysis of the Impact of Hedge Contracts on Bidding Behavior in a Competitive Electricity Market." *International Economic Journal* 14(2) (Summer 2000).

__________. "An Analysis of the June 2000 Price Spikes in the California ISO's Energy and Ancillary Services Markets." CAISO web site (September 2000).

__________. "Analysis of 'Order Proposing Remedies for California Wholesale Electric Markets' (Issued November 1, 2000)." Market Surveillance Committee of California Independent System Operator (December 1, 2000).

__________. "Measuring Unilateral Market Power in Wholesale Electricity Markets: The California Market, 1998–2000." *American Economic Review* 93 (May 2003): 425-430.

__________. "Diagnosing the California Electricity Crisis." *The Electricity Journal*, 16 (August/ September 2003): 11-37.

__________ and R.H. Patrick. "The Impact of Market Rules and Market Structure on the Price Determination Process in the England and Wales Electricity Market." *POWER Working Paper*, PWP-047 (1996).

Wolfram, C.D. "Strategic Bidding in a Multiunit Auction: an Empirical Analysis of Bids to Supply Electricity in England and Wales." *RAND Journal of Economics* 29 (Winter 1998): 703-725.

__________. "Measuring Duopoly Power in the British Electricity Spot Market." *American Economic Review* 89 (September 1999): 805-826.

Wood, P.H, III. *Asleep at the Switch: FERC'S Oversight of Enron Corporation*. Testimony in Transcript of Hearings before the Committee on Governmental Affairs, U.S. Senate, Volume 1. Washington, D.C.: U.S. Government Printing Office, November 12, 2002.

Yan, Dr. Joseph H., *Prepared Direct Testimony*, Docket No. EL00-95-248, Exh. CAX-141, August 25, 2011.

INDEX

Note: Page numbers with an *f* or *t* indicate a figure or table. Page numbers with an 'n' indicate the information is in the notes.

C

D

E

F

G

H

I

M

N

O

P

Q

R

S

T

U

V

W

Y

Z